THE TRIAL
AND EXECUTION
OF SOCRATES

THE TRIAL
AND EXECUTION
OF SOCRATES

Sources and Controversies

THOMAS C. BRICKHOUSE
NICHOLAS D. SMITH

New York   Oxford
OXFORD UNIVERSITY PRESS
2002

Oxford University Press

Oxford   New York
Athens   Auckland   Bangkok   Bogotá   Buenos Aires   Cape Town
Chennai   Dar es Salaam   Delhi   Florence   Hong Kong   Istanbul   Karachi
Kolkata   Kuala Lumpur   Madrid   Melbourne   Mexico City   Mumbai   Nairobi
Paris   São Paulo   Shanghai   Singapore   Taipei   Tokyo   Toronto   Warsaw

and associated companies in
Berlin   Ibadan

Copyright © 2002 by Oxford University Press, Inc.

Published by Oxford University Press, Inc.
198 Madison Avenue, New York, New York, 10016
http://www.oup-usa.org

Library of Congress Cataloging-in-Publication Data

Brickhouse, Thomas C., 1947–
      The trial and execution of Socrates : sources and controversies / Thomas C. Brickhouse
and Nicholas D. Smith.
      p. cm.
      Includes bibliographical references.
      ISBN 0-19-511979-7 — ISBN 0-19-511980-0 (pbk.)
      1. Socrates—Trials, litigation, etc. 2. Socrates—Death and burial. 3. Trials
(Blasphemy)—Greece—Athens. I. Smith, Nicholas D. II. Title.
B316 .B75 2001
183′.2—dc21

                                                                        2001036915

9 8 7 6 5 4 3 2 1
Printed in the United States of America on acid-free paper

Contents

Contents

PART II: RECENT SCHOLARSHIP

Preface

This book is divided into two parts. The first consists of new translations of the ancient Greek writings that shed light on how the trial and execution of Socrates were viewed throughout antiquity. These writings vary markedly in their length and in their degree of freedom from contamination by other sources of questionable reliability. Some are complete works, clearly polished before publication; others are quite fragmentary. Some were written by Socrates' contemporaries, by individuals who actually knew him well; others were written centuries after the death of the philosopher. Perhaps most important is the fact that these sources differ, often remarkably, in how they characterize the real animus against Socrates or in the degree to which he could honestly defend himself. In collecting these sources about Socrates' condemnation in a single volume, we wanted to provide easy access to materials of interest to those engaged in research on the famous trial. But we also invite readers to challenge their own understanding of Socrates' trial and its aftermath by testing their views against what the relevant ancient sources thought the evidence supports.

Although scholars are today deeply divided over whether any single source, or combination of sources, provides us with a historically accurate picture of the final episodes of Socrates' life, there is widespread agreement that the study of Plato's writings about the trial and execution of Socrates pay the greatest philosophical dividends. The second part of this book, then, concerns three issues that are fundamental to Plato's account of the trial, imprisonment, and execution: How well did Socrates respond to the charges against him? How did he understand his moral obligation to obey the law and to remain in prison? How accurate is Plato's account of Socrates' behavior when he was actually executed? To each of these questions we offer alternative answers that scholars have advanced in the secondary literature. By staging these three "contests of words," we hope to deepen the reader's own understanding of these three issues at the heart of Plato's account of how Socrates' life ended.

We would like to express our deep gratitude to those who provided new translations appearing in Part I: Jerise Fogel (Xenophon, selections from *Memorabilia*); Joel A. Martinez (Xenophon, *Apology*); Timothy J. O'Neill (Aristophanes, selections from *Clouds*); Hope May (Libanius, selections from the *Apology of Socrates*). All of the other translations provided in this collection are our own. Finally, we would like to thank our respective colleges for the many ways in which they have fostered our work. Thomas C. Brickhouse wishes to express his gratitude to the Lynchburg College Research Committee for the award of a summer grant in 1999. Nicholas D. Smith is grateful to Unhae Langis for assistance in preparing the manuscript.

Thomas C. Brickhouse
Lynchburg College

Nicholas D. Smith
Lewis and Clark College

THE TRIAL
AND EXECUTION
OF SOCRATES

Introduction

1. SOME QUESTIONS

The Athenian philosopher Socrates was brought to trial, convicted by the jury, and sentenced to death in 399 B.C.E. His execution, however, was delayed by a month because of a religious festival during which executions were not permitted.[1] After this delay, he was put to death by drinking poison derived from hemlock. About these facts there is no disagreement. But as the sources collected in this book and the scholarly essays that follow them show, several of even the most basic facts about these events were controversial in antiquity and remain so even today. Why was Socrates brought to trial? Why did the jurors—members of the world's first democracy—find him guilty? When he was given an opportunity to escape, even after he had been convicted and sentenced to death, why did he refuse to do so? How exactly did Socrates die? Differences of opinion on these and other questions about the trial and execution of Socrates continue to arouse our curiosity and to challenge new generations of scholars. Perhaps some of the answers given in this collection are the right ones; but our readers will soon see quite plainly that not all of the answers provided herein can be correct.

2. TRIAL PROCEDURES

In ancient Athens there were no public prosecutors who tried cases on behalf of the state. Instead, private individual citizens would bring criminal charges to a government official known as the King archon, who would determine if the charges were in accordance with law and would then forward the case to a jury trial. To prevent jury tampering or bribery,

---

[1]See section 5 of this introduction.

Athenian juries were quite large, from 200 members to perhaps ten times that many. In Socrates' case, the number seems to have been 500.[2]

Socrates' prosecutor was a younger man named Meletus. Assisting Meletus in presenting the case against Socrates were two other men: a well-known and highly respected politician named Anytus and a poet about whom very little is known named Lycon. The charge Meletus brought against Socrates was impiety. Because the law against impiety did not specify all of the ways one could be impious, as a part of his indictment, Meletus had to specify precisely how Socrates was supposed to be guilty of this charge. Meletus, accordingly, provided three specifications: Socrates was guilty of not recognizing the gods recognized by the city; Socrates invented new divine things; and Socrates corrupted the youth. It is sometimes said that there were three charges against Socrates, with these three specifications of the single charge of impiety no doubt in mind. But in fact Socrates was tried and convicted for the one charge of impiety—a charge made on the basis of these three claims, each of which allegedly explained ways in which Socrates was impious.

Different sources make different claims about the kind of defense Socrates offered against the charges. It was even claimed in later antiquity that Socrates simply remained silent and offered no defense at all. Plato and Xenophon—both of whom knew Socrates personally—contradict this much later claim, however, and we see no reason to doubt them. As our readers will soon see, however, Plato and Xenophon give somewhat different accounts of what Socrates did say in his defense, and this has given rise to many of our most difficult questions about the trial. One thing that seems clear in both Plato's and Xenophon's accounts of Socrates' defense (in fact, Xenophon makes this point explicitly) is that the general style and tone of Socrates' speech was perceived by many to have been quite haughty and proud—Xenophon characterized it as *megalegoria*, which translates literally as "big talk." Plato simply gives us a version of the speech without commentary, but readers of Plato's version have often thought that much of it seemed like "big talk." There is much speculation by scholars as to why Socrates would have defended himself in the way he does in Plato and in Xenophon.

In Plato's version, Socrates claims to be surprised that he was convicted by a fairly narrow margin: Had only thirty more jurors voted in his favor, rather than against him, he would have been found innocent. If indeed there were 500 jurors, as we have said, this means that the vote to convict Socrates was 280 to 220, since a tie vote of 250 for each side would have counted in Socrates' favor. In a much later (c. 250 C.E. or so) account, Diogenes Laertius says that the vote to convict Socrates was by the much

---

[2]Not 501, as some scholars have suggested. Only later did the Athenians use odd-numbered juries to avoid tie votes. When Socrates was tried, tie votes would be counted in favor of the defendant.

larger margin of 281 votes. There is no way to square this version with a jury of 500 members. If we assume an odd-numbered jury (of 501), the account in Diogenes Laertius would make the vote to convict Socrates 391 to 110.

Just as it did not stipulate all the ways in which one might be impious, the law against impiety also did not stipulate any particular penalty for those convicted of impiety—no doubt because some forms of impiety were regarded as far worse than others. The prosecutor in cases such as these, therefore, would also propose a penalty. This proposed penalty would be contained in the indictment itself, so even before Socrates went on trial, it was clearly known to all concerned that Socrates faced the possible penalty of death. But in trials of this sort—where the penalty is proposed by the prosecutor, but is not automatically imposed by the relevant law—the Athenian legal system provided for a second phase of the trial, in which those convicted could propose an alternative to the penalty given in the prosecutor's indictment. The ancient sources that have survived, unfortunately, give very different accounts of what Socrates said and did in this phase of his trial. According to Xenophon, Socrates simply refused to offer any counterpenalty, on the ground that to do so would be tantamount to a confession of guilt. According to Plato, however, Socrates first responded by saying that what he really deserved was to be treated as one of Athens' public heroes, who received free meals at a public building known as the Prytaneum (or Prutaneion). Socrates then went on to explain why he would not or could not offer several of the alternative penalties his jurors might have expected from him, and settled at last on a fine of 30 minas of silver, all but 1 mina of which would have to come from his friends and supporters (among whom Plato himself is named), because Socrates was so poor. Diogenes Laertius says that Socrates offered to pay either 25 or 100 drachmas (1 mina = 100 drachmas), but when this offer caused an uproar among the jurors, he changed his proposed penalty to that of free meals at the Prytaneum.

Translations and scholarly accounts used to depict the amount of the fine Socrates offers in Plato's version as a very small—even offensively small—sum of money, but more recent research has shown 30 minas to be a fairly substantial amount of money: something like 8½ years of wages for the average free Greek citizen worker. Perhaps more to the point, since jurors were paid for their services in Athens, 30 minas would have provided for the jury duty of 6000 jurors. The fine considered but later withdrawn in Diogenes' version, of course, is much lower, which would help to explain Diogenes' story as to why the jurors created an uproar when Socrates offered it.

Xenophon's version leaves no doubt as to why Socrates is then sentenced to death, having offered no alternative. Plato does not explicitly tell us about the next vote. He does provide a third speech—spoken by Socrates to his jurors after he has been condemned to death but before he is taken away to prison—in which Socrates seems to address his jurors in a way that suggests that all of those who had voted in favor of innocence had also voted in favor of his proposed penalty to pay a fine of 30 minas.[3] In Diogenes Laertius' version, in the vote to condemn Socrates to death, eighty of those who had found Socrates innocent of the crime actually went on in the next vote to favor the death penalty, which would leave only thirty votes in Socrates' favor—and 471 votes for death—in the final vote at the trial (again, assuming a jury of 501 members). If there is any sense to be made of Diogenes' version, it is that finding Socrates innocent is not the same as finding him worthy of the honor of free meals at the Prytaneum, which is the alternative penalty Socrates ultimately proposes in Diogenes' account. We think it is far more likely, however, that Diogenes has simply garbled Plato's version—note that both include some discussion of a fine of 1 mina (100 drachmas), of free meals at the Prytaneum, and of thirty significant votes. Even in the margin of the vote to convict, there is some appearance of confused overlap: In Plato's version 280 of the 500 jurors voted to convict; in Diogenes' version, the difference between the votes to convict and to release Socrates had been 281 votes. We provide translations of all of the applicable sources, in any case, so our readers can decide for themselves what makes the most sense.

3. SOCRATES' "BIG TALK" AND ITS EFFECT ON THE OUTCOME OF THE TRIAL

The different accounts of what Socrates said at his trial invite different understandings of his motives. In this, too, Xenophon's account is the most explicit: According to Xenophon, Socrates decided that he had lived long enough and would do better to end his life as a martyr than to allow old age and decrepitude to overcome him. This, claims Xenophon, explains Socrates' "big talk" at his trial. The account Diogenes Laertius gives seems to lend support to Xenophon's explanation, although it may do so only because Diogenes was convinced by Xenophon's account.

In Plato's version, Socrates claims that it is his duty as a defendant to instruct and persuade the jury. Until recently, however, scholars tended to see Plato's version of Socrates' defense as poorly suited to either of these ends—either because he avoided any serious discussion of the most serious concerns of the jurors or because the "big talking" tone of his speech was more likely to enrage the jurors than to persuade them. Recent scholarship, however, has been more divided on this issue. Some scholars now argue that the defense speech Socrates gives in Plato's version is actually well suited both to instruct his jurors about the activities that had led to his

---

[3]In his third speech, after having been sentenced to death, Socrates addresses two groups of jurors: one he identifies as "those who voted for my death" and one he identifies as "those of you who voted for acquittal." If any who had voted for acquittal had subsequently voted for the death penalty, Socrates' sorting of the two groups of jurors would make no sense.

being brought to trial and to persuade them to find him innocent. In these more recent accounts, Socrates was found guilty anyway because, as he says at the beginning of his speech, his jurors have been poisoned by too many slanders against him, some of which they have heard since they were children. The "big talk" in Socrates' defense, such scholars claim, is only the natural result of the firmness of his convictions—including especially his conviction that the very activities that had led to his trial were actually the result of a mission given to him by the god at Delphi (Apollo). The fact that he is charged with impiety for engaging in an exemplary life of pious duty to the god is a bitter irony. Scholars taking this position point to the closeness of the vote to convict, in Plato's account, as evidence of the persuasiveness of Socrates' defense. We invite our readers to consider the style and tone of Socrates' defense, in each of the ancient accounts, and to consider how they may have influenced the jurors. For comparison, readers may wish to take a look at other surviving defense speeches—in particular, the one by Andocides, "On the Mysteries," from a religious trial only a month or so before Socrates'—to see how Socrates' style and tone compare with a defense speech that we know was successful: Andocides won his case.

4. POLYCRATES' "ACCUSATION OF SOCRATES" AND THE MOTIVES OF THE PROSECUTION

Socrates was prosecuted on a charge of impiety. Some of our sources (Aeschines Rhetor, Aristides, Isocrates, Libanius, and Xenophon in the *Memorabilia*—but not in the *Apology*), however, claim that the motives of the prosecution were not, or at least not primarily, religious ones. Instead, they tell us that Socrates was tried for political reasons: It was because he was seen as despising the Athenian democracy and as one who taught politically subversive doctrines to some of Athens' most notorious traitors and criminals.

The arguments for and against this political interpretation of the trial can be somewhat complicated.[4] In favor of this interpretation, plainly, is that we have testimony to this effect from so many of our ancient sources. All but one of these, however, are later sources: Except for what we find in Xenophon's *Memorabilia*, the other evidence for the political interpretation comes from fifty years or more after the trial. One very important document, written at least six years—but probably in the first decade or so—after the death of Socrates, was the "Accusation of Socrates" by a speech

---

[4]Perhaps the liveliest and most widely read defense of the political interpretation can be found in Stone 1988. In this collection, Parker defends the view that politics was at least a part of what motivated the trial of Socrates. In our own work (especially Brickhouse and Smith 1989 and 1994), we have argued against this interpretation. We have included several sections from the later work in this collection.

writer named Polycrates. Unfortunately, this speech has been lost, but it is referred to in several ancient sources. A concerted and plausible effort to reconstruct at least the basic elements of this speech from the sources that refer to it was made in 1957 by Anton-Hermann Chroust.[5] Chroust argues, however, that the "charges made by Polycrates cannot possibly be based upon the actual events which took place at the trial [. . . and . . .] could not possibly have been part of the official indictment and proceedings which were instituted against Socrates in 399."[6] Even so, Chroust contends, Polycrates' "Accusation"

> apparently was a literary sensation. In any event, it unleashed a whole flurry of Socratic apologies, all of which took issue with Polycrates rather than the events that occurred during the official trial of Socrates in 399.[7]

Chroust's argument is an important one for understanding our sources, for if he is right that the charges made in this speech did not have anything to do with the actual trial, then we must be careful to distinguish those of our ancient sources that are really reactions to Polycrates from those (if any) that are not.

Now, one of the alleged political motivations for the trial of Socrates was that he was known as the teacher of Critias, the notorious leader of the so-called "Thirty Tyrants," who overthrew the democracy in 405 B.C.E., and Alcibiades, whom the Athenians attempted to prosecute for religious crimes in 415 B.C.E. but who escaped only to engage in a treasonous association with Athens' enemies during the Peloponnesian War. But this accusation is plainly identified by one of the sources cited in support of the political motivation for Socrates' trial—Isocrates—as having come from Polycrates.[8] Moreover, this and all of the other political prejudices against Socrates that we hear of are first mentioned by Xenophon in *Memorabilia* 1.2.9–64 and are said to have been made by one whom Xenophon refers to simply as "the accuser" (*katēgoros*). But when, at the very end of this section, Xenophon returns to the actual indictment and what charges Socrates actually faced at his trial, Xenophon changes his references to "the indictment" (*hē graphē*) and to the charges that "the author of the indictment" (*ho grapsamenos*) actually made (*Memorabilia* 1.2.64). As much as we are impressed with Chroust's argument in other ways, we find this distinction sufficient to show that Xenophon was well aware of the difference between the events that took place at the historical trial and the fabrica-

---

[5]Chroust dates the composition of Polycrates' "Accusation" around 393 or 392 B.C.E. (72).
[6]Chroust 1957, 135.
[7]Chroust 1957, 71.
[8]See Chroust 1957, 136.

tions of Polycrates.[9] If we are right about this, then we must attribute ulti-mately to Polycrates—and not to the trial itself or anything actually said by the prosecutors—all of the evidence for a political motivation for the prosecution of Socrates.

One very serious concern about the political interpretation of the trial is that it makes the defenses given to Socrates in both Plato's *Apology* and Xenophon's *Apology* almost entirely irrelevant to what is allegedly the main issue behind the prosecution. Plato's and Xenophon's versions both focus on the religious nature of the charge against Socrates and its three specifications. If one looks for them, one can find elements in these speeches that could be seen as pertinent to one or more of the supposed political motivations, but it can hardly be said that Socrates dwells on such motivations in either speech. If the political interpretation of the trial is correct, therefore, the sources closest to the trial itself—or at least two of them[10]—either obscure the main issues behind the trial or reveal that Socrates never bothered to address them. Although logically and histori-cally *possible*, we do not find this view particularly plausible, especially when both Plato and Xenophon showed themselves in other works to be perfectly capable of constructing forceful arguments critical of democracy and its institutions. Why then did they not give such arguments to Socrates in his defense, if the real issues were Socrates' supposedly sedi-tious ideas and influences on the young? If the answer is that the histori-cal Socrates did not bother to defend himself in a relevant way, then we are owed a convincing account of why Socrates would go to such lengths to avoid the most important issues and to neglect almost entirely the con-cerns that the advocates of the political interpretation claim must have been foremost in the minds of the jurors.

Indeed, as we argue in the selection reprinted in this collection, the indictment itself seems to count against the political interpretation of the trial. If the motivations for the trial of Socrates were primarily political ones, why was Socrates charged with impiety? Why, instead, was he not charged with sedition? The standard answer to this obvious question has been that his prosecutors could not charge him with crimes committed prior to the general Amnesty passed in 403 or 402 B.C.E.[11] This much is true, but nothing prevented Meletus or the others engaged in the prosecution from charging Socrates with sedition on the basis of crimes alleged to have

---

[9]*Contra* Chroust 1957, 136.

[10]The exact dates of Plato's *Apology* and Xenophon's *Apology*—and their chronological posi-tion relative to Xenophon's *Memorabilia*—are much disputed. Our own opinion is that Plato's *Apology* was written within a few years after the trial and Xenophon's was written at least five years after the trial (when he returned from a military campaign in Asia which he had begun in 403 or 402 B.C.E.). Xenophon's *Memorabilia*, we would argue, comes later still, composed at least partly as a response to Polycrates' "Accusation."

[11]See, for example, Stone 1988, 154.

been committed *after* the passage of the Amnesty—and if this charge was brought before a jury, then any evidence of crimes committed before the Amnesty could be introduced in court, as showing a continuing pattern (that is, before and after the Amnesty) of seditious activity. If Socrates was widely regarded as an enemy of democracy, as he seems to have been portrayed in Polycrates' speech, then the strategy we have just sketched would seem to be the obvious way to prosecute him. So, reference to the Amnesty of 403/402 B.C.E. in no way explains why Socrates was charged with a religious crime, rather than a political crime. The fact that the Amnesty was the legal brainchild of one of the members of Socrates' prosecution team—Anytus—is probably also noteworthy. Is it plausible to suppose that Anytus, who no doubt had to work hard to get the Amnesty passed, would so soon after its passage be engaged in prosecuting someone on an irrelevant charge, only because the Amnesty he had conceived outlawed the kind of prosecution he was, as a matter of fact, now engaging in?

Much recent scholarship has been devoted to the idea that the religious charge represented the actual concerns of the prosecution (and, presumably, the jurors who voted against Socrates). Those inclined to this position, and opposed to the view that the trial was essentially a political one, have tended to fall into two general categories: Some scholars think that Socrates was, in fact, guilty of the charge; others claim he was innocent. In this volume, the scholarly essays by Burnyeat and McPherran make the case for Socrates' guilt, and the selection from Brickhouse and Smith makes the case for Socrates' innocence. The main issue contested by these scholars is whether or not Socrates' own religious views or practices were sufficiently unorthodox as to make a charge of impiety a plausible one. Since the selections we have included make the relevant arguments in such detail, there is no reason to expand on this debate in this introduction.

5. SOCRATES IN JAIL: OBEDIENCE TO THE LAW

Having been found guilty and then condemned to death, Socrates was taken off to jail to await execution. But it so happened that Socrates' case had fallen during the religious festival in which a ship was sent off to the island of Delos to commemorate the return of Athens' mythical hero, Theseus. During the time that the ship was away from Athens, no executions were permitted. This had the effect of giving Socrates an extra month of life, which he spent in prison. According to Plato, he was visited there by Crito, with whom he has a conversation (in Plato's dialogue *Crito*) in which Crito tries to persuade Socrates to escape from jail. Socrates refuses. In one of the arguments he uses to explain to Crito why he should not escape, Socrates articulates a doctrine that has become known as the "persuade or obey" doctrine: The citizen should persuade the state or obey it. The correct interpretation of this doctrine has been, perhaps, one of the most disputed issues in Socratic scholarship. No doubt a significant feature of the attention this doctrine has received is that Socrates' attitude toward the law and legal authority in the *Crito* has appeared to many readers to be incompatible with one or more things he says in Plato's *Apology*. In the *Apology*, we find him proudly telling his jurors that, even if they offered to let him go free on the condition that he give up philosophizing, he would disobey them (29d). A little later, he recalls events that occurred under Athens' democracy and when the Thirty Tyrants were in power, in which he would not go along with what he was being told to do (32a–e). In these situations, we are told, Socrates seemed all too ready to disobey legal authority; so he must not mean what he seems to say in the *Crito*. This is what has come to be known as "the *Apology-Crito*" problem.

Xenophon's Socrates, too, seemed to claim that one ought never disobey the law or legal authority, even though legitimate governments can change the laws—thus requiring different or even conflicting actions at different times (*Memorabilia* 4.4.12–25). But scholars have nonetheless worried that such a strong doctrine of obedience to law puts Socrates' morality at risk and reveals his sometimes haughty moralism as no better than hypocrisy: Surely, it is claimed by some, we should all disobey a law that commanded some clear injustice, and surely Socrates was a thoughtful enough moralist to recognize this. The Athens in which Socrates lived was certainly not a morally immaculate place. During Socrates' lifetime, the Athenian democracy voted a number of times to commit genocide against the inhabitants of cities that refused to pay tribute to Athens' burgeoning (and in the increasing majority of historians' opinions unjust) empire. Can we really believe that Socrates, if he were called upon to take part in these campaigns, would obey such an order?

In this collection we offer two of the many attempts that scholars have offered to resolve the *Apology-Crito* problem. Richard Kraut argues that "persuade or obey" allows substantial—and morally appropriate—room for disobedience within the "persuade" disjunct of the doctrine. Brickhouse and Smith dispute Kraut's view, but go on to defend Socrates' consistency and the soundness of his doctrine as they understand it.

6. SOCRATES' DEATH

The ship returns from Delos, and Socrates remains in prison, having refused to escape. As his execution order required, a cup of poison derived from hemlock was prepared for him to drink, and Socrates drank it and died. But even on this topic there have been remarkably deep divisions among scholars—divisions that have been repeated in different forms for many generations now, as the research of the essay by Bloch included in this collection shows. The issue in this case has to do with the way Plato describes the effects of hemlock poisoning on Socrates. It turns out that there are actually several different kinds of poisonous plants that have been called hemlock. Ever since antiquity, this has created considerable confusion in those who read the death scene in Plato's *Phaedo,* for at least many forms of "hemlock" poisoning would have very different symptoms—symptoms not at all in keeping with the calm death scene we find in Plato's account. Given medical descriptions of violent seizures and the like, scholars were forced to explain away what seemed to be the patent fiction of Plato's *Phaedo.* One of the most noteworthy such attempts may be found in the concise and clear argument by Gill (included in this collection).

The evidence of Platonic fictionalizing in the death scene of the *Phaedo* was regarded as very significant for appraising Plato's accuracy as a source on the historical Socrates. Most scholars agree that Plato's dialogues provide the most interesting picture of Socrates; but there has been much less agreement on whether or not the portrait of Socrates we get from Plato is at all accurate. For those inclined to the view that Plato could not be taken as an accurate or historically trustworthy source, the apparently indisputable medical "fact" that the way Socrates' death is described in the *Phaedo* could not possibly be true appeared to be decisive evidence. Those who wished to argue for Plato's reliability as a source were forced to come up with explanations of how the *Phaedo* could be so wildly and demonstrably inaccurate, but no matter how sophisticated their arguments were, it is fair to say that the problem of the *Phaedo* remained a problem for—and an embarrassment to—their view.

Perhaps the most widely accepted argument for ignoring the contrary evidence of the *Phaedo* was that the *Phaedo* was generally agreed to belong to the group of dialogues scholars have called the "middle" group. A number of ways of giving relative dates to Plato's dialogues have been proposed, and although no unanimity has been achieved on this topic (some critics, indeed, have dismissed the entire effort, by any methodology, as hopeless and misconceived), there has been a more or less stable majority of opinion among scholars that the dialogues could be grouped into at least three general clusters: early, middle, and late. Few scholars have ever supposed that *all* of Plato's dialogues give a reliable picture of the historical Socrates; most have claimed only that the dialogues of the early group do so. In this way of thinking, Plato began his career writing dialogues in which he attempted to preserve the memory of Socrates and Socratic philosophy. But others, too, began writing "Socratic" works—works, that is, that made Socrates the main character—and some of these authors either did not know the real Socrates or did not concern themselves with historical accuracy. After a time, Plato began using Socrates, as others had been doing for some time in their "Socratic" works, simply as a recognizable character in whose mouth would be put all or most of the most interesting philosophical positions and arguments—whether or not these positions and arguments were consistent with those actually given by the real Socrates. Accordingly, even if there is no reason to dismiss as inaccurate everything in Plato's middle or late dialogues, the presumed fictionalizing of the end of the *Phaedo* did not deter those inclined to look to the earlier dialogues for evidence of the historical Socrates.

The essay by Bloch at the end of this collection—in print for the very first time in this book—contradicts what both sides of the "historicity" debate have now generally accepted for some time. It may be that the early dialogues are accurate, or it may not be. It may be that the middle and later dialogues are unreliable historically, or it may not be. But if Bloch is right, the end of the *Phaedo* provides no evidence for those who would find Plato guilty of fictionalizing in the middle or any other period. According to Bloch, the symptoms of hemlock poisoning that Plato gives could have come right out of a medical textbook. The problem with earlier accounts is that they confused the symptoms of poisoning by *conium maculatum*—the plant from which the poison given to Socrates was derived—with those of other (but very different) plants also called "hemlock." If Bloch's arguments are correct, then those engaged in the great debate over Plato's value as a historical source will have to find other evidence to dispute. But perhaps the happiest result of Bloch's argument is that we are no longer forced to imagine Socrates dying in a writhing, convulsing agony, and we are not forced to wonder at the ancient Athenians' choice of such a horrible and inhumane form of execution.

7. ARRANGEMENTS OF TEXTS AND SCHOLARSHIP IN THIS COLLECTION

We have arranged the texts in this collection by author and probable date, starting in Chapter 1 with the earliest of the known sources, Aristophanes (whose *Clouds* was first produced in 423 B.C.E.). According to Plato's *Apology,* the way Socrates was depicted in Aristophanes' *Clouds* was one important reason for the bad reputation he has with his jurors (see *Apology* 19c). We give three full dialogues and the last few pages of the *Phaedo* (all by Plato) in Chapter 2. The order of these dialogues follows their dramatic chronology: The *Euthyphro* depicts a conversation Socrates has as he waits at the office of the King archon to be given his court date; the *Apology* gives a version of his defense speech, followed by his counterpenalty proposal, and concluding with his last remarks to the jurors; the *Crito* reports a conversation Socrates has with a friend about escaping from jail as he awaits his execution; and the end of the *Phaedo* tells of how he died and what his last words to his friends were. The ordering of Plato's dialogues we give is not intended to make any claim about the order of their composition by Plato.

Following these works by Plato, in Chapter 3 we give the two works by Xenophon that are directly related to the trial and execution—the *Apology* and selections from the *Memorabilia*. We have put the *Apology* first because we believe the *Apology* was composed before the *Memorabilia*. We make no claim, however, about the relative dating of these works by Xenophon and the works we include earlier by Plato. Plato and Xenophon were contemporaries, and some—but not all—of the works we have included by each may have been written before some—but not all—of those by the other author, and we do not make any claim about which work by which author is the earliest.

Diogenes Laertius wrote perhaps six and one-half centuries after Socrates' death. Some of the minor sources we give after the selections from Diogenes in Chapter 4 are certainly known to have been written long before Diogenes was alive, but we give the selections from Diogenes first because he is the last of the major sources scholars tend to look to in piecing together information about Socrates. Although he writes much later, he claims to rely on sources that were close to—or contemporary with—the historical Socrates, and some of these sources seem to provide independent evidence from what we find in Aristophanes, Plato, or Xenophon.

In Chapter 5, we give a few pages of sources, the earliest of which are from perhaps half a century after the death of Socrates and the latest of which come from later antiquity. After these, we conclude our collection of sources in Chapter 6 with a selection of the late work by Libanius, which seems to have taken at least some of its inspiration from the lost work by Polycrates. Libanius' work has not been widely read or translated and has not been generally accepted as an important or independent source on Socrates. We make no claim about the accuracy or historical value of this or any of the other sources we have included—we claim only that those we have chosen to include are the most relevant and most informative of the ancient sources on our topic.

Following the ancient sources, we have included essays and chapters from books on three of the main topics of controversy about the trial, as summarized in this introduction. In Chapter 7, we provide a few scholarly opinions about why Socrates was brought to trial and why he was convicted. In Chapter 8, we offer a pair of contrasting views about Socrates' commitment to obedience to the law and legal authority. In Chapter 9, we provide the two most important papers on the way in which Plato portrays the death of Socrates. Other works by these and other scholars have been written on these and many other related topics. Indeed, there has been a remarkable increase in scholarship about Socrates in the last fifty years or so. We do not claim herein to have included the only, or even all of the best of, such scholarship. We claim only that the selections we offer provide fine examples of the kinds of controversies scholars continue to engage in about this very old, but always interesting, subject.

8. TRANSLATIONS AND TEXTS

All of the translations of works given in this collection are new. In several cases, we asked friends or acquaintances to provide the translations we would use; in other instances, we did the translations ourselves. In some cases, the works we have included are available in several different translations. We encourage our readers to compare those we have included here with others to see how differently the original Greek can be rendered in English by experts dedicated to getting it right. We hope and intend that the translations we have given here are as accurate and as readable as any available anywhere. We are pleased to offer new translations of a few sources, moreover, which are not easily found elsewhere—including especially the selections from Libanius. In preparing the translation we include here, Hope May actually translated the entire work. It was our decision as editors to include only selections of her new translation because the work itself is quite lengthy. Unless otherwise noted, the Greek texts used in every case were those of the Oxford Classical texts series.

PART I

ORIGINAL
SOURCES

CHAPTER 1

Aristophanes

Aristophanes (448–380 B.C.E.), Athenian comic poet. His family moved to a family farm on Aegina, an island just off the coast of Attica, when Aristophanes was still a youth. His fondness for rural life may explain the lampoons of city life in some of his plays and his apparent support of policies that would have protected the interests of those Athenians living outside the walls of the city during the Peloponnesian War. Of the forty or more plays he wrote only eleven survive. At the annual festivals at which plays were produced, Aristophanes won first prize at least six times. Aristophanes used the stage to lampoon Athens' imperial aspirations and her role in the Peloponnesian War. Cleon, the leader of the war party in Athens, was the target of many of Aristophanes' sharpest barbs. Cleon, for his part, apparently retaliated by prosecuting Aristophanes on two occasions. Although many of Aristophanes' jokes are obscene, his poetry can be exceptionally beautiful and poignant.

In Plato's *Apology* (19b–c), Socrates indicates that anyone who wants to know what accusations have victimized him for so many years need look no further than to "a play by Aristophanes." The play Socrates is referring to is the *Clouds,* first produced for the Greater Dionysia in 423 B.C.E. It failed to be popular either with the audience or with the judges and was substantially revised by Aristophanes after its initial production. It is the revised play that has come down to us. Aristophanes' target in the *Clouds* is the "new intellectualism," which included crude scientific speculation and the teachings of the various sophists. In the *Clouds* Aristophanes makes a character named Socrates represent both the nature-philosophers and sophists. Although the caricature seems plainly unfair to the nature of Socrates' activities and the motives behind them, it captures many of the same features of Socrates that we see in the early, "Socratic" works of Plato. The plot has a farmer named Stepsiades enroll in Socrates' *phrontisterion,* or "thinking shop," to learn how to use logic to cheat the many creditors he has acquired primarily through the debts incurred by his wastrel son, Pheidippides, who later in the play also enrolls in Socrates' school. The play features a contest in which Unjust Reasoning trounces Just Reasoning. Corrupted by Unjust Reasoning, Pheidippides assaults his own father, arguing that his father deserves the beating. Holding Socrates responsible for what his son has become, Stepsiades returns at the end of the play to burn down the *phrontisterion*.

All of the following translations are by Timothy J. O'Neill.

Clouds (lines 358–407)

CHORUS LEADER: Hail, most long-in-the-tooth old one! Hunter of the Muse-loved arguments! And also you, Socrates! Priest of nonsense! Tell us what you want. We would not give ear to any of the astronomers, except for Prodicus (on account of his wisdom and ideas). But to you we give ear because of your pretentious way of making your routes, barefoot and casting both your eyes askance. And, for us, you endure hardships and assume a solemn demeanor.

STREPSIADES: Oh goddess of the earth! The sound of your voice, it's so divine and holy and pompous!

SOCRATES: These are the only gods there are. All others are figments of your imagination.

STREPSIADES: Zeus too! Come on, by the goddess of the earth, Olympic Zeus is a figment of my imagination?

SOCRATES: *What* Zeus? No more of your nonsense! There is no Zeus.

STREPSIADES: Come again? Then who makes it rain? First of all, tell me that.

SOCRATES: The Clouds do, of course. I'll show you a solid proof. Tell me, have you ever seen it raining without seeing any clouds at the same time? If they are not responsible, then Zeus could make it rain on a clear day, while the clouds are gone on vacation.

STREPSIADES: By Apollo, your argument has just now conceived understanding in me. Imagine! I used to think it was just Zeus pissing through a sieve. But tell me this (and this question makes me shake): *Who* makes it thunder?

SOCRATES: The clouds, in their natural churning motions, make it thunder.

STREPSIADES: You lost me.

SOCRATES: Okay, listen up. Because they are full of water, indeed, filled to capacity. And free to move about, stretching to bursting, the rain is forced [by the laws of physics] from each cloud in torrents. And, when weighed down so greatly that one collides with another (each being saturated to bursting), it breaks asunder and explodes in thunder.

STREPSIADES: But who compels them to move? Isn't it Zeus?

SOCRATES: Hardly. It's obviously the ethereal vortex!

STREPSIADES: Vortex? *That's* escaped my notice. Hmmm. . . . So, where

Zeus was previously head-honcho, now it's the vortex who's boss. But what about the noise and thunder? You haven't taught me this.

SOCRATES: Didn't you hear me just now when I said that the clouds are filled with water and that, being full, when they draw near each other, they make a crash on account of their density and internal vortexicular action?

STREPSIADES: Come on! Why should I believe this?

SOCRATES: I'll teach you, using yourself as a model. You've had the stew served at the Panathenaic Festival. You know how it makes you expand when it's stirred up in your gut and then, out of the blue, all hell breaks loose from your ass?

STREPSIADES: By Apollo! It makes an awful commotion in me in no time. And this thunder, that little sauce, causes audible chaos and a terrible croak! At first, not frightening: *Bbbbbblast! Bbbbbbrrrrip!* And then it *really* goes: *Bbbbbbbbbbrappabbblappabbbbblast!* Whenever I shit, thunder's in attendance, *Bbbbbbburrrrp!* Much the same as with the raining clouds.

SOCRATES: Good! Considering this piddly flatulence in your intestines, of the sort that *you* have farted, is it not reasonable that the ether (being infinite in its farting) should make the fantastic thunder? After all, these names, "thunder" and "farting," are really homonyms.

STREPSIADES: Then where does lightning come from? Surely Zeus is carrying light-giving fire. Teach me this. For, throwing lightning, he burns to ashes some of us, others he leaves living, but merely singed. Clearly this is Zeus hurling lightning at oath-breakers.

SOCRATES: Well then, you remedial half-wit, if Zeus strikes down oath-breakers, why didn't he set Simon ablaze? Or Cleonymos? Or Theoros?[1] These, if any, are undoubtedly oath-breakers. But instead, he ignites his own temples, Athens' acropolis and shrines and the great oak tree! Why, I implore you? Surely oaks don't break oaths!

STREPSIADES: I don't think so. You're clearly making sense. But what *is* the lightning bolt?

SOCRATES: Basic physics. Whenever the dry wind is raised high and trapped, just as air is trapped inside of a bladder, it breaks out under extreme pressure. It farts violently [on account of its density and saturation] and, through the sheer force of this ethereal expulsion, it sets itself on fire.

---

[1]Contemporary Athenians whom Aristophanes seeks here to pillory in a comical way.

(lines 476–492)

CHORUS LEADER: Now then, take the old man, whom you want to teach, inside—sift through his mind and see what's in there.

SOCRATES: Come on and tell me about yourself. By knowing your ways, I can bring new devices against you.

STREPSIADES: "Devices?" By the gods! Do you intend to besiege me?

SOCRATES: No, but I do want to question you briefly. Is your memory good?

STREPSIADES: By Zeus, it depends. When someone owes me, I remember everything. But whenever I owe someone else, without fail, I tend to forget it all!

SOCRATES: Well then, do you have a knack for speaking?

STREPSIADES: Not for speaking . . . but I do have a knack for fraudulence.

SOCRATES: Then how will you be able to learn?

STREPSIADES: Don't worry—I'll manage beautifully.

SOCRATES: Let's see . . . whenever I throw out some piece of wisdom—about astronomy, let's say—will you quickly snatch it up?

STREPSIADES: "Snatch?" What? Should I lap up your wisdom like a dog?

SOCRATES: No . . . the man before me is an ignoramus and a barbarian! I'd feared this with you, old man: You need a whipping. Let me see . . . tell me, what do you do if someone is beating you?

STREPSIADES: Why, I get beaten. And then, after holding back a little while, I bear witness against him, and then, after that, sue the bastard.

(lines 627–680)

SOCRATES: By the divine Übermind! By Chaos and Ether! I've never seen such a yokel! Never so clueless, so clumsy, so absent-minded a hick as this one—who, studying a frivolous morsel of wisdom, completely forgets it before having learned it! But nevertheless, I'm going to summon him into the light. Where's Strepsiades? Will you drag your bed out here?

STREPSIADES: But the bedbugs won't let me carry it out!

SOCRATES: Hurry up, and put it down and pay attention.

STREPSIADES: Okay.

SOCRATES: Indeed, now what's the first thing you want to learn that you've never been taught? Tell me: Do you want to learn about measures, or words, or maybe rhythms?

STREPSIADES: I want to learn about measures. In fact, just the other day I was shortchanged about two measures by a barley dealer.

SOCRATES: That's not what I asked! I mean which measures you consider to be best: *poetic meter*. Throw me a bone—which measure do you want to learn about, the trimeter or the tetrameter?

STREPSIADES: I consider nothing before the yard.

SOCRATES: You're babbling. So, Brainiac, you say you want to learn neither trimeter nor tetrameter.

STREPSIADES: If neither one's a yard. I'll wager your trimeter isn't even three feet.[2]

SOCRATES: Oh, go to Hell! He's a hick *and* he's slow on the uptake. Hey, Speedy, maybe you could learn about rhythms.

STREPSIADES: What good will rhythms do for barley?

SOCRATES: Forget that! First of all, it can help you to be clever in social settings. You'll have a discriminating ear to tell which rhythm is for battle marches, and which again is a dactyl.

STREPSIADES: Oh, *dactyl!* That's another word for "finger," right? By Zeus, I know that one!

SOCRATES: Then show me.

STREPSIADES: Why, it's square in the middle. But before this, when I was a boy, it was this one down here that I'd show you!

SOCRATES: You're a hick *and* a moron.

STREPSIADES: You're pathetic! I'm not eager to learn any of these things.

SOCRATES: What *do* you want to learn?

STREPSIADES: *That* thing. You know—that *thing:* the most unjust argument!

SOCRATES: Look, friend, you must first learn the basics, such as the names of the several male quadrupeds.

STREPSIADES: But I know what's male, unless I'm out of my mind. There's the ram, the goat, the bull, the dog, and the rooster.[3]

SOCRATES: Do you see what you're doing? You're calling the female *and* the male of the species by the same name: "rooster."

STREPSIADES: Come again? I don't get it.

SOCRATES: You don't get it? There are, according to you, *male* and *female* roosters.

STREPSIADES: By Poseidon! Then, what am I supposed to call them?

SOCRATES: Naturally, the one is a "roosterette," and the other is a "rooster."

STREPSIADES: "Roosterette"? Well said, by Ether! As payment for this lesson alone, I'll fill your grainsack with barley 'til it splits from all sides!

SOCRATES: There you go again, but with this second noun! You're using "grain sack" as masculine when it's feminine.

STREPSIADES: How so? Shouldn't I use "grain sack" in the masculine?

SOCRATES: Yes, of course! It's just like Cleonymos.[4]

STREPSIADES: How do you mean? Instruct me.

SOCRATES: The grain sack of yours is equivalent to Cleonymos: Both use the *masculine* ending—omicron sigma.

---

[2]I borrow this rendition of the joke from Lattimore's translation.

[3]The following jokes play on the gender of Greek nouns, some of which, in Greek, have what are ordinarily feminine suffixes.

[4]There are several jokes in Aristophanes' comedies which portray this man as a homosexual who engages in anal intercourse, for which one could lose one's citizenship in Athens.

STREPSIADES: But, noble sir, a grain sack *isn't* like Cleonymos! You've handled that one before—it's a bag, open at one end for filling with grain—nothing like *him!* And yet, what should I call it from now on?

SOCRATES: What should you call it? Why, "sackette," of course—just like you'd say "tiskette" or "taskette."[5]

STREPSIADES: So, grain sack is *feminine:* "sackette," you say?

SOCRATES: Correct.

STREPSIADES: Then it is "Cleonymette's sackette."

(lines 723–756)

SOCRATES: What's *this* you're doing? Aren't you thinking?

STREPSIADES: Who, *me?* Of course I am, by Poseidon!

SOCRATES: What've you thought about?

STREPSIADES: Whether anything will be left of me after the bugs are finished!

SOCRATES: Oh, I fear *you'll* be most horribly devoured.

STREPSIADES: But I've already been totally eaten up by debt!

SOCRATES: Buck up, my man, and stay wrapped up tightly in those blankets. Otherwise your cheating mind will be discovered.

STREPSIADES: (Whining) Nooooo. . . . And who among the cheaters would've tossed whom out of the sheepskins with *this* knowledge?

SOCRATES: Okay, I should first observe. . . . What the hell is *this* you're doing? Are you sleeping?

STREPSIADES: By Apollo, I'm not.

SOCRATES: Do you grasp anything?

STREPSIADES: By God, no!

SOCRATES: Nothing at all?

STREPSIADES: Nothing more than my dick in my right hand.

SOCRATES: Fool! You'll think up *something* as soon as you're unwrapped from your blankets.

STREPSIADES: About *what?* You've got to show me this, Socrates.

SOCRATES: *Whatever* you want! First, discover this. Then, please *do* tell me.

STREPSIADES: You've heard what I want ten thousand times already! I'm concerned about my debts, and how I can avoid repaying a dime.

SOCRATES: Oh. Now go cover yourself, and let loose your frayed concepts and speculate down upon these minuscule mental manifestations; and, looking at the object of your inquiry, straightaway deduce.

STREPSIADES: (Speculating) I'm ruined!

---

[5]This joke is my own invention—the actual word Aristophanes uses here denotes a reward for some good or property saved and cannot be translated in any way that would be appropriate to the wordplay in the joke.

SOCRATES: Stop trembling. You should look away from some of your thoughts; and, having dismissed them, depart for a while. Then, go back to your brain; set it in motion again and weigh the issue.

STREPSIADES: (Looking away, then looking back) Oh! Dearest Socrates!

SOCRATES: What, old man?

STREPSIADES: I have a mind for welching on my debts!

SOCRATES: Display it.

STREPSIADES: Tell me now . . .

SOCRATES: Tell you what?

STREPSIADES: If I had a Thessalian witchwoman, I could have her take the moon by night, and then I could shut it in a round case, like a mirror; and having done so, I could watch over it night and day.

SOCRATES: Indeed. And what good would this be to you?

STREPSIADES: Some interest is due at the new moon. I would never have to repay my debts!

SOCRATES: Why exactly?

STREPSIADES: Because money is lent out to be returned at the end of the month, on the new moon, and I would be holding the moon hostage!

(lines 825–830)

STREPSIADES: You swore, just now, by Zeus.

PHEIDIPPIDES: I did.

STREPSIADES: Do you see how good learning is? There is, Pheidippides, no such thing as Zeus.

PHEIDIPPIDES: But, who then?

STREPSIADES: The Vortex is king. Zeus has been usurped.

CHAPTER 2

Plato

Plato (c. 427–c. 347 B.C.E.), Athenian philosopher. Plato was born into an aristocratic family and probably had the aspirations typical of a male of his social class until he became familiar with Socrates. It is reported that after the death of Socrates, Plato left Athens and lived for a time in Megara. His travels included three fateful trips, made at the behest of his friend Dion, to Syracuse on Sicily. His attempts to win over the tyrant Dionysius II to the causes of philosophy ended in failure, and Plato may have been imprisoned for a time in Syracuse before friends could secure his freedom. It was after his first visit to Syracuse that he founded what became known as the Academy, a school of sorts, over which he presided and, along with other leading thinkers, taught and wrote, probably until his death.

The Platonic corpus consists of some twenty-six dialogues. The dialogues are traditionally broken up into three groups, each corresponding to a different period in Plato's development. Many scholars now believe that the dialogues of the first (or early) group cast light on the views and philosophical approach of the historical Socrates and that the dialogues of the second and third (or middle and late) groups contain views that the historical Socrates had never considered. This interpretation of the corpus, however, is certainly not universally accepted. Three of the works included here, *Euthyphro, Apology of Socrates,* and *Crito,* belong to the first group. Plato's description of Socrates' death, which is the fourth piece of Platonic writing included here, is the concluding section of the *Phaedo,* a middle period work.

Euthyphro

The *Euthyphro* takes place in the agora, the Athenian marketplace, before the office of the King archon, a magistrate who decided whether charges of religious offense were to go forward for trial. Socrates is present to answer the charge of impiety brought against him by Meletus, and he meets Euthyphro, who was there to charge his father with murder for having killed a servant. An inquiry into the nature of piety ensues once Socrates professes not to have the knowledge Euthyphro claims to have about the nature of piety. Like most Socratic dialogues, the *Euthyphro* ends with both parties unable to provide a knowledgeable answer to the question that has been posed. The *Euthyphro* is an excellent example of the way Socrates engages in philosophy and of his interest in getting a suitable definition to a moral term.

EUTHYPHRO[1]: What's happened, Socrates, that would make you leave your regular place in the Lyceum, and hang around here at the King's stoa?[2] Surely you don't have a suit before the King archon,[3] as I do. 2a

SOCRATES: As a matter of fact, Euthyphro, the Athenians don't call it a suit—they call it an indictment.[4]

EUTHYPHRO: What are saying? I guess someone has indicted you; for I just won't believe that you're indicting someone else. b

SOCRATES: I'm not.

EUTHYPHRO: So someone else is indicting you.

SOCRATES: Right.

EUTHYPHRO: Who is this person?

SOCRATES: I myself don't even know much about the man, Euthyphro. He seems to me to be young and not well known. At any rate, they call him

---

[1]Euthyphro's name means "straight thinker," which he plainly proves *not* to be in this dialogue. Despite the irony of his name in this conversation, it is likely that there actually was an Athenian named Euthyphro and that he was known for his religious convictions and, perhaps, his interest in the origins of religious words. Plato portrays him in this dialogue as familiar with Socrates, although whether or not he ever actually discussed the nature of piety with Socrates we cannot say.

[2]The King's stoa was located in a corner of the agora and in front of the office of the King archon (see note 3).

[3]The King archon was one of nine Athenian magistrates. His primary function was to oversee charges of violations of religious law. Before a case was actually brought to trial, a preliminary hearing was held before the King archon whose purpose was to ensure that the accusations being made did in fact amount to legal charges.

[4]The distinction corresponds roughly to our distinction between a crime and a civil action, although many actions that we would consider to be crimes the Athenians would consider matters between private individuals.

Meletus,[5] I think. He's from the deme of Pittheus,[6] if you recall a Meletus of Pittheus, who has straight hair and only a slight beard and a somewhat hooked nose.

c EUTHYPHRO: I don't recall him, Socrates. But now what's he indicted you for?

SOCRATES: What sort of indictment is it? I think it's not trivial. For it's no small achievement for a young man to be knowledgeable about a matter such as this. For that man, so he says, knows how the youth are corrupted and who the corruptors are. And he's likely to be someone who's wise, and having noticed that, in my ignorance, I corrupt those who are his age, he's coming before the city to prosecute me, as if he

d were their mother. And he seems to me to be alone among the politicians to be starting in the right place. For he's right to care first and foremost that the young be as good as possible, just like a good farmer is

3a likely to make the young plants his first concern, and after them he turns to the others. And Meletus is really starting by weeding out those of us who are ruining the young seedlings, as he says. Then after this, it's clear that when he takes care of the older people, he'll be the cause of many great goods for the city, at least that's the reasonable outcome for someone who begins in this way.

EUTHYPHRO: I'd hope so, Socrates, but I'm afraid that just the opposite will happen. For it seems to me that by trying to wrong you, he's really beginning by harming the very heart of the city. So tell me, what does he say you're doing to corrupt the youth?

b SOCRATES: Absurd things at first hearing, my wonderful friend. For he says that I'm a maker of gods, and because I make new gods but don't believe in the old ones, he has indicted me, or so he says.

EUTHYPHRO: I see, Socrates. It's because you say that your spiritual voice[7] comes to you from time to time. So because you make innovations about divine matters, he's written this indictment, and he's taking it to court,

---

[5]The Athenian legal system did not provide for a state prosecutor. Instead, crimes were prosecuted by private individuals. The charges against Socrates were brought by the man mentioned here, Meletus, about whom nothing is really known. He may have been the son of a poet of the same name and, as Burnet 1924 points out (5), he may have been the Meletus who spoke against Andocides in an impiety trial that took place in the same year as Socrates trial, 399. One problem with identifying the Meletus who brought the charges against Socrates with the Meletus who spoke against Andocides is that Andocides says that Meletus was one of the four who participated in the arrest of Leon of Salamis. Were they the same person, Socrates could hardly say that Meletus is unknown to him, as he does at this point in the *Euthyphro,* since Socrates implies in the *Apology* (32c–d) that he knew those ordered to arrest Leon.

[6]One of the 139 political districts into which Athens had been divided since the end of the sixth century.

[7]That Socrates claimed to hear something divine, which Euthyphro here calls a "spiritual voice," was apparently well known. In the *Apology* (31c–d and 40a), Socrates tells the jury that it comes to him often and that he has heard it from childhood. It never advises him to

of course, to slander you, knowing that it's easy to slander before most people. In fact, even for me, whenever I say anything in the Assembly about divine matters, foretelling what's to happen to them, they laugh like I'm crazy. And yet there's nothing that I've foretold that wasn't true. Even so, they're jealous of everyone like us. But we shouldn't worry about them; instead, we should take them on. $\quad$ c

SOCRATES: Dear Euthyphro, being laughed at probably doesn't matter. It seems to me that the Athenians don't really care if they think someone is clever as long as he doesn't teach his wisdom. But they get angry with one who they think is making others wise, whether out of jealousy, as you say, or because of something else. $\quad$ d

EUTHYPHRO: I don't really care to test out what they think of me on this issue.

SOCRATES: Perhaps you seem to hold yourself aloof and don't want to provide instruction about your wisdom. I, on the other hand, am afraid that because of my good-hearted nature, they think that I've been eager to speak to everyone, only without taking a fee, but instead gladly paying if anyone would want to listen to me. If, then, as I was saying just now, they were really going to laugh at me, as you say they laugh at $\quad$ e you, it wouldn't be an unpleasant way at all to spend my time in court—laughing and joking. But if they're going to be serious, it's not clear how it'll turn out except to you soothsayers.

EUTHYPHRO: Surely it won't be a problem, and you'll conduct your trial intelligently and, I think, I will do so with mine.

SOCRATES: So now what's your case about, Euthyphro? Are you defending or prosecuting?

EUTHYPHRO: I'm prosecuting.

SOCRATES: Whom?

EUTHYPHRO: Someone whom I seem, again, to be crazy for prosecuting. $\quad$ 4a

SOCRATES: Why? Are you prosecuting someone who can fly away?

EUTHYPHRO: He can hardly fly away; he's already quite old.

SOCRATES: Who is he?

EUTHYPHRO: My father.

SOCRATES: Your father!

EUTHYPHRO: Absolutely.

SOCRATES: What's the charge, and what is the trial about?

EUTHYPHRO: Murder.

SOCRATES: By Heracles! Surely most people *don't* see how that's right! Indeed, I don't think this would be done correctly by just anyone, but I $\quad$ b suppose it takes someone *far* advanced in wisdom.

EUTHYPHRO: Far, indeed, by god.

---

do anything, but when it comes to him, it always "turns him away from" doing something that would be bad for him.

SOCRATES: But surely the one killed by your father is a member of your family. Of course, that's obvious. I suppose you wouldn't prosecute him for the murder of someone outside the family.

EUTHYPHRO: It's funny, Socrates, that you think it makes a difference whether the dead man's a stranger or a member of the family and it's not necessary to guard against this one thing—whether the killing took

c place justly or not, and if justly, let it go, but if not, prosecute, even if the killer shares your hearth and table. For the pollution's[8] the same either way if you knowingly associate with such a person and don't purify both yourself and him by going to court.

At any rate the one who was killed was a laborer of mine, and when we were working our farm on Naxos,[9] he was there as a worker hired by us. He got drunk and angry with one of our slaves and cut his throat. So my father bound his hands and feet, threw him in a ditch and sent a man here to inquire of the Religious Counselor[10] what should be done.

d During this time, he paid little attention to the captive and really didn't care much if he did die because he was a murderer, which is just what happened. He died from hunger and cold and being bound up before the messenger got back from the Religious Counselor. So that's what's upsetting my father and my relatives—because I'm prosecuting my father for murder on behalf of the one who was murdered. He didn't even kill him, so they claim, and even if he did, because the one who died was a murderer, we shouldn't be concerned on behalf of such

e a person, for it's unholy for a son to prosecute his father for murder— they know so little of the divine point of view concerning the pious and the impious.[11]

SOCRATES: Before god, Euthyphro, do you really think you know so exactly how things are concerning the gods, and about pious and impious matters that when things have happened as you say they have, you're not afraid that in bringing the case against your father, you're not also doing something impious?

5a EUTHYPHRO: Then I'd be useless and Euthyphro wouldn't be better than most people unless I had precise knowledge of all things of this sort.

---

[8]The notion refers to a kind of guilt that anyone who gives aid to someone who has offended to the gods would thereby take on. One of the oldest Greek religious notions held that anyone who becomes "polluted" in this way will receive some terrible punishment from the gods. Euthyphro wants to "cleanse" himself of any such pollution by prosecuting his father.

[9]An island in the middle of the Aegean. From this distance, it would take quite a long time to send a question to the Religious Counselor in Athens (see next note) and receive an answer.

[10]According to Burnet, Euthyphro is referring to one of three officials whose function it was to provide official interpretations of various religious laws and rules governing ceremonies.

[11]Socrates uses *hosiotes* and *eusebeia* and their cognates interchangeably. Although they are often translated as "holiness" and "piety," respectively, we have followed the reverse of this practice here to preserve better what ancient readers would have recognized clearly—the connection between the topic of the conversation here and the trial of Socrates.

SOCRATES: Well, then, most amazing Euthyphro, it's best that I become your pupil, and, before the court fight with Meletus, challenge him about this very thing, telling him that in the past I've thought that it's important to know about divine matters, and I do so now, when that man says I've committed a grave offense by speaking ill-advisedly and by introducing innovations about divine matters, I've, in fact, become your pupil. "And if, Meletus," I'd say, "you agree that Euthyphro is b wise about such matters, then you should accept that I too am thinking correctly and don't bring me to trial. But if you don't agree, bring the suit first against him, my teacher, rather than me on the ground that he's corrupting his elders, both me and his father, by teaching me, on the one hand, and humiliating and punishing him, on the other." And if I don't persuade him to drop his case or to indict you instead of me, it's best for me to use the same argument in court with which I have challenged him.

EUTHYPHRO: Yes, by god, Socrates, but if he tried to indict me, I think I'd c uncover where he's weak, and our discussion in court would be about him long before it was about me.

SOCRATES: And indeed, dear friend, because I understand this, I'm eager to become your student, knowing also that this Meletus and everyone else, I suppose, never seems to notice you, whereas he observes me so keenly and easily that he indicted me for impiety. So now, before God, tell me what you claimed just now to know clearly: What sort of thing do you say piety and impiety are as they apply to murder and to other d things, or isn't the pious the same thing in every action, and isn't impiety in turn the complete opposite of impiety, but in itself the same as itself, and doesn't all that is going to be impious, in fact, have a certain distinctive feature of impiousness?

EUTHYPHRO: Without any doubt, Socrates.

SOCRATES: So, tell me, what do you say the pious and the impious are?

EUTHYPHRO: I'll tell you right now that the pious is what I'm doing now, prosecuting the wrongdoer—whether it's for murder or for robbing temples—or one who has committed an offense in any other way such as these, whether it happens to be one's father or mother, or anyone else e at all; and not prosecuting is impious. Moreover, notice that I have powerful evidence that this is how the law is—just what I have already said to others—that what has happened is as it should be, namely, not to give in to one who is unholy, no matter who he happens to be. These 6a very people think that Zeus is the best and most just of the gods, and they agree that he bound his father because he unjustly swallowed his sons, and that Zeus' father, in turn, castrated *his* father for some other such reasons.[12] But they condemn me because I'm prosecuting my

---

[12]Euthyphro is referring to story told by Hesiod of Cronus's castration of Ouranus, and Zeus's later imprisonment of Cronus.

father when he is a wrongdoer, and in this way they say contradictory things about the gods and me.

SOCRATES: Is *this*, Euthyphro, why I'm being indicted—because whenever someone says such things about the gods, I have trouble accepting it for some reason? Surely it's for this reason that some, it seems, will say that I've committed a crime. Now if these things seem right to you, who has

b   a thorough knowledge about such things, surely it's necessary, it seems, for the rest of us to concur. What can those of us who agree that we know nothing about such things say? So tell me, in the name of Friendship,[13] do you really believe these things happened in this way?

EUTHYPHRO: And still more marvelous things than these, Socrates, which most people don't know about.

SOCRATES: Then you believe that the gods really do war among themselves, and that there are terrible feuds and battles and many other such

c   things, the sorts of things the poets talk about and as other sacred things are adorned by our good artists, and especially the robe filled with these adornments that's carried during the Great Panathenaea[14] up the Acropolis? Shall we say these things are true, Euthyphro?

EUTHYPHRO: Not only that, Socrates, but as I was saying just now, I'll describe many other things about divine matters for you, if you wish, which I'm certain will amaze you when you hear them.

SOCRATES: I wouldn't be surprised. But you can go through them for me

d   another time when we have time. For now, try to say more clearly what I asked you just now. For in the first thing you said, you didn't instruct me well enough when I asked what piety is, but you were telling me that piety happens to be what you're doing now—prosecuting your father for murder.

EUTHYPHRO: And indeed I was right to say that, Socrates.

SOCRATES: Perhaps. But yet you say that there are many other pious things, as well.

EUTHYPHRO: Indeed, there are.

SOCRATES: Recall then that this isn't what I requested of you—to instruct me about one or two of the many thing that are pious, but that form[15]

---

[13]This is an oath to Zeus, the patron god of friendship.

[14]One of the great religious festivals held every four years in Athens. The festival culminated in the placement of an elaborately embroidered robe on a statue of Athena Polias ("Athena of the City") in the Erechtheion, one of the temples on the Athenian Acropolis.

[15]The term used here is the same as the one Plato later uses in metaphysical discussions to refer to the Forms (or what we now call the Platonic Forms)—pure essences which exist in a nonphysical realm, and which concrete particular objects in this realm "imitate" or "participate in" or "share in" in such a way as (temporary and imperfectly) to have whatever characteristics they happen to have. Aristotle claims that Socrates did not separate forms from particulars but that it was Plato and his followers who first did so (Aristotle, *Metaphysics* M.4.1079b17–32; see also *Metaphysics* A.6.987a32–b12), and most scholars agree that there is no reason to see this metaphysical theory underlying Socrates' remark here, for the same term can be used—as it seems to be here—to identify the common character among

by which all pious things are pious. You were saying, weren't you, that all impious things are impious and all pious things are pious by reason of a single characteristic. Or don't you recall?

EUTHYPHRO: Indeed, I do.

SOCRATES: Instruct me then about what this very characteristic is in order that by looking at it and using it as a standard, I can say what either you or someone else might do is the sort of thing that is pious and that what is not of this sort I can say it is not pious.

EUTHYPHRO: Well, if you want it put this way, I'll put it this way for you.

SOCRATES: Indeed, I do want it.

EUTHYPHRO: What's pleasing to the gods is pious, then, and what isn't pleasing to the gods is impious.

SOCRATES: Excellent, Euthyphro. You are answering now in the way I was looking for. I don't know yet if you're right, but it's clear that you're going on to show that what you say is true.

EUTHYPHRO: Of course.

SOCRATES: Come, then, and let's consider what we're saying. Both what is beloved by the gods and the one who's beloved by the gods are pious, but what's hateful to gods and the person hated by the gods are impious. They're not the same but complete opposites—the pious and the impious. Is that it?

EUTHYPHRO: That's it.

SOCRATES: And does this appear to be right?

EUTHYPHRO: I think so.

SOCRATES: Then, Euthyphro, is it right that the gods fight and disagree with each other and that there is hatred among them for each other?

EUTHYPHRO: Yes.

SOCRATES: Is there disagreement about what things create the hatred and anger? Let's look at it this way: If you and I were to disagree about which number is greater, would the disagreement make us enemies and make us angry with each other, or would we quickly get rid of disagreement by resorting to calculation about these sorts of things?

EUTHYPHRO: Of course.

SOCRATES: Then if we were disagreeing about the larger and the smaller, by resorting to measurement, would we quickly put an end to the disagreement?

EUTHYPHRO: That's true.

SOCRATES: And by resorting to the scale, could we judge the heavier and the lighter?

EUTHYPHRO: Of course.

---

many things said to share a characteristic. The "form" of piety, in this case, simply refers to whatever it is that makes all pious things pious—whatever it is that is common to all pious things. This does not require the positing of Forms that are separate from individual particular things that have common characteristics.

SOCRATES: But then about what sort of thing are we enemies and become angry with each other when we've differed and haven't been able to find an answer? Perhaps it is not at the tip of your tongue, but consider what I'm saying—that it's the just and the unjust, noble and disgraceful, and good and bad. Isn't it when we disagree and aren't able to come to a sufficient answer that we become enemies to each other, whenever we do, I and you and everyone else?

EUTHYPHRO: Why, yes, Socrates, the disagreement's about just these things.

SOCRATES: What about the gods, Euthyphro? If indeed they disagree about anything, won't it be on account of these same things?

EUTHYPHRO: Absolutely.

SOCRATES: And about the gods, noble Euthyphro, according to your argument, don't they believe different things are just, noble and disgraceful, and good and bad. I don't suppose they fight with each other unless they disagree about these things? Isn't that so?

EUTHYPHRO: You're right.

SOCRATES: Therefore, what each believes to be noble and good and just, they love. But the opposites of these, they hate.

EUTHYPHRO: Certainly.

SOCRATES: So, according to you, the same things are believed to be just by some and believed to be unjust by others, and it's when they disagree about these that they fight and make war on each other. Isn't it so?

EUTHYPHRO: It is.

SOCRATES: So the same things, it seems, are hated by the gods and loved by gods, and the same things are hateful to gods and beloved by the gods.

EUTHYPHRO: It would seem.

SOCRATES: And, then, the same things would be pious and impious, Euthyphro, by this argument.

EUTHYPHRO: So it turns out.

SOCRATES: Then you haven't answered what I asked, as impressive as you are. For I wasn't asking what happens to be both pious and impious; yet what would be beloved of gods is hateful to the gods, it seems. The result, Euthyphro, is that it wouldn't be at all surprising if what you're doing now in punishing your father is pleasing to Zeus but hateful to Cronus and Ouranos, and dear to Hephaestus and hateful to Hera, and the same thing applies if any of the other gods differ with each other about this.

EUTHYPHRO: But I think, Socrates, that about this matter none of the gods differ with each other, namely, that the one who has killed someone unjustly needn't pay the penalty for it.

SOCRATES: What about human beings, Euthyphro? Have you ever heard someone disputing the claim that one who kills unjustly or who does anything else whatever unjustly needn't pay the penalty for it?

EUTHYPHRO: They never stop disputing about these things in the courts and elsewhere. For they commit all sorts of wrongs and then do and say everything to avoid paying the penalty.

SOCRATES: Is it that they agree, Euthyphro, that they've been unjust, and having agreed to that, they nevertheless say that they don't need to pay the penalty?

EUTHYPHRO: It is never *this*.

SOCRATES: Then they don't do and say exactly everything. I don't think that they would dare say that if indeed they have acted unjustly, they shouldn't pay the penalty. Rather, I think they say they've not acted unjustly. Isn't that so?   d

EUTHYPHRO: You're right.

SOCRATES: So, then, they don't dispute that the one who acts unjustly must pay the penalty. Rather, they dispute who the wrongdoer is, what he did, and when?

EUTHYPHRO: You're right.

SOCRATES: Then, do the same things occur to the gods, if indeed they fight about matters of justice and injustice, according to your account—one saying that the other is unjust and the other denying it? For surely neither god nor man would dare say that the wrongdoer need not pay the penalty!   e

EUTHYPHRO: Yes, Socrates, you've made just the right point.

SOCRATES: So when gods and men dispute—if the gods dispute—they dispute about each action that's been performed. And when they dispute about some action, some say that it was done justly and others that it was done unjustly. Isn't that so?

EUTHYPHRO: Of course.

SOCRATES: Come now, dear Euthyphro, so that I may become wiser,   9a instruct me about your proof that all the gods think that one has died unjustly when he was a worker and became a murderer and was bound by the dead man's master and who died from being tied up before the one who bound him could learn from the Religious Counselors what he needed to do about him. Show me how, on behalf of such a person, it's right for a son to prosecute his father and to bring against him a charge of murder. Come, then, and try to make this clear to me that all of the   b gods unquestionably agree that this is the right course of action. If you would make this sufficiently clear to me, I'll never stop praising you for your wisdom.

EUTHYPHRO: Well, that's perhaps no small task, though I could show you quite clearly.

SOCRATES: I understand. That's because I seem to you to be slower than the jurors, since it is clear that you'll show them that such acts are unjust and that all the gods hate such acts.

EUTHYPHRO: It'll be quite clear, if, in fact, they'll listen to what I say.

c   SOCRATES: They *will* listen if indeed you seem to be speaking well. In any case, I was thinking while you were talking and I put this question to myself: "Even if Euthyphro shows me convincingly that all of the gods believe that such a death is unjust, what more have I learned from Euthyphro about both the pious and the impious? This deed, it seems, would then be hateful to the gods. But it was revealed just now that the impious and the impious are not defined in this way, for what is hateful to the gods was manifestly what is beloved of gods." So I'll release you

d   from this point, Euthyphro. If you want, let all the gods believe this is unjust and let all the gods hate it. Well, then, is this what we're now correcting in our account—that what all of the gods hate is impious and what all of the gods love is pious, and what some love and some hate is neither or both? Do you then want us to define the pious and impious in this way?

EUTHYPHRO: What's to stop us, Socrates?

SOCRATES: Nothing at all is to stop *me*, Euthyphro, but consider your view to see if in setting it down in this way you'll most easily instruct me about what you promised.

e   EUTHYPHRO: I'd say that the pious is what all of the gods love, and the opposite of this—what all of the gods hate—is the impious.

SOCRATES: Should we consider this next then, Euthyphro, to see if you're right, or should we just allow it and accept what we ourselves or other people say, if someone only says it is, and concede that it's so? Or should we look into what the speaker says?

EUTHYPHRO: We should look into it. However, I think that this time I'm right.

10a   SOCRATES: We'll know better in a minute, my good man. But first think about this: Is the pious loved by the gods because it is pious, or is it pious because it is loved?

EUTHYPHRO: I don't know what you mean, Socrates.

SOCRATES: Then I'll try to say it more clearly. We talk about something's being carried and carrying, being led and leading, being seen and seeing; and do you understand that all such things are different from each other and in what way they are different?

EUTHYPHRO: I think I understand.

SOCRATES: Therefore, there is what is loved and it is different from what loves?

EUTHYPHRO: Of course.

b   SOCRATES: Tell me now: Is what's being carried something carried *because it's being carried,* or is it a thing that's carried for some other reason?

EUTHYPHRO: No, it's for this reason.

SOCRATES: And then a thing that's led is a led thing because it's being led, and a seen thing because it's being seen?

EUTHYPHRO: Of course.

SOCRATES: Therefore, it's not because it's a seen thing that it's being seen, but the opposite: It's because it is being seen that it's a seen thing. Nor is it because it's a led thing that it's being led, but it's because it's being led that it's a led thing. Nor is it because it's a carried thing that it's being carried, but it's because it's being carried that it's a carried thing. So, is what I want to say clear? I want to say this: If something becomes or undergoes anything, it does not become what it does because it's what becomes that, but rather it's what becomes that because it becomes what it does. Nor does it undergo what it does because it's what undergoes that, but it's what undergoes that, because it undergoes what it does. Or, don't you concede this? c

EUTHYPHRO: I do.

SOCRATES: Then is a loved thing either what's become something or undergoes something by something?

EUTHYPHRO: Of course.

SOCRATES: And is it just as it was with the previous items? It's not because it's a loved thing that it's loved by whom it's loved; rather, because it's loved, it's a loved thing.

EUTHYPHRO: Necessarily.

SOCRATES: So then—what are we saying about the pious, Euthyphro? Is it anything other than what's loved by all the gods, according to your account? d

EUTHYPHRO: Yes.

SOCRATES: Then it's in virtue of this—because it's pious—or for some other reason?

EUTHYPHRO: No, that's why.

SOCRATES: Then is it loved because it's pious, but it's not pious because it's loved?

EUTHYPHRO: It seems so.

SOCRATES: But it's because it's loved by the gods that it's a loved thing and beloved of gods.

EUTHYPHRO: Of course.

SOCRATES: Then what's beloved of gods isn't pious and the pious isn't what's beloved of gods, as you're claiming, but the one is different from the other.

EUTHYPHRO: How's that, Socrates? e

SOCRATES: Because we agree that the pious is loved because it's pious, but it's not pious because it's loved. Isn't that right?

EUTHYPHRO: Yes.

SOCRATES: But the thing that's beloved of gods is beloved of gods *by this very being loved*, that is, *because* it is loved by the gods. But it is not because it is beloved of gods that it is being loved.

EUTHYPHRO: You're right.

SOCRATES: But if being a thing beloved of gods and being pious were indeed the same thing, Euthyphro, and the pious is loved in virtue of its being pious, then the thing that's beloved of gods would be loved by them in virtue of being a thing beloved of gods. And if the thing beloved of gods is beloved of gods in virtue of being loved by the gods, then the 11a pious would be pious in virtue of being loved. But now you see that the opposite holds for them, since they are completely different from each other. The one is the loved sort of thing because the gods love it; in the other case, the gods love it because it is the loved sort of thing. When you were asked what the pious is, it turned out, Euthyphro, that you didn't want to make its essential nature clear to me, but you mentioned

b   a feature that *happens* to the pious—namely being loved by all the gods.[16] But what it is, you haven't yet said. So please don't hide it from me, but again, tell be from the beginning what the pious is—whether it's loved by the gods or whatever it takes on, for we don't differ about this—but tell me earnestly what the pious and the impious are?

EUTHYPHRO: But Socrates, I can't tell you what I know. What we propose somehow always moves around us and doesn't want to stay where we set it down.

c   SOCRATES: What you've said seems to have come from my ancestor, Daedalus.[17] If I were saying this and proposing these things, you would probably make fun of me since the results of my arguments run around and don't want to stay where they're put, on account of my relationship to him. But as it is, they're your claims. We really need another joke, because, as you yourself think, it's for *you* that they don't want to stay put.

EUTHYPHRO: I think the same joke fits what's been said, for I'm not the one

d   making them moving around and not staying put in the same place. But you strike me as the Daedalus, since it's because of you that they don't stay put in this way.

SOCRATES: I'm afraid, then, that I'm a more clever artist than he was, in so far as he only made his own creations move about, whereas I, it seems, make others' move about—as well as my own. Indeed, this is the most incredible aspect of my craft—that I'm wise unwillingly. For I wanted

e   my arguments to stay put and remain settled more than to have the riches of Tantalus in addition to the wisdom of Daedalus. But enough

---

[16]A similar consideration from a more modern viewpoint might help us to understand Socrates' argument. Consider what God wants us to do. If we say, as most contemporary theists do, that God wants us to do all and only good things, and (as an omnibenevolent being) that it is for this very reason—that they are good—that God wants us to do them, then even if it is true that all good things are, as a matter of fact, wanted from us by God, we cannot say they are good *because* they are the things God wants from us—that cannot be what *makes them good*—for that would make the property they needed to have *in order to be* wanted from us by God turn out to be *the result* of God's wanting them, rather than the *condition of* God's wanting them.

[17]One of the stories that made up Greek folklore claimed that Daedalus' statues were so lifelike that they would actually move around. It is not clear why Socrates would claim that Daedalus was his ancestor. Some ancient writers claimed that Socrates' father was a stone worker. If so, Socrates would probably have been trained in his father's occupation. However, there is no credible evidence that such was indeed his father's occupation.

of this. Since you seem not to be up to it, I'll be delighted to share my eagerness with you how you can instruct me about what the pious is. So don't give up on the task. See if it doesn't seem necessary to you that all of the pious is just.

EUTHYPHRO: That seems right to me.

SOCRATES: Then is all of the just pious? Or is all of the pious just but not all of the just is pious, but some of it is and some of it is something else?   12a

EUTHYPHRO: I'm not following what you're saying, Socrates.

SOCRATES: And yet you're wiser than I am, just as you're younger than I am. What I'm saying is that you've grown soft because of your wealth of wisdom. But, blessed one, steel yourself: For it's not difficult to grasp what I'm saying. I mean the opposite of what the poet meant when he wrote:

> One doesn't want to dispute with Zeus, the creator, who brought all things about. For where there is fear, there is reverence.

Thus, I disagree with this poet. Shall I tell you in what way?

EUTHYPHRO: Of course.   b

SOCRATES: Well, then, it doesn't seem to me that "where there is fear, there is reverence"; for many people who are afraid seem to me to fear sickness, poverty, or many other such things, but they don't have reverence for what they fear. Doesn't it seem that way to you?

EUTHYPHRO: Of course.

SOCRATES: But where there is reverence, there is fear, since hasn't whoever revered and felt ashamed about something at the same time both feared and worried about a bad reputation?

EUTHYPHRO: He'd surely be worried about it.   c

SOCRATES: Then it isn't right to say that "where there is fear, there is reverence," but where there is reverence, there is fear; however, it's not the case that everywhere there's fear, there's reverence. For I think that fear's more extensive than reverence, for reverence is a part of fear—just as odd is a part of, so that it's not that wherever there's number, there's odd number, but wherever there's odd number, there's number. Surely you follow now.

EUTHYPHRO: Of course.

SOCRATES: This is the sort of thing I was asking about when I was talking back then: Is it that where there's justice, there's also piety, or that where there's piety, there's also justice, but piety isn't wherever justice is? For piety is a part of justice. Should we say this, or does it seem to you to be otherwise?   d

EUTHYPHRO: No, this appears to me to be the right way.

SOCRATES: See now what follows: If the pious is a part of justice, we should, it seems, discover the sort of part of justice the pious is. Thus, if you asked me about one of the things we were discussing just now—for example, what sort of part of number is the even, and what sort of number this happens to be, I'd say that it is not the scalene triangle but the isosceles.[18] Or doesn't that seem to you to be that way?

EUTHYPHRO: It does.

e SOCRATES: Try to instruct me then about what sort of part of justice the pious is so that we may tell Meletus not to be unjust to us any longer and not to indict us for impiety since I've learned enough from you about what's holy and pious and what's not.

EUTHYPHRO: The part of justice that seems to me to be both holy and pious is what concerns service to the gods, and the remaining part of justice is what concerns service to men.

13a SOCRATES: It appears to me that you're right, Euthyphro. But I still need one little thing. I don't yet understand what you're calling "service." You probably don't mean one like services concerning other things. This is what we mean, for example, when we say that not everyone knows how to take care of horses, but the horse trainer does. Isn't that right?

EUTHYPHRO: Of course.

SOCRATES: For horsemanship is, I suppose, the service concerning horses?

EUTHYPHRO: Yes.

SOCRATES: And not everyone knows how to care for dogs, but the hunter does.[19]

EUTHYPHRO: Just so.

SOCRATES: And isn't huntsmanship, I suppose, the service concerning dogs?

b EUTHYPHRO: Yes.

SOCRATES: Isn't herdsmanship the service concerning cattle?

EUTHYPHRO: Of course.

SOCRATES: And now are piety and holiness a service concerning the gods, Euthyphro? Do you mean this?

EUTHYPHRO: I do.

SOCRATES: Doesn't every service achieve the same thing? For example, this sort of thing: It's for some good or benefit of what is served, just as you see when horses that are served by the art of horsemanship are benefited and become better. Or doesn't it seem that way to you?

EUTHYPHRO: It does to me.

c SOCRATES: So are dogs benefited by the craft of the hunter, and cattle by herdsmanship, and all other things in the same way? Or do you think that the service is to the detriment of what is served?

---

[18]The Greek word *isoskeles* means "having equal legs." An isosceles triangle, then, is one with equal sides. The Greeks must have used the isosceles triangles to refer to even numbers and scalene triangles—which have uneven sides—to refer to uneven numbers.

[19]The ancient Greeks did not own dogs simply as pets. Dog owners would have the animals only for their usefulness in hunting. This is why Socrates says that the service concerning dogs is huntsmanship—and not, as we would say, the business of the veterinarian.

EUTHYPHRO: By Zeus, I don't think so.

SOCRATES: But it's for their benefit?

EUTHYPHRO: Certainly.

SOCRATES: Then can it be the case that piety—since it's a service to the gods—is both a benefit to the gods and makes the gods better? Would you concede that whenever you do something pious, you accomplish a good for the gods?

EUTHYPHRO: By god, I don't agree.

SOCRATES: Nor did I think you meant this—far from it—and, in fact, that's why I asked you what you meant by "service to the gods," since I didn't think you meant that sort of thing.   d

EUTHYPHRO: And you're right, Socrates. I don't mean that sort of thing.

SOCRATES: Well then, what service to the gods is piety?

EUTHYPHRO: The very one, Socrates, by which slaves serve their masters.

SOCRATES: I understand. It is a kind of assistance given to the gods.

EUTHYPHRO: Absolutely.

SOCRATES: Can you tell me this: What is accomplished as a result of assistance given to physicians? Don't you think it's health?

EUTHYPHRO: I do.

SOCRATES: What about the assistance given to ship builders? What result does this assistance seek to accomplish?   e

EUTHYPHRO: It's clear that it's a ship.

SOCRATES: And, I suppose, the service rendered for house builders is for a house.

EUTHYPHRO: Yes.

SOCRATES: Tell me now, best one. The assistance to the gods is assistance for the accomplishment of what end? It's clear that you know, especially since you say that you know divine matters best of all men.

EUTHYPHRO: And I'm right, Socrates.

SOCRATES: So say, by Zeus, what is this all-glorious result which the gods accomplish by using our assistance?

EUTHYPHRO: Many wonderful things.

SOCRATES: And so do generals, friend. But all the same, can you easily say   14a what the point of their assistance is, namely, that they accomplish victory in war, or can't you say that?

EUTHYPHRO: Of course.

SOCRATES: And farmers, I think, accomplish many good things. But all the same raising food from the earth is the point of their accomplishment.

EUTHYPHRO: Absolutely.

SOCRATES: So what about the many good things that the gods accomplish? What is the point of their work?

EUTHYPHRO: And I told you a little earlier, Socrates, that it's quite a task to learn exactly how it is with all these matters. I'll simply tell you this: If   b anyone knows how to say and do what pleases the gods through praying and sacrificing, these are pious, and these things preserve private households and the common good of cities. And the opposite of what pleases the gods is unholy, which then overturns and destroys all things.

SOCRATES: You could have told me the point of what I was asking about much more quickly, Euthyphro, if you had wanted. But you're not eager to teach me; that's clear, for now just when you were right on top of it, you turned away. If you had answered that, I'd have learned all I needed from you about what piety is. But it's necessary for the questioner to follow the one who is questioned wherever he leads. So, again, what do you say the piety and piety is: Isn't it a kind of knowledge of sacrifice and prayer?

EUTHYPHRO: I think so.

SOCRATES: Then is sacrificing giving to the gods and prayer asking of the gods?

EUTHYPHRO: Obviously.

SOCRATES: By this account, the knowledge of asking and giving to the gods is piety.

EUTHYPHRO: You understand what I'm saying quite well, Socrates.

SOCRATES: I'm eager for your wisdom and I'm concentrating so that what you're saying won't be lost. So tell me: What's this service to the gods? You say it's asking them and giving to them.

EUTHYPHRO: I do.

SOCRATES: And isn't asking them for these things a matter of correctly asking what we need from them?

EUTHYPHRO: What else?

SOCRATES: And next is giving back to them in return giving correctly what they happen to need from us. For I suppose it wouldn't be very craftsmanlike to give to someone what isn't needed.

EUTHYPHRO: You're right, Socrates.

SOCRATES: So, the craft of piety is a kind of commercial business that men and gods engage in with each other.

EUTHYPHRO: A commercial business, if you like calling it that.

SOCRATES: I don't like calling it that unless it's true. But tell me, what benefit do the gods happen to get from the gifts they receive from us? What they give is clear to everyone. For we have nothing good that they don't provide us. But how are they benefited by what they get from us? Or do we get so much more from them from this business, that we get all good things from them but they get nothing good from us?

EUTHYPHRO: Do you believe that the gods benefit from what they get from us?

SOCRATES: Well then, Euthyphro, what in the world are these gifts from us to the gods?

EUTHYPHRO: Do you think it's anything but honor and respect and, as I was saying just now, gratitude?

SOCRATES: Then is the pious what gratifies but isn't beneficial or even loved by the gods?

EUTHYPHRO: I think that this is what's loved above all by the gods!

SOCRATES: Then the pious is, it seems, what's loved by the gods.

EUTHYPHRO: Absolutely.

SOCRATES: Would you be surprised, then, having said these things, if what you say doesn't stay put but walks around? And you accuse me of being the Daedalus who makes them walk when you're really much more skillful than Daedalus in making them go around in a circle? Or don't you see that, having gone around, our account comes back around to the same spot? You remember, surely, that earlier the pious and what is loved by the gods didn't appear to be the same thing but appeared different from each other. Or don't you remember?

EUTHYPHRO: I remember.

SOCRATES: Don't you realize that you're saying that what's loved by the gods is pious? But isn't this the same thing you were saying before?

EUTHYPHRO: Of course.

SOCRATES: Then either our agreement earlier wasn't a good one, or if it was, then what we are establishing just now isn't right.

EUTHYPHRO: It seems so.

SOCRATES: Then we must go back to the beginning to consider what the pious is, since I won't back off from this voluntarily until I understand. So, don't ignore me, but by all means set your mind to it and tell me the absolute truth. For you know if anyone does and you mustn't, like Proteus,[20] be set free before you say what it is. For if you didn't know clearly what the pious and the impious are, you couldn't possibly be trying to prosecute your elderly father for murder on behalf of a servant, and you'd fear that you'd be at risk with respect to the gods that you would be wrong in doing this and would be held in contempt by men. But now I'm quite confident that you think you know what the pious and the impious are. So tell me, good Euthyphro, and don't hide what you believe it is.,

EUTHYPHRO: Another time, Socrates. I must hurry off somewhere, and it's time for me to get out of here.

SOCRATES: What are you doing, friend? By leaving, you're tossing out my great hope that I'd learn from you what things are pious and what aren't and I could escape from Meletus' indictment by showing him that I've become wise about divine matters through Euthyphro and no longer speak off-handedly from ignorance or make innovations about them, and, especially, that I'd be a better person for the rest of my life.

---

[20]Proteus, a god of the sea, who could change shape at will. According to Homer's *Odyssey* (IV, 384–393), Proteus promised that he would tell the truth to anyone who could hold him down and keep him from transforming himself. Socrates, then, is threatening to hold on to Euthyphro and not let him go until he tells Socrates the right definition of piety.

Apology of Socrates

The title of this work in Greek is *Apologia Socratous*. We have given it the common title, *Apology of Socrates* (and refer to it generally as the *Apology*), because that is the way it is commonly referred to by scholars and readers around the world. This title is, however, somewhat misleading, for *apologia* in Greek simply means "defense"; it does not mean what we mean by "apology." Of course, one might well offer some sort of apology for one's behavior in a defense speech, but readers will not find such a tactic offered by Socrates in this work by Plato, which purports to be the defense Socrates gave at his trial. Socrates does *defend* the way he has lived his life, but he plainly does not *apologize* for anything here.

The extent to which Plato's writing is faithful to the actual speech Socrates gave is a matter of considerable controversy. (See our discussion in the Introduction to this book.) After first defending himself against the slanders that have been told about him for many years and then interrogating the prosecutor Meletus, Socrates makes his defense of philosophy, as he practices it, the centerpiece of the speech. He has, he says, been engaged in nothing less than a philosophical "mission," undertaken at the behest of the god. Over the years he tried to improve the souls of those with whom he has practiced philosophy by freeing them from any pretense to wisdom and exhorting them to make moral virtue and the perfection of the soul their first concern.

After he is convicted, Socrates is required to propose a counterpenalty to the prosecution's proposed penalty of death. Socrates is willing to have a substantial fine of 30 minas be paid on his behalf by four of his friends. The last part of the *Apology*, which follows the jury's rejection of Socrates' proposed counterpenalty, was not a formal part of the proceeding. However, it is possible that Socrates would be permitted to make final remarks to the jurors before leaving the court.

17a   I don't know what effect my accusers[21] have had on you, Athenians, but they were speaking so persuasively that I myself almost forgot who I am. And yet they said virtually nothing that's true. Of their many lies, one surprised me most of all: When they said you needed to be on your

b   guard against getting tricked by me, because I'm a clever speaker. Their not being ashamed of that seems to me to be the worst thing they did, because I'm immediately going to refute them by what I do—as soon as

---

[21]The speeches given by Socrates' accusers took place during the morning of the trial. Meletus was the man who actually brought the formal charges against him. But it was not uncommon to ask others to speak in court, as part of the presentations of the prosecution or the defense to the jurors. Apparently, speaking in support of Meletus' indictment were two others, Anytus and Lycon, which is why Socrates refers to more than one accuser. It does not appear that Socrates had anyone else give a speech as part of his defense.

I show that I'm not a clever speaker at all—unless they call a clever speaker one who tells the truth. If this is what they mean, I'd agree that I'm an orator, though not the way they are. As I say, they've said almost nothing that's true. But you'll hear only the truth from me, and yet not, by god, Athenians, in beautifully crafted language like theirs, carefully arranged with words and phrases. Instead, you'll hear things said by   c
me without any planning, in words as they occur to me—for I assume that what I say is just—and none of you should expect anything else. Nor would it be appropriate, I suppose, men, for someone at my age to come before you like a boy planning out what he's going to say. I really implore you to grant me one thing: If you hear me making my defense with the same language I'm used to using in the marketplace at the merchants' tables, where many of you have heard me, and elsewhere, don't   d
be surprised and don't make a disturbance because of it. The truth is this: Now is the first time I've come before a court, although I'm seventy years old. I'm a complete stranger to the language used here.[22] So just as if I really were a stranger, you would surely forgive me if I spoke in that dialect and manner of speaking in which I had been brought up, so   18a
what I am now asking is fair, it seems to me, namely, that you ignore the way I speak—it's not important—and you pay attention to and concentrate on this one thing: if what I say is just or not. This is the virtue of a judge; the virtue of a speaker is to tell the truth.

First, then, it's right for me to make my defense, Athenians, against the first of the false accusations made against me and against my first accusers, and then against the later ones and the later accusers. Many   b
have accused me before you, and have done so for a long time now, though they didn't say anything that's true. I'm more afraid of them than I am of Anytus and those with him, although they do worry me. But the earlier ones worry me more, men, who having gotten hold of many of you when you were children, convinced you with accusations against me that weren't any truer than the ones I now face. They said that there's a certain Socrates, a wise man, who thinks about what's in the heavens and who has investigated all the things below the earth and who makes the weaker argument appear to be the stronger. Those who   c
spread this rumor, Athenians, are the accusers who worry me. For the people who hear such things believe that those who inquire about such topics also don't believe in the gods. There are lots of these accusers and they've been at it for a long time already, telling you these things when

---

[22]Socrates is not claiming not to know how people speak or act in courtrooms, for later he shows that he does have some knowledge of such things (see 32a and 34c). His claim is only that he has never before been a litigant in a courtroom. In Athens' participatory democracy, those who did fancy themselves clever speakers would be very likely to have direct experience in litigation. Here and elsewhere, Socrates emphasizes the fact that he has not engaged in the sorts of political activities one would expect from him, if indeed he were the sort of "clever speaker" his accusers have made him out to be.

you were still at an age when you were most apt to believe them, when some of you were children and others were adolescents, and they made their case when absolutely no one presented a defense. But the most unreasonable part of all is that it's impossible to know and say their names, except one who happens to be a certain writer of comedies.[23] Those who persuaded you by using malice and slander, and some who persuaded others after they themselves had been persuaded—all are very hard to deal with. It isn't even possible to bring any of them up here and to question them, and it's absolutely necessary in making my defense to shadow-box, as it were, and to ask questions when no one answers. Trust me, then, that, as I say, two groups of accusers have arisen against me: the ones who are accusing me right now and the others who I say have been accusing me for quite a while. And please understand that I should defend myself against the latter group first. After all, you heard them accusing me earlier and with much more intensity than the ones who came later.

Well, then, I must make my defense, Athenians, and try to remove from your minds in such a short time the slander you accepted for a long time. I'd hope this happens, if it's better for you and for me, and that in making my defense I do it successfully. But it's not lost on me that this sort of task I'm facing will be difficult. In any case, let this turn out as the god wants; I must obey the law and make a defense.

Let's take up from the beginning what the accusation against me is from which the slander about me arose—the one that Meletus in particular put his faith in when he brought this indictment against me. Well, what did the slanderers say? I must read it as if it were the sworn statement of accusers: "Socrates does wrong and is too concerned with inquiring about what's in the heavens and below the earth and to make the weaker argument appear to be the stronger and to teach these same things to others"—something like this. For you yourselves saw these things in the comedy by Aristophanes: a Socrates being carried around there, saying that he's walking on air and all kinds of other nonsense which I don't understand at all.[24] And I don't mean to disparage knowledge of this sort, if anyone is wise about such things (may I not have to answer such charges by Meletus as that!), but, as a matter of fact, I don't possess a bit of that wisdom, Athenians. I'm supplying many of you as my witnesses, and I ask you to talk to and inform each other, as many of you as ever heard me carrying on a discussion—and there are many of you in this category—tell each other whether any of you have ever

---

[23]Socrates is referring to Aristophanes, the comic playwright. He refers to Aristophanes explicitly below, at 19c.

[24]The reference is to Aristophanes' play, the *Clouds,* which was first produced in 423 B.C.E. A central character named "Socrates" is made to look mischievous and silly to achieve a comic effect.

heard me discussing anything at all about things of this sort. And from this you'll know that the other things that most people say about me are no different.

In fact there's nothing to these claims, not even if you've heard someone say that I try to instruct people and make money that way. No, not even this is true. Although as a matter of fact I think it's impressive if anyone is able to instruct people in the way Gorgias of Leontini, Prodicus of Ceos, and Hippias of Elis pretend to do.[25] Each of them is able to go into any city and persuade the young—who can associate for free with any of their own citizens they want to—to abandon their associations with the local people and to associate instead with them and pay them and to thank them for it on top of it all. And then there's another wise man, a Parian, who I learned was living here. For I happened to run into Callias, the son of Hipponicus, a man who had paid more money to the sophists than anyone else. So I asked him—he has two sons—"Callias," I said, "if your two sons were two colts or two calves, and we could get hold of and hire an expert for them, who would make them admirable and good in the appropriate virtue? This person would be knowledgeable either about horses or farming. But now, since they're men, what expert do you have in mind to get for them? Who's knowledgeable about this sort of virtue, that of a human being and a citizen? I imagine you've looked into it, because you have two sons. Is there someone," I said, "or not?" "Of course," he said. "Who is he," I said, "and where does he come from, and how much does he charge for instruction?" "Evenus," he said, "a Parian, and 5 minas." And I called Evenus blessed, if he really has such a skill and teaches for such a reasonable fee.[26] I myself would certainly be pretty puffed up and would act like a bigshot if I knew these things. But the fact is that I don't know them, Athenians.

One of you, perhaps, might respond: "So what's the matter with you, Socrates? Where did these accusations come from? For surely if you weren't engaged in something unusual but were only doing something different from most people, these rumors and talk about you wouldn't have gotten started. So tell us what it is, so that we don't reach

e

20a

b

c

d

---

[25]Each was a prominent sophist. The sophists were teachers who traveled throughout Greece. It is difficult to generalize about the various subjects they professed to teach, but the most prominent of the sophists taught forensic and public speaking. Because some made extravagant claims about improving the character of their students, they were viewed with suspicion and outright contempt by many Athenians, who saw moral education as the province of the family and state (see 24d–25a).

[26]A mina was equal to 100 silver drachmae. One drachma was the average daily wage for a worker in Athens at this time, and so a single mina was equivalent to 100 days' wages for many Athenian workers. Even though 5 minas is, then, a considerable sum of money, Socrates is being sincere when he says that it is really quite reasonable if Evenus can indeed do what he claims, namely provide Callias with sons of good character.

a hasty judgment about you." I think this is a fair question, and I'll try to show you what produced both my reputation and the slander. So listen. No doubt, I'll seem to some of you to be joking. Rest assured, however, that I'll say only what's true. Athenians, I acquired this reputation on account of nothing other than a sort of wisdom. Well, what sort of wisdom is this? It is, surely, just human wisdom. It's likely that I really

e am wise in that sense. These men, to whom I was referring just now, might perhaps be wise in a way that's greater than human, or else I don't know what to call it. For I'm certainly not wise in that way, and whoever says I am is either lying or saying it to slander me. And don't interrupt me with your jeering, Athenians, not even if I seem to you to be bragging. The story I'm about to tell you isn't mine, but I refer you to a speaker you trust. About my wisdom, if it really is wisdom and what

21a sort of wisdom it is, I'll produce as a witness the Delphic god.[27] I suppose you know Chairephon. He was both my friend ever since we were young, and also a friend to your democratic faction, and he took part in your faction's exile, and he came back into the city with you.[28] And you know what sort of person Chairephon was and how impulsive he was about whatever he had an urge to do. Once, in particular, he had the nerve to go to Delphi and ask the oracle this question—and, as I say, don't interrupt me, men—he really did ask if anyone is wiser than I am. Then the Pythia responded that no one is wiser. His brother here will serve as a witness for you about these matters, since Chairephon is dead.

b Consider why I'm telling you this. I'm about to explain to you how the slandering of me came about. When I heard about what the oracle told Chairephon, here's what I thought about it: "What's the god saying and what's he hinting at? For I'm aware that, in fact, I'm not wise at all. What then does he mean in saying that I'm the wisest? He certainly isn't lying. That isn't divinely sanctioned for him." And for a long time I was puzzled about what he meant. And then, and with great reluc-tance, I undertook a search for its meaning in this way: I went to one of

c those who's reputed to be wise in order there, if indeed anywhere, to refute the oracle's response and show the oracle: "This person here is wiser than I am, but you claimed that I'm the wisest man." Then after thoroughly examining him—I needn't mention his name, Athenians, but he was one of the politicians that I had this sort of experience with.

---

[27]The Greek god Apollo was believed to communicate to humans through the oracle at Del-phi. Delphi is located in the mountains, about seventy miles northwest of Athens.

[28]At the end of the Peloponnesian War, a commission of thirty men was established to rewrite the laws of Athens. The group soon became known as the Thirty Tyrants, for they soon made it clear that they had no interest in recognizing the rights most Athenians enjoyed under democratic rule (see also note 38, below). Many who wanted to see democracy reestablished in Athens left the city and later retook the city by force from those loyal to the Thirty. Socrates' friend, Chairephon, was one who fought on the side of the democrats.

After conversing with him, I thought that this guy seems to be wise to many other people and, most of all, to himself, yet he isn't. And then I tried to show him that he thought he is wise, but he isn't. And so, as a result, I became hated by him and by many of those who were there. So, as I went away from him, I concluded to myself that I'm, indeed, wiser than this guy. I'm afraid that neither of us knows anything admirable and good, but this guy thinks he knows something when he doesn't, whereas I, just as I don't know, don't even think I know. At least, then, I seem to be wiser in this small way than this guy, because I don't even think I know what I don't know. From him, I went to someone else, one of those reputed to be wiser than the first guy, and the very same thing seemed to me to be true, and at that point I became hated by that guy and by many others too.   d   e

After that I went from one person to the next, and although I was troubled and fearful when I saw that I had become hated, nevertheless I thought I had to make the god's business the most important thing. In searching for the meaning of the oracle, I had to proceed on to all who had a reputation for knowing something. And, by the Dog,[29] Athenians—for I must tell you the truth—the fact is that I experienced something of this sort: Those who enjoyed the greatest reputation seemed to me, as I searched in accordance with the god, to be pretty much the most lacking, whereas those who were reputed to be less worthy of consideration were better men when it came to having good sense.   22a

Now, I must instruct you about my wandering, undertaken like labors, which resulted in my not refuting the oracle. After the politicians I went to the poets—those who write tragedies, dithyrambs, and the others, so that right in the very act of questioning them, I would catch myself being more ignorant than they are. Then when they read their poetry, which I thought they had really worked at, I asked them what they meant in order to learn something from them. Now I'm embarrassed to tell you the truth, but I must say it. Virtually everyone present could have given a better account of what they had written. After a little while, I realized this about the poets: They composed what they did, not out of wisdom but by some kind of natural ability and because they were divinely inspired, just like seers and prophets. For even though they in fact say many fine things, they don't know what they're saying. It was evident to me that the poets had been affected in some way like this. I found out that because of their poetry, they thought they were the wisest of people in other ways as well, which they weren't. So I left them, thinking that I'm superior to them in just the way that I'm superior to the politicians.   b   c

---

[29]The expression is uncommon. Socrates is clearly using it to signal to the jury the importance of what he is about to say.

d   And then finally, I went to the craftsmen. I was aware that I knew virtually nothing, but I also knew that I'd discover that they knew many admirable things. I wasn't deceived about this: They did know what I didn't know, and in that way they were wiser than I am. But, Athenians, the good craftsmen also seemed to me to make the same mistake the poets committed. Because of practicing his craft well, each one believed he was supremely wise in other things, the most important things—and

e   this very mistake of theirs seemed to me to overshadow that wisdom they did have. So I asked myself on behalf of the oracle whether I would prefer to be simply as I am, neither being wise in their sort of wisdom, nor ignorant in the way they are ignorant, or to be in both ways as they are. Then I answered myself and the oracle that I'd be better off being simply as I am.

23a   This very investigation, Athenians, has generated for me a great deal of hatred, which is most difficult to handle and hard to bear, and the result has been a lot of slandering, and the claim made that I'm "wise." It's because every time the people present think that I'm wise about the subject I refute someone else on. But what's likely, men, is that the god is really wise and that in this oracle he means that human wis-

b   dom is of little or no value. And he appears to mean that such a person is Socrates and to have used my name, taking me as an example, as if to say, "This one of you, O human beings, is wisest, who—as Socrates does—knows that he's in truth worthless with respect to wisdom." And so even now I go around searching and questioning, in keeping with the god, any citizen or stranger whom I think is wise. And when he doesn't seem to me to be so, I help the god out and show that he isn't wise. It's because of this occupation that I have no leisure time worth mentioning

c   to do anything for the city or for my family, but instead I'm in complete poverty on account of my service to the god.

But in addition to this, the young who follow me around, doing so of their free will, who have complete leisure—the sons of the richest people—enjoy hearing people examined, and they often imitate me, and then try to examine others. And then, I imagine, they find an abundance of people who think they know something but know virtually nothing. That's why those who are examined by them get angry with

d   me and not with them, and say that a certain Socrates completely pollutes[30] the land and corrupts the youth. And when anyone asks them what I do and what I teach, they have nothing to say and draw a blank, but so they don't appear to be confused, they say what's commonly said against all philosophers—"what's in the heavens and below the earth,"

---

[30]An ancient Greek notion that one who commits offenses against the gods "pollutes" the surrounding land and makes himself and everyone who inhabits the area liable to divine punishments until the land is "cleansed" by having the one who has offended undergo the proper punishment for the offense.

"doesn't believe in gods," and "makes the weaker argument the stronger." But I think they wouldn't want to say what's true, that they're plainly pretending to know, and they don't know anything. In so far, then, as they are, I think, concerned about their honor, and are zealous, and numerous, and speak earnestly and persuasively about me, they've filled your ears for a long time by vehemently slandering me. It was on this account that Meletus, Anytus, and Lycon came after me: Meletus, angry on behalf of the poets; Anytus, on behalf of the craftsmen and politicians;[31] and Lycon, on behalf of the orators. The result is that, as I was saying when I began, I'd be amazed if I were able to refute in such a little time this slander you accept and that has gotten out of hand. There you have the truth, men of Athens, and in what I'm saying, I'm neither hiding nor even shading anything large or small. And yet I know pretty well that in saying these things, I'm making myself hated, which is evidence that I'm telling the truth and that such is the slander against me and that these are its causes. And whether you investigate these things now or later, you'll discover that they're so.

Let this be enough of a defense for you about what my first accusers accuse me of. But regarding the good and patriotic Meletus, as he says, and the later accusers, I'll try to present a defense next. Just as if they were in fact a different group of accusers, let's take up their sworn statement in turn. It goes, I suppose, like this: They're saying that Socrates does wrong because he corrupts the youth and doesn't believe in the gods that the city believes in, but believes in other new divinities. Such is the charge. But let's examine each part of this accusation.

He says that I do wrong because I corrupt the young. But I say, Athenians, that *he* does wrong, because he's playing around in what's serious business, thoughtlessly putting people on trial, while pretending to be serious and troubled about matters which he has never cared about at all.[32] I'll try to show you this is so.

Come here, Meletus, and tell me. Isn't it true that you take it to be very important that the young be as good as possible?

I do.

Come on now and tell these people: Who improves them? It's clear that you know; at least it's a matter of concern to you. Since you've discovered me as the one who corrupts them, as you say, and you're bringing me to trial before these people here and you're accusing me. Come and tell us who improves them and show these people who he is. Do you notice, Meletus, that you're silent and can't say anything? And yet

e

24a

b

c

d

---

[31] Anytus was a craftsman who became one of the leading members of the democratic faction in Athens. Nothing is known about Lycon other than his participation as one who spoke against Socrates at his trial.

[32] Socrates is punning on the Meletus' name. "Meletus" sounds like *melein,* a Greek verb that means "to care about."

doesn't it seem to you to be disgraceful and sufficient proof of what I'm talking about, that none of this has mattered to you? But tell me, my good man, who improves them?

The laws.

I'm not asking you that. But who's the person who knows the laws to begin with?

These men, Socrates, the jurors.

What're you saying, Meletus—that they're able to educate the young and improve them?

Absolutely.

And which is it? All of them, or is it that some are able to do so and others not?

Everyone is.

What good news, by Hera! There's no shortage of those who provide help! But what about this? Do those who are here listening to the trial improve them or not?

They do, too.

What about the members of the Council[33]?

The members of the Council do, too.

But, then, Meletus, do those in the Assembly, its members, corrupt the youth, or do all of those people improve them?

They do, too.

Therefore, it seems, all Athenians except me make the youth admirable and good, but I alone corrupt them. Is this what you're saying?

That's exactly what I'm saying.

You've condemned me to a terrible fate! But tell me this: Don't you think this also holds with horses? Everyone improves them and an individual corrupts them? Or isn't it just the opposite of this, that one person or only a few are able to improve them—the horse trainers—whereas most people, if in fact they're around and use horses, corrupt them? Isn't that true, Meletus, both with horses and with all other animals? It's absolutely clear that it is, whether you and Anytus say so or not! The young would be fortunate indeed if only one person corrupts them and the others improve them! But the fact is, Meletus, that you're making it quite clear that you've never even thought about the young, and you're making your lack of concern readily apparent, because you haven't been concerned at all about what you're bringing me to trial for.

Anyway, tell me, in the name of Zeus, whether it's better to live among good citizens or bad? Answer, my good man, for I'm not asking

---

[33]The Council was the body of 500, selected by lot and rotated among the citizens, whose primary responsibility was the preparation of the agenda for the Athenian Assembly, the law-making body that all citizens could attend.

you anything difficult! Don't bad people always do something bad to those who happen to be closest to them, whereas good people do something good for those who are closest to them?

Of course.

Then is there anyone who'd rather be harmed by those they're around instead of benefited? Answer, my good man, for the law commands you to answer! Is there anyone who wishes to be harmed? d

Clearly not.

Come then. Are you putting me on trial here on the ground that I corrupt the youth and make them worse voluntarily or involuntarily?

I say you do it voluntarily.

What's that, Meletus? Are you at your age so much wiser than I am at mine that you knew that bad people always do something evil to those who are their closest neighbors, whereas good people always do e something good, but I've reached the point of such ignorance that I don't know this, because if I make someone I'm with bad, I'm likely to receive something bad from him, and so I'm doing such an evil voluntarily, as you say? I'm not persuaded by you about these things, Meletus, nor do I think anyone else is! Either I don't corrupt them, or if I do corrupt them, I do so involuntarily, so that, either way, you're not telling 26a the truth! If I corrupt them involuntarily, however, the law here isn't to bring people to trial for errors of this sort but to take them aside in private to teach and admonish them. For it's clear that once I understand, I'll stop what I'm doing involuntarily. But you've avoided associating with me and you didn't want to instruct me, and instead wanted to bring me here to trial where it's the law to try those who need punishment, not instruction.

Well, anyway, Athenians, what I was saying is obvious, namely, that Meletus has never cared anything at all about these things. Never- b theless, tell us now: How do you say that I corrupt the youth, Meletus? Isn't it in fact clear according to the indictment you wrote that I do so by teaching the young not to believe in the gods that the city believes in but instead to believe in other new divinities? Aren't you claiming that it's by teaching that I corrupt them?

That's exactly what I'm claiming!

In the name of these very gods that we're arguing about, Meletus, tell me and these men here still more clearly. I'm not able to understand c whether you're saying that I teach people not to believe that some gods exist—and therefore that I myself believe gods exist and am not a complete atheist, nor am not a wrongdoer in that way—and yet I do not believe in the ones that the city believes in, but others, and this is what you're accusing me of, because I believe in the others? Or are you saying that I don't believe in gods at all and that I teach others such things?

I'm saying that you don't believe in the gods at all.

Wonderful Meletus, why are you saying these things? Don't I even d believe that the sun and the moon are gods, as other people do?

No, by god, jurymen, since he says that the sun is a stone and the moon is earth.

Do you think you are prosecuting Anaxagoras,[34] Meletus? Are you being contemptuous of these men, and do you think they're so illiterate that they don't know that Anaxagoras of Clazomenae's books are full of these sayings? And, indeed, do you think the young learn from me what they can sometimes buy for at most a drachma in the stalls in the marketplace, and laugh at Socrates, if he pretends they're his own, especially since they're so absurd! In the name of Zeus, do you really think this about me, that I don't believe in any god?

No, by Zeus, you don't, not at all.

You're not to be believed, Meletus—and what's more, I think, not even to yourself! He seems to me, Athenians, to be completely insolent and out of control and this indictment is just the result of insolence, lack of self-restraint, and immaturity. He seems to be testing me by making a riddle, as it were. "Will the wise Socrates recognize that I'm fooling around and contradicting myself, or will I trick him and the others who are listening?" He seems to be saying contradictory things in his indictment, as if he were saying: Socrates is guilty since he doesn't believe in the gods, but he does believe in the gods. And this is the sort of thing someone says when he's fooling around.

So let's consider together, men, in what sense he appears to me to mean what he's saying. Answer us, Meletus; and you, members of the jury, as I requested at the beginning, bear in mind that you're not to interrupt me if I present my arguments in the way I'm used to.

Is there anyone, Meletus, who believes in what is associated with human beings, but who doesn't believe in human beings? Let him answer, men, and don't keep on interrupting. Is there anyone who doesn't believe in horses but who believes in what's associated with horses? Or is there anyone who doesn't believe in flute-players but who believes in what's associated with flute-players? There is not, O best of men! If you don't want to answer, I'll give the answer to you and to the others here. But answer the next one at least: Is there anyone who believes in the existence of what's associated with spiritual things, but who doesn't believe in spirits?

There isn't.

How helpful it was that you answered so reluctantly when you were forced to by the jurors here! Aren't you saying that I believe in and teach that there are spiritual things, whether new or old, and I believe in spiritual things, at least according to your argument, and you swore to that in your indictment. But if I believe in spiritual things, surely it

---

[34]A nature-philosopher who was at one time on friendly terms with Pericles and who may have been exiled. His views about natural change put him at odds with those who held traditional views about the way the gods cause many natural changes.

absolutely has to be true that I believe in spirits. Isn't that so? Of course it is! I take it that you agree with me, since you're not answering. But don't we believe that spirits are at least either gods or the children of gods? Do you say so or not?   d

Of course.

Then if I believe in spirits, as you're saying, and if spirits are gods, then this is what I'm saying that you're making a riddle of and fooling around about when you say that I don't believe in gods and then in addition to that, that I do believe in gods, since at least I believe in spirits. But if spirits are the illegitimate children of gods, either from nymphs or any others from whom it's also said they come, could someone believe that the children gods had with human beings exist, but not believe that gods exist? It would be similarly absurd if someone   e believed in the children of horses and donkeys, that is, mules, but didn't believe in horses and donkeys. Meletus, isn't it true that you wrote this indictment either to test us out or because you were confused about what actual wrongdoing you could accuse me of! It just isn't possible that you could persuade anyone who has even a little sense that the   28a same person could believe in spiritual and divine things and yet for the same person not to believe in spirits, gods, and heroes!

Well anyway, Athenians, that I'm not guilty according to Meletus's indictment doesn't seem to me to need much of a defense, and what I've said about it is enough. But what I was saying earlier—that there's great deal of hatred directed at me and by many people, you may be sure that's true. And it's this that'll convict me, if indeed I'm going to be con-   b victed—not Meletus nor even Anytus but the prejudice and ill will of most people. This is what's convicted many other good men and, I think, it'll do so in the future. And we needn't fear that it'll end with my case.

Perhaps someone could say, "But then aren't you ashamed, Socrates, of having been devoted to such a pursuit that's likely to lead to death at this time?" I should respond to this person as follows: "You're wrong, sir, if you think that a person who has any merit needs to consider the likelihood of life or of death and not to look only to this when he acts: Is he acting justly or unjustly and performing the deeds   c of a good or a bad person? By your argument, all those demigods who died at Troy would be worthless people, and especially the son of Thetis,[35] who scorned such danger when the choice was to endure disgrace, so that his mother, who's a goddess, spoke to him when he was eager to kill Hector, I suppose, in this fashion. 'My child, if you avenge the killing of your friend Patroclus and kill Hector, you yourself will

---

[35]The son of Thetis was Achilles, the Greek hero who, believing that it was right for him to avenge the death of his friend, Patroclus, went forth in battle to kill Hector, even though Achilles knew that the killing of Hector would eventually result in his own death.

die—for right away,' she says, "after Hector, your death awaits you."
But when he heard this, Achilles thought little of danger and death, but
instead since he had a much greater fear of living as a bad man and not

d of avenging his friends, he says, 'may I die after I dispense justice to the
unjust in order that I not remain here, a laughingstock, beside the
curved ships, a burden of the earth?' You don't really think *he* considered death and danger, do you?"

For it really is this way, Athenians, that wherever someone stations
himself, believing it to be best or where someone has been stationed by
his commander, I think, he must remain there to face danger, not weighing death or anything else more than disgrace.

e Thus, I would have done a terrible thing, Athenians, if, when my
commanders, whom you elected to command me, stationed me at
Potidaia, and Amphipolis, and Delium, and then remained where they
stationed me, like anyone else, and risked death and yet when the god
ordered—as I believed and understood myself to have been so ordered—
that I must spend my life philosophizing and examining myself and others, I would have abandoned my position through fear of death or any

29a other concern whatsoever. That would be terrible and then someone
might really bring me to court justly on the ground that I don't believe
the gods exist, since I disobey the oracle, fear death, and think I'm wise
when I'm not. In truth, the fear of death, men, is nothing but thinking
you're wise when you're not, for you think you know what you don't.
For no one knows whether death happens to be the greatest of all goods
for humanity, but people fear it because they're completely convinced

b that it's the greatest of evils. And isn't this ignorance, after all, the most
shameful kind: thinking you know what you don't? But in this respect,
too, men, I'm probably different from most people. If, then, I'd say that
I'm wiser than someone in some way, it would be in this way: While I
don't really know about the things in Hades, I don't think I know. But I
do know that it's evil and disgraceful to do what's wrong and to disobey
one's superior, whether god or man. Rather than those things that I know
are bad, I'll never run from nor fear those things that may turn out to be

c good. The upshot is that even if you let me go because you don't believe
Anytus—who said that either you shouldn't bring me here in the first
place or since you've done so, you have to kill me, telling you that if I
were acquitted, all of your sons will be completely corrupted by spending their time practicing what Socrates teaches—well, if you'd respond
to me: "Socrates, this time we won't do as Anytus says. We'll let you go,

d but on this condition, that you stop spending your time in this inquiry of
yours and philosophizing. But if you're caught still doing so, you'll die."
Thus, if, as I was saying, you were to let me go on this condition, I'd tell
you, "Athenians, I respect and I love you, but I'll obey the god rather than
you, and as long as I breathe and am able, I won't stop philosophizing
and exhorting you and pointing out to any of you I ever happen upon,
saying just what I usually do, 'Best of men, since you're an Athenian,

from the greatest city with the strongest reputation for wisdom and strength, aren't you ashamed that you care about having as much money, fame, and honor as you can, and you don't care about, or even consider wisdom, truth, and making your soul as good as possible?"' And if any of you disputes me on this and says he does care, I won't immediately stop talking to him and go away, but I'll question, examine, and try to refute him. And if he doesn't appear to me to have acquired virtue but says he has, I'll shame him because he attaches greater value to what's of less value and takes what's inferior to be more important. And I'll do this for whomever I come upon, young and old, foreigner and citizen, but I'll be more concerned with citizens insofar as you're more closely related to me.

e

30a

You may be sure that the god has commanded this, and I think that there's no greater good for the city than my service to the god. For the only thing I do is to go around trying to persuade you, young and old, not to care more about either your bodies or money, nor so passionately as you do about the perfection of your souls, saying, "Virtue doesn't come from money, but money and all other good things for human beings, both in private and in public, come from virtue." If I corrupt the young by saying these things, then this would be harmful. But if anyone maintains that I say anything else, he's lying. "Therefore," I would say, "Athenians, be persuaded by Anytus or not, let me go or not, because I won't do anything else, even if I have to die many times."

b

c

Don't interrupt me, but stick to what I asked you to do. Listen to what I'm saying and don't interrupt. I think you'll benefit by listening. For I'm about to tell you some other things that'll probably cause you to yell out. But don't ever do this. Rest assured that if you kill me—since I am the person I say I am—you won't harm me more than you harm yourselves. Neither Meletus nor Anytus could do anything to harm me; it isn't even possible. For I don't think it's divinely sanctioned for a better man to be harmed by a worse. Doubtless, he could kill me, or send me into exile, or take away my rights, and doubtless he and others also think these things are great evils. But I don't. In fact, I think that what he's doing now—trying to kill a man unjustly—is a much greater evil. Athenians, at this point I'm far from making this defense on my behalf, as one might think, but instead I'm making it on yours, so that by condemning me you don't make a terrible mistake regarding the gift the god has given you. For if you kill me, you won't easily find another person like me, simply put, even if it's funny to say so, who's been attached to the city by the god as if it were a large and well-bred horse, though one that's somewhat sluggish on account of its size and that needs to be disturbed by a gadfly. In some such way as this I think the god has attached me to the city—such a person who disturbs you and stirs you up and shames each one of you, I never stop landing on you everywhere all day long. Another one like me won't quickly come to you, men, and if you're persuaded by me, you'll spare

d

e

31a

me. But it's more likely that you'll be angry, like those who are disturbed when they're drowsy, and swat me—having been persuaded by Anytus—and easily kill me, then you'd spend the rest of your life asleep, unless the god, in his concern for you, were to send someone

b   else to you. That I am the sort of person who's been given to the city by the god, you'll see from what I'm about to say. For it doesn't seem to be human nature for me to have neglected all of my own affairs and endured not caring for my family's concerns all these years, and instead to have always done what's in your interest, coming to each of you individually like a father or an older brother, trying to persuade you to care about virtue. If I profited at all from these things and gave advice for a fee, it would make some sense. But now you yourselves see

c   that my accusers, while accusing me of everything else in such a shameless way, couldn't bring themselves to be so shameless as to produce witnesses that I ever made money from anyone or that I asked for any. I think that I'm producing a sufficient witness that I'm telling the truth: my poverty.

Perhaps it would seem odd that I go around giving advice in private and sticking my nose into other people's business but don't dare step up and give the city advice about your concerns in public. The rea-

d   son for this is the one you've often heard me give in many places, namely, something divine and spiritual comes to me, and it's this that Meletus made fun of in the indictment he wrote. It's come to me since childhood—this voice—and whenever it comes, it always turns me away from what I'm about to do but never turns me toward anything. This is what opposes my engaging in politics, and I think it's wonderful that it's done so. For you can be sure, Athenians, that if I'd tried to engage in politics earlier, I'd have been put to death earlier, and neither

e   you nor I would've benefited. Don't be upset at me for telling the truth: No one will survive who genuinely opposes you or any other populace

32a   and tries to prevent many unjust and illegal things from happening in the city. Instead, one who really fights for what's just, if he's to survive even for a little while, must live as a private and not as a public man.

I'm going to provide you with compelling evidence of this, not just talk, but what you respect—actions. Listen now to what happened to me so that you'll know that I'd give in to no one, under any conditions, out of fear of death, contrary to what's just, even if by not giving in I'd die

b   right away. I'm going to tell you some of the things one commonly hears in law courts, but they're true nonetheless. Athenians, I never held any other office in the city, but I was a member of the Council. My district, Antiochis, was in charge of the Council,[36] when you wanted to judge as a group the ten generals who failed to pick up those who died in the sea

---

[36]Each district had fifty representatives (selected by rotation and lot) on the Council (see note 33, above) each year and each group of fifty took a turn being in charge of the Council.

battle.[37] What you wanted though was against the law, as you all realized some time later on. At that time, I was the only one of the Councilors in charge who opposed you, urging you to do nothing against the law, and I voted in opposition. And though the orators were ready to denounce me and arrest me, and though you urged them to do so by your shouting, with the law and justice on my side I thought that, though I feared imprisonment or death, I should run the risk rather than to join with you, since you wanted what's not just. These things happened when the city was still a democracy. But when the oligarchy came to power, the Thirty summoned me and four others to the Rotunda and ordered us to bring Leon from Salamis to be put to death.[38] They often ordered many others to do such things, since they wanted to implicate as many as possible in their causes. At that time I made it clear once again, not by talk but by action, that I didn't care at all about death—if I'm not being too blunt to say it—but it mattered everything that I do nothing unjust or impious, which matters very much to me. For though it had plenty of power, that government didn't frighten me into doing anything that's wrong. So when we left the Rotunda, the other four went to Salamis and arrested Leon, and I left and went home. I suppose I'd have been killed for doing so if that regime hadn't been deposed shortly thereafter. You can also have many witnesses to these things.

So do you think I could've lasted all these years if I had been engaging in politics and by acting in a way that's worthy of a good man I had supported the right causes and, as one must, attached the greatest importance to this? Far from it, men of Athens. Nor could anyone else. For my whole life shows that I am this sort of person whether I did anything in public or in private, namely one who never gave in to anyone at all contrary to what's just, nor to any of those whom my accusers say are my students. I've never been anyone's teacher. But if anyone, young or old, wants to hear me talking or carrying out my own work, I never refused him, nor do I carry on a conversation when I get paid but not when I don't get paid. Instead, I make myself question rich and poor and by answering if anyone wants to hear what I have to say. And if any of those who listen becomes good or not, I couldn't rightly be held to be the cause, since I've never promised any of them any knowledge, nor have I ever taught anyone anything. If anyone says that he's ever learned anything from me or heard in private something that everyone else hasn't heard, you can be sure he's not telling the truth.

---

[37]Socrates is referring to the sea battle at Arginusae, which took place in 406 B.C.E., just two years before the end of the Peloponnesian War. The Athenian generals were charged as a group with a failure to retrieve the bodies of those Athenians who died during the battle.

[38]The arrest of Leon was by no means the only such illegal arrest that took place during the reign of the Thirty Tyrants, but it must have been especially egregious in the eyes of many Athenians.

c Why then do some enjoy spending so much time with me? Listen, Athenians, I'm telling you the whole truth. They enjoy hearing me examine those who think they're wise when they're not. It's not unpleasant. But, as I say, I've been ordered to do this by the god through dreams and oracles and in every way in which divine providence has ever ordered a human being to do anything whatever.

d This, Athenians, is the truth, and it's easily tested. If indeed I am corrupting some of the young and have corrupted others, then surely some of them who have grown up and recognized that I encouraged them to do wrong when they were younger ought to accuse me and take their revenge by coming forward. And if they don't want to, some of their relatives—their fathers and brothers and others who are close to them, if in fact any of their relatives suffered any harm from me— should make their complaint now and take their revenge. In any case, I see quite a few of them present here. First, there's Crito here, who's my

e age and from the same part of the city, the father of Critoboulus; then, there's Lysanias of Sphettus, the father of Aeschines here; and also Antiphon of Cephisus, the father of Epigenes, is here; and others still, whose brothers kept my company: Nicostratus, the son of Theozotides and brother of Theodotus—Theodotus is dead and so he couldn't beg

34a his father not to accuse me—and Paralius there, the son of Demodocus, whose brother was Theages. There's Adeimantus, the son of Ariston, whose brother is Plato here; and Ainantodorus, whose brother is Apollodorus here. And I can name many others for you, some of whom Meletus certainly should've called as witnesses when he gave his speech. If he forgot, let him call them—I yield up the time—and let him speak if he has anything of this sort to say. You'll find, however, that just the opposite's the case, men. All of those related to those I "corrupted"

b are ready to help me, the guy who did "bad things" to their relatives, according to Meletus and Anytus. Those who've been corrupted would probably have some reason to help me. But what reason could those who haven't been corrupted and who are already older men—their relatives—have except the correct and right one, namely, that they know Meletus is lying and I'm telling the truth?

Well then, men, this and perhaps other things like it are about all I

c can say in my defense. Perhaps some one of you may be angry when he thinks about himself if he went to trial on a less serious matter than this and he begged and pleaded with lots of tears with the members of the jury, and brought in his children, as well as many other relatives and friends in order to be shown as much pity as possible. But I'll do none of these things, and although in doing this, I appear to him to be run-

d ning the ultimate risk. Then perhaps when some of you consider this, you'll become more closed-minded about me and, having become angry, will cast your vote in anger. If indeed any of you is so disposed— I don't expect it of you, but if there is anyone—I think it's fair for me to say to this person, "I have a family, too, sir. This is just what Homer said:

'not from oak or rock' was I born, but from human beings. And so I do have a family, and sons, three of them, one in adolescence and two in childhood. Nevertheless, I won't bring them in here and beg you to   e
acquit me." Why won't I? Not because I'm indifferent, Athenians, nor out of disrespect for you. But whether I'm courageous in the face of death or not is another matter; but it seems to me not a good thing—for the reputation of me and you and of the whole city—for me at my age and with this reputation to do any of these things. Whether it's true or   35a
not, there's a view that Socrates is superior in some way to most people. If those of you who think they're superior—whether in wisdom or courage or in any virtue whatsoever—would act in that way, it would be disgraceful. I've often seen certain people put on trial, who, though they are reputed to be important, do surprising things, because they think their death is something terrible, as if they would be immortal if you didn't kill them. But I think they are bringing disgrace to the city,   b
so that a foreigner would suppose that those Athenians who're superior in virtue, whom they judge from among themselves to be worthy of getting offices and other honors, are no better than women. Such things, Athenians, those of you who seem to be important in any way whatever shouldn't do; nor, if we do them, should you allow it. But you should make this very thing clear: You'll do much better to condemn one who makes these pitiable scenes and who makes a laughingstock of the city than one who maintains his composure.

But apart from the issue of one's reputation, it doesn't seem to me right to beg the members of the jury, nor to grant acquittal to the one   c
who asks, but instead it's right to try to instruct and persuade. For the member of the jury doesn't sit for this reason—to make gifts out of what's just—but to judge what's just. He's taken an oath not to make gifts to whom he wants but to judge according to the laws. Therefore, we shouldn't get you in the habit of breaking your oaths, nor should you get in the habit of doing so. That wouldn't be pious for either of us. So please don't think that I, Athenians, should do for you what I believe   d
isn't noble, or just, or pious, and especially, by Zeus, when I'm being prosecuted by Meletus here for impiety. For it's clear that if I should persuade you and force you by begging when you have taken oaths, I'd be teaching you not to believe the gods exist, and in presenting a defense, I'd have simply made the charge against myself that I don't believe in the gods. But that's far from the truth. For I do believe in them, Athenians, as none of my accusers do, and I leave it to you and to the god to judge in what way it's going to be best for you and for me.

. . .[39]

---

[39]The jury now votes on whether or not to convict Socrates. He begins his next speech after the number of votes for guilt and for innocense is announced. For violations of this sort, the

e
36a

Many things contribute to my not being angry at what's happened—that you voted against me—and the result was not unexpected by me, but I was much more surprised by the total number of votes on each side. For I didn't think it would be such a small majority. I thought it would be much larger. Now, it seems, if only thirty votes had gone the other way, I'd have been acquitted.[40] I think that as far as Meletus is concerned, I've now been acquitted, and not only have I already been acquitted, but isn't it obvious to everyone that if Anytus and Lycon hadn't come forward to prosecute me, he would have incurred a 1000 drachma fine for not having received one-fifth of the votes?[41]

b

So the gentleman [Meletus] asks that the penalty be death. Well, what should I propose for you as a counterpenalty? Isn't it clear that it should be what I deserve? So, what would that be? What do I deserve to suffer or to pay for not having led an inactive life and for not caring about what most people care for—making money, managing my affairs, being a general or a political leader and any of the different offices and parties and factions that come about in the city? I believed that I was really too good to go down that path and survive. I didn't go where I would've been no help at all to you or to me, but went, instead, to each one of you in private to do the greatest good. As I say, I went there, undertaking to persuade each of you not to care about your possessions before you care about how you will be the best and wisest you can be, nor to care about what the city has, before you care about the city itself, and to care about other things in just the same way. Being this sort of person, what do I deserve to suffer? Something good, Athenians, if indeed I should truly assess my penalty according to what I deserve! Yes, and the sort of good thing that would be appropriate for me. What's appropriate for a poor man who's your benefactor and who needs to have the leisure to exhort you? There's nothing more appropriate, Athenians, than that such a person be given meals in the Prytaneum;[42] in fact, it's much more appropriate than for one of you who had won at Olympia with either a pair or a team of horses. For he makes you think you are happy, but I make you happy, and he doesn't need the

c

d

e

---

trial procedure was called an *agon timētos,* which meant that the law itself did not set the penalty for a conviction, leaving it for the defendant to propose a counterpenalty to whatever penalty had already been proposed by the prosecutor (in the indictment itself). Meletus had called for the death penalty. In this section of the *Apology,* Socrates explains why he chooses to propose the counterpenalty he does.

[40]Plato does not tell us exactly how large the jury was, but it is likely that the jury consisted of 500 citizens, in which case, 280 jurors voted to convict and 220 voted to acquit.

[41]Imposing this fine, which was quite substantial, served to discourage frivolous prosecutions.

[42]The Prytaneum was a building in which various Athenian heroes, Olympic victors, generals, and others were given meals at public expense. The privilege was, perhaps, the highest honor Athens bestowed on anyone.

food, but I do. So if I'm supposed to propose a penalty in accordance 37a
with what I deserve, I propose to be given meals at the Prytaneum.[43]

In speaking in this way I probably strike some of you as speaking
impudently pretty much as I did when I spoke about wailing and begging. But it isn't this sort of thing at all, Athenians, but in fact it's more
like this: I'm convinced that I've never willingly wronged anyone, but I
haven't convinced you of this. For we've conversed with each other for
just a little while. What I mean is, I think that if you had a law, as other
people do, about not judging death-penalty cases in a single day but
over many, you'd have been persuaded by me. But as it is, it isn't easy b
to destroy widespread slanders in a short time. Since I'm convinced that
I've never been unjust, I'm not about to treat myself unjustly and to say
of myself that I deserve something evil and to propose that sort of
penalty for myself. Why should I? Can it be that I should suffer the
penalty that Meletus proposes, which I say that I don't know whether
it's good or not? Or should I choose what I'm convinced is an evil, making this my counterproposal instead? Imprisonment? Why should I live c
obedient to those who happen to hold the office of the eleven prison
commissioners? Or a fine, and be imprisoned until I pay it? But that's
the same thing I was just talking about, for I have no money to pay it
with. Shall I now offer exile? Perhaps you'd impose that as my penalty.
I'd really have to be in love with living, men of Athens, to be so illogi-
cal as not to be able to see that if you, who are my fellow citizens,
weren't able to bear my activities and arguments—but they became so d
burdensome and hateful that you're now seeking to be free of them—
yet others will endure them easily. I think that's pretty unreasonable,
Athenians. A fine life I'd have to live, a man of my age, after going into
exile, going from one city to the next, always being sent into exile? You
can be sure that wherever I'd go, young people will listen to what I have
to say, just as they do here. If I drive them away, they themselves will
send me into exile by persuading their elders. But if I don't drive them e
away, their fathers and relatives will send me into exile for their sakes.

Perhaps some of you might say, "Can't you leave us to live in exile
and keep quiet and not talk?" This is the most difficult thing to convince
some of you of. If I say that this is disobedience to the god and that's 38a
why it's impossible to keep quiet, you'll think I'm not being sincere.
And if I say that this really is the greatest good for human beings—to
engage in discussion each day about virtue and the other things which
you have heard me talking about and examining myself and others, and
the unexamined life is not worth living for a human being—you'll be
persuaded even less by what I say. These things are true, as I say, but
it's not easy to persuade you. At the same time, I'm not in the habit of b

---

[43]Socrates does not actually propose "free meals at the Prytaneum" as his counterpenalty; he
only says that this is what he should propose, if he were to propose what he really deserves.

thinking that I deserve anything bad. If I had money, I'd offer what I could afford to pay; for I wouldn't be harming anything. But as it is, that isn't possible, unless you want to impose a penalty on me that I can pay. I suppose I could probably offer to pay you a mina of silver.[44] So I offer this amount.

Plato, here, Athenians, and Crito, Critobulus, and Apollodorus bid me to pay a penalty of 30 minas, and they'll guarantee that it's paid. I offer that much, then, and they'll be guarantors of the silver for you; they're good for it.[45]

. . .[46]

c   Just to gain a little time, Athenians, you'll be notorious and blamed by those who want to revile the city because you killed Socrates, a wise man—for those who want to hold you in contempt will say that I am in fact wise, even if I'm not. If you had held off for a little while, you'd have gotten what you wanted without having to do anything. For you see

d that I'm far along in life and that death is near. I say this not to all of you, but to those of you who voted for my execution. To them I have this to say: "Men, perhaps you think that I was convicted because of a failure to understand what words would have persuaded you, if I thought I should do and say anything that would gain my acquittal. That's far from accurate. I was convicted, not because of a failure to understand what to say, but because of not being brazen and shameless and because of not wanting to say the things you'd most like to hear—wailing and

e crying out and doing and saying many other unworthy things, which indeed, as I say, you're used to hearing from others. Nor did I think then that I should simply do anything slavish on account of the danger I was in, nor am I sorry that I've defended myself in this way, but I'd much rather choose to die having defended myself in the way I have than to live on in that other way. Neither in the law court nor in war should I or

39a any other person try to come up with plans to avoid death by doing anything we can. In battles it often becomes clear that one could avoid death

---

[44]See note 26 above. Because Socrates insists that he is at this point in his life a poor man and because he refuses to go to prison until money can be raised, it is reasonable to think that one mina is all that he could pay as a fine.

[45]See note 26, above. Thirty minas was the equivalent of 3000 days wages for an ordinary Athenian worker—hence, quite a substantial sum of money. It was not uncommon for others to provide assistance to those required to pay large fines—those who could not find sufficient resources to pay their fines would have all of their property confiscated and would be sent into exile. The four who encourage Socrates to raise the amount of his proposed fine to the much higher amount all come from some of the wealthiest families in Athens.

[46]A third speech of the sort Socrates now gives was not called for by Athenian legal procedure. If he spoke to the jury at all after the vote to execute him, he must have done so as they were preparing to leave the court.

by throwing down his weapons and turning to plead with his pursuers. And there are many other ways in each sort of danger to escape death if one would resort to doing and saying anything. For, men, it's surely not difficult to flee from death, but it's much more difficult to flee from evil; for evil runs faster than death. And now, being slow and old, I'm caught by the slower one, but my accusers, being clever and sharp-witted are caught by the faster one, evil. And now I go away, having been sentenced by you to death and they go away, sentenced by the truth to evil and injustice. I'll stand by my penalty and they, by theirs. I suppose it had to be this way, and I think it's appropriate.

Next I want to prophesy to those of you who voted against me. For I'm already here at that point at which people most often make their prophesies, when they're just about to die. I say, you who are putting me to death, that immediately after my death you'll have a much worse penalty, by Zeus, than the one you've imposed me by killing me. For you're achieving this now, thinking that you'll get off from having your life tested, exactly the opposite will happen to you, so I claim. There'll be more people who'll examine you—people I've held in check, but you didn't see it. And they'll be harder to deal with, in as much as they're younger, and you'll find them more irritating. If you think that by killing people you'll put a stop to anyone criticizing you because you don't live as you should, you're not thinking clearly. Escape is neither really possible nor admirable; the best and easiest course is not to restrain others, but instead to do what you need to do to be as good as possible. Now that I have made these prophesies to those of you who voted against me, I make my escape.

But to those who voted for me, I'd enjoy talking about what's just happened while the officers are taking a break and I'm not yet going to the place where I have to go to die. Stay with me during this time. For nothing prevents us from conversing while we can. As my friends, I want to show you the meaning of what's happened to me just now. Judges—for in calling you judges I'm referring to you as I should[47]— something wonderful has happened to me. In the past, the usual oracular voice of the spiritual thing has always come very quickly and has opposed me on quite trivial matters if I was about to do something that wasn't right. But now, as you can see for yourselves, what might well be thought—and is generally considered to be—the greatest of evils has befallen me. Yet this sign from the god didn't oppose me when I left home at dawn, nor when I came here to court, nor when I was about to say anything at all in my speech. And yet often at other times when I

b

c

d

e

40a

b

---

[47]Prior to this point in any of Socrates' speeches, he addressed his jurors only as "men," or "Athenians," reserving their formal title (*dikastai,* which we have translated as "judges") only for the subgroup of the jurors to whom he now speaks—those, that is, whom he thinks actually performed their duty as judges in the correct manner.

was talking, it held me back when I was in the middle of what I was saying. But today, concerning this matter, it hasn't opposed me at any point
in what I was doing or saying. What, then, do I take to be the explana-

c   tion? I'll tell you. What's happened to me will probably be something
good, and it can't be that we're right in supposing that death's an evil.
I've got strong evidence that this is so. It can't be that I haven't been
opposed by my usual sign unless I'm about to have good luck.

Let's also consider that we have good reason to be hopeful that this
is a good thing. Death is one of two things. Either it's like nothingness
and the dead have no awareness of anything, or it's, as they say, a

d   change and the soul migrates from this place to another place. If it's the
absence of sentience and is like sleep, as when someone sleeps and
doesn't even dream, death would be a wonderful gain. For I think that
anyone who picked a night in which he slept so soundly that he didn't
even dream and put it up against the other days and nights of his life,
and after thinking about it, had to say how many days and night were

e   better and more pleasant in his life than this night, why I think that not
just a private individual but even the great king[48] would discover that
such nights are easily counted compared to the other days and nights.
If death's like this, I say it's a gain; for the whole of time seems no more
than a single night.

If, on the other hand, death's like taking a journey from here to
another place, and what they say is true, that all the dead are there,

41a   what greater good could there be than this, judges? For if anyone who
arrives in Hades, having escaped those who claim to be judges here,
will discover real judges, who are said to sit in judgment there, Minos
and Rhadamanthus, and Aeacus and Triptolemus, and the other demigods who lived just lives, would the journey be a bad one? Or, in addition, how much would any of you give to be with Orpheus and

b   Musaeus and Hesiod and Homer? I'd want to die many times if this is
true! It would be wonderful for me personally to spend time there, since
I could fall in with Palamedes and Ajax, the son of Telemon, and any of
the other ancients who died on account of an unjust verdict, as I compare my suffering with theirs—I think it wouldn't be unpleasant—and
what's the greatest part of all, to spend my time testing and examining
those who are there, just as I do those who live here, to see if any of them
is wise and to see if any thinks he's wise when he's not. How much

c   would one pay, members of the jury, to examine the leader of the great
army at Troy,[49] or Odysseus, or Sisyphus, or countless other people one
could mention, men and women? Wouldn't it be unimaginable happiness to converse and associate with, and examine those who are there?

---

[48]This is a common way of referring to the King of Persia.
[49]Socrates is referring to Agamemnon, the legendary King of Mycenae and leader of the
Greek force that attacked Troy.

Surely those who are there don't kill people for that! For in addition to being happier than those who live here, those who are there are now deathless for eternity, if indeed what they say is true.

And so, members of the jury, you should be optimistic about death and think about this one truth, that no harm comes to a good man in life   d or in death, and his problems are not neglected by the gods. And what's happened to me now hasn't come about by chance, but it's clear to me that dying now and escaping these problems is better for me. This is why my sign hasn't turned me away from anything, and I'm not at all angry with those who condemned me or with my accusers. Yet, it wasn't with that in mind that they were condemning and accusing me,   e but instead they thought they'd injure me. They deserve to be blamed for that. At any rate, I do ask this of them. When my sons come of age, "punish" them, men, by disturbing them with the same things by which I disturbed you, if they seem to you to care about money or anything more than virtue. And if they think they've amounted to anything when they haven't, reproach them as I've reproached you because they don't care about what they should and because they think they've amounted   42a to something when they're worthless. If you'd do this, I myself and my sons will have been treated justly by you. But now the time has come to leave, me to die and you to live on; which of us is going to the better fate is unclear to anyone except the god.

. . .

Crito[50]

Athenian law forbade any execution from taking place during the so-called Delia, a religious festival in which a ship sailed to Delos and back to commemorate the legendary return of Theseus to Athens. Because Socrates' trial took place just as the Delia began, he was given a reprieve of approximately one month, during which time he continued to philosophize with his friends in his prison cell. In the *Crito*, Socrates' lifelong friend Crito has come to his cell early in the morning to urge him to escape that evening, for the ship has been seen on its return voyage not far from Athens. Unmoved by Crito's various arguments that it would actually be wrong for Socrates to remain in Athens to allow himself to be executed,

---

[50]It appears that Crito and Socrates came from the same deme, or precinct, in Athens. Unlike Socrates, however, Crito seems to have been a wealthy man. He was one of the four who guaranteed the fine of 30 minas that Socrates offered as his counterpenalty at his trial (see *Apology* 38b). Whether or not Crito urged Socrates to escape from prison or whether Socrates responded with the arguments Plato attributes to him, we cannot say. Xenophon, however, does confirm in his *Apology* (23) that some of Socrates' companions urged him to escape before he could be executed.

Socrates constructs an argument that justice requires that he stay in prison. Not only does the argument advance an interesting view of the nature of civic obligation, but it also reveals a number of the central doctrines of Socratic philosophy.

43a SOCRATES: Why have you come at this hour, Crito? Isn't it still early?

CRITO: Of course it is.

SOCRATES: Just what time is it?

CRITO: Right before dawn.

SOCRATES: I'm surprised that the prison guard was willing to answer your knock.

CRITO: Oh, he's well acquainted with me by now, Socrates, since I come here so often and I've taken good care of him.

SOCRATES: Have you come just now or did you come earlier?

CRITO: A bit earlier.

b SOCRATES: Then why didn't you wake me immediately instead of sitting quietly beside me?

CRITO: By the god, Socrates, I didn't want to. I wish I weren't so upset and unable to sleep. And I was amazed just now when I saw how peacefully you were sleeping. So I didn't disturb you on purpose so that you'd go on sleeping as peacefully as possible. Before now I've often thought you had a happy character throughout your whole life; but now, in this present disaster, I think so more than ever, since you are handling it easily and calmly.

SOCRATES: Well, Crito, it would be inappropriate for me at my age[51] to be worried if I have to die soon.

c CRITO: Others who are your age have been caught up in similar calamities, but their age doesn't free them at all from being worried about the problems they face.

SOCRATES: That's true. But why have you come so early?

CRITO: I've got bad news, Socrates—not for you, so it would seem—but bad and depressing news for me and all your companions ... and hardest of all, I think, for me to bear.

d SOCRATES: What is it? Has the boat arrived from Delos? For when it arrives, I have to die.[52]

CRITO: It hasn't yet arrived, but I have to think it'll arrive today, from what those who've come from Sounion[53] say, which is where they left

---

[51]In the *Apology* (17d) Socrates indicates that he is seventy years old. See also *Crito* 52e.

[52]Delos is a small island in the Aegean. Every year a ship was sent on a voyage to the island to commemorate the return of Theseus to Athens. During the time that the ship was en route, no executions could take place in Athens. Thus, in effect, Socrates was given a month's reprieve. According to Plato, he used this time to converse with his companions (see *Phaedo* 59d ff.)

[53]Ships coming back to Athens from the island of Delos would have to sail by Sounion, on the tip of the peninsula of land leading back toward Athens.

it. And it's clear from what they've said that it'll be here today. And then, Socrates, on the next day your life must end.

SOCRATES: Well, Crito, may it turn out for the best. If that's what the gods want, so be it. And yet I don't think it'll come today.

CRITO: What makes you think it won't? 44a

SOCRATES: I'll tell you. I gather I'm supposed to die the day after the boat arrives.

CRITO: Well, that's what the authorities say, at any rate.

SOCRATES: Well then, I don't think that it'll come today but tomorrow. I think this because of a dream I had a little earlier in the night.[54] You probably didn't disturb me at a crucial time.

CRITO: And what was the dream?

SOCRATES: I dreamed that a beautiful and graceful woman, wearing a white cloak, came toward me and called to me, saying: "Socrates, on the b third day you will come to fertile Phthia."[55]

CRITO: What a mysterious dream, Socrates!

SOCRATES: On the contrary; I think it's clear, Crito.

CRITO: Too much so, it seems. Yet, Socrates, you incredible man, even so, be persuaded by me and be saved. Since it's not just one disaster for me if you die, but apart from having been robbed of a companion such as I'll never find again, I'll appear to most people, who don't know you and me well, not to care—since I could've saved you had I been willing c to part with the money. And indeed what could be more disgraceful than a reputation for thinking that money is more important than friends? Most people won't be persuaded that you yourself didn't want to leave when we encouraged you to do it.

SOCRATES: But what do we care about what most people think, Crito? The most sensible people—the ones we ought to hold in higher regard—will think the matter's been handled just as it should've been.

CRITO: But surely you see, Socrates, that it's necessary to care about what d most people think. The circumstances we're in now make it clear that most people are able to do not just the smallest evils but virtually the greatest if someone's been slandered when they're around.

SOCRATES: I only wish, Crito, that most people were capable of the greatest evils so that they'd be capable of the greatest goods. That would be fine. But as things are, they're able to do neither. For they're not able to make anyone wise or ignorant, but they do whatever strikes them.

---

[54]It is likely that Plato intends the reader to take this remark seriously, for in the *Apology* (33c–d) Socrates indicates that he thinks dreams can indeed be a way in which divinities communicate with human beings.

[55]Phthia is the home of the great warrior Achilles, the central figure in Homer's *Iliad*. Many readers of Plato's time would have instantly recognized the allusion and would have seen that Socrates is suggesting that death will be a kind of homecoming for his soul and, hence, not something to be feared. Socrates also compares himself to Achilles in the *Apology* (28c–d).

e CRITO: I grant that. But, Socrates, tell me this. Surely your concern about me and your other companions isn't that if you leave this place, the blackmailers[56] will cause trouble for us for having sneaked you out of here, and we would then be forced to forfeit either all our property or quite a bit of money, or suffer something else in addition to these

45a things? If you're afraid of something like this, don't give it a thought. We're doing the right thing to run this risk in rescuing you and, if need be, to run an even greater one. So be persuaded by me and do nothing else.

SOCRATES: But I *am* concerned about these things, Crito, and about many others too.

CRITO: Don't worry about these things now—what people want to be paid to save you and get you out of here doesn't amount to much money. Anyway, don't you see how cheap these blackmailers are and

b that one wouldn't need much money for them? My money is enough, I think, and what's mine is yours. Furthermore, if, in your concern for me, you think I shouldn't spend my own money, these foreigners here are ready to spend theirs. One of them—Simmias, the Theban[57]—has brought enough money for this very thing. He's prepared, as is Cebes and a great many others, as well. So, as I say, don't back away from saving yourself out of fear of these things.

Nor should what you said in court bother you, namely, that you couldn't go into exile because you wouldn't know what to do with

c yourself.[58] People will welcome you in many of the places you may go. If you wish to go to Thessaly,[59] I have friends there and they'll provide for your safety and do many things for you so that none of the Thessalians will bother you.

Moreover, Socrates, it doesn't seem right to me to undertake what you're doing—betraying yourself when it's possible to save yourself—and you're speeding up for yourself what your enemies would be hurrying to do and what they've done their best to expedite in their desire to destroy you. In addition to these things, it seems to me that you're

---

[56]The Greek word which we are here translating as "blackmailers" is *sukophantoi,* from which we get the English word "sycophant." The Athenian legal system did not allow for public prosecutors. Instead, prosecutions for crimes were left to private individuals to pursue. Some individuals, however, made it their business to find out about allegations of crimes and, then, threatened the alleged perpetrators with prosecution unless they were paid a fee. Hence, the *sucophantoi* were blackmailers.

[57]Simmias and Cebes, referred to in the next line, were young men from Thebes, both devoted companions of Socrates. Plato chooses them to be Socrates' principal interlocutors in the *Phaedo,* the dialogue set in prison on the last day of Socrates' life and in which Plato discusses various arguments about the immortality of the soul.

[58]Crito is referring to Socrates' refusal to suggest exile as a counterpenalty the jury could impose on him. See *Apology* 37c–d.

[59]Thessaly was a large remote region north of Athens.

betraying your sons, whom you'll have left behind and abandoned, when it's possible for you to raise and educate them, and as far as you're concerned, they'll have to take whatever happens to them. And what'll happen to them, it seems likely, are the very sorts of things that usually happen to orphans. Either you shouldn't have children or you should share in their lives by nurturing and educating completely. You seem to me to be choosing the laziest way out. One should choose what a good and courageous man would choose, especially one who spends his whole life talking about caring for virtue. I'm ashamed for you and for us, your companions, that this whole matter involving you will seem to have been conducted with a certain lack of courage on our part—how the case was brought to court, when it was possible for it not to be; how the case itself was conducted; and last of all, there's this: As if we're making a joke of the matter, the opportunity appears to have escaped us through some fault and cowardice on our part—we, who didn't save you, and you, who didn't save yourself—when it was entirely possible to have done so if we'd been of any use at all. See to it then, Socrates, that this doesn't end badly and disgracefully for you and for us. So consider—or actually the time is past for considering but we need to have already settled on—a single plan. All these things need to have been done this very night; but if we're still waiting around, it'll be completely impossible. So by all means, Socrates, be persuaded by me and don't do anything else.

d

e

46a

SOCRATES: My friend, Crito, your concern will be worth a great deal if it is on the right side of this issue. But if not, the greater it is, the more difficult it makes things. So we need to consider whether we must do this or not. Because I'm not just now but in fact I've always been the sort of person who's persuaded by nothing but the reason that appears to me to be best when I've considered it. I can't now, when I'm in my present circumstance, set aside reasons I was giving earlier. If they seem to me to be virtually the same, I'll respect and honor the ones I did before. Unless we can come up with something better in the present circumstance than these, rest assured that I won't give in to you. Nor should the majority of people have any greater power to scare us in this present circumstance, like we were children by sending us to prison and death and confiscating our money.

b

c

What, then, is the most reasonable way to take up the matter? We could first take up the argument you were giving about opinions. Were we right or not each time we said that one ought to pay attention to the opinions of some but not of others? Or were we right before I was obliged to die, but now it's become clear after all that it was all done merely for the sake of argument and was really just for play and fooling around? I'm eager to investigate it together with you, Crito, to see if the reasoning seems different in any way to me since I'm in this circumstance or does it seem to be the same? Should we let it go or be persuaded by it?

d

I think that people who always think they have something to say, maintain, as I was saying just now, that, among the opinions people hold, one ought to think highly of some and not others. By the gods, Crito, doesn't this seem to you to be right? For you, in all probability, are *not* about to die tomorrow, and my present misfortune shouldn't skew *your* judgment. Consider then: Doesn't it seem to you to be correct that one shouldn't respect all the opinions people have but some and not others, nor the opinions of all people, but some and not others? What do you say? Is this right or not?

CRITO: It's right.

SOCRATES: Then should we respect the good ones but not the bad ones?

CRITO: Yes.

SOCRATES: Aren't the good ones are the opinions of the wise, and the bad ones the opinions of the foolish?

CRITO: Of course.

SOCRATES: Come, then. What did we used to say about these things? Does the trained athlete and one who's involved in such things pay attention to the praise and censure and opinion of everyone or of that one only who happens to be a doctor or a trainer?

CRITO: Of the one only.

SOCRATES: Therefore, we should fear the censure and welcome the praise of that one—but not the censure and praise of the many?

CRITO: That's quite clear.

SOCRATES: So one should act and exercise and eat and drink in the way that would seem best to him—to the one person, the one who has knowledge and expertise—rather than in the way that seems best to all the others?

CRITO: That's right.

SOCRATES: Well then. If one disobeyed the one and disdained his opinion and what he encourages, but respected those of the many, who understand nothing, won't he suffer some evil?

CRITO: Of course.

SOCRATES: What is this evil? Where does it achieve its effects and what part of the one who disobeys does it affect?

CRITO: Clearly, it's the body. It destroys it.

SOCRATES: You're right. Then in other areas too, Crito, isn't it this way as well? So that we don't have to run through them all, isn't it especially true that in what pertains to the just and unjust and the noble and good and evil—what we're now deliberating about—we should follow the opinion of most people and fear it, or that of the one, if there is anyone who understands, whom one ought to respect and fear rather than all of the others? If we don't follow this one individual, won't we corrupt and destroy what becomes better through justice but is destroyed by injustice? Isn't this so?

CRITO: I think so, Socrates.

SOCRATES: Come then. If we ruin what becomes better by health but is destroyed by disease when we're persuaded by the opinion of those who lack expertise, is our life worth living when this has been corrupted? This is, surely, the body, isn't it?

CRITO: Yes.

SOCRATES: Therefore, is our life worth living with a body in bad condition and corrupted?

CRITO: Certainly not.

SOCRATES: But is our life worth living with this thing being corrupted which injustice mutilates and justice improves? Or, do we believe that what justice and injustice concern—whatever it is of the things that makes us up—is inferior to the body?

CRITO: Certainly not.

SOCRATES: It is, rather, to be respected more?

CRITO: Much more.

SOCRATES: Well then, my good friend, we mustn't take very seriously what most people will say to us but rather what the one who understands justice and injustice will say—the one person, and truth itself. The upshot is that you didn't introduce the issue correctly when you started off by saying that one should consider most people's opinion about just, noble, and good things and their opposites. "But then surely," someone might say, "these 'most people' can kill us."

CRITO: Clearly, someone might say that, Socrates.

SOCRATES: You're right. But, my incredible friend, the argument we've gone through seems to me to be the same as before. Consider once more if we're still standing by it or not, namely, that one mustn't be much concerned with living, but with living well?

CRITO: We stand by it.

SOCRATES: And that living well and nobly and justly are the same—do we stand by it or not?

CRITO: We stand by it.

SOCRATES: Then from these agreements we must consider this: whether it's just or not for me to try to escape from here when the Athenians haven't released me. And if it seems just, we should attempt it; but if not, we should let the matter go. The considerations you mention—about the confiscation of money, reputation, and the raising of children—these, I'm afraid, are really the considerations of most people, who readily kill people and would bring them back to life if they could and would do so without even thinking about it. But since our reasoning requires this, we must consider only what we were saying just now: Would we, the ones who are escaping and the ones who are helping out, be doing what's just in paying our money and thanking those who'll get me out of here? Or would we really be acting unjustly by doing all of these things? If we'd clearly be bringing about an injustice, we shouldn't give any consideration to whether we need to remain behind to be killed and keep quiet about it or suffer anything at all rather than the injustice we'd be doing.

CRITO: I think what you said is right, Socrates, but think about what we should do.

SOCRATES: Let's consider it together, my good man, and if you can some-
e   how refute what I'm saying, refute it, and I'll try to do the same for you. But if not, stop giving me the same old speech—that I ought to go away from here against the will of the Athenians. For I think it's important to persuade you to do this and not act against your wishes. Think about whether what we said at the beginning of our investigation satisfies
49a   you, and try to answer what's put to you as you think best.

CRITO: I'll try.

SOCRATES: Do we say that we should by no means willingly do what's unjust, or do we say that we should act unjustly in some cases but not in others? Isn't injustice never good or noble, as we've often agreed before? Or, have all of our previous agreements been given up in these last few days, and have we, men at this age who have seriously discussed these
b   matters with each other, failed to see long ago that we are no better than children? Or is it absolutely what we said it was then? Whether most people agree with us or not, and whether we have to suffer harsher or more lenient things than what's going on now, injustice is still evil and disgraceful in every way for the one who's unjust? Do we say this or not?

CRITO: We do.

SOCRATES: One should never do what's unjust.

CRITO: Clearly not.

SOCRATES: Nor retaliate when one's been treated unjustly, as most people say, since one should never do injustice?
c   CRITO: It seems not.

SOCRATES: What follows then? Should we do evil, Crito, or not?

CRITO: Surely, we shouldn't, Socrates.

SOCRATES: What then? Is it just or not to do evil in return when one has suffered an evil, as most people say?

CRITO: Never.

SOCRATES: Treating men evilly does not differ from treating them unjustly.

CRITO: That's true.

SOCRATES: Therefore, we should neither retaliate nor treat anyone evilly, no matter what we have suffered from them. In agreeing to these things,
d   Crito, make sure that you don't speak contrary to what you think. For I know that these things seem and will seem true only to a few people. But to those to whom it has seemed right and to those to whom it hasn't, there is no common ground, but they can't avoid having disdain for each other when they see each other's conclusions. Consider very care-fully then whether you agree and share the same opinion with me and let's begin by deliberating from that point, namely that it's never right to do what's unjust or to retaliate or for one who has suffered an evil to avenge it by retaliating wrongly, or do you reject this and not share my

opinion about where to start? For it seems to be now the same as before,   e
but if it has appeared to you to be otherwise, speak up and instruct me.
But if you stand by what was said earlier, listen to what follows.

CRITO: I do stand by it and it seems to me the same as before. Go on, then.

SOCRATES: I'll tell you what comes next, or rather, I'll ask: Should one do
what one agrees to do for someone when it is just, or should one renege?

CRITO: One should do what one has agreed to.

SOCRATES: Now observe what follows. If we go away from here without
having persuaded the city, would we be doing anything wrong to any-   50a
one, and what's more, would we be doing it to those whom we ought
least of all be doing it, or not? Do we stand by what we agreed is right,
or not?

CRITO: I can't answer what you're asking, Socrates, because I don't
understand.

SOCRATES: Well, think about it this way: Suppose the laws and the state, or
however it should be called, came and confronting us as we were about
to run away from here were to say: "Tell me, Socrates, what are you
thinking about doing? Are you contemplating by this act that you're   b
attempting anything other than the destruction of us, the laws, and the
whole city insofar as you can? Or, do you think that the city can still exist
and not be destroyed when the decisions handed down in the courts
have no force but are left without authority by private citizens and are
destroyed?" What shall we say, Crito, to this and other things of the same
sort? For someone, especially an orator, could say a lot on behalf of the
law that has been destroyed which decrees that the decisions of the
courts be authoritative. Or shall we say to them, "The city was unjust to   c
us and did not judge my case correctly." Shall we say this or what?

CRITO: That's what we'll say, by god, Socrates.

SOCRATES: Then what if the Laws should say: "Socrates, is this the agreement between us and you, or was it to stand by the judgments that the
city hands down?" If at that point we'd be surprised when they said
this, perhaps they'd say, "Socrates, don't be surprised at what we're
saying, but answer, since you're accustomed to using question and
answer. Come, then. What's the charge against us and the city that leads   d
you to try to destroy us? First, didn't we produce you, and through us
didn't your father take your mother in marriage and give birth to you?
And tell us, what complaint do you have against those of our laws that
govern marriage?" "I have no complaint," I'd say. "And what about
those laws concerning the raising of offspring and the education which
you received? Or did our established laws for this not command the
right thing in ordering your father to educate you in music and physi-   e
cal training[60]?" "It was well done," I'd say. "Well then, since you were

---

[60]Music and physical training were standard forms of education expected of all free male
children in Athens. For an excellent discussion of what that education consisted in, see
Roberts (1984), 94–108.

born and raised and educated by us, could you say in the first place that you're not our offspring and slave, you and your ancestors? And if this is so, do you think that what's just for us and you is based on equality? And whatever we try to do to you, do you think it's right for you also to do in return? What's just for you in relation to your father, or to your master, if you happened to have one, wasn't based on equality so that you could do in return the very thing you suffered, whether to talk back when criticized or to strike back when struck, and many other such things? Yet, on the other hand, you are empowered to do such things against your fatherland and the laws, so that if we try to destroy you in the belief that it's right, you'll try to destroy us, the laws, and the country in return in so far as you're able. And do you, who really cares about virtue, maintain that in doing this you're doing what's just? Or, are you so wise that it's escaped you that, compared to your father and mother and all of your ancestors, your country is more honorable, more revered, more sacred, and to be held in higher esteem by the gods and by people with sense, and that you should revere your country and yield to it and cajole it when it's angry more than your father, and either persuade or to do what it orders and you should suffer in silence if it orders you to suffer something, whether it's to be beaten or to be imprisoned, and whether it leads you into war to be wounded or killed, you must do this, and it's just that you do so, and you shouldn't yield, or retreat, and abandon your post, but in war and in court and everywhere, you must do what your city and country orders, or persuade it as to the nature of what's just. But it's impious to use force on your mother and father; it's much more impious still to use it on your country." What shall we say to this, Crito? Are the laws telling the truth or not?

CRITO: It seems to me they are.

SOCRATES: "Consider, then, Socrates," perhaps the laws would say, "if we're right, then what you're now trying to do isn't right. Although we produced you, and raised you, and educated you, and gave all the other citizens and you, too, a share of all the good things we could, nonetheless we publically grant the power to an Athenian who wishes, as soon as he has been entered into citizenship[61] and sees the ways of the city and us the laws and who's not pleased with us, to pack up his belongings and go wherever he wants. Whether someone wishes to emigrate to a colony or to go somewhere else and live as an alien if we and the city should fail to please him, no law stands in his way or forbids him to go where he desires and keep his things. But he among you who

---

[61]At age eighteen, Athenian males who wished to become citizens actually went through a formal procedure in which they had to prove their eligibility and to declare formally that they wished to become citizens.

stays, seeing the manner in which we dispense justice and conduct the affairs of the city in other ways, we say that this person has already agreed with us by his actions that he'll do what we command, and we say that the one who does not persuade us acts unjustly in three ways: because he doesn't obey us who produced him; because he doesn't obey those who raised him; and because, having agreed to obey us, he neither obeys nor persuades us if we're doing something that's not right, 52a even though we offer him this alternative and don't order him about roughly to do what we command him to do. Although we permit him two options—either persuade us or do what we command—he does neither of these. We say that you, Socrates, will be ensnared by these charges if you do what you're thinking about, and of the Athenians you'll not be the least culpable, but among the most." If I were to say, "Why's that?" perhaps they would be right to attack me and say that I, more than any other Athenian, happened to have made this agreement with them. For they'd say, "Socrates, we have strong evidence that we b and the city were pleasing to you. For you wouldn't have stayed here more than all the other Athenians unless the city had been more pleasing to you. You never left the city to go to a festival, except once to go to the Isthmus,[62] nor to go to any other place except when you were serving in the army somewhere, nor did you ever make a trip abroad, as other people do, nor were you seized by a desire to know another city c or other laws, but we and our city were enough for you. You emphatically chose us and you agreed to be governed by us, and, in particular, you had children in it, because you were satisfied with the city. Besides, at the trial it was possible for you to have proposed exile as your counterpenalty if you wanted, and the very thing you're now attempting when the city is unwilling, it was possible for you to do then when the city was willing. You were trying to make yourself look good then by not being worried if you had to die, but you chose, as you were saying, death over exile. Now you aren't ashamed at those words. You don't d even respect us, the laws, since in trying to destroy them you're doing just what the lowest slave would do, trying to run away in violation of the compacts and agreements, according to which you agreed to be governed by us. First, answer this: Are we telling the truth or not when we say that you agreed—through your actions, not in words—to be governed by us, or aren't we telling the truth? What would we say to this, Crito? Do we agree or not?

CRITO: We have to agree, Socrates.

---

[62]Isthmus (near Corinth, west of Athens, in the small land connection—severed in modern times by a canal—between the Peloponnesus and the northern part of Greece) was the site of the Isthmian Games, a panhellenic athletic festival (similar to the now more famous Olympic Games) held every two years in April or May.

SOCRATES: "Isn't it also true," they'd say, "that you're breaking these compacts and agreements with us, though you weren't compelled to agree, and neither were you deceived nor were you given only a short time to deliberate about it, but you had seventy years, in which it was possible for you to leave if you weren't satisfied with us or if the agreements didn't seem right to you? You preferred neither Sparta nor Crete, which you're always saying are well governed, nor any other Greek or foreign city, but you left the city less than the lame, the blind, and other disabled people. So it's clear that the city and us, the Laws, pleased you more than other Athenians. Could anyone be satisfied with a city without being satisfied with its laws? Well do you not now stand by the agreements? You will if you're persuaded by us, Socrates; and you won't make yourself a laughingstock by leaving the city.

For consider: If you violate your agreements and commit any of these wrongs, what good will you be doing for yourself or for your companions? It's pretty clear that your companions are likely to be prosecuted themselves and be deprived of the city or lose their property. But first, you yourself, if you go to any of the nearest cities, Thebes or Megara—for both are well governed—you'll arrive as an enemy, Socrates, to their state. Those who care about their cities will suspect you, thinking that you're someone who destroys laws. Further, you'll confirm for the members of the jury their opinion, so they'll think they decided the case correctly. For whoever destroys the laws would probably seem to be someone who corrupts the young and who corrupts people who don't know any better. So, will you avoid well-governed cities and people who lead the most orderly lives? And in doing this will your life be worth living? Or will you approach these people and be so shameless as to discuss—what arguments, Socrates? Will you discuss the very ones you discuss here, that virtue and justice, and laws and customs are the most valuable things for people? Don't you think the 'Socrates affair' will appear unseemly? Surely you must think so. Or will you leave these places and go instead to Thessaly to be with Crito's friends? Now that place is filled with disorder and self-indulgence, and they might well enjoy hearing about you running comically from the prison, having put on a disguise and changing your appearance by wearing a leather hide or the other sorts of things that runaways use to disguise themselves. Is there no one who will say that you—an old man, who likely had only a short time left to live—dared to have such a greedy desire to live on in this way by breaking the greatest laws? Perhaps, if you don't disturb anyone. But if that's not the case, you'll hear many terrible things about yourself. You'll live a life of fawning and serving all people—what will you do in Thessaly other than feasting?— as if you had traveled to Thessaly for dinner! And what'll happen to our arguments about justice and the other virtues? Or is it that you want to live for the sake of your children, to raise them and to educate them? But why? By leading them off to Thessaly, you'll raise and educate them after you have made them exiles, and that is supposed to benefit them too? But if instead of that, they're raised while you're alive, will they be better brought up and educated than if you're not with them? For your companions will take care of them. Or is it that if you go away to Thessaly they'll care for them, but if you go away to Hades they won't? One   b has to think so if indeed those who say they're your friends are to benefit them at all.

"So, Socrates, be persuaded by us who raised you, and don't put your concern for your children or your life or anything else before justice, so that when you go to Hades you can use all of these things in your defense before those who rule there. For neither will it appear that it was better or more just or more pious for you or for any of your companions here that you did this, nor will it be better for you in Hades when you arrive there. But instead, now you'll leave—if you do leave— having been unjustly treated not by us, the laws but by men. If you   c escape after so disgracefully retaliating and returning wrong for wrong, and having broken the agreements and compacts with us, and having mistreated those whom you ought least of all to harm—yourself, your friends, your country, and us—we'll deal harshly with you while you're alive, and our brothers, the laws of Hades, won't receive you kindly there, knowing that, for your part, you tried to destroy us. So then,   d don't let Crito persuade you to do what he says instead of what we say."

Rest assured, dear friend Crito, that I think I hear this, just like the Corybantic revelers[63] think they hear flutes, and the same sound of these arguments buzzes in me and keeps me from hearing anything else. Know that if you say anything contrary to what seems now to be true, you'll be speaking in vain. Nonetheless, if you think it'll do you some good, say it.

CRITO: I have nothing to say, Socrates.

SOCRATES: Let it be so then, Crito, and let's act in this way, since this is the   e way the god[64] is leading.

---

[63]Corybantic revelers participated through frenzied dancing in rites celebrating the goddess Cybele. Socrates is here comparing the force of the argument the "Laws" have presented to the drums the revelers listened to while dancing.

[64]Socrates' reference to the god in the singular is controversial. (For contrast, see the reference to what the [plural] gods want, at *Crito* 43d). It is unlikely that he is referring to the divinity who communicates with him through the "voice" he hears, for, as he tells us in the *Apology* (31d), the voice always turns him away from what he is about to do. It does not lead him. Zeus is the divine protector of sworn oaths (which would be sworn in his name), and since Socrates' argument refers to the fact that he has sworn oaths of allegiance to the laws of Athens, and since Zeus' will might well be thought to represent the will of all the gods (assuming that they all agree) on matters of justice (see *Euthyphro* 6a–8e), Socrates' reference to "the god" may simply refer to Zeus as representative of the generic divine will. It is also clear that Socrates' discussion with Crito (unlike so many other discussions in which we find Socrates, in Plato's dialogues), is a discussion between good friends—and this, too, is a significant feature of the premises on which they rely in the argument (see *Crito* 49d). If

Phaedo

In the final selection by Plato, the concluding passage of the *Phaedo*, we find Socrates making his final preparations for death. Plato emphasizes how the philosopher's confidence in his arguments about how best to prepare the soul for dying give rise to utter calmness when the moment of death arrives.

116a PHAEDO: [Socrates] got up and went to a room to bathe and Crito followed him in and told us to stay put. And so as we waited by ourselves we talked and thought about what had been said, and then we discussed the catastrophe that had happened to us, since we absolutely believed that we would have to spend the rest of our lives just like orphans who had lost a father. And when he had bathed, his children were brought to him—he had two small sons and an older one—and the women of the house came, and when he had spoken to them in front of Crito and had instructed them about what he wanted, he told the women and children to leave, and he came back in with us. The sun was already near setting. He had spent a long time within. After bathing, he came

c out and sat down and didn't say much after that, and the servant of the Eleven came and stood near him and said, "Socrates, I won't think of you the way I think of others, because they made it difficult for me and cursed at me when I gave the order to drink the poison when the officers required it. But I know you to be the noblest and gentlest man who's ever come here. And now especially I know that you're not going to be upset with me—for you know who's responsible—but at them. So

d now you know what I came to tell you. Farewell and try to bear what you must endure as easily as possible." With tears in his eyes, he turned around and went out.

And Socrates looked up at him and said, "Farewell to you and we'll do what you say." And at the same time he said to us, "How kind this man is. Throughout my whole time here, he put up with me and talked with me sometimes, and couldn't have been better. And now how genuinely he's weeping for me! But come, Crito, let's obey him and let someone bring the poison if it's been ground up. If not, let the man go ahead and grind it up."

e And Crito said, "But, Socrates, I think that the sun is still on the mountains and hasn't gone down yet. And I know that others wait until

---

Socrates is referring to the god of friendship as the guide of this friendly conversation, his reference would again be to Zeus, the god of friendship (see *Euthyphro* 6b). In any case, it seems reasonable to suppose that Socrates' reference is to whichever god might be supposed to have led their argument.

well after they have been ordered to drink the poison, eating and drinking all they want, and even having sex with their lovers. Don't be in a hurry. There's still time." Socrates said, "It's understandable, Crito, that they do the things you're talking about, for they think that in doing them they're benefitting from it. But it wouldn't be a reasonable thing for me to do. For I think that by drinking the poison a little later, I'll have 117a nothing to show for it but looking ridiculous in my own eyes, hanging on to life and being 'stingy with the cup when there is nothing in it.' So, come, he said, obey, and don't refuse me."

And when Crito heard this, he motioned to a slave who was nearby, and after he'd delayed quite a while, he came, leading the one who was to deliver the poison, carrying what had been ground up in a drinking cup. And when Socrates saw the man, he said, "My good man, since you know about these things, what should I do?"

"Nothing but drink it and move around until your legs get heavy, b and lie down. It'll do its work." And then he offered the cup to Socrates.

And he took it quite gratefully, and without any fear and without changing the color or the expression on his face, looking at the man in his familiar bull-like way, he said, "What do you say about pouring a libation from the drink? Is it permitted or not?"

"We ground out, Socrates," he said, "what we think is the right amount to drink."

"I understand," he said, "but surely it is possible—and indeed one c ought to say a prayer to the gods that the journey from here to there will be a happy one. That's what I pray and may it turn out to be so." And as he said these things and was holding the cup, he drank it down quite easily and calmly. Most of us had been able to keep from crying reasonably well up 'til then, but when we saw him drinking and then after he had drunk, we were no longer able to do hold back. My tears came flooding out uncontrollably, so when I had bowed my head, I was weeping—not at all for him—but for my misfortune, such a companion d was I losing. Crito got up before me, since he wasn't able to hold back his tears. And Apollodoros had been crying all along and especially at this point exploded with wailing and anger and made everyone present break down except Socrates. "What are you doing?" he said. "That's just why I sent the women away, so that I wouldn't have to put up with e that! For I've heard that one should die in solemn silence. So keep quiet and bear up!" And when we heard this, we kept quiet and held back our tears. He walked around and when he said that his legs were heavy, he lay down on his back, for that's what the man told him to do. And then the one who administered the poison touched him, and after a time examined his feet and legs and after pressing hard on his foot, he asked him if he could feel anything. And he said that he couldn't. Next he touched his calves and going up in this way he demonstrated to us that 118a they were cold and stiff. And then he touched him and said that when it, the coldness, reaches his heart, he'll be gone.[65] And then the coldness was almost to his abdomen, and he uncovered his head—for he had covered it and he said his last words, "Crito, we owe a cock to Asclepius. Pay it and don't neglect it." Crito said, "It'll be done. Tell us if you want anything else." And after Crito said this, Socrates didn't answer. After a little while he moved, the man uncovered him, and his eyes were fixed. When Crito saw this, he closed his mouth and eyes. Such Echecrates was the end of our companion—a man, we could say, who was of those we knew living at that time the best and also the wisest and most just.

---

[65]The symptoms of hemlock poisoning described here have been much disputed by scholars, with some even claiming that Plato's description here is entirely misleading and inaccurate. However, it is anything but obvious what Plato would hope to gain by having the prison attendant explain the working of the most common form of execution at this period in a way that was patently (and demonstrably) false. In any case, the most recent work on this subject strongly supports Plato's accuracy (see the essay by Bloch in this collection).

CHAPTER 3

Xenophon

Xenophon (430–c. 356 B.C.E.), Athenian historian and mercenary soldier. Little is known of Xenophon's youth, and much of what can be said about his adult life has to gleaned from Xenophon's own writings. That he associated with Socrates and admired the philosopher greatly is clear from the four works (*Apology of Socrates, Memorabilia, Symposium,* and *Oeconomicus*) in which Socrates has a central place. In 401 B.C.E., Xenophon accepted an invitation to join the expedition of Cyrus the Younger in Persia. In the *Anabasis,* Xenophon recounts how, after Cyrus' defeat, he himself managed to guide the remaining Greek force to the sea and, hence, to safety. Xenophon subsequently served the Spartan king Agesilaus II as a military advisor. Banished from Athens for having sided with the Spartans at Coronae, Xenophon was later awarded by the Spartans with a large estate in Scillus in the western Peloponnese. Xenophon later moved to Corinth when his estate was overrun by marauders. There is some evidence that the Athenian degree of banishment was lifted and that Xenophon spent at least some of his final years in Athens.

Xenophon's accounts of Socrates and of Socratic philosophy differ sharply from Plato's in several important respects. Xenophon states that his purpose in writing about Socrates' remarks to the jury is not to persuade the jury of his innocence or to defend the life of philosophy, as Plato's *Apology* suggests. Instead, Xenophon wished to explain the haughty tone of Socrates' remarks by pointing out that Socrates actually sought his own death. Unlike Plato's Socrates, Xenophon's Socrates is interested in a wide variety of purely practical issues and is punctilious about conventional Athenian religion practices. Socrates, as Xenophon portrays him, was devoted to philosophy, but his arguments are rarely penetrating or persuasive.

Below we have Xenophon's *Apology of Socrates* in its entirety. The except from the *Memorabilia* shows that Xenophon was quite concerned about defending Socrates against the extralegal charge, probably brought by the sophist Polycrates, that Socrates had indeed corrupted Alcibiades and Critias.

Apology of Socrates

Translated by Joel A. Martinez

(1) It seems worthwhile to me to remember how, when he was summoned to court, Socrates deliberated about his defense and the end of his life. Others, in fact, have written about this and all have captured his boastful manner of speaking, which proves that he did in fact speak that way. But that he already believed death more choiceworthy for him than life they have not made clear, so that his boastful speech appears foolish.

However, his close friend (2) Hermogenes, son of Hipponicus, has given an account of him that makes his boastful speech seem suitable for his purpose. For, he has said that,[1] seeing Socrates conversing about everything but those things concerning the trial he said to him, (3) "Is it not necessary to consider, Socrates, something you can say to defend yourself?" And at first Socrates replied, "Do I not seem to you to have spent my whole life preparing my own defense?" When Hermogenes asked "How?"—"By going through life doing nothing unjust. I think attending to this is the greatest defense." (4) And when Hermogenes replied, "Do you not see how often the Athenian court is misled by a speech into putting to death one who has done no injustice, and how often one who has committed an injustice has given a speech that moved the court to pity or by speaking in a clever way has been acquitted?" "Yes, by Zeus," Socrates responded, "and twice now I have attempted to think about my defense, but my divinity opposes me." (5) And when Hermogenes said, "What an amazing thing for you to say?" Socrates answered, "Do you think it so amazing if to the god it seems best for me to be at the end of my life already? Don't you know that to the present day I have never conceded to any man that he has lived a better life than I have? For, what is pleasing is that I knew I had lived my whole life piously and justly, so that, while I have greatly admired myself, I have discovered that those close to me also recognize this about me. (6) And if I should now grow older, I know that I must face the frailties of old age—to see and hear less well, to be slow to learn and to be more forgetful of what I've learned. And, should I perceive

---

[1] What follows is Xenophon's account of Hermogenes' report of both a conversation between Hermogenes and Socrates as well as the events of the trial. I have only added the phrase "Hermogenes said" where I think it might help the reader keep in mind that the events described here do not come *directly* from anyone present at the trial.

myself becoming worse and blame myself, how," he said, "would I still be able to live pleasantly?"

(7) "Perhaps," he explained, "the god, out of good will, is protecting me by ending my life not only at an opportune age but also in the way that is easiest. For if I am condemned now, it is clear that I would suffer a death which is judged, by those who consider these things, easiest, least troublesome to loved ones, and productive of the most regret. For, whenever one leaves behind neither shameful or troublesome thoughts in the minds of those close to him, but passes away while his body has health and his soul is capable of kindness, how could he not be missed?"

(8) "And the gods," he continued, "rightly opposed inquiry into my defense at a time when we thought it best to seek for all the ways of escaping prosecution. For if I had accomplished this, it is clear that, rather than preparing to end my life now, I would be preparing to end it suffering from illness or old age, where all discomforts converge, void of any joy. (9) By Zeus, Hermogenes," he said, "I am not eager for these things, but as many fine things as I believe I have received both from the gods and from men, as well as the opinion I have of myself, if by making these things clear, I distress the jury, then I would prefer death to extending my life for a life worse than death."

(10) And Hermogenes said that Socrates, having come to these conclusions, when the prosecution made the accusations that he did not believe in the same gods that the state believes in but that he introduced other new deities and corrupted the youth, came forward and said:

(11) "But I, gentlemen, in the first place wonder at this about Meletus, judging by what he says: that I do not believe in the gods in whom the city believes, since anyone who happened to be around and Meletus himself, if he wished, have seen me sacrificing at the common festivals and the public altars. (12) Furthermore, how would I introduce new gods by saying that the voice of a god is made manifest to me, indicating what it is necessary to do? For, those who consult the sounds of birds and the voices of men form judgments based on sounds. And will anyone dispute that thunder makes sounds and is a great omen? And doesn't the priestess on the tripod at Delphi,[2] herself, announce the responses of the god with a sound? (13) And surely that the god knows beforehand what will happen and forewarns whomever he wishes; about this all say and think just as I say. However, while some name what forewarns them 'birds,' 'voices,' 'omens,' or 'prophets,' I call this a 'divinity' (*daimonion*), and I think by naming it thus, I speak more truthfully and more piously than those who attribute the power of gods to the birds. Indeed, I have the following proof that I do not speak falsely concerning the god: for, though I told the advice of the god to many friends, never once was I shown to have spoken falsely."

---

[2]The Pythia in the temple of Apollo at Delphi.

(14) And, Hermogenes said, when the jurors made an uproar, some disbelieving what was said and others being jealous that he should receive greater things from the gods than themselves, Socrates again said, "Come now, hear more, so that those who wish may disbelieve still more that I have been honored by gods. For, once when Chairephon[3] asked in Delphi about me, in the presence of many, Apollo answered that there is no man more free, more just, or more temperate than I."

(15) And since the jurors again, as was natural, made an uproar when they heard these things Socrates went on to say, "But, gentlemen, the god said greater things in oracles about Lycurgus, who made laws for the Spartans, than he did about me. For, they say that entering the temple the god said to him, 'I am considering whether to address you as a god or a man.' He did not liken me to a god but judged that I far surpass many men. All the same, you should not thoughtlessly believe the god even about this, but examine each thing the god said one by one. (16) Do you know anyone who is less a slave to bodily pleasures than I? Or any man more free than I, who accepts neither gifts nor wages from anyone? Who would you reasonably consider more just than the one who adapts to what he has so as to need none of anyone else's possessions? And how would anyone reasonably refuse to call me a wise man—I, who from the time I could first understand what was said have not stopped seeking and learning whatever good I could? (17) Don't the following seem to you to be proofs that I have not labored in vain, namely that many of our citizens who strive for virtue and many foreigners prefer to associate with me over everyone else? What shall we say is responsible for this fact, that although everyone knows that I, least of all, would have money to repay them, nevertheless many desire to give me some gift? And that it is never asked of me to return a favor, but many acknowledge that they owe me favors? (18) Or that during the siege,[4] while others pitied themselves, I lived no worse than when the city is happiest. And that while other men furnish themselves with expensive delicacies from the marketplace I produce, at no cost, more pleasurable ones from my own soul. If, having said all of this about myself, no one would be able to convict me of speaking falsely, how would I not be already justly commended by both gods and men? (19) Yet, in spite of all this, Meletus, do you say that in pursuing such things, I corrupt the youth? And yet surely we know what the corruptions of youth are; but speak up if you know of anyone under my influence who has fallen from piety to impiety or from self-control to licentiousness or from temperate living to extravagance or from moderate drinking to drunkenness or from loving hard work to softness or who has yielded to any other lowly pleasure." (20) "But, by Zeus," said Meletus, "I have known those

---

[3]See also Plato's *Apology* 20e–21a, which gives a significantly different account of the oracle to Chairephon.

[4]The siege that ended the Peloponnesian War. See Xenophon's *Hellenica* 2.2 for an account.

ones whom you have persuaded to obey you rather than their parents!" "I concede that," declared Socrates, "at least as regards education; for they know this has been a matter of thought for me. But, concerning health, men obey physicians rather than their parents; and in the assembly, at any rate, all Athenians surely obey those who speak sensibly rather than relatives. For do you not elect as generals, over fathers and brothers, and certainly, by Zeus, over your own selves, those who would be most prudent in the affairs of war?" "For this, Socrates," replied Meletus, "is both profitable and customary."

(21) "Therefore," Socrates said, "does this not seem to you to be amazing, that in these other affairs the best men obtain not only equal treatment but are preferred, yet I, because I am distinguished by some to be the best as regards the greatest good to man, namely education, on account of this I am being prosecuted by you on a capital charge?"

(22) It is clear that more was said by Socrates himself as well as by his friends who defended him. But I was not eager to relate everything from the trial; rather it was satisfactory to me to make clear that Socrates, on the one hand, put it before all else to be neither impious as regards the gods nor to appear unjust as regards men; (23) and, on the other, he did not think he should stubbornly resist dying, but he believed it was already an opportune time for him to die. And that he thought this way became even more evident after judgment was passed against him. For, in the first place, being ordered to propose a lesser penalty he neither proposed one himself nor did he permit his friends to do so, but he said that to propose a lesser penalty is for that one who admits he is guilty.[5] Secondly, when his friends wished to secretly free him from prison he did not follow them,[6] but he seemed to joke, asking if they knew of any place outside of Greece where death could not come.

(24) And as the trial came to a close Socrates said, "But, gentlemen, those instructing the witnesses that they should bear false testimony against me by lying under oath, as well as those witnesses who obeyed them, should be aware of their own great impiety and injustice. But, what cause do I have to think less of myself now than before I was condemned, since it was in no way proven that I did any one of those things of which they accused me? For, indeed, I have neither been shown to worship any new deities over Zeus and Hera, and those gods associated with them, nor to swear oaths to or name any other gods. (25) Indeed, how would I corrupt the youth by accustoming them to patience and frugality? And of the deeds upon which the penalty of death is laid down, sacrilege, burglary, enslavement, treason against the state, not even my accusers themselves claim I committed such acts. Hence, it seems amazing to me how it would

---

[5]Contrast Plato's account in his *Apology* (38b–c), according to which Socrates offered to pay a fine of 30 minas of silver.
[6]See Plato's *Crito* for an account of such an attempt.

in any way appear to you that I have committed a deed worthy of death. (26) However, nor should I think less of myself because I die unjustly, for this is not shameful to me but to those who condemned me. And the case of Palamedes,[7] who died in a similar way as myself, comforts me; for even now he occasions more beautiful songs than Odysseus who unjustly killed him. I know that for me also it will be confirmed by time to come and time past that I have never harmed anyone or made anyone worse off, but that I improved those who conversed with me by teaching them for free whatever good I could."

(27) Having said these things in a similar way as he had spoken before, he walked away with a cheerful look in his eye, his looks, and his gait. And when he perceived that those accompanying him were weeping he said, "What's this? Are you weeping now? Don't you know that long ago, before I was born, death was decreed for me by nature? But, surely, if I were killed while good things were pouring in, then it is clear that my well-wishers and I should feel pain. But, if I end my life while expecting more grief, I think you all must be cheerful that I am doing well."

(28) One who was present, Apollodorus—a great admirer of Socrates but otherwise simpleminded—then said, "But, for my part, Socrates, what I suffer most grievously is that I watch you going to die unjustly." To this, it is said that Socrates, stroking his head asked, "Would you rather, dearest Apollodorus, wish to see me die justly or unjustly?" And at the same time he laughed.

(29) It is also said that, seeing Anytus pass by, Socrates said, "This man is proud, as if he had accomplished something great and honorable by killing me. Because seeing that he was thought by the city to be worthy of great things, I said that he should not educate his son in the ox-hide trade.[8] How foolish this one is," he said, "who does not seem to know that whichever of us has accomplished that which is more beneficial and more noble for all time is the one who prevails. (30) But, indeed" it is said that he said, "Homer attributed to those who were at the end of life the ability to see things to come, and I wish to prophesy something. I was in the company of Anytus' son for a short time, and he does not seem to me to have a weak soul, so I say he will not remain in the servile occupation that his father has prepared for him. But, on account of not having any serious guardian, he will fall into some shameful desire and advance further into wickedness."

(31) And in saying this, he was not speaking falsely. For, the youth, taking pleasure in wine, did not stop drinking, day or night, and finally he

---

[7]A Greek warrior at Troy. Put to death for treason on a trumped up charge by Odysseus. See also Plato's *Apology* 41b, where Socrates compares his own situation to that of Palamedes.

[8]Meletus is said to have been in the ox-hide business. Mention is made of Anytus' wealth by Plato; see *Meno* 90a. This trade was by many regarded as an especially low and degrading one.

became worthless to the city, his loved ones, and to himself. And Anytus, on account of the poor upbringing of his son and his own lack of good judgment, still, though he is dead, has a bad reputation.

(32) As for Socrates, he brought envy upon himself by extolling himself in court and induced the jury to condemn him. It seems to me, however, that he received a fate dear to the gods. For, he left behind the most difficult time of life and he met with the easiest death. (33) And he exhibited strength of soul, for when he realized that it was better for him to die than to live, just as he had never resisted anything else that was good, nor was he soft in the face of death, but he accepted it and died cheerfully.

(34) Indeed, when I consider the wisdom and nobility of that man, I cannot help but remember him and in remembering him praise him. And if any of those desirous of virtue has met anyone more helpful than Socrates, I think that man most worthy to be deemed happy.

· · ·

Memorabilia 1.1.1–1.2.39, 1.2.47–1.3.15, 4.7.1–4.8.11

TRANSLATED BY JERISE FOGEL

1.1.1   I often wondered what the arguments could have been by which the prosecutors persuaded the Athenians that Socrates was worthy of death as far as the City was concerned. Now, the indictment of him was approximately this: "Socrates is guilty of the crime of not honoring the gods that the City honors, and of introducing other, new divinities; and he is also guilty of corrupting young men."

1.1.2   First, then: that he did not honor the gods that the City honors—what sort of proof did they use? For he was often seen sacrificing at home, and often on the common altars of the City, and he was seen not infrequently using divination. For it was commonly said that Socrates said that his divinity[9] signaled to him; this seems to me to be the main grounds they had for accusing him of introducing "new divinities."

1.1.3   But he did not introduce anything "newer" than the rest of the people who, believing in divination, make use of birds and words and chance meetings[10] and sacrifices. For these people understand that it is not the birds, or the people one meets by chance, who know what is best for those who are using divination, but that it is the gods who signal what is best *through* these entities—and this is also what Socrates believed.

---

[9]"Divinity" = *daimonion*.

[10]"Chance meetings": the Greek word is *symbola*—"omens" or "significant coincidences." Chance meetings of people were one of the chief "omens" for Greeks—and in the next sentence and in section 4 the word *symbola* is replaced by more concrete references to chance meetings, showing what sorts of "significant coincidences" Xenophon had in mind.

1.1.4   And yet most people *say* that they are "warned away" or "encouraged" by the birds and the chance meetings; and Socrates expressed it in the way he knew: He said that "the divinity signaled." And he advised many of his companions to do some things and not to do others, on the grounds that "the divinity was signaling." And those who followed his counsel profited, and those who didn't follow it had cause for regret.

1.1.5   And yet, of course (who wouldn't agree?), he didn't wish to appear to his companions to be either an idiot or a braggart. And he would have appeared to be both these things, if he had clearly lied when he claimed that the omens[11] were from God. Therefore, it is clear that he wouldn't have spoken out, if he weren't confident that he would speak truly. And in these matters who would have confidence in anything or anyone other than God? And if he had confidence in the gods, how could it have been that "he did not honor the gods"?

1.1.6   And moreover, he did the following also for his companions. On the one hand, he advised them to do what was necessary, when they thought certainly it was best for the thing to be done; on the other hand, when it came to actions of doubtful outcome, he sent them to go seek some divination about whether they should be done or not.

1.1.7   And he said that those who planned to manage their households and cities well had further need of divination. For if one were to become an architect, or a bronzesmith, or farmer, or a commander over men, or a critic of such professions as these, or an accountant or administrator or general, he thought that all such fields of learning were, in fact, to be chosen by human reason.

1.1.8   But he said that the gods reserved the most important aspects of these matters for themselves, and nothing of these aspects was clear to humans. For, to the one who has sown a field well, it is not clear who will reap it; nor is it clear to one who has built a house well who will dwell in it; nor to the general, whether his acts of generalship are profitable; nor to the political actor is it clear whether his command over the city is profitable; nor is it clear to one who has married a beautiful woman in order to have joy, whether the marrier will be grieved on her account; nor is it clear to the one who has acquired in-laws who are powerful in the city, whether he will be deprived of his city[12] because of them.

1.1.9   And he said that those who think that none of these things are due to divinity, but that they're all within the control of human reason,

---

[11]"the omens": In Greek, *ta phainomena*, "the appearances," that is, the omens that are being heeded.

[12]"Deprived of his city," that is, of his citizenship. In Greek, the word for city-state, *polis*, is also the word for citizenship in such a city-state. Xenophon's point is that one cannot know whether one's powerful in-laws will ever turn into enemies, even to the point of using their power to get one banished or exiled as a noncitizen.

are insane;[13] insane also however are those who use prophecy to distinguish among the things that the gods give humans to know by experience—as though someone should ask [the gods] whether it's better to have at the yoke someone who knows how to drive horses or someone who doesn't know; or whether it's better to have one who knows how to steer at the ship's helm or one who doesn't know—or what they're able to know by counting or measuring or weighing. He thought that those who asked such questions of the gods were acting impiously. For, he said, what the gods have given to us to know by learning, we should learn; but what is unclear to humans, we should attempt to find out from the gods by means of prophecy. For the gods signal to those who are gracious to them.

1.1.10   But Socrates, moreover, was *always* out in public. In the morning he went to the colonnades and the gymnasia, during the full market he was seen there, and for the rest of the day he was constantly in whatever place he thought he would meet up with the most people. And he talked quite a lot, and those who wished could hear him.

1.1.11   And no one ever saw Socrates do or heard him say anything unholy or impious.[14] For he didn't even speak about the nature of all things in the way that most of the others did, looking into how what the sophists call the "cosmos" was born, and by what necessary laws each of the entities in the heavens came into being; on the contrary, he even exposed those who pondered such matters as fools.

1.1.12   And first he questioned them about whether they were coming to ponder such subjects because they thought that they already were sufficiently knowledgeable about human affairs—or whether they thought they were acting appropriately by setting aside human affairs and questioning the affairs of the gods.

1.1.13   And he was amazed if it was not clear to them that it is not possible for humans to find these things out, since even the best thinkers, when speaking about these things, do not agree with one another's opinions, but rather behave toward each other like raving lunatics.

1.1.14   For, as among raving lunatics, some do not even fear what should be feared, while others are even afraid of what is *not* frightening—and some think it is not shameful to say or do whatever they like, even in a crowd, while others do not even think it appropriate to step forth among humankind. And some pay respect to neither temple nor altar nor anything else holy, while others worship even rocks and ordinary pieces of wood, and wild beasts. And among those who ponder the nature of all things, some think the universe is one single unit, while others think it is infinite in number. And some think that everything is always in motion, while others think that nothing ever moves. And some think that every-

---

[13]"Due to divinity" = *daimonion*; "insane" = *daimonion*, literally, "possessed by a *daimo an*," in a bad sense. The word-play is hard to capture in English.
[14]"Unholy" = *asebes*; "impious" = *anosion*.

thing is born and is destroyed, whereas others think that nothing has ever been born or destroyed.

1.1.15   And he also asked these questions of them: "Students of human arts think that whatever they learn to create they will then create for themselves and whomever else they wish.[15] Like them, do researchers of divine arts think that, when they gain knowledge of the necessary laws by which each thing comes into existence, they will create, whenever they wish, winds and waters and seasons and whatever other such things they find themselves in need of? Or do they not expect anything of this sort, and rather it is enough for them merely to know how each of these things arises?"

1.1.16   And so, such are the things he said about those who busied themselves with these matters. But he himself always discussed human affairs, asking what is pious, what impious; what is fine, what base; what is just, what unjust; what is wisdom, what madness; what is courage, what cowardice; what is a city, what a statesman;[16] what is rule over humans, what is a skilled ruler of humans; and other matters. When his interlocutors knew the answers to these questions, he considered them noble; those who did not know the answers he thought could justly be called slaves.

1.1.17   As for things, however, that it was not public knowledge that he believed, it is not surprising that the judges went astray in these matters in their judgment about him. But as for things that everyone knew [about him], isn't it surprising that they did not take *these* to heart?

1.1.18   For he had been a member of the Council once,[17] and sworn the Council oath, in which one says one will act in Council according to the laws; and when he had become chairperson in the Assembly,[18] and the Assembly wanted to put to death, in a single vote, Thrasyllos and Erasinides and their colleagues all at once, which was against the laws, Socrates refused to take the vote. And the Assembly was angry with him, and many powerful men threatened him; but he considered it more important to keep his oath than to please the Assembly in transgression against justice, and to take heed of those who were threatening him.

1.1.19   Moreover, he thought that the gods take care of humans, not in the way that most people think; for *they* think that the gods know some things, and don't know others. But Socrates thought that the gods knew everything, what was said and done and thought in silence, and that

---

[15]That is, arts such as carpentry, shoemaking, cooking, etc., which have as a result the production of some useful object.

[16]"city" = *polis*; "statesman" = *politikos*. The two words are closely related in Greek, a "statesman" being one who takes part in the life of the city-state.

[17]Council: the *Boulē*, the smaller body of officials chosen by lot for one year's service, who drew up the agendas for and took care of the smooth operation of the Assembly or *Ekklesia*.

[18]See Plato, *Apology* 32b.

they were present everywhere and signaled to humans about all human matters.

1.1.20   And so, I am amazed at how in the world the Athenians were persuaded that Socrates was not respectful of the gods—Socrates, who never said or did anything whatsoever impious toward the gods, and who moreover spoke and acted such that, if anyone were to speak and act this way, he would be thought to be extremely pious.

1.2.1   And it also seems amazing to me that some were persuaded that Socrates corrupted young men—Socrates, who, in addition to the things said about him above, firstly was the most moderate of all men in sexual matters and matters of the stomach; then, the most hardy and inured to winter cold and summer heat and all kinds of hardships; and moreover, he was so trained to moderation in his needs that even though he owned very little, he easily found it quite sufficient for living.

1.2.2   How then, when he had such qualities, could he have made others either impious, or lawbreaking, or greedy for delicacies, or sexually rapacious, or too soft-bodied to endure hardship? Rather, he held many men back from these vices, having made them desire virtue, and holding out hopes to them that, if they took good care of themselves, they would become noble.

1.2.3   And yet he never at all promised that he would teach this, but rather by clearly being such a man, he gave his companions hope that by imitating him they would become such men as well.

1.2.4   But further, he did not neglect his body, and he did not praise those who did neglect theirs. And so he disapproved of the overeater, as well as of overworking, and he thought that a sufficient workload was one that made one's soul content. He said that this bodily habit was sufficiently healthy, and that it did not get in the way of the care of the soul.

1.2.5   But he was not, on the other hand, delicate or vain, in clothing, footwear, or any other habit of life. No, he did not even make his companions into money-lovers. He kept them away from other passions, and he did not profit from the fact that their one passion was for being with him.

1.2.6   By refraining from this sort of profit, he considered himself to be preserving his independence. He reproached those who took pay in exchange for discourse as self-enslavers, because they of necessity held discussions [only] with those from whom they received their pay.

1.2.7   And he was astonished if anyone professed virtue but earned money for it, and did not consider his greatest profit to be that he would have made a good friend, but instead was [apparently] fearful lest the one who had become noble *not* return the greatest thanks to the one who helped him in this greatest of ways.

1.2.8   And Socrates professed nothing of this sort to anyone at all; but he trusted that those of his companions who took in carefully what he himself expressed approval of would be good friends for their entire lives to both him and one another. How, then, could such a man corrupt young men?—Only if concern for virtue is corruption!

1.2.9   "But, by god," the accuser said, "he made his companions despise the established laws, saying that it was foolish to establish the rulers of the city by lot, and that no one would want to make use of a captain chosen by lot, or a builder, or a flute-player, or any other arts, any of which do far less damage when their practitioners make a mistake than do those who make a mistake about affairs of the city." And such arguments, the accuser said, raised up young men to look down on the established constitution, and made them violent.

1.2.10   But in my opinion, those who make a practice of prudence and believe that they will be capable of teaching citizens what is fitting are least likely to become violent, since they know that enmities and dangers come with violence, while the same results may be achieved through persuasion without danger and even with friendship. For those who have suffered violence hate, thinking that they have been robbed; while those who have been persuaded respond in a friendly way, thinking that they have received a favor. To use force is not a characteristic of those who make a practice of prudence, but it *is* a characteristic of those who have strength without intelligence.

1.2.11   Again, one who dares to use force will need quite a few allies, but the one who is able to persuade will need none; for even alone, he would consider himself able to persuade. And murder happens least among such men; for who would prefer to kill someone rather than persuade him and make use of him while he is alive?

1.2.12   "But," the accuser added, "Critias and Alcibiades became intimates of Socrates, and the two of them did the city the most grievous wrongs. Critias became the biggest thief and the most violent and murderous of all those in the Oligarchy, while Alcibiades became, for his part, the most irresponsible and high-handed and violent of all those in the democracy."

1.2.13   And I, for my part, will not speak in their defense, if those two men did in fact do some evil to the city; but I *will* discuss how their comradeship with Socrates came about.

1.2.14   For these two men were in fact naturally the most desirous of public honor of all the Athenians, and they wanted to achieve everything on their own, and become the most famous of all men. On the other hand, they knew that Socrates lived quite self-sufficiently off the most meager of possessions, and that he was quite self-controlled with respect to all pleasures, and that in his discussions he influenced those who spoke with him in the way he wished.

1.2.15   And seeing these things, and being the sort of men described above, it is unclear whether one should say that they strove for his companionship because they were desirous of the way of life of Socrates and of the prudent wisdom that he had, or whether they did it because they thought that if they associated with him they would become very proficient in speech and action.

1.2.16　In *my* opinion, if God had given them the choice of either living their entire lives the way they saw Socrates living, or dying, they would both have preferred to die. And their actions made this clear: for as soon as they thought themselves more powerful than their fellow-companions, they immediately leapt away from Socrates and began to take an active part in politics, which was why they had yearned for Socrates in the first place.

1.2.17　Now, perhaps someone might object to this that Socrates should not have taught his companions political subjects before he taught them prudent wisdom. I don't dispute this: but I observe that all teachers present themselves as examples to their students, in how they practice what they teach; and I see that they simultaneously lead them along by means of reasoning. And I know that Socrates too presented himself to his companions as a noble man, and one who conversed in the finest way about virtue and other human matters.

1.2.18　And I know that Alcibiades and Critias, too, were temperate while they were with Socrates, not because they were afraid of being charged a fee or struck by Socrates, but because they believed at that time that this was the best action to be taking.

1.2.19　Then, perhaps many of those who claim to be philosophers might say that the just man could never become unjust, nor the temperate man rash and high-handed, nor was it possible that a person who learned anything that *could* be learned might ever *un*-learn it. But this is not what I understand to be the case about these matters. For I observe that, just as those who don't exercise their bodies are not able to do physical work, so also those who do not exercise their soul are not able to do spiritual work; they can neither do what they need to do, nor can they hold themselves back from what they should keep away from.

1.2.20　This is the reason, too, that fathers, even if they themselves are temperate, nevertheless keep their sons away from wicked men, on the grounds that association with good men is the practice of virtue, while association with bad men undoes virtue. And of the poets, one also witnesses this, saying:

"*Learn good things from good men; if you mix with bad men,*
　　you will lose even the good sense you already possess,"[19]

and another says:

"*But a good man is sometimes evil, and at other times excellent.*"[20]

---

[19]The couplet comes from Theognis, vv. 35–36, and is again put by Xenophon into Socrates' mouth in *Symposium* 2.4; Plato also quotes it at *Meno* 95d.

[20]The author of this hexameter verse is not known; Plato (*Protagoras* 344d) quotes it as proof of the same assertion.

1.2.21   And I am also a witness to this: For I observe that, just as those who create poetry in meter forget how to do this when they do not practice the art, so also forgetfulness of their teachers' words sets in for those who do not take care to practice them. And when someone forgets the words that remind him of it, he also forgets what his soul had felt that made it long for virtue. And it is no wonder that someone who has forgotten this also forgets prudent wisdom.

1.2.22   And I further observe that those who have been led by their passion into philosophy and those who have gotten involved in love affairs are less capable of both taking care of what they should do, and refraining from what they shouldn't do. For many men who are quite wealthy are frugal before falling into lust, and after having fallen are no longer wealthy; and once they have spent all their money, they no longer refrain from the kinds of money-making they *had* refrained from in the past, in the belief that they were disgraceful.

1.2.23   It is, therefore, clearly possible that one who was temperate before might not be temperate at another time, and that one who was capable of acting justly before might be incapable of it later. As a consequence, it seems to me that all noble and good habits must be practiced, and especially temperance. For desires for pleasure have been planted in the same body along with the soul, and these desires persuade the soul not to be temperate, but rather to cater to them and to the body as quickly as it can.

1.2.24   And, in fact, Critias and Alcibiades, as long as they were with Socrates, were able to control their non-noble lusts, since they had him as an ally in their struggle. But when they had left him, Critias fled in exile to Thessaly and lived there with people who practiced lawlessness rather than justice. Alcibiades, in his turn, was hunted out by many prominent women because of his beauty, yes-sirred into moral oblivion[21] by many powerful men on account of his power in the city and among the allies, and honored by the people and excelling with ease. Just as athletes in the gymnastic contests who excel with ease neglect practice, so Alcibiades also neglected himself.

1.2.25   When events turned out this way for the two of them, and they, swelled up on account of their birth, were lifted into haughtiness by their wealth, were puffed up by their power, and were toadied into weakness by many men, and on top of all these circumstances, they had also been away from Socrates for a long time, why is it surprising if they became arrogant?

1.2.26   Then, if they went wrong in some way, does the accuser really blame this on Socrates? And the fact that while they were both young, when they were most likely to be extremely ignorant and intem-

---

[21]"yes-sirred into moral oblivion": Greek *diathruptomenos,* literally "broken," here in the sense of "weakened" or "made effeminate."

perate, Socrates made them prudent—doesn't the accuser think that he is worthy of any praise for this [feat]? Indeed, other [arts] are not judged this way.

1.2.27   For what flute-player, what citharist, what other teacher who has made his students proficient, is blamed if they seem to become worse when they have come to someone else? And what father, if his son associates with someone and is temperate, but later becomes wicked when he associates with someone else—what father would find fault with the first companion, rather than *praise* the first companion in direct proportion to how much worse the son appears to be while he is with the second? Moreover, the fathers themselves do not bear the blame for their sons, when their children make mistakes, if they themselves are wise.

1.2.28   And so, it is also just to judge Socrates: If he himself did something base, it would be reasonable to think that he was wicked. But if he himself was consistently temperate, surely he could not justly take the blame for wickedness that was not in him.

1.2.29   But even if he made no one wicked, if he praised those who did base things when he saw them, it would be right to take him to task. Now, when he perceived indeed that Critias was in love with Euthydemus and was trying to have him in just the way of those who enjoy bodies sexually, Socrates tried to turn him away from his desire, telling him that it was not the desire of a free man, and that it was not appropriate for a noble man to beg favors of his beloved, in front of whom he wishes to appear worthy, supplicating him as beggars do and entreating him to grant things that were not to be granted by a good man.[22]

1.2.30   And when Critias did not heed these warnings and refused to be turned away, it is said[23] that Socrates, in the presence of Euthydemus and many others, said that he thought Critias was seeming a little swinish of late, desperately wanting to rub up against Euthydemus, the way that little pigs rub up against stones.

1.2.31   Critias hated Socrates because of this incident, so much so that even when, as a member of the Thirty, he became Reviser of the Laws (*Nomothetes*) along with Charicles, he remembered it against Socrates, and among the [revised] laws, he wrote that it was illegal to teach the art of speaking, wanting to act spitefully against him and not having a way to reach him, except for bringing up against him the charge that is commonly brought up against philosophers by the common crowd, and slandering him with it in front of the common crowd. [And it *was* slander,] for neither I myself ever heard Socrates say this, nor do I know of anyone else who says he heard him.

---

[22]"things that were not to be granted by a good man," i.e., anal penetration.
[23]"it is said": Xenophon is careful not to give credence to this funny quip, although he illogically uses it also to explain Critias's actions against Socrates while in office under the Thirty; see next section.

1.2.32   But it was clear [that this was Critias' aim]: For when the Thirty were in the process of killing many of the citizens, including some of the best, and were forcing many to do wrong, at some point Socrates said that he thought it would be amazing if a shepherd, made cattle-driver, rendered the cows fewer and worse, and yet was not generally considered to be a bad herdsman; but that it would be even more amazing if someone who had become caretaker of the city rendered its citizens fewer and worse, and yet was not ashamed, and did not consider himself a bad caretaker of the city.

1.2.33   And when this comment was brought back to them, Critias and Charicles summoned Socrates, and the two showed him the law and forbade him to speak with young men. But Socrates asked the two whether it was permitted to ask a question, if he didn't understand one of the published laws. And they consented.

1.2.34   "Well, now, I," he said, "am prepared to obey the laws, but in order that I do not through my ignorance inadvertently break any law, I want to learn clearly from you, whether when you order that we refrain from 'the art of speaking,' you are considering that art to be associated with truthful sayings or with false sayings. If with truthful sayings, I would clearly have to refrain from speaking the truth. But if you mean with false sayings, it is clear that I must try to speak the truth."

1.2.35   And Charicles, angered with him, said, "Socrates, since you are ignorant, we are proclaiming these rules to you more simply: not to converse at all with young men." And Socrates said, "Wait—so that there is no doubt—define for me up to how many years old should one consider men to be 'young men?'" And Charicles said, "For as long a time as they are not permitted to be members of the *boule*, since they are not yet sensible; so, to be explicit for you, don't converse with men younger than thirty years old."

1.2.36   "Not even if I am buying something," he said, "and if a man younger than thirty years old is selling it? I cannot ask how much he is selling it for?" "That sort of thing, yes," said Charicles. "But you, Socrates, are in the habit of asking questions for the most part when you already know what the answer is; so don't ask that kind of thing." "Should I not even answer, then," he said, "if some young man asks me a question, if I know the answer, for example where does Charicles live, or where is Critias?" "That sort of thing, yes," said Charicles.

1.2.37   But Critias said, "But Socrates, you will need to refrain from the following sorts of topics—shoemakers and builders and blacksmiths. For I believe that they are already worn out, since you constantly talk about them." "Hmm," said Socrates; "then [I also need to avoid] the topics that follow on the heels of these, namely justice and piety and other sorts of things like these?" "Yes, by god," said Charicles, "and also the subject of cowherds; and if you don't, be careful that *you* aren't making the cattle fewer."

1.2.38   And it became clear from this that they had become angry with Socrates when the story about the cows had been relayed to them.

1.2.39   We have now told what kind of companionship Critias had with Socrates, and how they treated one another. And I would say, myself, that no one gains any education from a person he does not find pleasing. Critias and Alcibiades did not find Socrates pleasing to them even for the time when they associated with him, but rather they were eager right from the beginning to stand out in city politics. For even while they were associating with Socrates, they tried especially to converse with none other than those who were practicing politicians.

[sections 1.2.40–1.2.46 omitted]

1.2.47   Now, as soon as they suspected that they were more powerful than the other politically minded citizens, they no longer went to Socrates; for he didn't please them for any other reason, and whenever they came to him they became aggravated when they were caught in their errors. But they acted in the affairs of the city, and for this reason they also came to Socrates.

1.2.48   But Crito was a companion of Socrates, and Chairephon, and Chairecrates, and Hermogenes, and Simmias, and Cebes, and Phaidondas and others, and they spent time with him not in order to become assembly or lawcourt speakers, but in order to be able to treat their household and slaves and family and friends and city and fellow-citizens in a fine way, once they had become noble themselves. And of these, not one, whether younger or older, either did any evil or incurred any blame.

1.2.49   "But Socrates," said the accuser, "taught them to abuse their fathers. He persuaded his companions that he was making them wiser than their fathers, and he claimed that if one convicted one's father of insanity it was even legally permissible to bind the father. And he used this fact to argue that it was lawful for the more ignorant to be bound by the wiser."

1.2.50   But Socrates thought that it would be just for the man who bound others up on account of ignorance to be bound up himself by those who knew what he himself did not know. And on account of such considerations he often examined the question of how ignorance was different from insanity. And he thought that it was convenient for the insane to be bound, both for their own sakes and for the sake of their friends and family, while it would be just for those who did not have the knowledge that was needed to learn from those who did have it.

1.2.51   "But Socrates," said the accuser, "dishonored not only fathers but one's other relatives among his followers, saying that relatives did not help those who were sick, nor those who were attacked in court, but rather that doctors helped the first, and those who knew how to argue in court helped the second."

1.2.52   And [the accuser] said also that Socrates said about friends and family that it was not at all useful to be a well-wisher, unless they are also going to be able to give some actual help; and that he said that only those men were worthy of honor who knew what was needed and were able to articulate it. So, he said that by persuading the young men that he himself was most wise and most capable of making others wise also, he put his companions in such a frame of mind toward him that for them all other people were of no account in comparison with him.

1.2.53   And I do know that he said these things about fathers and other relatives and about friends and family. And indeed, in addition to these things, that when the soul, in which alone understanding resides, has left [the body], they take the body even of their nearest kinsman and hide it in a tomb as quickly as possible.

1.2.54   And he said that even while living each person gets rid of whatever part of his body (and of all things belonging to him he most loves his body) is useless and unhelpful, and permits another person to get rid of these parts for him as well. They themselves get rid of their own nails and hair and calluses, and they allow doctors to cut and burn them away in very painful ways, and in exchange for this they even think it appropriate to pay them money. And they spit out saliva from their mouth as far away as they can, because it does not help them at all when it is in there, and is more likely to do harm.

1.2.55   Therefore, he said these things not by way of teaching that one should bury one's father while he is still alive, or cut oneself into pieces, but rather, as he demonstrated that that which is foolish is dishonorable, he advised that one take care to be as wise as possible and as helpful as possible. The point was that, whether one wishes to be honored by father or brother or anyone else, one should not be lax, trusting merely in the fact that one is "related," but rather should try to be useful to the people by whom one wishes to be honored.

1.2.56   And the accuser said that Socrates also chose out from the canonical poets the most wicked excerpts and used these as proofs to teach his companions to be evil-doers and tyrants. He said that he quoted Hesiod's "no kind of work is a reproach, but lack of work *is* a reproach,"[24] and said that the poet was commanding that one not refrain from any type of work, even if it be unjust or shameful—that one should do even such things as long as there is monetary gain.

1.2.57   But Socrates, when he agreed that to be a worker was useful and good for a person, and to be lazy was harmful and bad, and to work was good, and to slack off bad, said that those who were doing something good were working and were workers, while he reproached as lazy those who were playing at dice or doing anything else wicked and hurtful. And from this basis it might rightly be said that "no kind of work is a reproach, but lack of work *is* a reproach."

---

[24]*Works and Days* 311. If Xenophon is accurate, the accuser misread the line—I have translated it the way the accuser would have wanted it to read. In the context of *Works and Days*, the line would sound more like this: "Work is no reproach, but lack of work *is* a reproach."

1.2.58   And the accuser said that he often quoted these lines of Homer, to the effect that Odysseus:

> ...whenever he encountered some king, or man of influence, he would stand beside him and with soft words try to restrain him: "Excellency! It does not become you to be frightened like any coward. Rather hold fast and check the rest of the people."

> ...When he saw some man of the people who was shouting, he would strike at him with his staff, and reprove him also: "Excellency! Sit still and listen to what others tell you, to those who are better men than you, you skulker and coward and thing of no account whatever in battle or council."[25]

And he said he interpreted these lines in fact, saying that the poet was recommending that common men and the poor be struck.

1.2.59   But Socrates was not saying this. For if he had been, he would have thought that he himself should be struck. Rather, he said that it was necessary for those who were helpful neither to the army nor to the city, and who were not capable of helping the populace itself, if it needed anything of them, and especially if they were also arrogant, to be stopped in every way, even if they happened to be quite wealthy.

1.2.60   But Socrates himself was clearly the opposite of this type of person—he was a man of the people, and a lover of mankind. For he took in many enthusiastic followers, both citizens and foreigners, and never charged anyone any fee for his companionship, but rather gave of his own goods unstintingly to everyone. Some of them, receiving small portions from him as a gift, sold them to others for much money, and were not men of the people as he was; for they refused to speak with those who could not give them money.

1.2.61   But Socrates even in his relations to other men was an adornment to the city, much more so than Lichas was to the city of the Lacedaimonians—and Lichas was famous on this account. For Lichas, during the Spartan Boys' Festival,[26] feasted the foreign visitors in Sparta, but Socrates throughout his whole life helped all those who wished it in the greatest way, expending his own resources; for he made those who stayed with him better men and then sent them off.

1.2.62   In my opinion, Socrates, being this sort of man, was worthy of honor from the city rather than death. And one could discover this even by examining [the matter] according to the laws. For according to the laws, if someone is clearly a thief or clothes-stealer or cut-purse or burglar or

---

[25]*Iliad* 2.188–191 and 198–202. (Translation by Richmond Lattimore.)
[26]"Spartan Boys' Festival": the *Gymnopaidiai*, at which nude boys danced and went through various physical exercises.

slaver or temple-robber—*these* are the people for whom death is the penalty. Socrates was the farthest away of all men from these types.

1.2.63   Moreover, he was never responsible, as far as the city was concerned, for a war that turned out badly, or civil strife, or treachery, or any other kind of evil. And in private affairs, he never deprived any person of goods, nor did he ever involve anyone in catastrophic debt—he was never even remotely responsible for any of the things mentioned.

1.2.64   How then could he be liable to the indictment? Instead of not honoring the gods, as was written in the indictment, he clearly served the gods best of all men; and instead of corrupting young men, of which the author of the indictment did accuse him, he clearly held back those of his companions who had evil desires from these desires and turned them around to desire the most noble and magnificent virtue, by which cities and households are well governed. Since he did these things, how could he not be worthy in the city's eyes of great honor?

1.3.1   Now, in order to show that he was even beneficial to his companions, as I think, both in his actions by showing himself to be the person he was, and also in conversation, I will write as much as I can remember about these matters. Now, in regard to the gods, he clearly acted and spoke according to the answer the Pythia gave to those who asked her how one should act either concerning sacrifice, or concerning the care to be taken of dead ancestors, or concerning any other of these sorts of things. For the Pythia gave answer that they would act piously by acting in accord with the law of the city. And Socrates both did this himself and advised the others to do it, and he thought that those who did otherwise were worthless meddlers.

1.3.2   And he prayed to the gods asking simply that they give good, since the gods know what is most beautiful, and what is most beautiful is good. And he thought that those who prayed for gold, or silver, or kingship, or anything else of this sort, prayed no differently than if they were praying about a game of dice, or a battle, or anything else that is obviously unclear as to outcome.

1.3.3   And he did not think that one who made small sacrifices from small possessions fell short [in the gods' eyes] of those who made many large sacrifices from their many large possessions. For, he said, the gods would not be noble if they received more pleasure from great sacrifices than from small ones. For then it would often happen that they were more pleased by sacrifices from wicked people than by sacrifices from good people. Nor would it be worthwhile for people to live justly, if sacrifices from the wicked were more pleasing to the gods than those from the good. Rather, he thought that the gods were most pleased with the honors given them by the most pious. And he was also an admirer of this verse:

And make sacrifices as you are able to the immortal gods.[27]

---

[27]Hesiod, *Works and Days* 336.

He said that "as you are able" was noble advice with respect to our treatment of friends and relatives, and guest-friends and strangers, and the rest of life as well.

1.3.4   And if he thought something was being signaled by the gods, he was less easily persuaded to act against the signs than he could have been persuaded by someone to take as a pathfinder a blind person who did not know the way rather than a sighted person who *did* know it. And he accused other people of folly, if they acted at all against the signs given by the gods, and stuck by the perverse folly of people instead. He himself ignored all human advice in favor of the counsel of the gods.

1.3.5   And he schooled his mind and body in a way of life by which, except for some acts of the gods, he was able to continue confidently and without trouble, and would not lack the means for necessary expenditure. For his way of life was so frugal that I find it difficult to believe that anyone could work so little as not to be able to earn enough to satisfy Socrates. For he took as much food as was pleasant for him to eat; and he tended to consider his desire for food a sort of condiment. And all sort of drink was sweet to him because he did not drink unless he was thirsty.

1.3.6   And whenever he was invited to and wished to attend a dinner-party, he quite easily refrained from filling himself up at it beyond the mere satisfaction of his hunger, which for most people is quite difficult to do. And he advised those who were unable to do it to ward off the impulses that persuaded them to eat when they were not hungry and to drink when they were not thirsty; for he said that these were the impulses that harmed stomachs and heads and souls.

1.3.7   And he said jokingly that he thought that Circe too used these impulses to make many[28] into swine when she feasted them; whereas Odysseus did not become a swine both through the advice of Hermes and because he himself was temperate and refrained from engaging in such things as she offered beyond satiety.

1.3.8   This was the way he joked about these matters—but at the same time he was serious. And he advised that one strictly refrain from sex with beautiful people; for he said it was not easy to remain sober when engaged in such activities. Moreover, when he once found out that Critoboulus, the son of Crito, had kissed the son of Alcibiades, who was beautiful, he asked Xenophon (Critoboulus was present),

1.3.9   "Tell me, Xenophon; did you not used to think that Critoboulus was to be counted among the sober people rather than among the rash, and among the responsible rather than the foolish and headstrong?" "Very much so," said Xenophon. "Now, however, you must consider him to be hotheaded and villainous. This man would play with swords, and set himself on fire!"[29]

---

[28]For the story of Circe's turning Odysseus' men into swine, see *Odyssey* 11.229ff.

[29]"play with swords, and set himself on fire": these are meant to translate two proverbial expressions in Greek for taking extreme and foolish risks.

1.3.10   "And why indeed," said Xenophon, "do you charge him with this, once you saw him do what he did?" "Well," he said, "isn't this the man who dared to kiss the son of Alcibiades, who is exceptionally good-looking and in the prime of his youth?" "Yes, but let me tell you," said Xenophon, "that if *that* is a headstrong deed, I think I'd also want to run the risk!"

1.3.11   "Reckless!" said Socrates. "And what do you think you are submitting to when you kiss a beautiful boy? Don't you think that it is to become immediately a slave instead of a free man, and to pay a great amount for pleasures that do you harm, and to have no time for caring for anyone who is noble, and to be forced to take seriously matters that not even a madman would take seriously?"

1.3.12   "Heracles!" said Xenophon. "What awesome power you attribute to a kiss!" "And this amazes you?" said Socrates. "Don't you know," he said, "that phalanx-spiders, even though they are no bigger than a half-obol's size, when they merely touch one's mouth wear humans down with sharp pains[30] and deprive them of their good sense?" "Yes, by god," said Xenophon. "The reason is that phalanx-spiders have some poison in their bite."

1.3.13   "You foolish one!" said Socrates. "Don't you think that beautiful boys also have some poison in their love, which you don't see? Don't you know that this beast, which they call 'the beautiful boy in the prime of his youth,' is so much more dangerous than phalanx-spiders that the spiders at least have to touch you, whereas this beast does not even need to touch you for there to be some poison in it? and that from quite far away such a beast causes one to become mad? But I advise you, Xenophon, whenever you see some beautiful boy, to flee with all speed. And you, Critoboulus, I advise to go into exile for a year. For perhaps (although it will be difficult) you might recover your health in that amount of time."

1.3.14   This, too, is how he thought those who were not steadfast toward sex ought to indulge their lust: with such objects as the soul would not find acceptable at all unless the body stood very much in need of them, while they would not cause problems for the soul if the body did need them.[31] And he himself was clearly prepared toward these dangers: He

---

[30]"sharp pains" = *odunai*, the word also used of birth pangs.

[31]Xenophon uses a rather circumlocutory expression to explain Socrates' attitude toward sex, which does *not* (as he wants to imply with the word "too"), apparently, exactly mirror his attitude toward food and drink as discussed above. Xenophon says that Socrates thought that one should indulge oneself sexually, only if one's body really needed the sex, with persons who utterly repulsed one's soul, and so did not threaten to ensnare it—beautiful boys were to be avoided because if their physical beauty led one to make sexual use of them, one would be doing violence to one's own soul by forcing it into a situation of prolonged love-enslavement. The subtext is that one cannot treat beautiful (i.e., upper-class, free-born) boys as sexual objects, then make one's escape afterwards—their "beauty" is therefore a snare for the soul in that it calls up a physical desire that one cannot get rid of through mere physical

held himself back from the most beautiful boys and ones most in their prime more easily than others were able to hold themselves back from the ugliest and those least in their prime.

1.3.15   This is how he was disposed on the questions of eating and drinking and sex, and he thought that he enjoyed himself no less satisfactorily than those who worried themselves much about them—and that he got much less grief than they did from them.

[sections 1.4–4.6 omitted]

4.7.1   Now, the fact that Socrates declared his own opinion to his fellow-discussants in a plain and simple manner seems to me to be clear from the things that have been said already. The fact that he also strove to have them be independent in carrying out appropriate practical actions,[32] I will now discuss. For of all the men I know, he was the one most concerned to know what each of his companions knew. And of the things that it was fitting for a noble man to know, if he knew about the matter, he was absolutely eager to teach it to them; but if he himself were ignorant of it, he urged them to go to those who were knowledgeable about it.

4.7.2   And he taught also the extent to which a person correctly educated should be conversant with each subject. For example, he said that it was necessary to learn geometry to the point where one was able, if he ever needed to, to measure correctly in order either to receive land as an inheritance, to transmit it legally to another, to apportion it [e.g., to one's sons or tenants], or to calculate its worth [e.g., for a public land survey or census, or to draw up one's own accounts]. And he said this was so easy to learn that someone who put his mind to measurement would at one and the same time get to know how large his property was and go away knowing how it is measured.

4.7.3   But he did not think it wise to learn geometry to the point of difficult diagrams. For he said he didn't see how these were of any help; and yet he was not ignorant of them.[33] But he said that these were capable

---

contact. Presumably Xenophon's Socrates would not have objected so strenuously to a man's making sexual use of a slave now and again.

[32]"be independent in carrying out appropriate practical actions" = *autarkeis en tais prosekousais praxesin.* The strong contrast is between Socrates' sharing of his opinion in words and his exhorting his companions to act self-sufficiently. The Greek here could be taken to mean either of two things: (1) Socrates wanted his companions to act independently in doing things that they were suited to do (so Marchant); (2) Socrates wanted his companions to act independently in a practical manner, taking actions that befit the theory he had shared with them (and to which they had consented, so making it their own)—or even simply to act on their own knowledge and well-thought-out opinions. I favor the second interpretation. The key term is *prosekousais,* an adjective that means "appropriate" or "suitable," and more strongly "belonging to."

[33]Theodorus the geometrician, called *agathos* by Socrates at 4.2.10, was said to have been Socrates' teacher. Contrast the attitude toward advanced study of geometry (and below, of astronomy) that Xenophon attributes to Socrates here with that reflected in the educational curriculum Plato's Socrates proposes in Book VII of the *Republic.*

of filling up a person's lifetime, and of stopping one from pursuing many other useful kinds of learning.

4.7.4   And he strongly advised them also to become familiar with astronomical measurement,[34] however only to the point of being able to know the time-divisions of night, of the month, and of the year,[35] for the sake of journeying and sailing and keeping the watch. And for whatever other things are done either over the course of the night or according to the month or the year, he advised they discern and use as orienting signs the time-divisions of the aforementioned periods. And he said that even these refinements were easily learned by night-hunters and ships' captains and many others whose business it was to know them.

4.7.5   And he strongly advised against learning astronomy to the point of knowing the bodies that do not remain in the same trajectory, and the planets, and the changeable stars;[36] and against spending time searching out their distances from the earth, and their orbits, and their sources. For he said he did not see any use at all in these things. And yet he was not ignorant even of these things; but he said that these things too were capable of filling up a person's lifetime, and of stopping one from pursuing many useful kinds of learning.

4.7.6   And he entirely advised against becoming a student of the heavens, and of the way in which God contrives each thing in them. For he didn't believe they could be discovered by humans, and he also thought that someone who searched out what the gods had not wished to make perfectly clear would not be pleasing to them. And he said that one who gave careful thought to these matters ran the risk of going mad, no less than Anaxagoras had gone mad, who had pondered most deeply the explanation for the contrivances of the gods.

4.7.7   For Anaxagoras, when he said that fire and sun were the same, did not understand that people easily strike up fire (unlike the sun), and that they cannot look directly at the sun, and that when they are shone upon by the sun they have darker skin, while this is not the case with fire. And he was also ignorant of the fact that none of the things that are born from the earth can grow well without the ray of the sun, while all things die when they are heated by fire. And when he claimed that the sun was a fiery rock, he also was ignorant of the fact that a rock when it is in fire does

---

[34]The Greek word is *astrologia*, but from the discussion Xenophon's Socrates clearly has in mind the measurement of celestial phenomena such as orbits and revolutions, for the sake of time-keeping, rather than what we would call "astrology."

[35]That is, to the point of being able to calculate what hour of the night, day of the month, and month or season of the year it was.

[36]"the changeable stars": that is, celestial phenomena that do not remain in a fixed place in the sky, but "wander" erratically like the planets over a period of time—comets might be an example. Socrates' point is that celestial phenomena that are changeable do not help anyone calculate time-periods, and thus do not need to be learned.

not give off light or last for a long time, whereas the sun remains the brightest of all things for all time.

4.7.8   And he advised also that they learn mathematics. And, as in the other sciences, he advised them to avoid the empty practice of this area, but he himself looked into and discussed all types of learning with his companions up to a useful point.

4.7.9   And he very strongly recommended that his companions take care of their health, by learning as much as they could from those who were knowledgeable; and he recommended that each one pay attention throughout his entire life to the kind of food or drink or exercise that was good for him, and to how he should make use of these in order to live in the healthiest way. For he said it was the task of one who took this kind of care of himself to find a doctor who best understood the things that were good for his health.

4.7.10   And if someone wished to make use of some sort of science other than that which concerns human beings, he advised him to study divination. For he said that a man who knew the means by which the gods signal to humans about their affairs would never be bereft of the wise counsel of the gods.

4.8.1   And if anyone thinks that he was caught lying about the divinity (*daimonion*), since he was condemned to death by the judges for saying that the divinity signaled to him in advance about what he should and should not do—first, let him recall to mind that Socrates was already at that time so advanced in age that even had he not died then, he would have ended his life not long afterwards. Second, he escaped the most oppressive period of one's life and the period during which all people become weakened in mind, and instead of this he displayed the strength of his mind and achieved good fame for it in addition; and he delivered his lawcourt speech most truthfully and liberally and justly of all men, and received his condemnation to death quite mildly and bravely.

4.8.2   For it is generally agreed that no man in memory received a death sentence with more nobility. To illustrate the point: It was necessary for him to remain alive for thirty days after the judgment, because the embassy to Delos occurred in that month, and by law no one was allowed to be publicly killed until the procession returned from Delos. And he was seen openly during this time by all his companions living in no way differently from what he had done in the time before—and yet during the time before he was of all men most wondered at for living so cheerfully and contentedly.

4.8.3   And how could anyone die more nobly than this? That is, what kind of death could be nobler than one that is undergone most nobly? And what kind of death is happier than the noblest? And what kind of person is more loved by the gods than the one who is most happy?

4.8.4   And I will tell also the story I heard from Hermogenes the son of Hipponicus about him. For he said, when Meletus had already indicted him, that when he heard him speaking about everything but the court case he said to him that it was necessary to think about what defense he would make. At first Socrates said, "Don't you think I have spent my whole life practicing my defense?" And when he asked him what he meant, he said that he had gone through his life doing nothing other than analyzing justice and injustice, and doing justice and refraining from injustice. He thought living in this way was the noblest sort of practice for one's defense.

4.8.5   But Hermogenes replied, "Don't you understand, Socrates, that the judges at Athens in the past have killed many men who had done no wrong, persuaded by a speech—and that they have acquitted many who *have* done wrong?" "But, by god," he said, "Hermogenes, when I tried to think about my defense speech for the judges, the divinity said, 'no.'"

4.8.6   And Hermogenes said, "That's amazing." And he said, "Are you amazed if it seems better to the god that I end my life now? Surely you know, up to this point in time, I would concede to no person that he had lived better or more pleasantly than I have. For I consider those to be living the best who take the most care that they become as good persons as possible. And I consider those who are most aware that they are becoming better people to be living the most pleasantly.

4.8.7   "Up to this point in time it was my perception that these things were the case for me, and when I happened to meet other people and compared myself with others, I have constantly thought this about myself. And it's not just my opinion: My friends too constantly think this about me, not because they love me—for then those who love others also would think this about *their* loved ones—but because they themselves are of the opinion that they are becoming good people when they associate with me.

4.8.8   "But if I live a longer time, perhaps it will be necessary for me to pay the debts of old age, and have worse vision and be weaker of hearing, and worse at understanding, and to become slower to learn and more forgetful, and to become worse than those whom I first was better than. But truly, if I were not to perceive these things happening, life would be no life at all; but again, if I did perceive them, of course, by necessity I would be living a worse and less pleasant life.

4.8.9   "If I die unjustly, this would be a shameful thing for those who have killed me unjustly; but what is shameful for *me* about the fact that others are not able to recognize or do justice in my case?

4.8.10   "And it is my perception at least that, of those who have done and suffered injustice, the reputation of those who came before is a legacy held in greater esteem among those who came after them; and I know that I also will enjoy esteem among men, even if I die now—a reputation that will not be shared by my killers. For I know that it will always be a witness in my favor that I never did injustice to any person or make anyone worse—and I tried always to make my companions better people." This is what he said to Hermogenes and to the rest.

4.8.11 And of those who know what kind of person Socrates was, all those who aim at virtue even now live in longing for him above all men, since he was the most useful to them in the consideration and practice of virtue. In my opinion, indeed, since he was such as I have described—that is, so reverent that he did nothing without consultation of the gods, so just that he did not harm anyone, no matter in how small a way, but rather helped in the greatest way those who kept his company; and so temperate that he never chose the pleasurable instead of the good; and so intelligent that he did not err when he judged the better and the worse, nor did he stand in need of someone else but rather was independent in his knowledge of these matters; and competent both in articulating in speech and defining such matters, and in examining others and bringing them into self-contradiction when they were in error, and turning them toward virtue and nobility—for all these characteristics, I think he was such a person as the best and most blessedly happy man would be. And if anyone does not agree, I challenge him to judge the matter by comparing the character of others with these characteristics.

CHAPTER 4

Diogenes Laertius

Diogenes Laertius (c. 200–250 C.E.), Italian biographer and historian of Greek philosophy. All that is known about the life of Diogenes is that he lived in Laete in Cicilia and authored *On the Lives and Opinions of Eminent Persons in Philosophy,* a ten-book work, written in Greek, about some eighty-one Greek thinkers. His accounts consist essentially of anecdotes and brief summaries of Greek thinkers, much of which is found nowhere else in antiquity. For this reason, Diogenes' claims are often difficult to assess. Whether Diogenes himself fabricated certain stories or whether the sources on which he relied, many of whom go unnamed, exaggerated, or invented what they had heard others say cannot be determined.

On the Lives and Opinions of Eminent Persons in Philosophy

BOOK ONE, CHAPTER FIVE—SOCRATES

18   Socrates was the son of Sophroniscus, a stone worker and Phainarete, a midwife, as Plato states in the *Theaetetus.* He was an Athenian, from the deme of Alopece. It seemed that he assisted Euripides, which is why Mnesimachus says:

> The Phrygians is this new play by Euripides . . . in which Socrates supplies the kindling.

Or again, "Euripides was held together by 'Socrates-nails.'" And Callias says in the *Captives,*

A. Now why are you so solemn and so very high-minded?
B. I am entitled to be. Socrates is to blame.

Aristophanes says in the *Clouds*,

This is the one who makes the tragedies of Euripides so full of chatter, and [so bereft of] of wisdom.

[Socrates] didn't need to travel, as most philosophers do, unless he had to   23
go on a military expedition. The rest of the time, he remained right where
he was, eagerly seeking people to converse with, not to alter their opinion,
but to try to understand the truth. They say that when Euripides gave him
a writing by Heracleitus and asked him, "What do you think of it?" he
said, "What I understand is noble and so is what I don't understand.
Except it needs a Delian diver [to plumb its depths]."

He was good about getting exercise and he was in good shape. He
served at Amphipolis, and when Xenophon fell from his horse at the battle of Delium, he picked him up and saved him. And when the Athenians
were in retreat, he stayed calm and quietly turned around, preparing to
defend himself if anyone attacked him. And he served at Potidaea by trav-
eling across the sea, for it wasn't possible to go on foot because the war
prevented it. They say that he lasted a whole night in a single position, and
when he won the prize for valor there, he turned it over to Alcibiades, with
whom he was in love, so Aristippus says in the fourth book of *On Ancient
Luxury*. . . .

That he was firm in his opinions and a proponent of democracy is   24
made clear from the fact that he didn't yield to those who were with
Critias, the ones who ordered him to bring Leon of Salamis, a man of
wealth, before them in order to have him killed. And he was the only one
to vote to acquit the ten generals. And when it was possible for him to
escape from prison, he didn't want to. He reproached those who wept [at
what was to happen to him] and, while a prisoner, gave his best talks to
them.

He was equally able to persuade and dissuade people. Thus, after dis-   29
cussing knowledge with Theaetetus, he sent him away filled with enthu-
siasm, according to what Plato says. And after discussing something about
piety with Euthyphro, who had indicted his father for the murder of a
stranger, he diverted him [from what he had set out to do]. And through
persuasion, he made Lysis quite ethical. For he was able to fashion arguments out the matters at hand. When Lamprocles, his son, became violent
with his mother, he calmed him down, so Xenophon said. When Plato's
brother, Glaucon, wanted to go into politics, he stopped him on account of
his lack of experience, as Xenophon says. But he imposed the opposite on
Charmides, for whom [politics] came naturally.

When Alcibiades said that Xanthippe's abuse was too much to bear,   37
[Socrates] said, "I'm used to it; it's like listening to the unceasing sound of

a pulley." "And do you mind the noise that geese make?" "No," he said, "for they offer me eggs and goslings." "Well, Xanthippe," he said, "gave birth to my children." When she tore off his cloak in the agora, his acquaintances urged him to punish her with a beating. "By Zeus," he said, "so that while we are fighting, each of you could say, 'that's a good one, Socrates,' 'that's a good one, Xanthippe.'" He used to say that he lived with a difficult woman just as horseman like spirited horses. "But as when those people master them they can easily be around other [horses], so I, by dealing with Xanthippe, shall be ready for other men."

The Pythia bore witness to these things and things like them when she gave that oracle to Chairephon.

Of all men Socrates is wisest.

And for this there was considerable ill will against him, especially because he refuted those who thought highly of themselves in order to show they were foolish, just as he slighted Anytus, according to Plato's *Meno*. And when he couldn't bear being scoffed at by Socrates, he got Aristophanes' friends agitated about him. And then he helped persuade Meletus to assent to the indictment [of Socrates] for impiety and corrupting the youth.

He did assent to the indictment, but Polyeuctus conducted the trial, as Favorinus says in his *Multifarious History*. Polycrates, the sophist, helped with the speech, so Hermippus says, or Anytus, as some say. Lycon, the demagogue, prepared everything. Anthisthenes says in his *Succession of Philosophers*, as does Plato in his *Apology*, that [Socrates] had three accusers: Anytus, Lycon, and Meletus. Anytus was angry on behalf of the craftsmen and politicians; Lycon, on behalf of the professional speakers; and Meletus, on behalf of the poets, all of whom Socrates really tore to pieces. In the first book of his *Remembrances*, Favorinus says that Polycrates' account of Socrates isn't true. There, [Favorinus] says, he recalls the reconstruction of the walls of Conon, which didn't happen until six years after the death of Socrates. And it is so.

The plaintiff's oath in the trial was like this. It is still in the posted even now, so Favorinus says, in the Metroon. Meletus, the son of Meletus, of the deme of Pitthos, has written down these things against Socrates, the son of Sophroniscus, of the deme of Alopece, and swears to them. "Socrates is guilty of not believing in the gods which the city believes in, and of introducing other new divinities, and he is guilty of corrupting the youth. The penalty is to be death." When Lysias wrote a defense speech for him, the philosopher said after having read it, "It's a fine speech Lysias, but it surely not suitable for me. It was clearly more lawyerly than philosophical." Then Lysias responded, "How it is, Socrates, that if it is a fine speech, it can't be suitable for you?" [Socrates] said, "A fine cloak and shoes would not be suitable for me, either."

In his *On the Wreath*, Justus of Tiberius says that while [Socrates] was being tried, Plato stepped onto the platform and said, "though I am the youngest, O men of Athens, to step onto the platform . . . ," whereupon the

39

40

41

jurors shouted out, "Get down, get down!" Then Socrates was convicted by two hundred and eighty-one votes more than those for acquittal. And when the jurors were demanding what it is necessary for him to suffer or to pay, he said he would pay 25 drachmas. Eubulides says that he agreed to pay 100 drachmas. And when the jurors made an uproar at this, he said,   42 "For my services, I am proposing free meals at the Prytaneum."

They condemned him to death, by an additional eighty votes. He was put in prison and when not many days had passed, he drank the hemlock after he carried on a long and wonderful conversation, which Plato recounts in the *Phaedo*. And according to some, [Socrates] wrote a paean, which began:

> Hail Delian Apollo, and Artemis, famous sons

But Dionysodorus denies that the paean was his, and says instead that Socrates wrote a not very well organized fable in the manner of Aesop, which began:

> Aesop once said that the citizens of Corinth are not to judge the city's virtue by wisdom of the human law-court.

And so he left humanity. The Athenians immediately had a change of   43 heart, which resulted in their closing the Palaestra and the Gymnasia. They banished the others, but they gave Meletus the death sentence. They honored Socrates with a bronze statue, made by Lysippus, which they set up in the Pompeion.[1] On the very day Anytus arrived [in Heraclea], the Heracleans announced that he was to be banished from their community. The Athenians were not only affected in this way about Socrates but also about many other such matters.

---

[1]The storehouse where sacred artifacts used in processions were kept.

CHAPTER 5

Minor Sources

Aeschines of Sphettus

Aeschines of Sphettus (fl. early fourth century B.C.E.), Athenian philosopher. Little is known of Aeschines' life. The way he is mentioned in Plato's *Apology* (33e) and again in the *Phaedo* (59b) should make us confident that Aeschines was one of Socrates' most devoted associates. He may have been present later in life at the court of Dionysus of Syracuse, where Plato also visited. Aeschines wrote at least seven dialogues featuring Socrates as the central character. Of these only fragments have survived. To what extent Aeschines was trying to capture the actual views of Socrates is a matter of conjecture.

In the passage below, Socrates is explaining to an unnamed listener why he associated with Alcibiades. It is interesting that Aeschines thought it was important to explain Socrates' motives in associating with Alcibiades, no doubt in reaction to Polycrates' *Accusation of Socrates* (see the Introduction to this collection).

FRAGMENT 1K

(from Publius Aelius Aristides, *In Defense of Oratory*)
110D335 I wonder how one ought to deal with the fact that Alcibiades and Critias were the associates of Socrates, against whom the many and the upper classes made such strong accusations. It is hard to imagine a more pernicious person than Critias, who stood out among the Thirty, the most wicked of the Greeks. People say that these men ought not be used as evidence that Socrates corrupted the youth, nor should their sins be used in any way whatsoever with respect to Socrates, who does not deny carrying on conversations with the young.

Isocrates

Isocrates (436–338 B.C.E.), Athenian orator. As a young man, Isocrates was influenced both by Socrates and some of the sophists. After a period of self-imposed exile, Isocrates returned to Athens and founded a school whose fame quickly spread throughout the Greek world. Although he wrote many speeches on behalf of litigants, Isocrates is best known for his political discourses in which he advanced the view, unpopular with many in Athens, that the Greeks would be wise to unite in order to thwart any Persian incursions. Later, he took the Macedonian side against Athens, believing that Phillip would achieve the goal of protecting Greece.

The passage below comes from Isocrates' *Busiris,* an *epideixis,* or display piece intended to demonstrate the author's rhetorical skill. The target is the fourth-century B.C.E. sophist Polycrates, who is being taken to task for the ineptness of his "Accusation of Socrates." For further discussion of the influence of Polycrates' "Accusation," see our discussion of this topic in the Introduction to this book.

BUSIRIS[1]

[4] Although I see that you are quite proud of the "Apology for Busiris" and the "Accusation of Socrates," I shall try to make clear to you that you have fallen far short of what is appropriate in both speeches. For everyone knows that it is necessary for those who wish to praise people to reveal more good things about them than is fitting and for those who wish to make [5] an accusation to do the opposite. But you have failed to make use of such [principles] in your speeches [. . .]. So, when you were accusing Socrates, as if you were trying to praise him, you gave him Alcibiades as a pupil, and although no one saw him being educated by [Socrates], all would agree that he was better by far than the others [who were around Socrates]. [6] Indeed, if the dead were to acquire the power to consider what has been said, he would give such thanks to you for the accusation as to any of the ones who are accustomed to singing his praises.

· · ·

Aeschines (Rhetor)

Aeschines (Rhetor) (c. 390–c. 320 B.C.E.), Athenian orator. Aeschines was born to a family of limited means. Whether his father at one time had con-

---

[1]Isocrates is addressing Polycrates' "Accusation of Socrates." See the Introduction to this book for discussion.

siderable property and lost it during the Peloponnesian War, as Aeschines claimed, cannot be known. His position as secretary to the Council probably gave him his knowledge of Athenian governmental practices and the details of Athenian law and legal procedure. He took a leading role in organizing the resistance among the various Greek cities to the rise of Macedonian power, although differences about how to conduct Macedonian policy led to his bitter rivalry with the orator Demosthenes. At one point Demosthenes brought a formal charge of treason against Aeschines, a charge that Aeschines successfully rebutted. Much of the rest of career was spent attacking Demosthenes, who assumed the leading role in Athens' resistance to Macedonian control.

The following passage is evidence that the case of Socrates was still on the minds of Athenians even half a century or so following Socrates' execution. Aeschines says that Socrates' association with Critias was the cause of his having been brought to trial. But see the Introduction to this book about how that issue may have been introduced.

ORATIO 1

173 Men of Athens, then you killed Socrates, because it appeared that he educated Critias, one of the Thirty who destroyed the democracy.

· · ·

Aristotle

Aristotle (384–322 B.C.E.), Greek philosopher. Born in Stagira in Calcidicia, in northern Greece, Aristotle was sent to Athens in 367 B.C.E. to become a student in Plato's Academy. He remained at the Academy for twenty years, until Plato's death. Aristotle lived in a number of places in the eastern reaches of the Greek world for several years until he was returned to Macedonia in 342 at the request of King Philip to become one of the teachers of Philip's son Alexander (the Great). In 335 Aristotle returned to Athens to start his own school, known as the Lyceum. When Alexander died in 323, Aristotle left Athens to escape increasingly hostile anti-Macedonian sentiments. Aristotle died in Calchis in 322.

His surviving works provide ample testimony to the encyclopedic scope of Aristotle's interests. It is likely that he offered both technical lectures intended for small audiences of dedicated students and informal lectures for larger audiences whose interests were more casual and utilitarian. The works that have survived are, for the most part, notes and remarks that provided the basis of the former lectures. Early in his career, Aristotle wrote a number of dialogues in the Platonic manner, of which only fragments survive.

Although Aristotle's remarks about Socrates are brief and scattered, they provide an invaluable source of information about the philosophy of the historical Socrates, for in a number of passages Aristotle is careful to distinguish between the views of Socrates and Plato. Moreover, given the length of his stay in Plato's Academy, it is only reasonable to assume that Aristotle carried on discussions with various persons, including Plato, would could verify what the historical Socrates believed and how it differed by the views of the mature Plato.

The first passage below shows that Socrates questioned the democratic practice of appointing persons to governmental positions by lot. Scholars continue to dispute about the extent to which this was seen as symptomatic of a more general anti-democratic sentiment of Socrates. The second passage tells us something about the scope and focus of Socrates' philosophical interests. It is significant in that many Athenians would have been deeply mistrustful of anyone who questioned their own competence to make their children good.

THE ART OF RHETORIC

Then there are the sort of comparisons Socrates used. For example, if some- 1393b4–8
one says that people shouldn't be chosen by lot to hold office, that's just
like someone appointing athletes not based on ability to compete by lot, or
that one should choose the captain from those in the crew because we need
one chosen by lot and not one who possesses knowledge of sailing.

METAPHYSICS A

Socrates busied himself with ethical matters and not with nature as a 987b1–4
whole. By searching for the universal in these matters [i.e., the ethical], he
was the first to see the importance of definitions.

• • •

Diodorus Siculus

Diodorus Siculus (c. 40 B.C.E.), Italian historian. Nothing is known of his life other than his authorship of the *Library of History,* Diodorus' attempt to write a history of the world. Most of the forty-volume work has been lost, but what has survived reveals that Diodorus was reporting the views of others and contributing little himself.

The brief passage below here records and unverified story of the fate of Socrates' prosecutors.

BOOK IV, 37.7

In Athens, Socrates the philosopher was prosecuted by Anytus and Meletus for impiety and corrupting the youth; he was sentenced to death, and he met his end by drinking hemlock. But the prosecution was unjust—the people had a change of heart when they saw that such a great man had been destroyed. So it was that they were angry at the prosecutors and, in the end, put them to death without a trial.

. . .

Dio Chrysostum

Dio Chrysostum (c. 40–c. 120 C.E.). Dio was born into a wealthy family in Prusa, a city in Asia Minor. His writing showed that he was well trained in classical philosophy and rhetoric. In Rome, he acquired his reputation as an orator and sophist. Banished in 82, he turned to philosophy and was influenced by both Cynics and Stoics. His extant writings consist of some eighty orations. Some concern various aspects of Greek culture and daily life during the classical and Hellenistic periods; others address political affairs in his native Bithynia; yet others express Dio's moral views.

In this passage, the author compares himself favorably to Socrates, suggesting that, like Socrates, he has been a misunderstood servant of the state. The forms of corruption that Dio says the youth of Athens were involved in may reflect the forms of corruption with which his own enemies had charged him.

THE FORTY-THIRD DISCOURSE

[8] I am not surprised at my current problems. For Socrates, whom I often think about, did everything on behalf of the city during the reign of the Thirty Tyrants and shared in none of their evil deeds, but, in fact, when he had been sent by them to get Leon of Salamis, he refused to obey, and he made no secret of his contempt for them, saying that they were like bad shepherds, who take lots of strong cattle and then make them few and weak. [9] Nevertheless, it was at the hands of the democracy, when it was prospering and on account of which he had risked the danger he did that he later suffered after having been slandered by some blackmailers. His accuser was Meletus, a vile man and a blackmailer. He says that Socrates is guilty of corrupting the youth, and of not honoring the gods that the city honors, and of introducing new divinities. These things were virtually the opposite of what [10] Socrates did. He honored the gods as no one else did, and he wrote paeans for Apollo and Artemis, one which even now I sing, and he not only tried to keep the young from being corrupted, but he chas-

tised and reproved them if they started wanting too much and became out of control, or made money from the city—some did this by taking bribes for an acquittal, others by being blackmailers, and yet others by plundering the wretched islands by claiming it was for taxes or by enlisting their men as soldiers, just as some are doing with us. That is why some people hated him and said that he corrupted the young.

· · ·

Maximus of Tyre

Maximus of Tyre (late second century C.E.), Roman sophist and literary figure and a student of Platonism. His surviving works are forty-one public lectures he delivered in Rome during the reign of Lucius Aurelius Commodus (180–192 C.E.).

In this selection, Maximus suggests that Socrates refused to make any defense of any kind, preferring to "remain silent." Given the testimony of those alive at the time of the trial, this surmise seems quite implausible, but it may derive from a corruption of the tradition—which goes back at least to Xenophon—of apologists trying to explain why Socrates, although a brilliant thinker and speaker, was not able to persuade his jurors to release him.

ORATION III

Whether Socrates Did the Right Thing When He Did Not Defend Himself
[1] It is a terrible thing that each of the other crafts escapes the court of public opinion. Certainly the ship captain, when he takes command of the ship and employs his craft according to its own principles, is not called to account by laymen, nor does the doctor put up with the sick examining and testing what he does—the cures and regimens—nor do potters, cobblers, and hand-workers, who engage in more lowly activities than these have any other judge of what they do except the craft itself. But despite the fact that not even Apollo, who knows the number of the grains of sand and who can divine the ways of the sea, could convict Socrates of ignorance, this has not freed him even now from being accused and investigated. The accusers who came on the scene later are even harsher to him than Anytus and Meletus and his actual Athenian jurors. If he had been a painter or a sculptor, like Zeuxis, or Polycrates, or Phidias, the reputation of his craft would have ensured that his accomplishments were met with adulation. And when men saw them, they wouldn't dare to condemn or even question them, but praise for such recognized spectacles would come forth automatically. But what if there was a person who was good, not with respect to a handicraft—not a painter or a sculptor—but who put his life together

proportionately and precisely with reason, labor, habituation, frugality, courage, self-control, and all of the other virtues, but who then happens not to have a sound reputation, universal praise, or unanimous judges? Quite a different result would come about because of what he says.

[2] The issue before us now is of this. Meletus wrote the indictment against this Socrates; Anytus stated the case against him; Lycon prosecuted him; the Athenians judged him; the eleven imprisoned him; and a servant killed him. [Socrates] was condescending to Meletus when he wrote the indictment; he was contemptuous of Anytus when he stated the case; he laughed at Lycon when he spoke; he condemned the Athenians in return when they condemned him; he offered a counterpenalty after they stated the penalty they wanted him to suffer;[2] and when the eleven imprisoned him, he granted them his body, for it was weaker than their many bodies. But he didn't give them his soul, which was stronger than all the Athenians. He didn't make it difficult for the servant, and he didn't flinch when he was presented with the poison.[3] The Athenians didn't want to condemn him, but he died voluntarily. That he acted voluntarily is proven by the fact that when it was possible for him to pay money and flee when he was imprisoned, he chose instead to die.[4] The involuntariness of what they did is shown by the fact that they immediately changed their mind.[5] What could be a more ridiculous position for jurors to be in?

[3] Do you still want to ask about whether Socrates acted correctly or not? Suppose someone came to you and told you about an Athenian, an old man who spends his time in philosophy, poor in luck but formidable by nature, good at speaking and a quick thinker, alert and sober, the sort of person who would neither do or say anything rashly, who was now far from youth and who had, on the one hand, won praise for his character from not the worst of the Greeks, and, on the other, from Apollo among the gods. When some arose against him with envy and hatred and anger at his good deeds—Aristophanes from the theater,[6] Anytus from the sophists, Meletus from the blackmailers, and Lycon from the orators[7]—one made fun of him. [. . .] And yet [are we to believe that] when he came before the court, he spoke against [his accusers] and made an exceptionally lengthy oration, a defense so well constructed for what the jurors were to conclude, preparing the court with an introduction, persuading [the jurors] with his version [of events], making the case with proofs, evidence, and probabilities, calling up certain witnesses from among the Athenians who were the wealthiest and most admired by the jury? And then with his conclusion

[2]See Plato, *Apology* 38b; contrast Xenophon, *Apology* 23.
[3]See Plato, *Phaedo* 117a–118a, Xenophon, *Apology* 33.
[4]See Plato, *Crito.*
[5]See Diodorus Siculus in this collection.
[6]See Aristophanes in this collection. See also Plato's *Apology* 18d.
[7]See Plato, *Apology* 24a.

supplicating, entreating, begging and, perhaps, at just the right time, shedding a tear, and, after this, bringing it to a close by calling up a wailing Xantippe, his weeping children, and though all these things that he manipulated the jury, and they acquitted him and showed pity for him and released him?[8]

[4] Oh, you good man who carries off the prize! Perhaps Socrates then hurried back [from the court] to the Lyceum and then to the Academy and the other places where he spent his time, exuberant, like those who have been saved from a storm at sea. How could philosophy have beared to have this man return to her? No more than the athletic trainer could bear to see the competitor back from the stadium, anointed with myrrh, having been crowned a winner without having broken a sweat and without having exerted any effort, untouched and unwounded, and having none of the marks of the excellence [of a contestant]. And what purpose could Socrates have had in making his defense before those Athenians? Because they were jurors? But they were unjust! Because they were wise men? But they were ignorant! Because they were good? But they were corrupt! Because they were well disposed? But they were filled with anger! Because they were like him? But they could not have been more unalike! Because they were his superiors? But they were his inferiors! Because they were his inferiors? What superior ever defended himself to an inferior? What could he say in making his defense? That he did not practice philosophy? But that would be untrue! Or that he did practice philosophy? But that is why they were angry with him!

[5] Well, by God, since it was none of these things, it was necessary, then, for him to refute the charge—that he neither corrupted the young nor introduced new divinities. Yet what craftsman persuades the layman in what concerns his craft? How were the Athenians to understand what the corruption of the young amount to? Or what virtue is? Or what his *daimonion* is or how it is to be respected? Officers chosen by lot did not concern themselves with these issues. Solon didn't draft anything about them, nor did the august laws of Draco. Summonses, declarations, indictments, audits, oaths, and all such things were brought before the court,[9] just like battling and talking that goes on among bands of children over dice when they steal from each other and treat each other unjustly and are treated unjustly. But truth and virtue and the well-lived life call for other jurors, other laws and other speakers—persons among whom Socrates prevailed, was crowned, and was held in high regard.

[6] How could an old man and a philosopher not look laughable playing dice with children? What doctor has ever persuaded the feverish that thirst and hunger are good? Who has ever persuaded the intemperate that pleasure is evil? Who has ever persuaded the money-maker that he is not

---

[8]Contrast Maximus' hypothetical version here with the accounts given in Plato's *Apology* and Xenophon's *Apology*.

[9]The Heliaia—the court in which Socrates' case was tried.

pursuing anything worthwhile? It wouldn't have been difficult for Socrates to persuade the Athenians that the pursuit of virtue is different from the corruption of the young or that divine knowledge concerning spiritual matters is not against the law. Either they knew theses things along with him, or he understood and they did not. And if they understood, what need was there to give an account to those who know? But if they did not understand, it was not a defense-speech they needed to hear; they needed knowledge. With respect to other defense-speeches, witnesses are called, there is proof, arguments, testimony, interrogation, and other such things, so that in time the obscure will be revealed in court. But there is a single test for virtue and nobility and goodness, namely, the reverence one has for them, which had been driven out of Athens at that time, so what need did Socrates have of giving an account?

[7] By God, perhaps [he acted as he did] so that he would die.[10] But if a good man must be concerned about that above all, then the right thing for Socrates was not to make a defense before the jurors, but not to have become so hated by Meletus and not to have refuted Anytus and not to have caused trouble for those wrongdoers among the Athenians, and not to have gone around the city conversing with every person and about every craft, pursuit, and desire, a chastiser of all alike, sharp and relentless, never meek, neither fawning, nor slavish, nor saying anything to avoid upsetting anyone. And if anyone has ever been contemptuous of death in battle, like a ship captain is contemptuous of death on the sea, and if he wanted to die nobly while involved with their craft, are we to believe that a philosopher needed to become a deserter, jumping ship, so in love with life, throwing away virtue as if it were a shield in battle. What juror would have praised one who did such things? What juror could have accepted Socrates standing in the court meek and fearful, his hope for life contingent upon others? This would have to have been the form of his defense. Or, must he have said nothing meekly or out of fear, but only what is worthy of a free man and of philosophy? You are not telling me of a defense, but of a provocation and an inflaming of [the jurors'] anger. How could a corrupt democratic court bear such a defense, having been twisted by freedom, intolerant of what people want to say, accustomed to uninterrupted flattery? Why, no more than an intemperate drinking party could bear a sober man taking away the drinking cup, leading away the flute girl, seizing the garlands, and putting a stop to the drunkenness. Therefore, Socrates was doing the safe thing by keeping silent when it was not possible for him to say what is true, guarding virtue and guarding against their anger, giving them a sharp rebuke because they convicted him although he kept silent.

[8] Of course, the Athenian jurors needed him to say something. Socrates was seventy years old, and during this time he enjoyed philoso-

---

[10]See Xenophon, *Apology* 1, 5–9, 32–33, *Memorabilia* 4.8.1, 4.8.6, 4.8.8.

phy and uninterrupted virtue, an unfalteringly healthy life, a pure way of living, useful encounters with others, beneficial meetings, and good associations—when these things did not save him from the courtroom, prison, and death, was he going to be saved by a water clock, measuring the short time for Socrates to make a speech? It was not possible, and even if it had been, Socrates would not have accepted it. It is intolerable, oh Zeus and the other gods. Why, it would be like some adviser standing alongside Lenities, the Spartan, and suggesting that he retreat a little and give way to Xerxes' attack as if he were some blackmailer in a full suit of armor! But [Lenities] refused, and preferred to lie there with his virtue and his arms rather than to live and show his back to the barbarian king. What else would the defense of Socrates have been than a turning tail, running from being struck, cowardice trying to look like it is the right thing. Therefore, he held his ground and received the blows, and was the best of all of them. The Athenians thought that they were condemning him. Xerxes thought he had beaten Lenities. But though Lenities was killed, it was Xerxes who was defeated. And though Socrates was killed, it was the Athenians who were condemned—God and the truth being their judge. Such was the indictment of Socrates against the Athenians: The city of the Athenians is unjust, for the gods Socrates believes in, *it* does not, and *it* introduces other new divinities. Socrates believes in the Olympian Zeus, and the city of Athens believes in Pericles. Socrates trusts in Apollo, and the Athenians voted to condemn him. The city is also unjust by corrupting the youth. [Socrates] corrupted Alcibiades, Hipponicus, Critias, and countless others. What a true indictment! What a just court and what a sharp condemnation! In return for their impious treatment of Zeus came a plague and a war with the Peloponnesus. On behalf of the young who had been corrupted came the Decelaia[11] and the misfortune in Sicily,[12] and the disaster at the Hellespont.[13] So it is that God judges and so it is that he condemns.

---

[11]The last part of the Peloponnesian War, which ended in the surrender of Athens to Sparta.

[12]A catastrophic expedition undertaken toward the end of the Peloponnesian War by the Athenians against Sicily, Sparta's most powerful ally, undertaken in 415–413 B.C.E. The mission resulted in the loss of perhaps a third of Athens' navy. All of the men and ships were lost.

[13]The Hellespont is the narrow strait where the Black Sea meets the Aegean. An ugly episode occurred here in 387 B.C.E. after the end of the Peloponnesian War, at a time when the Athenians were attempting to rebuild their military power. Spartans and Persians defeated an Athenian naval squadron, whereupon the Persians gained absolute authority over several Greek colonies in islands in the Aegean near Asia Minor.

CHAPTER 6

Libanius

Libanius (314–393 C.E.), Greek orator. Libanius was born into one of the more privileged families in Antioch. His early training was in classical literature and rhetoric, which he pursued for a time in Athens. It was there that he may have developed his interest in the fate of Socrates. He moved to Constantinople, where he established a school. He also had a close relationship with the emperor Julian. Libanius' career as a writer and teacher blossomed when he returned to Antioch. His reputation as a leading sophist spread and he attracted many students, including some who would themselves later become accomplished orators and thinkers. He maintained an active interest in politics, often attempting to mediate between the emperor and the people of Antioch.

The passages below are taken from one of Libanius' declamations, *Apology of Socrates.* Here Libanius images that he is a *sunêgeros* of Socrates, that is, someone who speaks on behalf of Socrates at his trial. The speech is important for the insight it provides us into what a learned author, writing some six centuries after the trial, took to be the causes behind the trial of Socrates. The selections we have included may well cast light on issues that Socrates' fourth-century B.C.E. detractor, Polycrates, introduced when he took up the case against Socrates during the debate about whether Socrates deserved to be put on trial (see our Introduction to this collection).

Apology of Socrates

TRANSLATED BY HOPE E. MAY

1   Not even if someone introduced more accusations against Socrates, men of Athens—in an attempt to persuade you that unless he is punished the city is bound to come to ruin—would I think it's proper to stand here and deny

that I am and have always been his friend. Nor is it right to attach greater weight to the outrage perpetrated by those who unjustly conspired against him than to what I know to be the justice of what he says and does. And it would be a terrible thing to abandon this person who was my companion in days gone by and whom I made my counselor in my personal affairs now that things are going badly for him.

[. . .] Anytus attacked not out of any goodwill toward you nor out of concern for the moral fiber of your children but from another motive entirely. But, Athenians, I want to say how things are, just as Anytus did. If I show that Socrates never instructed anyone about theft, lying, temple robbing, perjury, laziness, breaking the laws, or overturning the city, but instead thought only of self-control and justice and was, of all people, the most concerned about you, you must instruct Anytus to hang his head in shame. 13

Socrates knew that living as a manual laborer, tilling the land, sailing the seas for money, mining for silver, courting political office, using rhetoric against private citizens and reaping the spoils through its use, convey powers and benefits on those who engage in these things that are admired by most people and create fear among the rich. But Socrates just couldn't believe that any of them led to great happiness. He believed instead that of all that a human being could own the soul is the most divine and that the one who renders the soul free of evil is truly the happiest man. Further, he believed that philosophy frees the soul from evil, and he found it to be the greatest medicine for those who could engage in it. He gave away to others the things from which luxury and power come, and he was attracted to what gives the body no pleasure but instead improves the soul in every way. 15

Socrates avoided spending his time in investigation of the nature of the heavens and the sun—which is something one can look at any time— and discovering calculations about the moon, and where lightning comes from and what makes thunder, since he believed that all inquiries are silly if they result in nothing for their practitioners. But instead he eagerly sought justice, how to conceive courage, who is rightly called wise, what is the greatest good for the household, the city, and the whole country, and he was steadfast about these things, never calling himself a teacher of anything, nor exacting money like a wicked sophist, but he conducted his life by examining the nature of each issue along with those who associated with him. 16

And then there are his encounters with those spell-binders, the sophists—Protagoras, Gorgias, Prodicus, Thasymachus, and the others who are dragged everywhere for pay, which acts on them just as a young plant attracts hungry pests. And when he showed these men by his questioning that they were less intelligent than the reputation they had and that they weren't able to teach others anything whatever of what they said they knew, then at once the youth of the city were freed from their worthless ties to the sophists. At the same time he spread your reputation for 22 wisdom among people. If these sophists were admired everywhere for their speeches they read for profit, he showed that they were offering up an empty collection of words. They utterly lacked thought and knowledge of the nature of what they were trying to talk about. It would have been more just for them to pay to learn rather than getting money as if they were able to teach something that is needed.

33   I think I've made clear from what's been said that it wasn't to shield the youth from corruption or from thinking that he would suffer a penalty if anyone brought harm to your children that Anytus persuaded Meletus to write the indictment against Socrates. It's also clear that even though it was possible to get Socrates out of the current predicament he is in,[1] he came to the court, confident in his knowledge that he had done nothing bad nor that he was deserving of any punishment. Moreover, I was delighted when I heard some of you talking when you were being selected for jury duty. For it struck you as amazing that if Socrates had engaged in evil and in spending his time corrupting the youth such a long time ago, Anytus would have appeared so upset on account of these things at such a later time, and you asked each other how this might be.

48   Then I will ask this of him, men, although I have left it alone so far. Does Socrates hate the democracy, Anytus, and would he gladly see a tyrant appointed to the city? Who is this man? Or, by Zeus, is it himself? For the man would have easily paid bodyguards, and organized an army of mercenaries, and armed many relations.

53   But consider this. Socrates hates democracy, Anytus says, and he's persuading the partisans of the democracy to mock it. What was he doing, Anytus, against the gods? Did he read arguments which he constructed against the democracy to his companions? But he neither wrote them nor read them! And did it come from his mouth that one should change the state? Did someone hear him saying that the city has become bad because it's directed by laws, whereas it would be great if it was ruled by the powers of tyrants? At what Lyceum did he approve of arguments such as these? At what school? At what workshop?

59   No one ever saw Socrates happy that the government was altered nor was he seen praying with those who held power as if he were someone who cowardly avoids associating with the wrongdoers but who enjoys it when the people suffer. He wasn't one of the Thirty, either as a co-ruler or

---

[1]In sections 26–32, Libanius says that Socrates had approached Anytus to question him about his craft. Anytus, says Libanius, made his wealth in the leather industry (which was widely regarded as degrading and filthy work), and became defensive when asked about his trade (presumably because it would be an embarrassment to Anytus's political ambitions). This, explains Libanius, was the source of Anytus's anger against Socrates. Moreover, Libanius claims, Anytus actually offered to drop the prosecution against Socrates, if only the philosopher would promise never again to bring up Anytus's leather trade, but Socrates declined, on the ground that he would never give in to anyone at the expense of truth.

as a supporter, but they so disliked each other that Socrates condemned what they did, whereas Critias, his "disciple and friend," sought to punish his teacher by silencing him.[2] How is it possible that one could plan a tyranny when there isn't one and then be disgusted with it when it came about? Could he pray to see the people disenfranchised, but then when he saw it come about, be distressed?

Saying that he would become bad on account of Socrates, what father 103 disinherited his son? Has anyone shut up his son at home so that he wouldn't hear the corrupting words? They knew all about the other things that I've described to you and that I'm now discussing—about the theft, sacrilege, and deceit. Socrates didn't believe that they were always so terrible and contrary to law. These things have a place in midst of battles, and a general who steals to secure victory is better than one who is afraid to do so. If you bring deception to bear, just like an engine of war, you have acted lawfully.[3]

Themistocles[4] engaged in two deceptions: one fortified the city [of 104 Athens] and one saved Greece. We see this especially with doctors who change the desires of the afflicted with deception, and sometimes we do this even with healthy people whenever it would be better to mislead them than to have them hear the truth.

So what did Socrates say that he shouldn't have [. . .]? Let there be 105 deception in battle, for one who engages in a contest where one's life is at stake expects some trickery. And was it wrong to say how Odysseus was honored for his theft of the statue of Pallas?[5] He stole from the Trojans who had earlier stolen from Menelaus what was most to be honored.[6]

Do you think that if Socrates was trying to incite the young against citizens and friends, he would have done what enemies who have made war with enemies do? Wouldn't the audience have told him that the example does not fit the general idea? I think there is nothing new in his mention of the Trojan War while demonstrating that theft is sometimes useful. And what you did when the Spartans and you were at war—indeed, what everyone does when they destroy enemy cities—why you make off with things held to be sacred, since you judge every gain taken from those who are hostile to be pious.

You have testified, sir, that the man has often sworn falsely and violated confidences. So now you must say that the others have been taught

---

[2]See Plato, *Apology* 32c–e and Xenophon, *Memorabilia* 1.2.31–38.

[3]In Plato's *Republic,* Book I (331c–d), Socrates argues that it is not always just to pay back debts or to tell the truth, giving as examples refraining from returning borrowed weapons or telling nothing but the truth to a friend who had gone mad.

[4]A great leader of the Athenians and early supporter of Athens' democracy, whose advice allowed the Athenians to prevail over the invading Persians during the Persian War.

[5]An epithet for Athena.

[6]Menelaus' wife, the famous Helen.

by him to regard the gods lightly. And regarding the remaining accusations, I say the same thing. You have testified that he committed a sacrilege, that he has stolen. You say, then, that he works by doing violence to many men. But if you say that his words are wicked, yet you can't show that he has this effect on others, you aren't able to censure with deeds, which of necessity prove how one has lived. Then with these you are refuted.

111   We don't see a man praising robbery or adultery, although keeping away from the goods of others; rather, we see him breaking up marriages and breaking in people's houses. In these sorts of men, their deeds are wholly consonant with their words. But if someone should think it appropriate to guide other men toward these things, but keeps himself as far away from them as possible, he has refuted his own advice in words with the advice given by his deeds. [. . .] For instance, if someone advising others to give money to the people should himself draw back from giving his own, he would hinder the voluntary contribution from those who were advised by his words. Similarly, if someone should desert his post when in battle to join his enemies, although he orders against desertion in words, he has made all of his words worthless; causing fear by deed, more than encouraging by word. Inevitably, in these sorts of men, one who is a persuasive advisor must undertake the actions that he recommends.

112   If then, Socrates taught to swear falsely and to steal and to do violence, and the rest that Anytus says he did—in fact, he has argued the opposite: that respecting the gods and disdaining money are suitable and moderate and equitable—then he would have appeared to play with his own words, since he would show by his deeds that he is not this sort of man [. . .] on the one hand, showing to the men conversing with him the ways to the better life, but, on the other, choosing for himself the road that leads to the worse.

127   But, it is said, Socrates was making men lazy. In what way? Did he ever say that idleness and making nothing is better than pursuing work? Did he ever advise the craftsmen to give up their trades? The farmers to hate the earth? The traders to abandon the sea? The sailors to sleep? The ship owners not to prepare ships? And, in a word, for all to free themselves from every business? To look up to the sky, as if they would come to a livelihood in that place? Let one, from all the Athenians, come forward as a witness and I will be silent. But if Socrates does not approve of doing nothing, or if he supposes that being eager for the acquisition of money is greater than being eager for virtue of the soul, what strange claims these are, since he said that the soul is the most honorable possession, the body the second, and money the third. How was this persuading others to be idle?

136   In accusing Socrates of being someone who teaches others how to do evil and saying that he corrupts your young, Anytus can't recall any examples except Alcibiades and Critias. For these a defense is easy: I ought to

be ashamed, however, if I lumped Alcibiades in with the reputation Critias had for doing harm intentionally. After all, Alcibiades did many good things but was often kept from doing the right thing and was compelled to cause the pain he did.[7] [. . .]

Athenians, I've described these things not for Alcibiades and Socrates but for you and your reputation. You ought to appear not as if you have reconciled with an impious person and that you have received such a one back into the city, but as having reconciled with one who did nothing wrong. But . . . let's suppose Alcibiades is no better than Critias, and let Socrates be their teacher, although he never claimed that he was anyone's teacher. So consider this: Should anyone who wishes to teach be liable for the evil of those who do not want to learn or who are not able to do so? If Socrates told them what would benefit them if they did what he said, but they didn't pay attention, since there were other things that would bring them more pleasure, why are we to despise Socrates instead of them? It's just as if a farmer did everything he could to work the land, and used his hands, implements, oxen, and seed as he should have, and then received nothing from it because the land was no good, and then one believed that he was responsible for what happened, surely it is open to him to account for this—to reveal his skill and his land.

Let me speak now about your anger directed at the sophists— Anaxagoras, Protagoras, and Diagoras. Why wasn't Socrates also the object of that anger, especially if he did the same things that angered the people? One ought to have punished him for engaging in the same pursuits. [. . .]

Anaxagoras was rightly imprisoned for his impious views about the sun and the moon. And you rightly and fittingly exiled Protagoras when he inquired about whether the gods exist. And you were wise when you promised a reward to the one who killed Diagoras, for he made a mockery of the Eleusinian mysteries and the secret rites. But can someone mention a book by Socrates—or can anyone mention something he said—about the gods that's in violation of the laws? But if, Anytus, you're not able to show this, even if you would mention countless sophists who have been killed, you won't have refuted Socrates. For the punishment of the unjust cannot be turned into the wickedness of those who have done nothing wrong.

Then whereas great rewards in Hades wait for him because of his temperate and orderly life, let him take even the debts from you, Athenians, because he is a man of poverty who is married to a woman, and who is rearing his children. He did not turn to collecting money even when by doing so he could lived in luxury, but he taught the men in his country to

142

153

154

168

---

[7]Libanius goes on for several paragraphs listing the good things that Alcibiades did for Athens, and in the next section reminds his audience that the Athenians had eventually recalled Alcibiades under full amnesty, after having banished him earlier.

rise from misfortune. As a common guardian, he is over and above the citizens, since he investigates and learns if their child has been corrupted from wine or from gambling, or from any other evil. He cries out against careless fathers, rouses up slumbering generals, urges the political speakers toward thoughtfulness, and causes pain that is advantageous. For I have seen even doctors doing the same.

170 Go ahead and cry, you unlucky children of Socrates. Cry, wretched Xantippe. But Socrates will never do this. He is confident about the end and does not fear the voyage. There are much better places there in Hades, as the saying goes, for one who has been prepared by just acts, than there are here. And so he'll not seek a disgraceful way of saving himself, nor will he throw aside in prison the courage he has cared about. He thinks that to beg for his life would be disgraceful both to the city and to himself; it would be disgraceful for one who is reputed to be wise to cringe before death like a barbarian. [. . .]

172 How many men do you suppose would have neglected their sons, but paid attention to them on account of this man? How many men who would have quarreled with their siblings did not have the heart to do so? How many men who would have mistreated their parents, instead took care of them? For they feared Socrates' criticisms instead of the law courts, since they knew that it was possible to buy off a legal accuser. On the other hand, they knew that escaping reasoning, such a guardian of just things, was impractical, as was persuading Socrates to be silent. Then, on account of this, is he to die and will he pay a penalty, because those whom he stung were left in a better state?

174 Now some of you who are looking at him while he is alive wish to see him dead. But when he is dead, and the anger passes, and the affair is viewed with reason, all of you, I think, will lament the fact and will blame the prosecutors, your vote against Socrates and everything connected with the prosecutors, whenever the voice of Socrates and his arguments come to memory . . . whenever those well acquainted with him mourn, whenever his friends cry out . . . whenever strangers sail over to be with him and discovering that he's dead, look for his tomb . . . whenever one says to another, while pointing to a location, "There he constructed the arguments about self-control, there he constructed the ones about courage, and there he constructed the ones about justice. There he spoke and defeated Prodicus, there Protagoras, the one from Elis there, and the one from Leontini there."

175 Who will bear the memory of these victories without tears? How will we look at each other after the hemlock? Many things, Athenians, vex us greatly when they are around, but they are missed when they're not here. [. . .] Don't let it appear that the possession of wisdom is a dangerous thing here in Athens, the place allotted to it. Don't abide the terrible spectacle—an affront to the city—of Socrates being carried out of the prison, and the city bereft of his voice, just like a song bird, and of others cursing you in silence at his tomb, and then fleeing to one place or another, some

to Megara, some to Corinth, some to Elis, some to Euboeia. Carrying with them the flower of Athens, saying wherever they go, "Receive us Athenian exiles, men, we who are not traitors or deserters. We were not negligent, not did we commit any of the things for which the law sets penalties. Instead, we are charged with love of argument and education. Lycon persuaded you about these matters. Meletus wrote the indictment about these matters, and Anytus prosecuted for these reasons. We have seen Socrates tried; we have seen him convicted; we have seen him imprisoned; we have seen him killed. These are the things that counseled us to flee and to seek asylum."

PART II

RECENT
SCHOLARSHIP

CHAPTER 7

Why Was Socrates Prosecuted?

The Impiety of Socrates

M. F. BURNYEAT

One day in 399 BC Socrates went on trial in Athens, charged with impiety and corrupting the young, and spoke certain words to the jury in his defence. Some time later—no-one knows how much time later—Plato wrote *The Apology of Socrates,* in which Socrates again speaks certain words to the jury in his defence.

No sensible scholar believes that the relation between the first set of words and the second is the relation of identity. It is most unlikely that what Socrates said and what Plato wrote are exactly the same, if only for the trivial reason that unprepared spoken discourse very seldom comes out as a sequence of syntactically perfect, complete sentences.[1] The written and the spoken speeches could of course be partly the same. Plato could have preserved the gist of what Socrates said and re-presented it in his own inimitable prose. That indeed is what many scholars think the *Apology* does. But it is equally possible that Plato, like Xenophon and perhaps others as well,[2] devised his own independent defence of Socrates, which had little or nothing in common with what Socrates said on the day.

The scholarly literature on this topic is a paradise of inconclusive guesswork. I have no new guesses to offer here. Instead, I want to propose another way of reading Plato's *Apology.* Rather than taking the text as a historical challenge and wondering about its relation to what Socrates actually said on the day, or, more generally, about whether it gives a historically faithful account of Socrates' life and thought, I suggest that it

M. F. Burnyeat, "The Impiety of Socrates," *Ancient Philosophy* 17 (1997), 1–12.

would be more appropriate to the present occasion, and to everything George Steiner has stood witness for over the years, to read it as a personal challenge.[3]

If the words spoken by Socrates in the written defence are not identical with the words spoken by Socrates on the day of his trial, then the jury to which the written defence is addressed need not be identical with the jury of 501 (or 500) male Athenians to whom the spoken defence was addressed. Plato's writing the *Apology* in the form of a defence speech by Socrates puts the reader—any reader—in the position of juror. To read the *Apology*, whether in ancient times or today, is to be challenged to pass judgement on Socrates.

He is charged with impiety and corrupting the young. Is he guilty or not guilty? And if he is guilty, what should the punishment be? How would you have voted if you had been on the jury in 399 BC? How in your imagination do you vote now?

This, I propose, is the challenge the written defence presents to its reader, by virtue of the forensic form—the standard form of a court speech—that Plato gave it. Xenophon's *Apology*, by contrast, is plain narrative, like an investigating journalist's account of the trial, with sound-bites from the most dramatic moments of Socrates' speech and interviews with various interested parties. Plato's *Apology* opens with one of the common forms of address to jury or assembly, 'You, men of Athens' (ὦ ἄνδρες Ἀθηναῖοι),[4] and continues throughout in the forensic mode we are used to from surviving speeches of Lysias or Demosthenes. This is decidedly not a dialogue. Readers are not invited, as the dialogues properly so called invite us, to join in a philosophical discussion about virtue, knowledge, and reality. We are invited to reach a verdict on the case before us.

Very well. Let us start reading. At the end of the first paragraph (18a) Socrates says that the virtue (ἀρετή) of a juryman, what a good juryman will do, is to concentrate his mind on the justice of the defence he will present. The manner and rhetorical skill with which it is presented should be disregarded. In other words, if you are sitting—in reality or in imagination—on this jury, the only thing that should weigh with you is the justice of the case.

Imagine, then, that you are a good member of the jury in the sense defined. You already know something of Socrates' activities, from listening to him in person or from reading the dialogues of Plato. How, let me ask, do you now think you would have voted then? Guilty or not guilty?

> [At this point the audience in Geneva voted 'Not guilty' by a majority of many to one. Other audiences in Durham, Lille, and London, and in biennial lectures at Cambridge, have invariably voted 'Not guilty' also, though not always by so dramatic a margin.]

In 399 BC the vote was something like 280 against Socrates, 221 in favour. If only 30 votes had gone the other way, he would have been acquitted (36a).[5] All the same, 280 or so to find him guilty is a large number of people.

They will not all have voted 'Guilty' for exactly the same reasons.[6] Some, perhaps, were motivated by political hostility to Socrates, because of his association with Alcibiades and the tyrant Critias; others perhaps by malice, having had the unpleasant experience of being made to look a fool by Socrates' questioning; others again may have been swayed by the caricature of Socrates in Aristophanes' *Clouds*, which Socrates at 18a–19c says is the chief prejudice he has to combat. But how far do these still standard explanations take us?

Socrates says that many of the jury have heard him talking and know the sorts of things he says (17c, 19d). Many of you have read him talking in Plato's dialogues and know the sorts of things he says. They know—you know—he is not like the Socrates of Aristophanes' *Clouds* who studies things in the heavens and under the earth and who teaches people to make the weaker argument the stronger (19b–c). Socrates was such a familiar figure in the community, for so many years, that we have to probe deeper.

Imagine a reasonably conscientious member of the jury: one who has heard Socrates in discussion, who understands the difference between him and the Socrates of the *Clouds*, who is not activated by political vengefulness or personal malice, who concentrates as a good juryman should on thinking exclusively about the justice of the defence Socrates offers. Someone who genuinely cares about the welfare of the city and about whether it is good or bad for the young to listen to Socrates. My question is: Could *such* a person have voted to find Socrates guilty of impiety and corrupting the young?

I want to suggest that the answer is 'Yes'. Indeed, that we shall not understand Socrates, or the enormous and permanent impact he has had on human thought, unless we realize that he was guilty of the impiety charge for which he was condemned. But first, a word of caution.

Socrates' impact on subsequent thought is due largely to the writings of Plato, so it is the Socrates of the writings of Plato we have to understand, and that same Socrates whose guilt I propose to argue for. This will be no historical hypothesis about the flesh-and-blood snubnosed personality who died in 399 BC, but an invitation to make your own imaginative judgement on the literary Socrates whose defence Plato immortalized in the *Apology*, perhaps many years later.

The exact charge is specified at 24b: Socrates ἀδικεῖ (does wrong, sc. to the city) by corrupting the youth and not believing in the gods (θεοί) which the city believes in but other new divinities (δαιμόνια καινά). I suggest it is true that Socrates does not believe in the gods the city believes in, and that a large part of what is involved in his corrupting the young is that they end up not believing in them either (so 26b and *Euthyphro* 3a–b). Part of my evidence is that the written defence never rebuts this part of the charge. Nowhere in the *Apology* does Socrates say he does believe in the gods the city believes in.

He proves to his prosecutor Meletus that if he believes in new δαιμόνια (divinities) he believes in gods, because δαίμονες are θεοί (gods) (27a–28a). On the strength of this proof he claims the indictment is self-contradictory: it says that Socrates does not believe in gods but believes in gods (27a). The question before the jury, however, is whether Socrates believes in the gods the city believes in, not whether he believes in gods. Socrates makes fun of Meletus for confusing him with Anaxagoras and claiming he says the sun is a stone and the moon earth, not gods as other people believe (26d-e). But he does not say he does believe that the sun and moon are gods.

He *refers* constantly to ὁ θεός, which can mean 'god' in a generic sense or 'the god'. It is ὁ θεός who told Chaerephon at Delphi that no one is wiser than Socrates (21b), which Socrates eventually interprets to mean that ὁ θεός has ordered him to philosophize, testing himself and others (28e-29a; cf. 33c). It is also ὁ θεός who is responsible for Socrates' 'divine sign', that mysterious inner voice which from time to time warns him off something he is about to do (31c–d, 40b). Since the first mention of ὁ θεός is the phrase 'ὁ θεός at Delphi' (20e), the jury will assume he is talking of Apollo. But he never speaks of Apollo by name.

Apollo, of course, is one of the gods the city most centrally believes in. He presides over the basis of its social structure. Each member of the jury can speak of 'my Apollo Patroos (Ancestral Apollo)', meaning the altar to Apollo that is focus to the organization of his 'fratry' (group of families, subdivision of a tribe) through which he has his citizenship. Apollo is as important at Athens as he is at Delphi. But nowhere in the *Apology* is he mentioned by name.

When interrogating Meletus Socrates makes a point of swearing by Hera (24e), by Zeus (25c, 26e), and by 'these very gods of whom we are speaking' (26b). On the other hand, in his address to the jury the only time he names a deity is when he mentions that Achilles' mother Thetis was a god (θεός, 28c). This is to explain why she could foresee what would happen if he avenged Patroclus; it has nothing to do with Thetis being one of the gods the city believes in. (There is in fact no evidence of Thetis having had a shrine, or any civic role, in ancient Athens.) All the important references to divinity in the *Apology* are indeterminate references to ὁ θεός or, once or twice, to θεοί—'gods' in the plural, without the definite article (35d; 41d).[7] Socrates might as well be speaking of 'god' and 'gods' in a quite generic sense. He might almost be a monotheist. There is little or nothing to show that *the* gods, the numerous particular and highly individual gods the city believes in, mean anything to Socrates at all. Yet that was the central charge of the indictment, the part on which the rest depends.

How is a conscientious 'juror-reader' to interpret Socrates' silence on the central issue we have to make up our minds about? Would it be unjust to interpret it as an admission that the charge as levelled is true?

What Socrates does say about divinity is as damning as what he does not say. His central theme is that his philosophical activity is undertaken at the bidding of ὁ θεός, whom it would be wrong to disobey (23c, 28d–30a, 33c; 37e). That is his interpretation of the oracle. Ὁ θεός wants him to go around Athens asking his questions and showing people they do not know what they think they know. Socrates is a gadfly god-sent to sting the Athenians into caring for virtue above all else (29d–31b; 36c; 41e). And the best way to exercise this care is to spend every day in philosophical discussion about virtue: 'For a human being the unexamined life is not worth living' (38a). Ὁ θεός wants everybody every day to be *questioning*: examining and re-examining the values by which their life is led.

In other words, what divinity minds about, in Socrates' view, is two things: (1) that people should try to be virtuous, (2) that they should realize they do not yet know, but have to find out, what it is to be virtuous. In yet other words, Socrates' divinity lays it down that the accepted values of the Athenian community are to be put in question. Neither in private nor in public life are the Athenians living as they should—the *Apology* is one long counter-indictment charging the Athenians with rampant injustice. Few modern scholars have seen this as clearly as the author of the following excerpt from an ancient rhetorical treatise:

> Since we are on the subject of deliberative and judicial speeches, you may also take from Plato examples of further complex disputes, which combine, in some fashion, all the branches of rhetoric. The *Apology of Socrates* has as its primary purpose (πρότασις) an apology, as its title makes clear, but it is also an accusation of the Athenians, seeing that they brought such a man to court. And the bitterness of the accusation is concealed by the moderation (τῷ ἐπιείκι) of the apology; for the things spoken in self-defense are an accusation of the Athenians. These are two strands (συμπλοκαί) in the speech.[8] A third is this: the speech is an encomium of Socrates, made inoffensive by being covered up as a requirement of self-defense. This is the third strand. The result is two interconnected judicial themes (ὑποθέσεις), the apology and the accusation, together with one encomiastic theme: the praise of Socrates. The fourth strand, which was, as Plato saw it, the most important theme, with a deliberative or counselling function and philosophical content, is this: the book is an exhortatory proclamation (παράγγελμα) of what sort of a person the philosopher ought to be.[9]

Seldom has the *Apology* been summed up so well.

I am sure this ancient rhetorician is right that accusation is as important a theme as defence. Witness especially the section 31d–32e where Socrates says it would be impossible for anyone who puts justice first to take part in Athenian politics (or democratic politics anywhere) without perishing (cf. also 36b–c). The death sentence at the end of the *Apology* is the most vividly present reminder of how vice and injustice dominate the city (see 39a–d). But everything Socrates says about the value of his philosophic mission is by implication an indictment of the Athenians for resisting the call to virtue. And in making this counter-indictment Socrates claims to be speaking on behalf of divinity. What his divinity wants from the Athenians is their singleminded dedication to justice and virtue.

But would not Zeus want the same? Yes and no. In the *Iliad* Zeus sends Athene to *break* the truce sworn in his name (iv 71–72 with iii 276–280, 298). In due course he will punish the violation he has himself decreed (iv 168, 235–240). Apollo, god of medicine, is also god of the plague. The traditional gods both help and harm in the relationships and activities they are interested in.[10] Socrates' divinity, by contrast, appears to be as singleminded as Socrates.

Now let us return to our conscientious, decent-minded jurors, be they many or few, listeners then or readers today. When they have heard all this that Socrates says about ὁ θεός, they are bound to agree that Socrates is not ἄθεος (godless). It is clearly not the case that he believes in no gods at all, that he has no religious beliefs. But does he believe in the gods that the city believes in? Does he share the religion of the Athenian people? Recall how closely a Greek community's sense of its own identity and stability is bound up with its religious observances and the myths that support them. If Socrates rejects the city's religion, he attacks the city. Conversely, if he says the city has got its public and private life all wrong, he attacks its religion; for its life and its religion are inseparable.[11] Let our jurors ask themselves this question: What would be left of traditional (fifth century) religion, hence what would be left of traditional (fifth century) Athenian life, if the city accepted Socrates' view that what divinity demands from human beings is not propitiation and sacrifices, festivals and processions, but the practice of moral philosophy? I submit that our jurors are bound in good conscience to say to themselves: Socrates has a religion, but it is not ours. This is not the religion of the Athenians.

Socrates almost said the same at 35d: 'I believe in gods as do none of my accusers'. These words can be understood to mean that he believes more piously than they do. But they can also be taken to mean that he believes in a different way from them.

Perhaps the most disturbing statement, calculated to make the jury roar, is that Socrates is immune from harm by the court (30c). Nothing they inflict—death, exile, disenfranchisement—will touch him where it counts. Rather, they will be the ones to suffer—from the injustice they will have committed. Even a juror who does not roar could be disturbed by this. The jury's task, remember, is not to admire Socrates' courage and strength; still less to attempt, as modern scholars do, a rational reconstruction of Socratic moral philosophy. It is to judge whether Socrates does harm to the city he claims cannot do harm to him. And that claim clearly goes against the grain of the traditional culture, as expressed by and mediated through the poets. One of the reasons poetry will be censored in the ideal city of the *Republic* is precisely because the poets instill the idea that a good and just person can suffer harm and tragic loss through divine or human agency and thereby lose their happiness (379d–380b, 387d–e, 392b with 364b; the tale of Zeus and Athene breaking the truce is expunged at 379e).

Socrates' rival claim is not of course that you cannot lose your money, your children, be struck by disease, and so on, but that a good and virtuous person will cope with whatever happens in the best possible way, turning it to something good: 'Virtue does not come from possessions but from virtue possessions and *all other things* come to be good both for individuals and for a city' (30b).[12] And it is clear that one becomes virtuous, in Socrates' view, by one's own efforts, through philosophizing.

Now it is a traditional idea that humans cannot prosper without the help of the gods. The paradigm of hubris (arrogant pride) is the belief that you can. When Ajax boasted he could succeed without the gods, and spurned Athene's aid, her anger struck him with madness and death (Sophocles, *Ajax* 756–778). Connected with this is that the word εὐδαι-μονία, which we translate 'happiness', originally meant 'being favoured by divinity (δαίμων)'. Yet in the written speech Socrates comes perilously close to saying you must and can prosper on your own, by your own efforts: you are to gain *eudaimonia* without the help of god or gods. Divinity's role is an ancillary one only, to protect the just—or at any rate to protect Socrates through the 'divine sign'—from certain unforeseeable worldly consequences of their own justice. If the 'divine sign' is a special gift to Socrates (as is implied at *Republic* 496c), even so the just will not suffer harm for the lack of its protection. Being just, they will always prefer death to doing what is unjust, and will never regard death as a harm that matters. But divinity cannot make people just and virtuous. It can only wait upon humans to be virtuous by their own efforts, and then it is well pleased. The question is, might not our decent-minded juror think this the most frightful hubris? And does not hubris land not only the hubristic individual but also his city in trouble? The city of Athens has recently been through terrible troubles. Are not the jurors menaced, directly or indirectly, as a consequence of having this hubristic philosopher in their midst?

I have argued that Socrates' god demands a radical questioning of the community's values and its religion. I want now to move the discussion to a more theoretical level, to gain a better understanding of the confrontation between traditional Athenian religion and the singleminded divinity of Socratic religion. The text that seems designed to help us reach this understanding—although we do not know whether it came out after, in conjunction with, or before the *Apology*—is Plato's *Euthyphro,* to which ancient editors gave the subtitle 'On piety: a testing dialogue'.

Euthyphro, whose ideas about piety Socrates will put to the test, is prosecuting his own father. At their farm on the distant island of Naxos a hired labourer killed one of the house slaves in a drunken brawl. Euthyphro's father tied the man up, threw him into a ditch, and sent a messenger to Athens to ask the religious authorities what he ought to do. By the time the messenger returned, the labourer was dead from hunger and cold. One question a reader of this dialogue is invited to think about is this: Does Euthyphro act piously in bringing a charge of homocide against his own father on behalf of the labourer?

The magistrate before whom Euthyphro has come to lay his charge is about to give a preliminary hearing to the charge against Socrates, who is accused, so he tells Euthyphro, of corrupting the young by making new gods and not believing in the old ones. So another question a reader of this dialogue is invited to think about is the question, Is Socrates guilty of impiety?

Clearly, both questions should be thought about together. They invite a contrast between the standards of the old religion, strongly—even fanatically—supported by Euthyphro, and those of Socratic religion. It would be difficult to imagine a more dramatic context for the theme-question of the dialogue: 'What are piety and impiety both in relation to murder and in relation to other things?' (5c–d).

Euthyphro's first properly formulated answer to the question 'What is piety?' is: Piety is what is pleasing to the gods (6e). Now if by 'definition' you mean what many modern philosophers mean by it, an analysis of the meaning of a word in ordinary discourse, then Euthyphro's definition is as good a definition as you will find in the Platonic corpus. Greek religion was much occupied with propitiating and pleasing gods. The snag was, how can humans know what gods want? Worse, different divinities often want different and incompatible things, as when Euripides' Hippolytus was caught in the cross fire between the chaste goddess Artemis and Aphrodite, goddess of sexual love. The conflict of religious obligations may be tragically unresolvable.

More troubling still is the prospect of conflict between different aspects of the same divinity. At a difficult moment on the way back from his expedition, Xenophon sacrifices to Zeus Basileus (Zeus the King) and dutifully does what the entrails prescribe (*Anabasis* vii 6.44). Not long afterwards, and still struggling, he learns from a seer that his difficulties are due to Zeus Meilichios (Zeus the Merciful): he has not sacrificed to *him* (vii 7.4).[13]

In the *Euthyphro* it is enough for Socrates to fasten on the first type of conflict. Not on the lack of singlemindedness in an individual god but on the fact that the gods quarrel and disagree—at least according to the stories that Euthyphro believes. Socrates has already said he is reluctant to accept the religious narratives of his community (6a–b—a very significant admission for the question before us). But, given Euthyphro's beliefs, Socrates is entitled to argue:

> It would not be surprising if, in punishing your father as you are doing, your action is pleasing to Zeus [who tied up his father, Cronus,

for eating his own children] but hateful to Cronus and Uranus [Zeus' grandfather, whom Cronus castrated], pleasing to Hephaestus but hateful to Hera, and similarly with respect to any other gods who are at variance with one another over your action. (8b)

In short, the same things may be both pious (because pleasing to some gods) and impious (because displeasing to others).

I need not remind you that these very stories of the gods and goddesses doing violence to one another are the paradigm examples of what will be banned by the censors of the ideal city of the *Republic* (377c–378d), who will not even permit an allegorical interpretation of these central narratives of Greek religion. Plato knew very well that he was proposing an ideological reconstruction of the entire Greek tradition. What Euthyphro, as a fanatical spokesman for the old ideology, should have replied when faced with Socrates' conclusion that the same thing may be both pious and impious is: 'Yes, that's life. Remember the story of Hippolytus.' Instead, Plato asserts his authorial control and makes Euthyphro allow Socrates to change the definition of piety so that it now reads: 'What is pious is what is pleasing to *all* the gods' (9e).

This is fatal. Why have many gods if they think and act as one? Were this revised definition of piety to gain acceptance at Athens, it would destroy the community's religion and its sense of its own identity.

Worse follows. Socrates asks: Are the gods pleased by what is pious because it is pious, or is it pious because it pleases the gods? This is the intellectual ancestor of the question that exercised the theologians of later, monotheistic times: Does God command what is good because it is good, or is it good because God commands it? A knotty, abstract, but enormously influential piece of reasoning forces Euthyphro to endorse the first alternative and reject the second. He accepts that the gods are pleased by what is pious because it is pious, not the other way round. This is another blow to traditional polytheism. Piety becomes a moral quality prior to and independent of divine pleasure or displeasure. The gods not only think and act as one. They all singlemindedly love virtue and hate vice. If you want to know how to please the gods, moral philosophy will tell you more than the sorts of divination on which Xenophon had to rely.

Such gods would never have brought about the Trojan war, which goes back, you remember, to the judgement of Paris and Aphrodite's promise that, if he gave the prize for beauty to her rather than to Hera or Athene, she would get him the love of Menelaus' wife Helen. And where would we be now without the Trojan war? I am tempted to say that, with gods as singlemindedly moral as Socrates', Greek culture would have been impossible and, in consequence, Western civilization would not be what it is today.

A less flamboyant way of putting the same point is to quote Gregory Vlastos:

What would be left of her [Hera] and of the other Olympians if they were required to observe the stringent norms of Socratic virtue which require every moral agent, human or divine, to act only to cause good to others, never evil, regardless of provocation? Required to meet these austere standards, the city's gods would have become unrecognizable. Their ethical transformation would be tantamount to the destruction of the old gods, the creation of new ones—which is precisely what Socrates takes to be the sum and substance of the accusation at his trial. (Vlastos 1991, 166)

Back, then, to the trial. The question before us as 'juror-readers' of the *Apology* is not whether Socrates has a better religion than the Athenians, but whether he believes in the gods the city believes in. The discussion in the *Euthyphro* may—or again it may not—leave you siding morally and/or intellectually with Socrates, but it was Socrates himself at the beginning of the *Apology* who said that a good jury member should consider nothing but the justice of the case presented. And the case for the prosecution is that Socrates does wrong to the city by rejecting its religion, not believing in the gods the city believes in and corrupting the young by leading them not to believe in them either. So I ask you again, Is he guilty or not guilty as charged?

[The vote at Geneva now was 26 against Socrates, a few in his favour and a number of abstentions. Previous versions of this speech have invariably secured a similar reversal of opinion. A good illustration for Plato's strictures on the power of rhetoric.]

After the verdict, the penalty. In ancient Athens this was decided by the jury too, and they accepted the death sentence the prosecution had demanded from the start. Although I have argued that Socrates was guilty as charged, I certainly would not ask anyone to support the further decision to impose the death penalty. What I want to do, by way of concluding, is to connect the case of Socrates with a recent, continuing tragedy of our own society.

Socrates was put to death by and on behalf of a traditional religion that was both polytheistic and (let us say) not particularly focussed on what we would call morality. When in book 10 of Plato's *Laws* an ideal society is recommended where the gods are conceived in terms Socrates would approve, as 'good and honouring justice more than humans do' (887b), Plato is quite happy to impose the death penalty on those who refuse to adhere to the creed of his new religion if they cannot be cured of their unbelief (909a). In this sense, the new religion ushered in by Socrates and Plato proved even less tolerant than the old. We know that Christianity turned out no better. A few years ago an English newspaper (the *Independent*) published a letter in which the Pope of the time of Queen Elizabeth I advised two Catholic English noblemen that, were they to assassinate the

Queen, Head of the Church of England, it would increase, rather than decrease, their prospects of everlasting bliss in Heaven.

That, of course, was a conflict between two brands of Christianity. But in the fictional world of Salman Rushdie's *Satanic Verses* we meet again a confrontation between a traditional polytheistic religion and a new highly moralistic monotheism. In all that has been written about the Rushdie affair, I have not seen it sufficiently emphasized that the now notorious scenes of blasphemy in Gibreel's dream are not a mindless insult to the Prophet and his wives, but an act of symbolic, passive resistance by the adherents of the traditional polytheistic religion, after this has been prohibited by the Prophet, the old gods' statues thrown down, and their temples closed. 'There were more ways than one of refusing to Submit' (p. 381). The death sentence which in the novel's dream is actually carried out on Baal, the poet at the centre of the resistance, is a fictional anticipation of the sentence pronounced upon Rushdie in the real world of our day—the world in which it was appropriate to remind *Independent* readers of religious conflict in their own European past.

Both Socrates and Rushdie's polytheists speak, think, and act in ways that the opposing religion is bound to consider impious. But the converse is also true. One group's piety is another's impiety. The *Euthyphro* lays the groundwork for Plato's own denunciation in the *Republic* of the impiety of traditional Greek religion, from which in turn he derives his notorious proposals to censor literature out of existence. Euthyphro himself may be a fanatical enthusiast, but what he is an enthusiast for is the traditional religion. (In the *Cratylus* his 'expertise' enables him to understand the meaning and significance of the names of lots and lots of gods.) Numenius of Apamea (second century AD), the first pagan philosopher we know of to take an interest in the Bible, imagined that Plato chose so 'boastful and dull-witted' a character in order to be able to criticize 'the theology of the Athenians' without incurring the same fate as Socrates (frag. 23 Des Places). A fanciful idea, perhaps, but better than denying all connection between Euthyphro's views and the religious basis for accusing Socrates of impiety.[14]

It is perhaps less obvious that the *Apology* is on the same side as the *Euthyphro* and *Republic*. We are so accustomed to reading it as the testimony of one who dies for the freedom of inquiry and the freedom to proclaim in the marketplace the results of inquiry, no matter how upsetting to received opinion. Indeed, as an unreconstructed liberal I like to think of the historical Socrates as doing just that, dying for the cause of free thought and free speech. But here I am speaking of the Socrates of Plato's *Apology*. And there is no doubt that the relation between the author of the *Apology of Socrates* and the author of *Euthyphro, Republic,* and *Laws* x, is the relation of identity.

This brings me to the final suggestion I want to leave you with. I offer it as no more than a possibility to think about, a rather sobering hypothesis concerning the verdict Plato himself had in view when he wrote the *Apology*. The verdict was this:—

Yes, Socrates was guilty as charged of not believing in the traditional gods and introducing new divinities. But what is shown by the fact that so good a man as Socrates was guilty of impiety under Athenian law? The impiety of Athenian religion. What the Athenians, from within that religion, inevitably saw as his wronging the city was the true god's gift to them of a mission to improve their souls, to educate them into a better religion. They judged as they did, and could do no other, out of ignorance. For they had the wrong religion, and he was the first martyr for the true religion. So what we should do, as readers of Plato's brilliant and moving defence, is join with him in promoting the new religion. *In cauda venenum.* If we can get political power, we will make this new religion compulsory for all—especially the poets.

Notes

1. We need not believe either Xenophon's statement (*Apol.* 4) that Socrates was prevented by his 'divine sign' from preparing the defence beforehand, or the report in Diogenes Laertius ii 40 that he turned down an offer from Lysias to write the speech for him. It is nevertheless evident that the interrogation of Meletus at 24c–28a could not have been fully prepared ahead of time, yet syntactic propriety is preserved as beautifully as in any Platonic dialogue, even with the audience interrupting at 27b. The same holds for Socrates' response to the verdict (35e ff.). It would be absurd to try to read the *Apology* as a verbatim transcript of the spoken speech.
2. Xen. *Apol.* 1 refers to others (plural) who have written about Socrates' defence and death, but gives no indication as to who they were or the character of their writings save that they all conveyed the lofty (or haughty) tone (μεγαληγορία) of his speech.
3. 'The present occasion' refers to a colloquium at Geneva in honour of George Steiner. This address in a slightly different version originally appeared in the colloquium proceedings. Dykman and Godzich 1996, 13–36.
4. The main alternative, 'Gentlemen of the jury' (ὦ ἄνδρες δικασταί), is used only in Socrates' valedictory address to the jurors who voted against the death penalty (40a, 40e, 41c); they have earned the title 'juror'.
5. On the problems of determining the exact figures, see the still unsurpassed edition by Burnet 1924, *ad loc.*
6. For more on the importance of this point, see my review of Stone 1988.
7. I say 'once or twice' because at 35d the word θεοί is a semi-quotation from the indictment; in the next and final sentence Socrates restores ὁ θεός in the singular.
8. A bold translation, but forced upon me by the context. The enumeration 'one, two, three' prevents συμπλοκή carrying its normal meaning 'combination'; despite the dictionaries, here it must mean 'element in a combination'.
9. From the first of two books 'On figured speeches' (Περὶ ἐσχηματισμένων, date and author unknown) which have come down to us in the corpus of Dionysius

of Halicarnassus (Usener and Radermacher 1904–1929, 305.5–23. For the reference and help with the translation, I am indebted to Janet Fairweather.

10. For more on this principle, I may refer to Padel 1992, esp. 166.
11. One way to gain some sense of this inseparability is to read through Parke 1977.
12. Burnet's construal of the sentence, my italics. Both the construal and the italics are confirmed by the negative expression of the same idea at 41c–d: 'To a good man nothing bad happens either in life or in death, nor are his affairs uncared for by gods'. This famous declaration of faith (it is introduced as something the worthy jurors ought to hold true) is the closest Socrates comes in the *Apology* to the idea of divine providence. But you must acquire virtue first.
13. For more on the conflictedness of Greek divinity, see Padel 1995, ch. 20.
14. For an extreme case of this denial, see Burnet 1924, 5–7.

• • •

The Trial of Socrates
And a Religious Crisis?

ROBERT PARKER

In 399 B.C., Socrates was condemned and put to death on a charge of impiety, having declined to suggest that counter-penalty of exile which the jury would doubtless have preferred to impose. Around that bizarre and tragic event cluster a series of quite fundamental questions about the character of Athenian society, and the historical development of Greek religion. Perhaps no execution has been as much discussed as Socrates',[1] except that of Jesus; and a detailed discussion of the related issues would spring the bounds of this book by far. All that can be offered is a sketch-map of the terrain. We will begin with the condemnation of Socrates, pass to other acts of repression against religious unorthodoxy, and ask whether and in what sense it is legitimate to speak of a religious crisis in the late fifth century. And we must raise again from a new perspective the issue of "new gods"; for a charge of "introducing new gods"—a standard practice of the Athenian people, as we saw in chapter 9 [of Parker 1996]—figured nonetheless in the formal indictment against Socrates. An underlying issue that still evokes strong feelings is that of intellectual dissent and the Athenian democracy's response to it. To what extent was there in fact freedom of thought or freedom of religion or freedom of the intellectual (revealingly anachronistic terms) in the vaunted home of *parrhesia* and *isegoria*, political free speech?

Robert Parker, "The Trial of Socrates: And a Religious Crisis?" from *Athenian Religion: A History* (New York: Oxford University Press, 1996), pp. 199–217.

But, it may be objected, is it not anachronistic, in a study of the religion of a people, for a chapter to take its start from the trial of one eccentric individual? Would not a contemporary of Socrates have named quite different events as the "religious crises" of his experience? The second part of the objection, at least, must be allowed. In a sense, Socrates was just one trouble-maker or bad citizen among many put to death by the Athenians.[2] The truly spectacular religious trials of the period related to the mutilation of the Herms and profanation of the Mysteries in 415, a pair of crimes that stunned all Athens.[3] And Thucydides tells how the great plague that began in 430, against which all religious remedies proved vain, drove men to nihilism and despair (just as the Lisbon earthquake of 1755 caused Voltaire to renounce the optimistic doctrine of Leibniz and Pope what "whatever is, is good"[4]). About the effects of both events in the longer term we can only speculate. Did the experience of 415 make many Athenians more prone to lash out against persons of suspect piety, including perhaps Socrates? Had the trauma of the plague, by contrast, left a residue of disbelief? The two influences in combination might have tended to create a polarization of attitudes.

On the surface, however, civic religion very soon picked itself up from the plague, any interruption in celebration of the festivals being very temporary;[5] from the cheerful piety of an Aristophanes one would never guess that such an event had ever occurred. Believing societies seem in fact normally to respond to huge natural catastrophes not by loss of faith but with such reactions as anger against "the authorities," search for scapegoats, and, above all, forms of self-blame and mutual accusation that confirm existing religious assumptions: the Black Death brought the Church, the Jews, and, of course, man's sinfulness into disrepute, not God himself. "Only this antidote apply/Cease vexing heaven and cease to die," advised Thomas Dekker in the early seventeenth century.[6] In a sense the plague strengthened the faith of the Athenians, if it is right to see, for instance, the purification of Delos and the introduction of Asclepius as responses to it.[7] As for the impious citizens of 415, a surprising number were permitted to return to Athens in due course. To surmount these two crises nothing perhaps was required but time. A deeper readjustment may have been needed to cope with the issues raised by supposed impieties of thought such as those of Socrates. And the ground for singling out Socrates is that we happen to know more about the popular prejudice against him than against any other impious intellectual—Diagoras, as it might be, or Anaxagoras. He owes his prominence here to Aristophanes' attacks, not to anachronistic reverence for the pagan saint.

The official charge ran: "Socrates does wrong by not acknowledging the gods the city acknowledges, and introducing other, new powers [*daimonia*]. He also does wrong by corrupting the young."[8] The exact legal position is unclear, but fortunately little hangs by it; most probably, the practices in the charge were not formally forbidden by a specific law, but were cited as evidence that Socrates was guilty of the broad and undefined offence of "impiety."[9] A much more serious difficulty is that we know the arguments of Socrates' accusers only as they are refracted through his various defenders. Very broadly, we have to choose between two main interpretations; or rather, since both surely contain some truth, where to place the emphasis between two extremes. According to one, the jurors condemned Socrates because they mistook him for an embodiment of all that was worst in the type of the impious intellectual or sophist. For the other, the general charge of "corrupting the young" concealed one much more specific: that it was Socrates' teaching which had produced the two men who had harmed the city most, Alcibiades and Critias. And since the memory of the tyrant Critias was the fresher and more bitter of the two, Socrates was particularly liable to be thought, like Critias, a "hater of the people." As Aeschines was to tell a jury half a century later, with memorable lack of nuance, "You [i.e., the Athenian people] put the sophist Socrates to death because he was shown to have educated Critias."[10] On this latter view the issue was fundamentally one of politics rather than of religion. In either case, the decision to prosecute an old man for saying and doing what he had been saying and doing unmolested for so many years must have been a response to the wounds of recent history:[11] a lost war, a lost empire, an oligarchic coup. The problem is to decide whether the Athenians' diagnosis was more specific—"Socrates taught subversives"— or more general—"Socrates embodies the moral malaise that has brought Athens low."

Before addressing that problem, let us note that the interweaving of religious and political factors is far from being unique to this case. On the contrary, it may be that an accusation of impiety was almost never brought before an Athenian court without political anxiety or hatred being present in the background.[12] But the relation between the two kinds of motivation is not a simple or single one. One possibility is the accusation of "impiety" or something similar brought against persons whose political attitudes were widely resented, but who had unfortunately failed to commit any other identifiable offence. The attacks at the end of the fourth century on various anti-democratic philosophers were doubtless primarily of this type.[13] Here the formal charge was a screen not just for the prosecutors but for the jurors. But those who supposedly brought similar charges against "the friends of Pericles" in the 430s had no such reserve of general hostility to draw on. If they were to achieve their own political aims, they had to convince the jurors that the associates of the brightest political star of the day were indeed impious and dangerous men. Different again was the crisis of 415, where a conspiracy to mock the gods was taken as proof of a conspiracy against the state, and the two terrors stoked each other's fires. It will not do, therefore, to deny a given incident all religious content simply because political factors also intrude.

We return to Socrates. The apolitical interpretation of course gains in strength if the accusation of impiety had a foundation in reality. Was Socrates prosecuted, as has lately been suggested, because of a true perception that his teaching subverted the basis of traditional religion? One feature of the historical Socrates certainly was exploited by his accusers: for the charge that he "introduced new powers [*daimonia*]" must, as Plato and Xenophon recognize, allude to his "divine sign," *daimonion,* though seeking also to implicate him in further innovations left threateningly vague.[14] But stereotype and distortion intrude even here. The prosecution must have argued that Socrates had abandoned the gods of the city in favour of his personal divine voice; but no one who knew anything of the real character of Socrates' sign could suppose that it was in any kind of rivalry with the traditional gods.[15] Possibly a prosecutor could have exploited the kind of sharp remark about revered Athenian myths with which Socrates is credited in Plato's *Euthyphro;*[16] but this too would have been most unjust, criticism of myth being an accepted, and indeed in some ways a pious, practice. Socrates was unorthodox, it has been suggested, in declaring justice, not sacrifice, the key to divine favour, or in postulating gods who were wholly benevolent to mankind.[17] But it is strange to suppose that the fellow countrymen of Solon would have been stirred to outrage by sentiments such as these. Socrates' actual religious position would never, surely, have caused him to be singled out as a target for attack.

Religious resentment against Socrates was, however, not necessarily the less acute for being misdirected. The portrait of "Socrates" in Aristophanes' *Clouds* becomes, therefore, a document of prime importance. For our purpose, it does not matter at all whether "Socrates" bears much relation to the historical figure. What is important is that the play is treated in Plato's *Apology* as a typical expression of the popular prejudices against him.[18] For many jurors, therefore, "Socrates" was, in caricature, Socrates. And the portrait of Socrates in *Clouds* has an intrinsic interest for our theme which makes it worth pausing over here. Popular fears of impiety are here displayed, much more fully and clearly than in any other source.

"Socrates" is head of a school. He is, in fact, literature's first don. This very obvious fact is also very important. Traditionally, young men had been "trained in virtue"—that is, "the ability to manage one's own affairs and those of the city"—by informal association with older men: relations, family friends, and lovers. The sophists, by contrast, are the founding fathers of Higher Education, formal instruction purveyed by an outsider; and it has rightly been argued that this educational revolution, which of course undermined traditional familial authority in some degree, is at the root of the Athenians' profoundly ambiguous attitudes to philosophers and sophists and Socrates. Though Socrates was unique in being condemned by an Athenian court "for words" (as Hyperides put it) not actions, the point was that he was a teacher and his were action-inspiring words.[19]

In "Socrates"' school are taught both strange doctrines about the heavens, and also the art of "making the worse appear the better cause" (Ar. *Nub.* 94–99, 112–115). His prospective pupil Strepsiades assumes that, as one who "contemplates the sun," he will "look down on the gods"

(225–226). And indeed Socrates declares that the conventional gods "aren't currency with us" (247–248), and undertakes to introduce Strepsiades to "our gods," the Clouds, and to reveal "the true nature of things divine" (250–253). He argues in some detail that rain, thunder, and lightning, the phenomena that cause Strepsiades to fear Zeus, have natural causes; and points out that lightning, far from picking on Zeus' enemies, spares perjurers and strikes inanimate objects, even Zeus' own temple (366–411). Socrates' tone is light, but the arguments he uses remained, throughout antiquity, fundamental to the case against gods who intervene in the world.[20] (Interestingly, his atheism is wholly based on scientific arguments of this kind. He seems unaffected in this area by Protagorean scepticism, and by sophistic speculations about the origin of belief in the gods.) His own gods, we soon learn, are Chaos, Clouds, and Tongue (424), and these novel deities recur as a comic leitmotif throughout the play (627, 814, 1150). The strength of his reverence for the new gods does not excuse but underlines his turning away from the old; "kainotheism" is not an alternative to atheism but the form it takes. Similarly, admission to his school is portrayed as a form of initiation into Mysteries (255 ff.),[21] but the effect is much less to present Socrates as a man of strong if misguided piety than to stress the secret, elitist, anti-social character of his teaching.

But what harm is there in atheism? That it angers the gods, a factor often stressed in modern accounts, is not stated in the play. What is stressed instead is how, allied with rhetoric, it subverts social morality. Strepsiades laughs in the face of a creditor who reminds him of his oath to make repayment (1228–1241). "Those are not at all to be tolerated who deny the being of God. Promises, covenants and oaths, which are the bonds of human society, can have no hold upon an atheist. The taking away of God, though but even in thought, dissolves all": the words are John Locke's,[22] but the thought is also Aristophanes'. The overthrow of morality reaches its climax when Strepsiades' son Pheidippides, also initiated in the mysteries of the school, begins to beat his father, scorning, of course, his pathetic appeals to "Zeus of Fathers" (1468).[23] Strepsiades now repents (it is in fact the comi-tragic motif of Strepsiades' delusion and repentance that gives the play its coherence and bite[24]), and realizes "how mad I was to renounce the gods because of Socrates" (1477). He leads a violent attack on the school, designed to eradicate it from the community and expel (though not destroy) its occupants.[25] Strepsiades speaks the final words of the play: "Well, why did you insult the gods, and inspect the seat of the moon? Chase them, hit them, pelt them for a hundred reasons, but most of all remembering how they wronged the gods." The obscene pun on "inspecting the seat of the moon" only slightly mitigates the grim violence of this ending.

Clearly, the Socrates of the play and the Socrates of the indictment are the same man. Both are atheists; both corrupt the young. And these are the prejudices that, very largely, the *Apologies* of both Plato and Xenophon seek to dispel.[26] According to Plato, Socrates was hated because he

exposed the ignorance of older men in the presence of his younger followers;[27] the same charge of setting the younger generation against the old
is translated into comic fantasy in the father-beating scene in *Clouds*.

We hear of the political charges not from Plato but from the point-by-
point rebuttal of an unnamed "accuser" in the first two chapters of
Xenophon's *Memorabilia*. According to a long-accepted view, Xenophon is
there responding not to any of the actual speeches for the prosecution but
to an *Accusation of Socrates* published by the rhetorician Polycrates at least
six years after the trial. That consensus has recently been strongly challenged; but even if the challenge is correct, we still have in Xenophon not
a faithful transcript of the arguments actually employed by the prosecution, but a re-creation of them made after an uncertain interval of time during which the celebrated case had been repeatedly discussed.[28]
Xenophon's "accuser" emphasized (among many others) the charges that
Socrates had educated Critias and Alcibiades, that he constantly ridiculed
the use of that key democratic device, the lot, and was in general hostile to
the "people and the poor."[29]

Can any of these resentments be declared irrelevant to the actual condemnation? The ancient prejudice against sophists as atheists and teachers
of unjust arguments is surely not to be dismissed: such was, as we know
from Aristophanes, the popular perception of Socrates, and the prosecution had no reason at all not to exploit it to the full, even if they also wished
to appeal to political anger. We see from the trials of 415 how ready Athenians were to suspect the same individuals of impiety and of treacherous
disloyalty to the constitution; indeed, since five of the persons convicted in
415 were associates of Socrates,[30] some responsibility for the earlier impious outrage may well have been laid at his door in 399. And we have, as it
happens, in Lysias 6 a spectacular demonstration of the virulence with
which religious arguments could still be deployed in this same year of
Socrates' trial. [31] Are the political factors similarly uneliminable? It has
been suggested that they were first brought into the debate by Polycrates,
several years after Socrates' death.[32] But, even if the influence of Polycrates
on subsequent tradition is allowed, there are no strong reasons to doubt
that political arguments were already used in 399. Because of the Amnesty
of 403, Socrates could not be charged with spreading anti-democratic sentiments before that date; but there was no bar to the argument that, having
corrupted Alcibiades and Critias in the past, he was liable to go on corrupting the present generation.[33] Plato's *Apology*, of course, does not imply
that political factors had any importance (except perhaps in one passing
aside[34]). But we have no reason to take Plato's defense any more seriously
as a historical record than whatever accusation underlies the "accuser" of
Xenophon.[35] It is, therefore, hard to doubt that the names Critias and
Alcibiades, and the word "hater of the people," were spoken at the trial.
Beyond this point we can scarcely go. Different arguments will have had
different weight with different jurors; and the motives of most individual

jurors were surely also mixed. It is pointless to attempt to clarify that complex mess of human resentment, and declare religious or social or political factors decisive.

We turn to the other instances of repression. It was believed in later antiquity that Socrates was not alone: His death was only the culmination of a series of trials and other attacks on intellectuals dotted through the second half of the fifth century. But the evidence is extraordinarily difficult and untrustworthy.[36] Only in one case is it contemporary; and here it appears that it was for mocking the Eleusinian Mysteries, not for preaching atheism, that the Melian poet Diagoras was outlawed from Athens with a price on his head. (It looks as if he had been notorious for impiety for some years but was only indicted in 415/4, just when sensitivity to any slight to the Mysteries was at its height.)[37] We have early fourth-century evidence that Pericles' mistress Aspasia was prosecuted (unsuccessfully) for impiety, but no indication of the details of the charge.[38] Protagoras was supposedly condemned to death for writing his sceptical *On the Gods*, while the book itself was burnt in the market-place; but these reports begin in the Hellenistic period, and appear simply incompatible with a remark in Plato that Protagoras had lived out his life in high repute throughout Greece.[39] For the most striking claim of all, that shortly before the Peloponnesian war the well-known seer Diopeithes proposed a decree which was to make "those who do not acknowledge the divine" or who "teach about things in the air" liable to prosecution, we have only the testimony of Plutarch; apart from the lack of supporting evidence, there is no very strong reason to be suspicious.[40] There is fourth-century testimony that Anaxagoras was "prosecuted for impiety" by the enemies of Pericles (but the later accounts that give details of the actual trial are mutually contradictory in a very suspicious way), and that Diogenes of Apollonia "came close to danger."[41] Finally, we have further fifth-century evidence that natural philosophers were resented (though not necessarily attacked): "who, seeing this, does not recognize a god, and does not hurl far from him the crooked deceits of talkers about the heavens [*meteorologoi*], whose mad tongue makes random throws about what is hidden, devoid of understanding?" enquires a chorus in Euripides.[42] It was to sentiments such as these that those who attacked the great scientist Anaxagoras (if such indeed there were) must have appealed, however political their own motivation may have been.[43]

Clearly, enough uncertainties remain (and doubtless will always remain) to prevent any confident conclusion. If Anaxagoras was never tried, if the decree of Diopeithes was passed only on the comic stage, if it was for political crimes that Socrates was executed, we are left with little more than resentful talk, as heard in Aristophanes and Euripides. (No argument, however, can remove the charge of atheism from the formal indictment against Socrates.) On a less sceptical view, talk became action more than once, though still not with great frequency. One general observation can perhaps escape these specific uncertainties.[44] We are not considering the extent to which the Athenians in practice restricted a liberty which in principle they allowed. On the contrary, no Greek surely would have supposed that an impious opinion should be permitted to circulate out of respect for freedom of speech. In practice, no doubt, the Athenians very rarely moved against verbal impiety. A wide variety of opinions about the gods could be comfortably accommodated, in a religion that lacked dogma and revelation; and it is easy to think of intellectuals, such as Hippon, whose views would doubtless under investigation have seemed impious to some, and who nonetheless went unmolested. But in such cases we are dealing not with principled tolerance but with a failure to live up to intolerant principles. Fortunately such failures seem to have been very regular.

Was there, as has often been supposed, a "religious crisis" in the second half of the fifth century? In the sense that traditional religion was seriously undermined, certainly not; there is any amount of evidence, from inscriptions, dedications, oratory, and comedy, that it continued to flourish in the fourth century just as before. But in the sense that speculative thought was perceived by some as a threat, perhaps for the first time, a kind of crisis did arise (though its extent is partly veiled by the various uncertainties that we have just discussed).

Several difficult problems arise in connection with this crisis. Late fifth-century opinions about the divine can sound, to a modern ear, like a babel of unorthodox and critical voices. We hear scientific determinists; critics of myth, or of divine morality, or of divine justice, or of divination; various kinds of allegorists; speculative theologians prepared to declare, for instance, that "Earth and Mother and Rhea and Hera are the same"; thinkers of another stamp who offer explanations of how men first came to form a conception of the divine.[45] We need to ask what in all this was truly threatening or "impious"; what constituted an attack from without rather than from within the traditional religious framework, that loose and accommodating structure within which certain forms of doubt, criticism, and revision were, in fact, traditional.[46]

From the contemporary evidence, beginning with *Clouds* and ending with Plato's important discussion of atheism in *Laws*, it emerges that one position above all was feared: that of the "atheist" scientist, who substitutes chance and necessity for the gods as an explanation of celestial phenomena—and so deprives Zeus of his thunderbolt.[47] (Scepticism about divination certainly also created unease, but we hear nothing of repression of sceptics. And Socrates is scarcely to be taken seriously when, in *Euthyphro*, he moots the possibility that a critic of certain myths of divine conflict might be prosecuted for impiety.[48]) Now, in a certain illuminist perspective, science and religion may appear as natural enemies, destined to come into conflict. But in Greece they were able, as a rule, to maintain good neighbourly relations. Provided science stayed clear of militant atheism (as it did),[49] there was no obvious need for hostilities between it and the undogmatic, ever-changing Greek theology, protected by no Holy Office. Scientists could even borrow the characteristic argument "from within" of the religious reformer, and reveal that their new position was, behold, actually more pious than its traditional precursor: thus the Hippocratic author of *On the Sacred Disease* urges that it is impious to suppose (as most people in this case did) that gods, the source of good, can inflict disease.[50] Hippocratic medicine is in fact a prime example of a science that lived in easy harmony with traditional religion.

Conflict, therefore, was scarcely inevitable. But, it may be countered, the particular point in dispute between, say, Anaxagoras and the Athenian people was too fundamental to admit of compromise: it was the very power of Zeus, or any other god, to intervene in the world. It was no use merely acknowledging "the divine," if this "divine" had no purchase on the affairs of men. "Who ever refrained from wrongdoing from fear of Air or Aither?" as a critic of Stoic theology was later to enquire.[51] Yet even if this is conceded, we have still to ask why the conflict arose when and where it did. Ionian philosophers had been offering such mechanistic explanations of the natural order since the sixth century, without, to our knowledge, arousing protest. And at no other time or place in the Greek world were philosophers put on trial for the impiety of their physical theories.[52] Why did Athens fear what Miletus had applauded, what Megara was to tolerate?

Part of the answer must be that, even if the natural philosopher was not a new phenomenon in the fifth century, he enjoyed a new prominence. Scientists were rare enough in the sixth century to be admired and patronized, brilliant eccentrics ever in danger of tumbling down wells. By the fifth they were common, and influential, enough to be felt as a threat.[53] It is obviously tempting to add that it was through association with the threatening intellectual movement par excellence, that of the sophists, that natural philosophy acquired a taint. Earlier philosophers, it can be argued, attacked religious tradition constructively and from within: the sophists advanced much more radical criticisms and drew more radical conclusions; or at the least such radical criticism first emerged in the sophistic period. Protagoras denied that secure knowledge is possible about the existence of the gods; Prodicus argued that early man had acquired his gods by deifying natural products and the inventors of techniques; a character in a play by Critias declared that the gods were an invention of a "wise lawgiver" eager to discourage secret wrongdoing.[54] If theories such as these were put about in association with mechanistic accounts of the workings of the universe, the ugly atheistic implications of the latter would be starkly revealed. The "atheism" of Socrates in *Clouds* is so dangerous because he is also a sophist and a moral relativist. And Plato too says that the typical atheist combines "scientific" belief in a mechanistic universe with the characteristic "sophistic" commitment to a life led according to nature, not convention.[55]

In broad outline this explanation is likely to be correct: natural philosophy became offensive only once it was felt to be combined with moral relativism or antinomianism. But it is very uncertain whether prominent sophists did in fact make provocative attacks on traditional belief. In later antiquity, the theological positions of Protagoras and Prodicus, taken perhaps out of context, were certainly adjudged impious; no such charge is brought against them in Aristophanes or Plato, for whom, as we have seen, the archetypal atheistic position is primarily scientific rather than sophistic.[56] We have no more than uncertain hints that some of Protagoras' *Overthrowing Arguments* may have been designed to overthrow "ancestral traditions, coeval with time" in the matter of religion, such as belief in divination.[57] It is impossible, therefore, to fill in the details of the alliance between a scientific determinism that was pushed to an atheistic extreme and sophistic antinomianism. We are left with Plato's unsubstantiated testimony that such an alliance occurred[58] (perhaps among hearers of philosophers and sophists rather than the thinkers themselves), and the general likelihood that this was the source of public fear of the impious scientist.

If a kind of religious crisis did indeed occur in the late fifth century, one may reasonably ask how it was resolved. "By Stoicism" is doubtless the answer in the long term; in a shorter perspective we would need to consider how key elements in the Stoic solution were already being developed in the fourth century: the argument from design; the "double determination" theory of causality (whereby god works through natural process); that other compromise, best known from Roman sources, by which traditional forms of cult (*theologia civilis*) are accepted by the educated as the proper way to honour a divine principle that is intellectually quite differently conceived (*theologia physica.*) Plato in old age could already claim that actual atheism was in decline.[59] These issues in religious philosophy cannot be discussed here: let us merely note that traditional religion surrendered none of its rights, explicitly at least. Plutarch indeed describes how, as early as 430, Pericles allayed his troops' religious fears by explaining the physical causes of a terrifying eclipse. But the incident is chronologically impossible;[60] and everything we know of the permissible tone of public life in the fourth century suggests that politicians and generals still paid respect to divination, still acknowledged the traditional divine signs as signs. It is possible that a preference for natural over theological explanations of certain phenomena made a creeping advance, plausible certainly that such was now the preference of some of the educated. But scientific determinism neither sought nor won any victories in the open field. According to Plutarch again, an eclipse of the moon in 357 left Dion and his entourage, graduates of Plato's Academy, unalarmed; but one of them, the seer Miltas, offered a heartening interpretation in religious terms to the frightened troops. The formal victor was certainly traditional religion.[61]

We revert to "new gods." At first sight Socrates has little in common with the great courtesan Phryne. Yet they shared the fate of being accused of "introducing a new god"; Socrates, however, too proud to supplicate the jury, was condemned, while a novel and most impressive appeal secured the acquittal of fair-breasted Phryne. Was "kainotheism" therefore formally proscribed by law (as two unreliable late sources declare)?[62] A broader question is whether Athenian law identified specific forms of impiety, such as kainotheism, or merely laid down penalties and procedures for use against an offence, "impiety", the content of which it was left to jurors and tradition to decide. Not only Socrates and Phryne but also Demades and Aristotle were charged with "introducing new gods," in their case by deifying mortals: the recurrent complaint implies, it has been urged, a formal prohibition.[63] But it remains possible that a charge of introducing new gods was simply one of the accepted ways in which one could seek to persuade a jury that an individual was guilty of impiety, not part of a formal definition of the offence.

But how could a prejudice (whether codified or not) against kainotheism coexist with the Athenians' famous "hospitality" towards foreign gods? This is a much more serious problem than that concerning the exact terms of the law. A simple solution to the paradox is available: new gods could be introduced by the city (Pan, Bendis, and others),[64] perhaps in consultation with the gods themselves via an oracle, but ultimately by the city alone; though individuals or groups could establish new cults at their own expense, they could do so only with the authorization of the people. All religious practice undertaken on Attic soil occurs therefore by gracious permission of the assembly.

At the deepest level this simple solution is probably correct.[65] The principle that the individual should worship no gods other than those approved by the state would doubtless not have been controversial. In practice, however, things seem to have run on in a less regulated way. It is not clear, for instance, that individuals ever did approach the assembly with a request for permission to "introduce a new god". Was it with authorization that Themistocles founded his offensively vainglorious shrine to "Artemis Aristoboule"? Perhaps the case is not relevant, since Themistocles did not introduce a new god but applied a new epithet to an old one.[66] Our key example ought therefore to be Asclepius, unquestionably a new god[67] imported by private initiative; alas, on the point that concerns us nothing explicit is recorded. It would no doubt have been bold for Telemachus to build a sizeable sanctuary just below the acropolis without authorization; but the subsequent claim to the site lodged by the *Kerykes* might be taken as evidence that he did just that. (If so, the claim also suggests that his procedure was hazardous. The grandson of the Egyptian priest who introduced Sarapis to Delos in the third century was prosecuted when he built a fixed shrine for the god, who had hitherto lived unmolested in rented accommodation.[68] In such a case a court that decided in favour of the new god provided a kind of retrospective authorization.)

Asclepius had a precinct; other foreign gods such as Sabazius and Adonis lacked one, and it is surely out of the question that their disreputable rites had ever received the authorization of the people. An immigrant community, wishing to found a shrine in Athens to its native god, had to apply to the assembly, since otherwise it could not buy land on which to build it;[69] but what was sought was right of ownership, not of worship, and the cults in question may have been carried on in rented accommodation before the shrine was thought of. Plato in a famous passage of *Laws* both attests and proscribes the practice of founding private shrines, often no doubt to "new gods."[70] In practice, therefore, individuals seems to have "introduced new gods" with some freedom (though it may have been uncommon, and for non-citizens was certainly illegal, to lodge such a god in a substantial shrine without approval). They were called to account only if they or their religious associations proved objectionable on other grounds. The accusation brought against Socrates of "acknowledging new powers" is only a counterpoise to that other and much more damning one of "not acknowledging the gods the city believes in." And it was as a priestess in what we have called an "elective" cult, a "leader of lawless revel bands of men and women," that Phryne was attacked. Against such revel bands—centres, as they saw them of social subversion and crime—the Athenians were indeed always ready to strike.[71] And in charging their leaders with, among other things, "introducing new gods," they were affirming their right of ultimate control over all the religious practices of Attica. But Phryne would scarcely have been spared even if she had dedicated her troupe to an honest Attic god. When such groups were suppressed, as when the *Bacchanalia* were suppressed at Rome, the issue was not fundamentally one of theological orthodoxy.

Notes

1. There is an extensive bibliography in Brickhouse and Smith 1989.
2. So Wallace 1994, 144.
3. So Todd 1993, 312; on the crisis, cf. Parker 1983, 168–170; Ostwald 1986, 537–559; Murray 1990, 149–161.
4. Breidert 1994 is a collection of contemporary responses to the tragedy (also discussed by Kendrick 1956).
5. See Mikalson 1984, 423–431.
6. Cited by Slack 1985, 39–40—a superb study which charts the gradual and partial supersession of such attitudes, but not in favour of explicit atheism; bibliography on "Disaster Studies" ibid., 344–345, and cf. Ziegler 1969, chs. 5 and 17. On the plague as *flagellum dei* see the sections on Cyprian and Gregory in Grimm 1965.
7. Cf. Parker 1996, ch. 8 n. 115, and ch. 9 n. 97; for other responses that have been suggested in ancient and modern times see ibid. ch. 8 n. 51, and ch. 9 n. 121; and note too Thuc. 1.118.3. on Apollo's involvement. Thucydides, 2.64.1, makes Pericles say he was "hated" because of the plague: cf. Marshall 1990, 169, who suggests that it was blamed on Pericles' pollution (Thuc. 1.126–127). Impious citizens: cf. Parker 1983, 170 n. 148.

8. Favorinus *ap.* D.L. 2.40. In the phrase νομίζειν θεοὺς the verb is poised between a reference to "custom, customary [worship]" (so, e.g., Hdt. 4.59.19) and "belief" (so, e.g., Eur. *Supp.* 732, rightly so taken by Collard ad loc.): see Fahr 1969; Yunis 1988, 62–66.

9. See below, n. 63.

10. 1.173. For doxography see Brickhouse and Smith 1989, 70 n. 29; they cite Hackforth 1933, 73–79, as unique to their knowledge in denying the importance of political factors (which they too doubt, 69–87; and cf. Finley 1968, 58–72).

11. Finley 1968 stresses that the trauma was not just that of the tyranny of the Thirty.

12. As Robin Lane Fox suggests to me. The hierophant Archias, condemned for a technical offence of impiety (Dem. 59.116), warned the Theban oligarchs of Pelopidas' impending coup in 379/8 (Plut. *Pelop.* 10.3, cf. 14.1), an act that must have been unpopular, however complicated the Athenians' public attitude to the coup had to be (Buck 1994, 72–78; Hornblower 1985, 209). The political record of the speaker of Lys. 7 was perhaps poor (Todd 1993, 308). About the cases known from Dem. 57.8 and Lys. 5 we know little. See in general Todd 1993, 307–310. The use of charges under the "Statutes of Recusancy" against persons suspected of treason in sixteenth-century England has been compared (see "Statutes, of Recusancy" in the index to Elton 1974).

13. Discussed in Parker 1996, ch. 12; on the friends of Pericles see below.

14. Pl. *Euth.* 3b; Xen. *Mem.* 1.1.2, etc. Cf. Versnel 1990, 126 (and the works he cites).

15. Contrast Garland 1992, 149 (with an interesting citation of Kierkegaard). That Socrates participated in civic rituals in the usual way cannot strictly be proved. But to doubt it we must reject both Xenophon's explicit statement that he did (*Mem.* 1.1.2) and the whole presentation in all the works of both Xenophon and Plato of Socrates' attitude to Delphi and to cult more generally; we must also discount the biographical fact that pious Xenophon admired him.

16. 6a; but the remark has much too clear a place in Plato's strategy in that dialogue (see n. 48 below) to be good evidence for the historical Socrates.

17. See Connor 1991, 49–56; Vlastos 1991, ch. 6.

18. 19b–c; note too Xen. *Symp.* 6.6–8.

19. Educational revolution: cf. the portrayal of Anytus' attitude in Pl. *Meno* 91c–92b, and Havelock 1952, 95–109. Mrs Thatcher was quoted in the 1980s as being distressed at the way in which "young people who were absolutely thrilled at getting a place at university have every decent value drubbed out of them when they get there" (I quote from memory but am sure of "drub"). That Socrates was in this broad sense a true sophist is rightly stressed by Nussbaum 1980; Kerferd 1981, 55–57. Hyperides: fr. 55 Jensen, cited by Hansen 1980. Note too, with Wallace 1994, the ostracism of Damon, another teacher (Arist. *Ath. Pol.* 27.4.).

20. See, e.g., Lucretius 6.379–422, with C. Bailey's notes in his commentary ad loc. (Oxford 1947).

21. Cf. Bowie 1993, 112–124.

22. In *A Letter concerning Toleration.*

23. For the importance of the father-beating theme, see the probable allusion to this play in Ar. *Vesp.* 1037–1042.

24. See Macleod 1983, 49–51.

25. See Davies 1990.

26. As did that of Socrates himself, if Hansen 1980 is right to revive the view that coincidences between Plato and Xenophon derive from this common source rather than from imitation.

27. E.g., *Ap.* 23c-d; cf. Xen. *Ap.* 20, *Mem.* 1.2.49; Strauss 1993, 199–209.

28. For Polycrates, Chroust 1957, 69–100; against Hansen 1980, and independently N. Livingstone of Christ Church, Oxford, in a doctoral dissertation in preparation on Isocrates. A coincidence of detail (citation of *Il.* 2.188 ff.) between Xen. *Mem.* 1.2.58 and Polycrates *ap.* Σ Ael. Arist. III, p. 480.30 Dindorf is one of the indications usually held to prove their interdependence; on the other view, it attests, on this point, fidelity on the part of both to the actual prosecutor.

29. *Mem.* 1.2.9–11, 12, 58.

30. For a prosopography see most recently Ostwald 1986, 537–550; he stresses that most of the persons accused were youngish men, of an age to be seen as products of the new education.

31. J. Burnet (note on Pl. *Euth.* 2b9) described Lys. 6 as "almost the only monument of religious fanaticism that has come down to us from antiquity." For the possibility that the Meletuses involved in the prosecutions of Socrates and Andocides are the same see Blumenthal 1973; cf. Brickhouse and Smith 1989, 27–28. Note too Lys. 30, a milder instance from the same year.

32. So, tentatively, Brickhouse and Smith 1989, 80. Ar. *Av.* 1281–1283 is sometimes cited to prove that Socrates was already renowned for philolaconism in the fifth century, but also makes sense on the view that he merely symbolized austerity (as we know that he did).

33. So Hansen (1980), who stresses how implausible it is that the prosecution should have failed to raise political issues.

34. The reference in 33a4–5 to "those who people slandering me claim are my students," which is often taken as an allusion to Critias and Alcibiades: see Brickhouse and Smith 1989, 194–197. Note too the admission in 23c that he associates with rich young men.

35. Contrast Brickhouse and Smith 1989, 2–10. The recent publication (*P. Köln* 205, in Gronewald, Maresch, and Schäfer 1985) of a fragment of a Socratic dialogue in which the philosopher, conversing on his deathbed as in *Phaedo*, demonstrates that "pleasure is the goal," ought to serve as a caution (admittedly in a not quite comparable context) to those who believe in the historicity of any Socratic literature.

36. The basic discussion is now Dover 1975; Kerferd (1981, 21 n. 7) judges it "excessively sceptical"; but the case for less scepticism would need to be made out point by point. Note, however, with Kerferd, Arist. *Rhet.* 1397b25–27, where Aristotle appears to say that "sophists" are often put to death. (I do not understand Dover's view of the passage [Dover 1988, 148 n. 25].) For another sceptical discussion, see now Wallace (1994), who recognizes only the ostracism of Damon and possibly (Pl. *Tht.* 171d) a prudent withdrawal by Protagoras.

37. See Ar. *Av.* 1071–1073, Lys. 6.17–18; Melanthius, *FGrH* 342 F 16 (both in Σ Ar. *Av.* 1073). A book containing explicitly atheistic doctrines appears first in Aristoxenus fr. 45.I Wehrli[2] (superseded text) *ap.* Philodemus *PHerc.* 1428 col. xi.5 ff. (*Cronache ercolanesi* 4, 1974, 21–22; cf. ibid. 18, 1988, 122), who apparently doubts its authenticity (*aliter* Henrichs, *Cronache ercolanesi* 4, 1974, 28; but both ἐπεμφέρω and the following contrast with "his only genuine writings" suggest that spurious writings are alluded to: read perhaps [ἀληθὲ]ς in line 10, cf. D.L. 1.39.12). For an excellent brief account of the problems concerning Diagoras

see Wehrli 1961, followed in the essentials in the full studies by Winiarczyk 1979 and 1980; cf. id. 1981, and Smarczyk 1990, 278 ff. As to chronology, the natural inference from Ar. *Av.* 1071–1073 that his banishment was recent has ancient support (Σ Ar. *Av.* 1073; Diod. 13.6.7; and the Mubassir life, T 10 Winiarczyk), which is, however, itself likely to be based on inference from the *Birds* passage (cf. Jacoby 1959, who sets the banishment much earlier); but there is already an allusion to his notorious impiety in *Clouds* (Ar. *Nub.* 830; the relevance of Hermippus fr. 43 KA, of 430, is less certain), even the rev. version of which is generally and probably rightly held (see Ar. *Nub.* 551–559; Kopff [1990] disagrees) to antedate the ostracism of Hyperbolus in 416. See further Bremmer 1995 (with a fresh translation of the Mubassir life).

38. Antisthenes fr. 35 in the edn. of F.D. Caizzi (Milan 1966) *ap.* Ath. 589e; but cf. Wallace 1994, 132.

39. *Meno* 91e; the growth of the book-burning legend can be traced with much plausibility step by step: see Dover 1988, 142–145, 158; and for another sceptical treatment of the tradition, Müller 1967; cf., however, n. 36 above.

40. Plut. *Per.* 32.2; note, however, Dover 1988, 146–147, who points out that the verbal formulation in Plutarch is unlikely to be original. That the decree was remembered though never passed is a rather remote possibility. Ostwald (1986, 528–532) argues that it was in fact the first Athenian law against impiety.

41. Anaxagoras: Ephorus *FGrH* 70 F 196 *ap.* Diod. 12.39.2; cf. Dover 1988, 140–141 (who doubts even this); Yunis 1988, 66–68 (who, however, makes too much of an ordinary narrative imperfect in Ephorus); attempts are still made to sort out the later tradition, and believe parts of it, by Mansfeld, 1980, Woodbury 1981; cf. Ostwald 1992, 339. Diogenes: Demetrius of Phaleron *ap.* D.L. 9.57 (fr. 91 Wehrli); but on Demetrius' motivation and reliability, see Dover 1988, 145–146.

42. Fr. 913 Nauck; see too Cratinus fr. 167 KA = DK 38 A2, a supposed attack (not verbatim) on Hippon for impiety; and Eupolis fr. 157 KA, ἔνδον μέν ἐστι Πρωταγόρας ὁ Τήιος | ὅς ἀλαζονεύεται μὲν ἀλιτήριος | περὶ τῶν μετε ώρων. A whole tradition of attacks by poets (in various genres) on philosophers is attested by Pl. *Rep.* 607b–c, with *Laws* 967c-d (cf. Pind. fr. 209 Snell/Maehler). For the popular association of astronomy with atheism, see Pl. *Ap.* 18b-c, 26d, and *Laws* 967a; Plut. *Nic.* 23.3–4.

43. So rightly Derenne 1930, 41.

44. Cf. the conclusion to Derenne, ibid. 254–267; Decharme 1904, 179—"la loi sans doute a été sévère pour les libertés de la pensée, mais, dans la pratique, l'esprit public le fut rarement"; D. Cohen 1991, 210–217 (the work by Garnsey that he cites appears in Sheils 1984).

45. See in general Burkert 1985, 311–317. On allegorists see Richardson 1975. Speculative theologian: see the Derveni papyrus, *Zeitschrift für Papyrologie und Epigraphik* 47, 1982, after p. 300, col. XVIII 7, tentatively ascribed to Stesimbrotus by Burkert 1986.

46. In particular, the criticisms of divine justice and morality aired in the plays of Euripides have numerous antecedents (cf. Drachmann 1922, 52, cf. 16: "in so far . . . he is still entirely on the ground of popular belief"), though Euripides presses them unusually hard. For recent discussions which stress the traditional aspects of Euripides' theology see Heath 1987, 49–64; Lefkowitz 1989b; for the unusual pressure see Yunis 1988, pt. 2.

47. See n. 42 above, and Pl. *Laws* 886d–e, 889b–890a, 967a–d.

48. Divination: cf. the defensive or threatened tone of Hdt. 8.77; Soph. *OT* 897–910;

Xen. *Eq. Mag.* 9.7–9, *Cyr.* 1.6.46; for an attack, Eur. *Hel.* 744–760 (of, perhaps significantly, the year after the Sicilian disaster: cf. Thuc. 8.1). Myths: Pl. *Euth.* 6a. Socrates is merely "teasing" Euthyphro with this whimsical suggestion, according to Guthrie 1975, 110 n. 1; rather, the issue is raised, in a way characteristic of a dialogue that is in part a *retorsio criminis impietatis*, to stress the division between true Socratic piety and the traditional version, in fact impious, that has presumed to arraign him. The attack on the panathenaic robe (of all things) in 6b-c sharply separates Socrates from civic piety. Note too the hint contained in the reference to secret doctrines (of Orphic type?) in 6c that the truly dangerous innovators in religion (cf. the charge made against Socrates of καινοτομεῖν, 16a) are soi-distant experts such as Euthyphro.

49. Indeed, most pre-Socratic philosophers are demonstrably theists, if of a quite untraditional type: see, e.g., Kahn 1960, 155–159; Barnes 1979, I. 94–99; II. 156–159, 279–280.

50. Loeb Hippocrates, ed. Jones, vol. 2, p. 144 § 3. For the type of argument cf. e.g., Pind. *Ol.* 1.35 ff.; Xen. *Ap.* 13.

51. Philodemus *De Pietate* in *PHerc.* 1428 col. xiii.8 ff. (*Cronache ercolanesi* 4, 1974:23).

52. Expulsions of philosophers, usually Epicureans, are, however, attested from a few Greek states (in the Hellenistic period when datable): see Habicht 1994, 237. On later Athenian impiety trials, see Parker 1996, ch. 12.

53. I owe this point to Edward Hussey.

54. 80 B4; DK 84 B5 + *PHerc.* 1428 fr. 19 (n. 56 below); DK 88 B25 = TrGF I.43 Critias F 19 (on which see most recently Winiarczyk 1987 and Davies 1989).

55. *Laws* 889b–890a. Sophists did sometimes, it seems, discuss scientific topics (see Pl. *Prt.* 318e and Kerferd 1981, 38–40); at all events, the man in the street was convinced that they did, as we see from *Clouds* (cf. Ar. *Av.* 692 and n. 18 above).

56. For the atheists recognized in later antiquity, see Winiarczyk 1984. That Protagoras' attitude was not polemical is argued by Müller 1967, 140–148; Lloyd-Jones 1971, 130–131; Kerferd 1981, 164–168; that Prodicus was a "modernist," not an atheist, by, e.g., Drachmann 1922, 42–44, and Dodds in his note on Eur. *Bacch.* 274–285. The "modernist" view of Prodicus is confuted by the new evidence of *PHerc.* 1428 fr. 19, where he is credited with explicit atheism (Henrichs 1975, 107; 1976), only if the doxographer is directly reporting rather than, as is perhaps more plausible, interpreting his views; it is, however, hard to see what ground Prodicus could have had for believing that gods of traditional form existed, once the origin of men's belief in them had been explained away. On Prodicus' contemporary reputation, see Willink 1983, who detects an allusion to his impiety in the comparison with Tantalus in Pl. *Prt.* 315b–c; this is possible, no more. Epicurus certainly treats him as an atheist, fr. 27.2 Arrighetti.

57. Namely, the language of Hdt. 8.77, χρησμοῖσι δὲ οὐκ ἔχω ἀντιλέγειν ὡς οὐκ εἰσὶ ἀληθέες, οὐ βουλόμενος ἐναργέως λέγοντας τειρᾶσθαι καταβάλλειν ... (the word ἀντιλογία recurs later) and Eur. *Bacch.* 199–203, esp. πατρίους παραδοχὰς ... οὐδεὶς καταβαλεῖ λόγος (see Radermacher 1898).

58. *Laws* 889a–890a. The evidence of this text is more slippery than it at first appears. No philosopher can be identified who held the amalgam of views that Plato here attacks and describes as common (see Guthrie 1969, 115–116). It is probably Plato's own synthesis of tendencies he perceived as threatening (so de Mahieu 1964, 16–47); but Plato was too imaginative and too emotional to be a very careful reporter of other people's views.

59. Pl. *Laws* 967a-b. Design: see, e.g., Henrichs 1975, 105 n. 53; Jaeger 1947, 167–171;

Parker 1992. Double determination: Plut. *Per.* 6 is the classic illustration (cf. Babut 1969, 521). *Ratio civilis* and *physica:* Jaeger 1947, 2–4, with notes; Lieberg 1982. On the whole issue see Burkert 1985, 317–337; Gerson 1990. Of course questions about the social role of schools of philosophy are also relevant.

60. Plut. *Per.* 35.2 (a story repeated in philosophical schools, Plutarch notes); cf. Dover 1988, 47, 141. Plutarch also claims that Demosthenes forbade the Athenians to attend to oracles, and reminded them that Pericles and Epaminondas had regarded such things as mere pretexts for cowardice (*Dem.* 20.1). But his story is probably spun out of Demosthenes' denunciation of the philippizing Pythia (Aeschin. 3. 130), a specific and not a general attack, no more a sign of theoretical scepticism than pious Hector's attack on Poulydamas in *Il.* 12.231–250. For appeals by Demosthenes to oracles, see 18.253, 19.297–299, 21.51. About Pericles' own religious attitude (discussed by Schachermeyer [1968]) little can be learnt from scraps of his public speeches (Plut. *Per.* 8.9; Lys. 6.10) and questionable anecdotes (Plut. *Per.* 8.6, 13.12–13, 35.2, 38.2), the only sources.

61. Cf. Burkert 1985, 305. Dion: Plut. *Dion* 22.6, 24.1–3; Pritchett 1979, 111.

62. Joseph. *Ap.* 2.267; Serv. on Virg. *Aen.* 8.187; cf. Hausrath 1970, no. 56.

63. So Derenne 1930, 223–236, and Rudhardt 1960; for Demades and Aristotle, see Parker 1996, ch. 12 nn. 5 and 87, for Demades esp. Ath. 251b, "the Athenians penalized him ὅτι θεὸν εἰσηγήσατο Ἀλέξανδρον". But for the view that the law against impiety was non-specific see MacDowell 1978, 197–202; Ostwald 1986, 535; Cohen 1991, 207–210; for the view that Athenian law was typically procedural, not substantive, see Todd 1993, 61 n. 14, 64–67.

64. Such a formal civic recognition of the divinity of heavenly bodies ("foreign gods" though they are) is what the author of the Platonic *Epinomis* recommends, according to Festugière 1972, 129–137. The text is remarkable in containing an explicit proposal to "introduce new gods." The author therefore stresses that existing cults should not be tampered with (καινοτομεῖν, 985c–d) and that the barbarian worship will be much improved by the cultured and experienced Greeks, aided by the Delphic oracle (987d–988a).

65. Cf. Sourvinou-Inwood 1988, 270–273.

66. Contrast Garland 1992, 115, 151; on Themistocles see Parker 1996, ch. 9.

67. Unless indeed the Zea foundation (of which we know nothing) is prior: on all this see Parker 1996, 175–185.

68. *IG* XI.4.1299 (= M. Totti, *Ausgewählte Texte der Isis- und Sarapis-Religion* [Hildesheim 1985], no. 11; an extract in *SIG*³ 663, commentary in Engelmann 1975.) The legal ground for the charge is uncertain: "introducing new gods"? or failure to seek the special permission required by a non-citizen to own land? (see Vial 1984, 155en156). Pouilloux 1954, no. 24 (first cent. B.C.) has been compared: an Antiochene has appealed (successfully) to the *boule* against the attempts of "certain persons" (Rhamnusians?) to debar him from celebrating rites of Agdistis.

69. Permission to own land: cf. Parker 1996, 170, 243, 337–338; and for a Delian instance, *Inscriptions de Délos: Période de l'Amphictyonic attico-délienne, actes administratifs* (nos. 89-104-33), ed. J. Coupry (Paris, 1972). 1519. 11–16. Wilamowitz (1881, 273, 177) points out that the Athenians had no choice but to allow foreigners to worship their own gods if they allowed them to reside at all.

70. *Laws* 909d–910d; cf. Festugière 1972, 136.

71. Cf. Parker 1996, ch. 9 n. 34.

Does Piety Pay?

Socrates and Plato on Prayer and Sacrifice

MARK McPHERRAN

Plato's *Apology* offers a perennial challenge to its readers, prodding them to ask inter alia whether its Socrates is really guilty of the formal charge of impiety by failing to "recognize" the gods of Athens (*Ap.* 24b8-c1).[1] If one turns to Xenophon for assistance in answering this question, however, the response will be an unequivocal "not guilty," for as his portrait has it: "[Socrates] never said or did anything impious (*asebes*), and his speech and actions in respect of the gods were those of a truly religious (*eusebestatos*) man" (*Mem.* 1.1.20). Naturally, such straightforward ripostes have been found utterly unconvincing by a score of modern critics who, dismissing Xenophon's categorical affirmations of Socratic piety as instances of tell-tale overkill,[2] detect in the pages of Plato's early dialogues an utterly revolutionary, completely heterodox Socrates.[3] This Socrates conceives of the gods as being so perfectly just that—unlike the gods of the civic cult—they cannot be magically "bribed" or persuaded with prayers and sacrifices to procure any "good which without that gift their own will for good would not have prompted them to do."[4] As a result, religious ritual is reduced to the status of idle play. Socratic piety replaces such vain external machinations with the inner demand that we serve the gods though the improvement of our souls—something the gods allegedly cannot do on their own.[5] Time spent on prayer and sacrifice, on this account, is simply time wasted, time stolen from the more demanding, truly pious task of elenctic self-examination. It is no wonder, then, that this Socrates should now find himself in a situation not unlike that of a "free-thinking radical Christian preacher . . . defending the bona fides of his gospel before a church-court packed with Bible-belt fundamentalists."[6]

In this essay I shall show that—despite its attractions—this representation of Socrates' relation to the traditional cult is too simplistic and conflicts with too much of our textual evidence to be adopted. Among other things, any right-thinking Athenian (Socrates included) would have seen such a complete denial of the efficacy of prayer and sacrifice as clearly atheistic,[7] thus rendering Socrates' denial of guilt of the formal charge of non-recognition (and later, atheism [*Ap.* 26b–28a]) an outright lie. In addition, such an account also appears to cast the mature Plato as a retrograde

Mark McPherran, "Does Piety Pay? Socrates and Plato on Prayer and Sacrifice." In Nicholas D. Smith and Paul Woodruff, eds., *Reason and Religion* in *Socratic Philosophy* (New York:) Oxford University Press, 2000, pp. 89–114.

thinker on the topic of religious ritual, since he clearly does foresee a role for sacrifices, prayers, festivals and so on in the cities of the *Republic* (e.g., 415e) and, especially, the *Laws* (e.g., 738b-c, 828b). Indeed, in this latter, Cretan City, there will be an official sacrifice every single day of the year (828b; cf. 807a). In what follows, then, I will argue for a more complex reading of the evidence; one that not only preserves the radical revisioning of traditional attitudes Socrates and Plato intended, but also secures a genuine role for the central, constitutive practices of ancient Greek religion. I will also offer a concluding sketch of how Plato's view developed ingeniously upon Socrates' account in response to the non-Socratic tenets of his moral psychology and mystical theology.

1. SOCRATES AND THE CHARGE OF NON-RECOGNITION

Let us recall the first formal charge against Socrates: "The gods the state recognizes, [Socrates] does not recognize (*hous men hê polis nomizei theous ou nomizôn*)" (*Ap.* 24b9-c1). The meaning of this phrase is somewhat unclear.[8] Is Socrates being charged with neglecting or violating the religious practices of the Athenian *polis* (for example, not "recognizing" gods like Athena Polias by failing to pay appropriate cult to them) or is he charged with not believing in the existence of the civic gods (that is, not "recognizing" their existence intellectually)?[9] If we assume (as we should) that the best gloss on *nomizein* is one that captures its essential link to *nomos*, then *nomizein* bears the broad meaning "to accept" (or "treat," "practice") as is customary.[10] On this reading, the expression *theous nomizein* should be understood to mean "to accept the gods in the customary way," indicating that both traditional religious behavior *and* the set of attitudes that are taken to underlie such behavior are implied. Of course, since Plato has Socrates focus his defense on the nature of his *beliefs* and the views he purportedly *teaches* (never having him address the issue of cult-observance), the primary aspect of *theous nomizein* at issue here would seem to be its attitudinal, intellectual component (whose central concern is whether one believes that the Athenian gods in question *exist*; cf. *Ap.* 26b8-d5, 29a1-4, 35d2-5).[11] Nevertheless, given the clear orthopractic dimension of *theous nomizein*—as well as the jurors' probable expectation that charges of impiety would be countered with testimony of correct religious practice[12]—whether Socrates failed to observe proper cult practice will have been an issue for *some* jurors. As the trial progressed, these jurors and others will also have been caused such concerns by Socrates' apparent failure to cite his cult observances as a defense, and some might have additionally recalled that the Socrates of Aristophanes' *Clouds* rejects the practices of the ancestral cult (Ar. *Nub.* 425-426), sacrificing *solely* to illegitimate deities (namely, "the Clouds" [365]). What, then, can we say about Socrates' actual conformance to traditional religious practices?

Xenophon, as we saw, provides a zealous defense of Socrates on this topic, portraying him as "the most visible of men" in cult service to the gods (*Mem.* 1.2.64; cf. 1.1.2, 1.1.9, 1.1.18–20, 1.3.1–3) and having him testify that he often sacrificed at the public altars (Xen. *Ap.* 10–12; cf. *Mem.* 1.1.1–2, 4.8.11). Although some have seen this defensive effort as indicating that there was serious pre-trial concern as to whether Socrates *was* conventionally observant,[13] the silence of the *Apology* on the topic of Socratic sacrifice and the difficulty of believing that someone so publicly pious in his behavior could be indicted on a charge of non-recognition suggests that Xenophon may give this testimony prominence due to an intensely apologetic (and conventionalist) agenda. Nonetheless, again, it would be appropriate to combat charges of impiety with testimony of cult observance—that would be *prima facie* evidence that the accused was neither an atheist nor a non-conforming innovator—and since it receives such an emphasis in Xenophon there is arguably something to it: it seems unlikely that Xenophon would offer as a defense a portrait of Socrates that simply no Athenian could take seriously.

There is, additionally, some corroborating Platonic evidence on this point. For example, Socrates' famous request for the sacrifice of a cock to Asclepius at *Phaedo* 118a testifies to an orthopractic bent, and at 61b we also find him offering a hymn to a god (probably Apollo; note also the libation and hymn at *Symp.* 176a; cf. 220d). Moreover, Plato is willing to put twelve prayers into the mouth of his Socrates.[14] Note, finally, the stage-setting of the start of the *Republic* (327a), where Socrates has traveled down to the Piraeus in order to pray to the goddess Bendis and observe her festival.[15] This much testimony is, of course, not entirely compelling.[16] However, we may infer from the modest lifestyle Plato attributes to Socrates, as well as Xenophon's explicit reports, that Socrates' sacrifices were humble (*Mem.* 1.3.3). If so, that—together with Plato's focus on Socrates' thought and dialectical encounters (not his solitary activities)—gives us an explanation why Plato did not dwell on the matter.[17] In any case, *Euthydemus* 302c–303a (cf. *Ap.* 35d), *Menexenus* 243e–244b, *Phaedrus* 229e, and, again, the numerous references in Xenophon's *Memorabilia* (1.1.2, 1.1.19, 1.3.64, 4.3.16–17, 4.6.4–6; cf. Xen. *Ap.* 11–12) all testify to some extent to Socrates' orthopraxy.[18] Although Xenophon's reports may, again, exaggerate the extent of his religious conformity out of apologetic fervor, Xenophon nonetheless seems to authenticate a degree of traditional practice to which Plato independently testifies. Thus, it appears that the civic sacrifices, religious festivals, and ancestral and household gods that were such a large and prominent part of everyday Athenian life would probably have been part of Socrates' life as well.[19]

Thus far, then, our results suggest that Socrates saw his philosophical convictions to be somehow compatible with traditional religious observance. Nevertheless, whether and how that might be so requires serious rethinking in view of the conceptual case that has been made for Socrates' actual rejection of the utility of traditional prayer and sacrifice.

2. POPULAR RELIGION AND THE SOCRATIC REFORMATION

It is helpful to begin our foray into this topic with some familiar truisms. Greek religion did not comprise a unified, organized system of beliefs and rituals distinguished from the social, political, and commercial aspects of life we would now ordinarily term "secular." Rather, it was a complex tangle of practices and attitudes seamlessly integrated into everyday life, especially public communal life. Greek religion also did not take any particular set of texts as foundational (not even Hesiod's *Theogony* had anything like the status of a Bible) and there was no organized church and clergy to interpret or regulate them.[20] Rather, a city or individual would be deemed pious (*eusebês*—that is, in accord with the norms governing the relations of humans and gods) not primarily by virtue of conforming to a set of beliefs or dogmas, but through the correct observation of the ancestral religious practices (*ta patria*). The most fundamental and indispensable of these practices was the sacrifice, typically accompanied by prayer (*euchê*).[21] Such sacrifices ranged from an individual's libation of wine at the start of a meal—pouring a small amount on an altar or the ground while invoking the protection of a deity in prayer—to the great sacrifices of cattle held during civic religious festivals, culminating in a communal banquet that renewed each citizen's ties with the city-protecting deities (a portion of meat being set aside as a burnt offering for the gods as part of the shared meal; see, e.g., *Od.* 3.417–472).[22] Besides such examples of what we might think of as "white magic," however, we must also set those other rituals which aimed to harm, not help, others—in particular, curses (*arai/katarai*) and other such prayer-imprecations (see, e.g., Pind. *Ol.* 1.75 ff.; *Il.* 3.299–301, 9.456; *Od.* 2.134 ff.; *Rep.* 394a; *Crit.* 119e; *Laws* 854b, 876e, 930e–932a, 949b).[23]

Traditional religious practice, then, often centered on prayers to a divinity, and these almost always involved a request for a *particular* (not general) and materially manifested good (for example, that one's crops flourish or be cured of blight, or that one's enemies be harmed).[24] However, like any superior, it was thought useful to put such supernatural assistants in one's debt first in order to "enlist" them in one's cause (or to reward them subsequent to their services). Thus, it was typical to accompany a prayer of request with an offering of some sort designed to establish a claim on the "helper": a farmer should offer wine to the god before he calls on his or her aid, and having sacrificed richly he could then remind the god that something was now owed to him in return.[25] As Euthyphro confesses to Socrates (*Euth.* 14c–15a), this *do ut des*—"I give so that you will give"—conception of reciprocity between gods and humans is rather like an art of commerce (*emporikê;* 14e8).[26]

These practices appear to rest on the traditional and fundamental assumption that justice consists in reciprocation, in repayment in kind (that is, the *lex talionis* conception of justice): a gift for a gift, a loss for a loss, an evil for an evil[27] (as, for example, when Zeus asks from Hera one of her favorite cities in return for abandoning Troy [*Il.* 4.40–43]; cf. Soph. *Ajax* 79). Tied to this idea as its most prominent corollary is the moral imperative "Help your friends and harm your enemies."[28] With this second, negative component, we are encountering not the notion that those who do evil should be *punished* (for example, as part of a program of moral therapy), but rather the idea that it is fitting to exact a revenge against personal enemies when motivated by hate and by a desire to relieve one's feelings of resentment (e.g., *Il.* 21.423; Thuc. 7.68.1 ff., Arist. *Rhet.* 1370b30). Although this is a norm of *justice* in some sense—since without its notion of repayment *in kind* there would be no moral constraints at all on the methods and amounts of harm one might visit upon a hated enemy (cf. Eur. *Ion* 1046–47; Demos. 23.69)—it could nonetheless be used to justify helping a friend to win an unjust law suit (e.g., Isae. 1.7; Hyp. 1.10) or to sanction savage civic actions—for example, the proposed execution of all the males of Mytilene, selling their wives and children into slavery (Thuc. 3.40.7; cf. 3.38.1).[29]

In respect of this venerable principle, Socrates must be counted a moral revolutionary (and a self-conscious one: *Cri.* 49b–d).[30] For, as he sees it, since we should never do injustice, we should never do evil, and from that it follows that we should never do an evil in return for an evil, even one done to us (*Cri.* 48b–49d, 54c; cf. *Rep.* 335a–d).[31] An average Athenian would no doubt have been astonished when confronted by this innovation: to forgo the pleasures of fully harming one's enemy (including, perhaps, an infliction of physical harm on his innocent relatives) in favor of the intellectual pleasures of doing the just, non-harmful thing would have seemed an unlikely, inverted way of looking at things.[32] Thus, as we consider Socrates' view of the gods and the nature of appropriate prayer below, it will be important to remember that for Socrates, no one should request—and no just god can assist—the return of one evil for another.

This point is only useful, of course, if the gods are thought to be just, and whether this was so for an average Athenian is difficult to gage. We can begin to approach this complex issue by recognizing that on the traditional picture of things, there is a radical split between the realm of humanity and that of the gods. These latter, mysterious beings vastly exceed us in knowledge and power, and in ways and for reasons we cannot hope to fathom they might cause any manner of disaster: droughts, financial ruin, epidemics, military defeats, or shipwreck (e.g., Hes. *Op* 242 ff.; *Il.* 1.1–5, 9.456). Indeed, the gods were often credited by the poets with behavior that would be deemed capricious and immoral in ordinary humans—for example, the adulteries of Zeus, the thefts and deceits of Hermes, the jealousy of Hera, and other seemingly malicious and vengeful fits. In this picture, the gods are to be conceived analogically by comparison to the chief powers of this world, kings and their nobles.[33] Like an earthly ruler, Zeus should be credited with an overall plan of how to accomplish his self-centered goals, and given his status as the divine strongman, this would be a plan to which, in the end, he could force his divine inferiors to submit.[34] Chief among such interests was Zeus's desire to secure from all lesser beings that foremost of all Homeric goods, honor. Humanity—conceived of as a kind of indentured peasant class, and so reliant on the judicial functions of their rulers—would then naturally speak of Zeus's justice and would appeal to it against the transgressions of both lesser deities and other humans (with cult then an extension of the Homeric practice of gift-giving, aimed at fostering harmonious relations between unequals).[35] However, in this same picture Zeus and the other divinities do not govern the universe in the interests of humans, but in their own, and so "the justice of Zeus" is not always to be understood by us mortals and cannot be counted on to coincide with our own moral presuppositions and assessments.[36] The gods, for example, might well respond to a prima facie unjust curse-imprecation or, while responding to a just one, pay back a wrongdoer with a misfortune far in excess of what the *lex talionis* would call for (for example, wiping out an entire person's family line for one member's having defaced a tomb [*IG* 3.1423.7–13]; cf. Eur. *Pho.* 66 ff.).[37]

This picture is clearly problematic. On the one hand, to think of the gods in this fashion is to portray their actions as willful *incursions* into the separate moral order of *this* world, and when subjected to the categories applicable to human superiors, these acts will often have appeared haphazard and *unjust*.[38] As such, these actions could even be explained as resulting from a *lack* of power and knowledge.[39] On the other hand, it was part of the popular conception of the gods that—just as with any set of superiors who have an interest in maintaining the flow of goods from their chattel—these beings would put up with only just so much misbehavior. Oaths, for example, were essential to the orderly maintenance of life's major transactions (e.g., marriages and treaties), transactions without which there would be no *polis* and thus no gift and honor-giving *polis*-cult. Hence, one common epithet applied to Zeus was "Zeus of Oaths": Zeus in his oath-overseeing role (a being who ensures that oathbreakers or their offspring suffer severe punishment).[40] Existing alongside the conception of divine unpredictability, aloofness, and "immorality," then, there was a conviction that behind the apparently willful and seemingly chaotic actions of the gods there existed a knowledgeable Zeus, a deity whose interferences in human affairs are not capricious violations of our moral order, but rather contributions to a larger, coherent plan of events that constitute one overarching scheme of justice (conceived of in a retributory fashion).[41]

Socrates, it seems, emphasized this latter view, assuming that the traditional outlook of two realms was mistaken insofar as it presupposed two distinct moral codes (one for humans, one for gods), and insofar as it sanctioned not just the return of good for good, but also the return of evil for evil.[42] Moreover, he takes it as a given that the gods are (by definition?) perfectly wise, and thus far wiser than human beings (*Ap.* 23a5-b4; *Mem.* 1.1.19; cf. *Hip. Ma.* 289b). But because there is but one moral domain, wisdom entails the possession of virtue, in a god as much as a person (and implies the unity of the virtues; see, e.g., *Prt.* 361b, 329e ff.). Hence, the gods are supremely virtuous (*Mem.* 4.4.25). But since perfectly virtuous persons—knowing the good as they would—could only do good and can never cause evil to anyone, and since there is but one moral domain, the gods also cannot be at odds with each other, and must be the causes of only good and never evil (*Euth.* 15a1-2; *Rep.* 379b–c; cf. *Rep.* 379c2-7).[43] We need, then, to ask whether belief in the existence of gods such as these can be thought compatible with both the intellectual and the behavioral recognition of the gods of the Athenian state.

In order to be in agreement with the everyday "belief-demands" of Athenian *polis*-religion, it is clear that one must believe (1) that there exist gods denoted by the names of those gods possessing publicly funded cults (e.g., Athena Polias), (2) that these gods take notice of the affairs of humans (e.g., by observing our oath-breaking, prayers, and sacrifices), and (3) that the gods will respond to some of our actions (e.g., by visiting disaster on oath-breakers), especially our prayers and sacrificial offerings (that is, they are gods with a *do ut des* cult).[44] How, then, does Socrates stand in respect of these three commitments?

It seems evident that Socrates satisfied condition (1), believing that the civic gods of Athens *exist*. For example, *Apology* 26b–c—"before these very gods of whom we now speak" (a remark made prior to any clarification of the charge of not recognizing the gods of the state [26c–d])—and his many positive references to "the god" who has stationed and ordered him to philosophize to the Athenians (a fairly unambiguous reference to Delphic Apollo, disobedience to whom *would* convict him of religious nonconformity [29a]) provide good prima facie evidence that Socrates had an intellectual commitment to the existence of the gods of Athens. In fact, the texts of Plato and Xenophon are filled with many such direct and undisguised religious references. To remove them from our texts would be to gut them, and there is no reasonable interpretive principle that would allow us to read them all as mere verbal pandering or unannounced allegory. In addition, Socrates would have taken several civic oaths during his life, all of which called the gods of the state as witnesses: the ephebic oath (to maintain the fatherland, to honor the ancestral sanctuaries, et cetera), those taken as a juror, and those taken as a member of the Boulē (*Mem.* 1.1.18) and as a litigant at the *anakrisis* of his own trial.[45] This observation, together with the probability that Socrates conceives of his *daimonion* as the voice of Delphic Apollo, testify additionally to a Socratic belief in the existence of the civic gods.[46] The items above also give good support to his holding the view that (2) the gods pay attention to human conduct.

It is with the final core belief—(3) the relationship of reciprocity—that we encounter significant difficulties. Besides the notion that the gods provide moral reciprocity by visiting retribution on those who violate various norms of behavior, this relationship was best exemplified in the popular imagination by the phenomenon of petitionary prayer and sacrifice, followed by a return: a sacrifice of goods accompanied by the hope or expectation of having thereby maintained or obtained divine favor.[47] But this latter idea encounters the problems outlined earlier: while it seems clear that Socrates' perfectly just gods are *compatible* with gods who serve as moral enforcers,[48] it is problematic as to whether they can also be squared with the quarreling and seemingly capricious gods of the popular religion, gods who can be influenced to "help friends and harm enemies" by means of imprecations and material sacrifice.

3. SOCRATES AND RECIPROCITY

First, it seems unlikely that Socrates' disbelief in divine enmity and injustice per se would put him at risk of disbelief in the civic gods. Although *Euthyphro* 6b–c suggests that Socrates rejected the substance of the scenes depicted on the festival robe offered to Athena Polias (cf. *Rep.* 378b–380c, 381e–382e), this "Battle of the Olympians and Titans" does not seem to have been a required article of civic belief, but simply one tale of the poets with which anyone might disagree with relative safety.[49] Pindar, for example, was able to speak plainly of "Homer's lies," (*Nem.* 7.23) without incurring any legal sanctions, and we have no evidence of there having been prosecutions for disbelieving the stories found in Homer or Hesiod—for example, the adultery of Ares and Aphrodite (*Od.* 8) and Zeus' deception of Metis (*Thg.* 872–906).[50] Thanks to their exposure to the works of Hesiod, Sophocles, and Aeschylus, most Athenians were acquainted with affirmations of the gods' justice, and we hear of no one demurring at these expressions.[51] It also would have been no great shock to an Athenian to hear skepticism regarding the poets' tales of divine immorality. They had been exposed to such doubts and denials for years by thinkers such as Hecataeus, Solon, Pindar, Xenophanes, Euripides, and Heraclitus.[52] It is, rather, with his rejection of the negative side of the *lex talionis* (that is, the "return of an evil for an evil") and some of the propitiatory *do ut des* aspects of cult that Socrates' doctrine of divine justice seems to present a threat to the civic gods and cult of Athens.

Gregory Vlastos, as we saw in the introduction (cf. nn. 4, 5, 6), provides the extreme version of this threat. He portrays Socrates' conceptions of piety, justice, and the gods as demanding *only* that we serve the gods though the improvement of our souls, gods who are by their very nature "relentlessly beneficent" (irrespective of our prayers and sacrifices) since they are perfectly good and completely cognizant of our needs.[53] On this account, Socrates thoroughly undermined the linchpin of Greek popular religion, namely, the idea that the gods can be "bribed" with a gift of sacrifice to help oneself or one's friends to procure goods that the gods might otherwise have neglected to provide.[54] For these same reasons, Socrates' gods also cannot be persuaded to harm one's enemies: the gods do what they must do in response only to what virtue commands, paying no heed to sacrificial curses or imprecations (whether Socratically just or not).

Here, then, it may seem that there is simply no room for prayer and sacri-fice in the life of the Socratic philosopher: such activities are incapable of influencing the gods to perform any action, and instead steal precious time away from the life of elenctic self-examination. Thus, it might even appear that the true philosopher will have to oppose religious ritual on eudai-monistic grounds.

To see at last if this account accurately captures Socrates' relation to traditional religious practice, we need to discover: (1) under what condi-tions the traditional presupposition of divine reciprocity included the notion that the gods can be influenced to do our wills for both good and ill; (2) whether Socrates' gods can respond in a similar fashion to prayer and sacrifice; and (3) whether there might be Socratic motivations for engaging in prayer and sacrifice that are independent of a concern for divine reciprocity.

As is typical in Greek religion, the evidence pertinent to item (1) appears contradictory, suggesting that the Greeks had conflicting attitudes concerning the susceptibility of the gods to petitionary prayer and sacri-fice.[55] Although the idea that gods with an established cult can be counted on to respond *eventually* to material, sacrificial requests is basic and virtu-ally unquestioned,[56] whether they can be persuaded contrary to the justice of the *talio* is unclear. However, we do find at *Iliad* 9.497–501, for example, Phoenix assuring Achilles that the gods' wrath *can* be diverted by means of sacrifice. Likewise, Euripides' Medea is confident that she can exact "just repayment with God's help" (*Medea* 803) against Jason (and even though that means his just "repayment" for infidelity is three innocent lives taken "impiously" [796]). Next, at *Republic* 364b–c we hear that there were wandering priests and soothsayers who promised to expiate past wrongdoing or to harm enemies—justly or not—by means of sacrifice; while the following section (364e–366b; cf. 419a) indicates that there are some who even believe those poets who claim that the gods can be "swerved" from punishing wrongdoers by getting a "cut of the take" (that is, sacrifices purchased through unjustly-acquired gains). Along the same lines, there is the anonymous Athenian's mention at *Laws* 885b–e of those many people who require proof that the gods are "too good to be diverted from the path of justice" by gifts (cf. 888a–d, 908e–909d), which strongly suggests that such requests were common.[57] At *Laws* 948b–948e, he even goes so far as to claim that the creed of the *majority* is that for the cost of a small sacrifice the gods "will lend their help in vast frauds and deliver the sinner from all sorts of heavy penalties" (948c4–7). There is, finally, an instance of retributive civic religion to be found in the opening ceremonies of the Boule. There, before each meeting, a herald would recite a prayer that included a curse on those who plotted evil against Athens, requesting that such enemies meet a miserable end.[58] These examples all suggest that it was common to think that one's sacrificial requests for good things— even virulent curses on others—were likely to be fulfilled, perhaps even irrespective of their actual justice.[59]

Against all this, however, we need to recognize that within the tradition there existed another strand that emphasized the idea that the size and performance-details of a sacrifice are of use only in displaying and advancing one's social status and are thoroughly *irrelevant* to the gods.[60] We hear, for example, of a visitor to Delphi who, after offering a lavish sacrifice, asked the Pythia who of all men most pleased the gods with sacrificial honors (assuming that *he* would be named). Naturally, the priestess named another, much more obscure man who, although his sacrifices were modest, never neglected the proper rites (Porphyry *Abst.* 2.16). In addition, it is important to note that sacrificial activity was often not so much aimed at obtaining specific goods or evils as at maintaining an ordered relationship with the gods and ensuring their general good will, a will that (it was generally agreed) could not be *reliably* influenced by such activity.[61]

So then we find, existing parallel with the more material and mercantile (and perhaps justice-indifferent) dimensions of Greek religion, another aspect that emphasized the petitioner's inner motivation, his or her intention to perform the rites of request or thanks as best they can (for example, in a timely, scrupulous manner). Here a god's reciprocity would be understood to be a response not to the size or quality of the material offering but to the petitioner's desire to honor the god, and (thus) his or her inner propriety and justice.[62] In view of the intensity of our human (and certainly Athenian) inclination to self-assertion, however, this non-mercantile attitude was in all likelihood an intermittent, minority phenomenon. Our initial question then becomes whether and to what extent Socrates' views support or undermine the notion of reciprocity in both mercantile and non-mercantile senses and whether Socrates' gods can be *counted on* to respond in at least some situations to prayer and sacrifice (and how that could be so).

The first part of this question is not too difficult to answer. In view of his commitment to the idea that the only real (or at least the most central) good is virtue (and that an object's goodness hinges on its wise, virtuous use),[63] Socrates must reject the *purely* mercantile tendencies of popular religious practice—namely, those resting on the incorrect assumptions that sacrificial items are themselves god-valued and that our requests for particular material gains and physical protection will be given significant weight by the gods. Rather, Socrates' gods cannot care for any material sacrifice per se, and whether or not any particular request will be granted depends on whether the gods' doing so will further the overall good. Confirmation of this analysis is provided by Xenophon, who attributes to Socrates the argument that if the gods cared about the size or frequency of a sacrifice, then they would have to be more pleased by the gifts of the wicked than by those of the virtuous (which, he assumes, is absurd) (*Mem.* 1.3.3).[64] Naturally they also will not respond to unjust requests, and curse-imprecations in particular would seem most ineffective on his account.[65]

I want to argue, however, that Socrates did manage to retain and recast the internal, non-mercantile dimension of the tradition, emphasizing the petitioner's intentionality and piety over his or her particular material gift-offerings and requests.[66] On this reading, Socrates admits reciprocity between gods and humans, sanctioning our requesting certain things of the gods and demanding that we *honor* them (internally and in our behavior), without endorsing any mercantile, *do ut des* cult. He also thinks that a divine response to such honors is likely (in certain cases), while not making it a *strict requirement* of piety that the honoring involve a material sacrifice. Our texts also make it apparent that he revolutionized the traditional notions of piety and "honoring," recasting them in terms that emphasize the priority of acting justly and engaging in philosophical "soul therapy" (as kinds of pious "honoring") over petitionary prayer and material sacrifice.[67] Socrates is thus, *contra* Vlastos, a wholesale threat not to the actual practice of cult, but to the narrow, self-aggrandizing *motivations* of many of its practitioners: those who give priority to *material* sacrifice as they seek to gain external goods, thereby neglecting the form of "belief-sacrifice" ("self-examination") mandated by Apollo ("caring more for bodies and money than for the improvement of the soul": *Ap.* 30a–b; cf. *Phdr.* 279b–c). For certain jurors then—jurors who could not embrace a reflective life informed by motivations beyond their usual ones—Socrates could have been recognized as a genuine threat to cult *as they conceived of it*. Let me justify and elaborate on these claims.

According to Socrates, from perfectly good gods we, of course, have nothing to fear (*Mem.* 4.3.5–7), and they will spontaneously provide us with many and important goods at the right moment, irrespective of whether we deserve them or have actively requested them (*Ap.* 41c8-d2; *Euth.* 15b1–2; *Mem.* 1.1.19, 1.4.5–18, 4.3.3–17; Xen. *Ap.* 5–7; cf. *Alc.* 2 149e3–150b3). Moreover, since the gods wish to promote justice, and since for Socrates, piety is the part of justice that requires us to serve the gods (assisting them to produce good in the universe),[68] they may aid us in doing so irrespective of our requests (for example, by sending us a helpful divine "sign"). Such assistance would come *in response to* the justice and piety of our actions or intentions, and not to the size or kind of any material offering that accompanied any request we might have made (*Mem.* 1.3.3; 2.1.28).[69] The gods, of course, *need* nothing from us (e.g., *Euth.* 13c; *Mem.* 1.6.10), and since they cannot be in conflict with one another *or* with true justice, they cannot be magically influenced to serve as vengeful *lex talionis* helpers against the forces that oppose our wills, especially when our plans involve the commission of Socratic injustices (cf. *Rep.* 364a–c; *Laws* 905e).[70] Nevertheless, there is a place in this picture for a Socratic conception of effective petitionary and thanking prayer, and a modified, positive *do ut des* notion of human-god reciprocity.

Although it would seem that Socrates could not consider prayers or sacrifices alone to be *essentially* connected to the virtue of piety (since, independent of the right intention, such actions in themselves do not necessarily serve the ends of the gods), their performance is nonetheless compatible with the demands of piety, especially if they are accompanied by a correct god-honoring intention. After all, since Socrates embraces the positive side of the *talio*—the return of one good for another[71]—we should (as the tradition holds) reciprocate as best we can the gods' gifts by *honoring* the gods in fitting ways through performing acts with the inner intention to so honor them (acts which are also virtuous: *Mem.* 1.4.10, 18; 4.3.17).[72] While, again, serving the gods via philosophical self-examination has pride of place in providing such honors, there is no reason why such actions cannot include thanks-offering prayers and material sacrifices.[73] In addition, such actions serve both ourselves and the gods: they help to induce our souls (and those of others who are encouraged to imitate us) to follow the path of justice (thus producing god-desired good in the universe and eudaimonia for ourselves) by habituating us to return good for good (and not evil for evil). Of course, no such action can be expected to establish a claim on any deity that would give us a right to expect any *specific* or immediate return.

Nevertheless, Socrates does appear to think that the gods aid those who do what is virtuous. Xenophon, for example, represents Socrates as accepting the view that he receives goods from the god(s) (namely, portents such as his *daimonion*) *because,* apparently, of the piety of his mission to the Athenians.[74] Hence, since petitionary prayers and sacrifices that offer honor to the gods *are* virtuous by attempting to offer good for good, Socrates will expect that good things will be returned to us for such efforts in some fashion (though not necessarily in the fashion we would choose for ourselves: *Mem.* 1.3.2, 2.1.28).[75] Socrates, thus, must also think that the gods will provide some goods to us if and only if we actively request (in the right fashion) that they provide them. Just as a master-craftsman offers guidance, nourishment, and tools to his assistants when they ask, so— Socrates would have thought—the gods may be expected to aid us in a similar way.[76] By waiting for our proper god-honoring requests for help in doing virtuous actions before granting them, the gods would thus help to train our souls to be virtuous (by rewarding our "inner work"). Moreover, since such assistance would naturally be withheld from us until we are in a position to put that gift (e.g., divine advice) to a virtuous use, the gods must await our active and properly pious requests before giving such assistance. Such requests in the pursuit of virtue, it is arguable, spring only from a condition of the soul that is correlated with being in a position of sufficient wisdom to put that help to the right, good-producing use.[77]

In addition to such justifications for performing prayer and sacrifice connected to the notion of reciprocity, we finally need to remember that Socrates also appears to have had a highly developed and conservative sense of obligation to both the written and the unwritten *nomoi* of Athens. Thus, we can expect him to enjoin and practice those rituals required or expected by such *nomoi* for that reason alone (*Mem.* 1.3.1, 4.3.13, 4.3.16, 4.4.25; cf. *Cri.* 48d–54d).[78] These actions also help to foster and maintain a general belief in the existence of good and helpful gods and an awareness of our inferior status in respect of wisdom and power, attitudes that

Socrates is clearly interested in promoting (see, e.g., *Mem.* 1.4.1–19, 4.3.1–17; *Ap.* 21d–23c).[79] Again, however, although for Socrates the gods are always pleased in some sense by the honor such sincerely motivated practices display toward them, they—quite unlike the gods entertained by some Athenians—are not responsive to either the material basis of the sacrifice (e.g., its *size*) or the specifics of the request (since any particular item requested might not be conducive to one's real good: *Mem.* 1.3.2) or to Socratically unjust petitions (cf. Ar. *Peace* 363–425).

We need also to remember again that Socrates seems to have reinterpreted the concept of cult in such a way that it would include the practice of elenctic, self-examining philosophy; and such "cult" is a kind of "ritual purification" of the soul which is not only compatible with Socratic piety, but positively demanded by it.[80] For those jurors disposed to hear things his way, Socrates gives eloquent and emphatic testimony that he is—just as Xenophon and Plato later portrayed him—the most conspicuous and constant acolyte of the gods to be found in Athens. He may even claim to be among the most generous of "sacrificers," having foregone the external goods of leisure, money, and family life for the sake of his pious service to the god (*Ap.* 23b–c, 31b–c), a service that, with his trial and conviction, includes the sacrifice of his very life.

4. THE THREAT OF SOCRATES

We can conclude, then, that with the perfectly wise and just deities of Socrates we have few specific or *materially rewarding* imprecations to make: beyond the sincere, general prayer that one be aided in pursuing virtue, there are few requests or sacrifices to which all-wise deities can be *counted on* to respond (since in our ignorance *we* can never know if any specific request would be virtue-aiding and since the gods have no need of material things).[82] Surely *this* implication of Socrates' moral theory cuts straight at the root of some of the popular traditional motivations underlying many cult practices.[83] Socrates' position applies not only to the civic gods and the sacrifices of the major religious festivals but also to the lesser deities of everyday cult, those beings regarded by most Athenians as more intimately involved in their own lives and more directly helpful than the "High Gods" of the city. But if Socrates rejected the efficacy of particular and/or improperly motivated material sacrifice requests, then he was a quite threatening figure—whether he was recognized as such by any of his jurors. After all, to many Athenians the assistance of a Heracles would have meant, above all, help against the unseen, non-human (and so less easily dealt with) forces bearing down on one, and for most of them this meant help against oppressive *other deities*. By taking away the enmity of the gods, then, the need for and the efficacy of *this* Heracles is also removed. But again, even more worrisome still to some pious sensibilities, there is no point and no hope in invoking a Heracles bound by the chains of Socratic justice against life's *particular* vicissitudes, especially if one requests a Socratically unjust response (e.g., the harm of enemies). After all, any seeming disaster one might try to avert may in fact be a disguised, virtue-producing challenge in Socrates' picture of things.[84]

Given all the above, it seems clear that those jurors able to recognize the implications of Socrates' views for sacrificial cult would have seen him as threatening the stability of both state and household: for when everyday particularized, materially oriented and self-interested (even retaliatory) motives are the primary ones underwriting its performance—and this seems in fact to have often been the motivation behind various public and especially private sacrifices and dedications[85]—then what Socrates offers *is* a virtual repudiation of cult.

Against this view, however, it has been argued that Socrates' account of the origin of the formal charges out of the first, "informal ones" in the *Apology* (20c4–24b2)—especially in view of his explicit commitment to truth-telling (e.g., 18a5–6, 20d5–6)—means that he is a *liar* if his Socratized gods actually threaten some of the motivations underlying the civic cult (since such a threat is never mentioned there).[86] This should not worry us unduly. Although it is true that Socrates never makes explicit his attitudes towards religious cult when he spells out the prejudices that led to his trial, we can, in the first place, understand these as covered by the generalizations he uses when he connects his alleged "investigation of the things aloft" with atheism at 18c, when he speaks of unspecified "slanders" connected with the allegations that he has "wisdom" at 23a, and when he notes the charge that he teaches about "the things aloft" at 23d. After all, Socrates' claim that the slander and envy that will convict him has convicted others in the past and will do so in the future (28a8–b2) indicates that his specification of this chief cause is quite general; that is, it is not limited to simply the specific ill will created by the "first accusations" against him, but also includes whatever elaborations and distortions those early rumors may have generated among the populace of Athens. Secondly, Socrates does refer to Aristophanes' *Clouds* as a "first accuser" (19c), recalling for the jurors that its Socrates "spouts much drivel"—drivel which we know included that character's accepting without a murmur Strepsiades' wholesale rejection of traditional sacrifice and prayer (*Nub.* 425–426). Thirdly, this objection to my thesis presupposes that Socrates' citation of his antihubristic elenchus-wielding activity as a source of prejudice cannot be inclusive of any worries over religious conformity that may have been motivating some of the hostility that began to focus on Socrates during the course of his mission. But there is no evidence for this assumption, and the text of the *Euthyphro*—replete as it is with hints that Socrates' view of piety is reformist—gives us reason for thinking that not all of Socrates' encounters with, say, the poets, were purely purgative and contained no indirect dialectical nudges towards a view at odds with the idea that the gods can be enlisted in un-Socratic, retributive causes.[87] Finally, I think it is (and probably must remain) a live issue whether and to what extent the "first accusers," the prosecutors, and the jurors (and even Socrates himself) were able to consciously apprehend the threat to traditional cult motivations latent in Socrates' thought. The fact that this threat is not explicitly mentioned in the *Apology*, however, does not constitute justification for dismissing the influence it could have had upon the minds of the various parties to the trial and, in view of the forensic limits imposed on Socrates, it cannot lead us to the conclusion that Socrates was engaged in either deceit or negligence.

Socrates, then, is not being derelict or disingenuous in failing to point out how his conceptions of the gods, justice, and the philosophical life pose a threat to some traditional motivations for participating in traditional religious practices (thereby threatening "guilt" on the charge of non-recognition under its popular interpretation).[88] Rather, Socrates expresses exactly those beliefs necessary to his defense, despite the fact that a few of them might have hinted to some of the more traditionally minded jurors his actual guilt on the non-recognition charge (under their interpretation of it)—for example, that Socrates' gods care more for philosophical argumentation than for burnt offerings, and that even their infliction of disasters upon us may be a good from the Socratic perspective. Socrates is under no obligation to convict himself of impiety as it may be construed by some of his jurors (or even by the majority), especially since he holds that he does recognize the *real* gods, the ones that Athens *should* (or really does) prefer to those that the many take to be connected to "the lies of the poets" (*Ap.* 35c7–d7).

More importantly, though, Socrates does not address concerns about how his views undermine everyday propitiatory religion because, as we have just seen, he simply does *not* undermine *all* motivation for religious ritual.[89] Besides, and regardless of what actually transpired at the trial, if Plato were to have portrayed Socrates as citing his own cult observances, he would have deceptively suggested that—contrary to his and Socrates' own conceptions of things—such traditional *actions* actually *do* constitute good evidence of a person's piety, when clearly *they do not* for Plato or Socrates. Rather, for them piety—like any other virtue—is an internal matter pertaining to the soul, and no behavioral criteria are sufficient for fixing either its definition or its instantiation in the soul of another.[90] Traditional religious practice can thus be part of the life of the Socratic philosopher—even an epiphenomenon of his or her inner piety—although it cannot serve as sufficient evidence that his soul is in a virtuous state.

It should be clear, then, that Socrates had in essence proposed important reformations of a linchpin of traditional religion: take away the conflicts of the deities and the expectations of particular *material* rewards and physical protection in cult, and you disconnect the religion of everyday life from its practical roots. To offer then those not already centered on the development of their inner, intellectual lives the substitute of the difficult, often pain-producing activity of elenctic self-examination is to offer little solace in the face of life's difficulties. Socrates, in short, raised the stakes for living a life of piety considerably by making its final measure not correct and timely religious practice, but rather, the actual state of one's philosophically purified soul.[91] He thus represented a profound challenge to a fundamental aspect of traditional Athenian life, and constituted a dangerous threat to those unprepared to understand or change.[92]

5. PLATO, PRAYER, AND SACRIFICE

If the preceding resembles what Plato learned from Socrates,[93] then it is no surprise to find that "Plato deliberately pours . . . new wine into old bottles,"[94] by proposing in the *Laws* a system of religious observances quite comparable in their external respects to those familiar to his own countrymen. One of his reasons for doing so seems vaguely Socratic: Plato understands that the weight of such traditional observances can be a useful prop to the new institutions of his imagined state. Religious festivals, for example, will continue to function as a way of bringing a city's citizens into a joyous association with one another and with what they take to be the *polis*-preserving gods. Naturally, he as well as Socrates rejects the idea that the Olympians honored by these rites are fully identical to the deceitful, vengeful, warring gods described by the poets (*Rep.* 377e–390e; *Laws* 941b, 636c–d, 672b–c). In fact, their images are but pictorial representations of a divine nature better grasped by nonsensuous thought (930e–931a). As a result, Plato, like Socrates, was able to vigorously reject the widespread idea that the gods can be magically influenced by prayer and sacrifice to expiate past wrongdoing or unjustly harm one's enemies (905d–907b).

Plato's weightier justification for the retention of cult, however, rests on his more complex, non-Socratic psychology. First, although Plato intends that there should be significant attention paid to rationally persuading the guardians and others of God's existence (885d–e, 996c–d), he knows that his citizens will initially acquire their religious views while young and malleable, and so he will make use of this fact by constructing religious devices that appeal to our non-rational elements. For Plato, charming tales, impressive festivals, seeing ones' parents at prayer, and so on are all effective ways of impressing upon the affective parts of the soul a habit of mind whose rational confirmation can only be arrived at in maturity (887d–888a). Even then, observing and participating in such forms of activity is recommended for all periods of life as delightful in itself—as simply a kind of "serious play" (803e). Thus far, however, we have seen no connection between worship, divine response, and moral development, and it may seem as though Plato has discarded Socrates' partial retention of the traditional idea of reciprocity and exchange of services.

To address these issues, the key text to consider is *Laws* 715e ff. Here Plato asks "What conduct . . . is dear to God and reflects his wishes?" The answer is:

There is but one sort, summed up in the ancient saying that "like approves of like," apart from excess (which is both its own enemy and that of due measure). . . . It is God who is pre-eminently the "measure of all things," much more truly than any man, as they say. So he who would be loved by such a being must himself become such to the utmost of his might, and so, by this argument, he that is temperate among us is loved by God, for he is like God, whereas he that is not temperate is unlike God and at variance with him. The consequence of all this is the doctrine [that] . . . if a good man sacrifices to the gods and keeps them constant company in his prayers and offerings . . . this will be the best and noblest policy he can follow; it is the conduct that fits his character as nothing else can, and it is his most effective way of achieving a happy life. But if the wicked man does it, the results are bound to be just the opposite. (716c–717a; cf. *Rep*.613a–b)

Clearly, we should also consider this account in relation to the famous passage from the *Theaetetus* (176a–177a), where we are told that evil "has no place in the divine world," which explains why

we should make all haste to escape from earth to heaven; and that means becoming as like god as possible, and that again is to become righteous with the help of wisdom. (176a8–b3)[95]

In both this and our key passage, there are simply no remnants of a *do ut des* exchange of material goods. Indeed, later on in the *Laws* (995e), Plato gives detailed prescriptions on the kinds of offerings that are appropriate, all designed to constrain the impulse to make immoderate sacrifices in hopes of a divine payoff. Moreover, the sort of emphasis placed on the notion of *homoiôsis* indicates that this idea takes precedence over those few places in the *Laws*, where direct god-to-individual rewards are projected (in this life, that is) (631b–d, 718a). What we have here instead is some sort of method of assimilation to divinity via prayer and sacrifice, coupled with the moral character of the worshipper. What link, then, does Plato postulate here between worship and imitation of God?

The feature of God that is first identified in the passage is "measure," an indication that this God should be identified with the Demiurge of the *Timaeus,* a Mind that imposes limits on the unlimited, giving order to the universe, and, in particular, its moral order (715e–716a). Thus, we should associate the operations of prayer and sacrifice as ways of becoming like God with the idea of moral ordering. Next, this ordering cannot be simply a matter of the external form of a ritual, since its effects are said to differ according to the character of the practitioner. So, then, we need to specify the relations Plato sees between correct ritual behavior, character, and the production of internal order.

To begin with, Plato characteristically associates self-control with virtue and *eudaimonia,* and maintains that it is through the correct channeling of pleasures and pains that we are first able to acquire virtuous habits

(644b, 653a–b). Such channeling involves associating pleasures with the maintenance of the internal order constitutive of virtue. For Plato, religious festivals, songs, and so forth ideally fill this role. They are potent devices—"charms" and "enchantments" he calls them—that provide virtue-training pleasures, pleasures that can be associated as stimuli with the self-control and internal harmony that are productive of virtuous behavior (653c–d, 654c–d, 659d–e, 665a–c, 887d). Such activities typically involve pleasing sights and sounds, social cooperation, and the repetition of movements springing from and reinforcing an internal attitude that desires to do what is virtuous (e.g., honor God). Next, Plato understands that such performances are to be governed by those same considerations that caused him to restrict poetry in the *Republic;* that is, they involve both the expression of one's own character and an element of imitation (655a–b, 668b). Here, it seems, we have the connection between cult and the "imitation of god."

We recall that in the *Republic*, Plato differentiates pure narration from "imitation" (*mimêsis*), characterizing the latter as dangerous because of its potential negative effects on character (e.g., 392d ff.). First, imitation of the bad will foster habituation into the ways of the bad (395c–396b), and secondly, it can thus fragment and disorganize the soul (394e–395b). However sensitive to the negative consequences of role-playing this may be, Plato is here able only to glimpse, at best, its positive possibilities (*Rep.* 394–7, 402b–d). By the time he composed the *Laws,* however, he was able at last to discern and apply these possibilities in some detail. At 655d–656b, for example, we are told that chorus members cannot escape taking on the character of what they enjoy portraying, and that what they enjoy is a sign of their character; hence, that good character may be promoted by pleasurable imitation of what is good.

We should thus conceive of Platonic cult practice as a kind of theatrical portrayal of divinity, a virtue-training imitation of God made pleasant by a harmonious employment of both external and internal factors. First, the close attention Plato pays to establishing the regularity and ceremonial features of his cults should be interpreted as a recognition that repeatedly having to meet the demands of ritualized repetition on a regular basis will foster the virtues of steadfastness and intellectual *andreia* in each practitioner. Externally one emulates God by the use of orderly, pleasant movements, involving material offerings of thanks that mimic the giving of those goods which God bestows on us. In this way, order, pleasure, and return of good for good are associated with one another. Petitioning God for internal goods rather than things of equivocal value such as wealth (801a–c, 955e), on the other hand, imitates God's own desire for the flourishing of the good. Both sorts of sacrificial action encourage in each practitioner the virtue of temperance, the central virtue mentioned in our key passage. The material sacrifices involved in cult are, in addition, literal sacrifices of good things which one might have retained for oneself, and so this mimicry has the added effect of modeling and thus, through repetition, habituating us to a key component in all the Platonic virtues, namely, self-sacrifice and the avoidance of *philotimia* and *pleonexia*. We are told, for example, that the Demiurge is good, and that there is consequently no self-serving envy or jealousy (*phthonos* in Him. As a result, He "desires that all things should be as like Himself as can be" (cf. *Phdr.* 247a, 253b–c). By training citizens to model this sort of self-sacrificing activity, then, Plato provides training in obtaining a state of individual happiness correlated with a self-sacrificing desire to shape oneself and others in a fashion that approximates to the nature of the Divinity. This ritualized struggle to establish and maintain the correct polity within the soul also has a direct and reflexive effect on the actual *polis* as well. The Athenian of the *Laws*, for instance, informs us that his Cretan city will produce citizens who harbor no envy, and who thus pursue their lives on the basis of a virtuous disposition, and not through competitive, jealous, harmful attempts to obstruct others (731a).

In the operations of Platonic cult, then, the prescribed external motions are inducements and models for developing matching internal movements that aim at a harmonious relationship between the soul's parts. These motions are to be orderly and guided by the virtues, and are thus internally imitative of the divinity's own Reason (e.g., 963a ff.). This Reason is an active causal principle which aims at what is best, governing the universe as a principle of virtue. The internal imitation of divinity occasioned by cult is thus an opportunity to play the role of Demiurge, bestowing order and beauty on the material world through one's physical motions, while simultaneously aligning one's character in the direction of virtue. As a harmonious movement of the soul, this will also attach character-reinforcing pleasures to such mimetic movements. Naturally then—and just as Plato claims—the cult activity of the unjust will be ineffective, for they will presumably experience such orderly movements not as pleasurable, but as painful, as cutting against the grain of their disorderly souls.

The inner dimension of these rites must also be understood in view of the way Platonic piety developed in contrast to Socratic piety. Socrates, on the one hand, advises the traditional and sober Apollonian virtue of "knowing that we are all worth nothing with respect to [divine] wisdom" (*Ap.* 23b; cf. 20d–e), offering no hopes of ecstatic visions of the divine and rejecting aspiration to divine status as a form of the same dangerous hubris he observes in his interlocutors. On this picture, it is then natural that Socrates would rest his picture of cult on the traditionalist notion of a reciprocity involving distant, different, superior beings. Platonic piety, on the other hand, advises us to storm the heavens with an erotically passionate, epistemic optimism, convinced of the possibility of an ascent to a vision of the Forms that is both cognitive and mystical (e.g., *Phdr.* 249b–d). So, although Socrates raised the religious stakes in Athens by making self-examination and not votive sacrifice the test of true piety, Plato went one step beyond by making the ascent of the soul into the realm of divinity the real measure of religious success (cf., e.g., *Rep.* 490a–b; *Symp.* 211e–212a). We should then, as a result, entertain the idea that the inner movements of a Platonic ritual can include—for those sufficiently talented and pre-pared—a theurgic dimension, fostering the sort of likeness to the divine that focuses more specifically on the cognitive reordering of the soul.

The preceding sketch, I hope, indicates the way in which Socrates and then Plato, building on his teacher's innovations, were able to reconceive the meaning of existing religious forms. Plato's adumbration of cult as an imitation of god, in particular, contains a revolutionary psychological grasp of one possible relation between ritual behavior and moral psychology not unlike a number of more highly developed Eastern models. Rejecting the age-old model of prayer as barter, Platonic religion is able to reinforce through repetition and role-playing the virtue-guiding sentiments and the sovereign reason they rely on, investing both with the authority of a transcendental source of political and cosmic order (in addition to the prudential considerations supporting virtue: *Laws* 732e–734d). However naive we may find Plato's attempt to harness this idea to his social engineering, we must, I think, recognize its profound psychological and religious sophistication.

NOTES

This essay developed out of work gathered in my 1996 book, *The Religion of Socrates*, presentations delivered to the Workshop on Reason and Religion in 5th Century Greece, University of Texas, Austin, September 1996, and the 1998 Arizona Colloquium on Ancient Philosophy, Tuscon, February 1998. I am very grateful to the organizers of the Workshop, Nicholas Smith and Paul Woodruff, for their invitation to participate. My thanks as well to Nicholas Smith, George Rudebusch, and Jennifer Reid for their helpful comments on previous versions of this essay.

1. Attempts to answer such questions in respect of the historical Socrates are, of course, inevitably plagued by the paucity and unreliability of the evidence. Hence, in what follows I shall treat the dialogues of Plato (primarily the *Apology*) and the works of Xenophon as constituting a mosaic of the characteristics, methods, views, and activities of a transdialogical, fictional Socrates. This approach, whether or not it manages to refer accurately to the flesh-and-blood individual teacher of Plato, still allows us to confront many of the most interesting questions that Plato's and Xenophon's work provoke—in this case, those having to do with the relation between Socrates as a literary character and the fifth-century Athenian religious attitudes of our authors (and their intended audiences).

   Whether or not we can use the testimony of Aristotle in conjunction with that of Plato's "early" dialogues and Xenophon's work to triangulate the views of the historical individual Socrates in the manner of Gregory Vlastos is a thorny matter which I cannot take up here. However, see, e.g., Vlastos 1991, chs. 2 and 3, and McPherran 1996, ch. 1.

2. Xenophon's account of Socratic piety "refutes itself," claims Vlastos, since "had the facts been as he tells them, the indictment would not have been made in the first place" (Vlastos 1971, 3). See also Vlastos 1991, 163 n. 29.

3. The most recent examples are Vlastos 1991, ch. 6, and Burnyeat in chapter 7 of this collection.
4. Vlastos 1991, 176.
5. Vlastos 1991, 173.
6. Vlastos 1989a.
7. See, e.g., Momigliano 1973.
8. See Brickhouse and Smith 1989, 30–34; Fahr 1969; Yunis 1988, 63–66.
9. See, e.g., Burnet 1924, 184; cf. Garland 1992, 14, 142–144, who makes the charge out to be "one of nonconformity in religious practice, not of unorthodoxy in religious belief," while Brickhouse and Smith (1989, 30–31) and Reeve (1989, 78), on the other hand, see the charge as focusing on the nature of Socrates' beliefs.
10. Yunis 1988, 65; Dover 1968, 203; Fahr 1969, 15–17, 107, 138–139.
11. Yunis 1988, 39, 63–66; Fahr 1969, 153–157; Brickhouse and Smith 1989, 31; Connor 1991, 50 n. 10; Reeve 1989, 78; Versnel 1990, 125; Derenne 1930, 217–223.
12. See Isoc. 15.281–282; Mikalson 1983, 92; MacDowell 1978, 197–202.
13. Burnet 1924, notes on *Euth.* 3b3 and on *Ap.* 18c3, 24c1; Allen 1970, 62; Chroust 1957, 235 n. 119.
14. Listed and discussed in Jackson 1971: *Euthd.* 275d; *Phd.* 117c; *Symp.* 220d; *Phdr.* 237a–b, 257a–b, 278b, 279b–c; *Rep.* 327a–b, 432c, 545d–e; *Phlb.* 25b, 61b–c.
15. Based on the state of the evidence, however, we are not in a position to establish a specific motive for Socrates wishing to pay cult to Bendis in particular. On Bendis and her introduction into Athens c.432 (as an exotic, Thracian Artemis), see Garland 1992, 111–114, and Versnel 1990, 111–113.
16. Scholars like Vlastos, for example, will argue that "middle-dialogue" texts such as the *Phaedo* and *Symposium* are useless in determining the religious attitudes of the more historically accurate "early-dialogue" Socrates.
17. Plato would also not be likely to think that such testimony would be a philosophically relevant matter to bring up in the *Apology,* just because of its irrelevance to the substantive issue of whether someone possesses the correct intellectual attitude to the gods. Plato surely recognizes that truly impious people may still sacrifice, and he would have expected his sophisticated audience to know this as well. Xenophon, on the other hand, should not be expected to distinguish clearly between practice and belief, and in his zeal to defend Socrates to all and sundry, may be expected to emphasize his sacrificial practice. This is just what we find in the *Memorabilia,* e.g., *Mem.* 1.3.1–4.
18. A practice that would likely have begun with youthful attendance at sacrifices and similar occasions; see *La.* 187d-e. It must be conceded that the ancestral cult-objects referred to at *Euthd.* 302c–d merely come with the *oikos* and certify one's membership in the phratry and other civic bodies, and hence, have minimal religious significance; see Aristotle, *Ath. Pol.* 55.3, and Lacey 1968, 25 ff. Nonetheless, in the same section of text (302d) Socrates declares that as much as any Athenian he has family prayers and altars, and that the gods associated with these (e.g., "family Apollo" [*Apollôn patrôos*] and "courtyard Zeus" [*Zeus herkeios*]) are not only his ancestral gods, but his *masters* as well, thus indicating genuine belief in the gods associated with the cult-objects and giving weight to the idea that Socrates engaged in traditional cult practices.
19. Reeve 1989, 67. See also Burkert 1985, 216–275, and Parke 1961.
20. See, e.g., Burkert 1985, 8; Dodds 1951, 140–144; Lloyd—Jones 1971, 134; A. E. Taylor 1911, 15–16.

21. For examples of prayer, see *Il.* 1.37–42, 1.446–458; Hes. *Op.* 724–726, 465–468; Aesch. *SAT* 252–260, *choe.* 124–151; and Thuc. 6.32. Although there are indications that a person might experience a personal relationship with a deity akin to the sort a trusted servant might have with a kindly master (see, e.g., Eur. *Hipp.* 948–949; *Ion* 128–35)—especially in the case of sects such as the Orphics and the various mystery cults (e.g., that of Eleusis)—the predominant popular sentiment seems to be that of distant respect; see, e.g., Dodds 1973; Versnel 1981; Zaidman and Pantel 1992, 13–15.

22. For surveys of sacrificial practice (and other forms of religious ritual), see, e.g., Burkert 1985, ch. 2; Mikalson 1983, ch. 11; Zaidman and Pantel 1992, 28–45.

23. It appears that most fifth-century Athenians took it for granted that curse-imprecations were an effective means of causing others harm, such as loss of material goods, pain, illness, and destruction of human life (cf. *Laws* 933c–e); see, e.g., Luck 1985, ch. 1, and Watson 1991, ch. 1. Watson (1991, 3–4) notes that there was considerable blurring between the notions of "praying" and "cursing" in antiquity, since both were conceived of as requests (accompanied by sacrificial gifts) for a benefit to be granted the petitioner (or community) (e.g., harm to one's enemy).

24. For the majority of Greeks, the most significant divinities were those tied to one's immediate situation—heroes and lesser gods with more local, partisan interests than the Olympians (e.g., Asclepius and Heracles); Dodds (1973), 153–154. Even the Olympians themselves, however, were thought to be involved in the centrally important task of fulfilling curse-imprecations: either Zeus (Soph. *Phil.* 1183) or all the gods (Soph. *OT.* 269) could be called upon to fulfill one's retaliatory aims (although there was, apparently, a preference for seeking the help of the gods of the Underworld—e.g., Hades, Persephone, and [especially] the Erinyes). See Watson 1991, ch. 1 (esp. 1.14).

25. The gods were clearly thought to delight in sacrificial gifts; for example, in the *Iliad* Iris insists that she must not miss her share of "the sacred feast" (23.205–207), while Hera proclaims, "No more joy for us in the sumptuous feast when riot rules the day" (1.575 ff.).

26. On the ancient self-interested attitude toward cult, see Dodds 1973, 144–155; Dover 1974, 246–249; Vlastos 1991, 176–177.

27. Cf. e.g., Hes. fr. 174; Aesch. *Choe.* 306–314, *Ag.* 1564; Arist. *Nic. Eth.* 1132b21–27, *Top.* 113a2–3, *Rhet.* 1367a19–20. See Blundell 1989, ch. 2, and Vlastos 1991, ch. 7, for additional citations and analysis.

28. See, e.g., *Meno* 71e; *Rep.* 332d; Pind. *Pyth.* 2.83–85; Eur. *Medea* 807–10. For extensive documentation and discussion of this corollary, see Blundell 1989, ch. 2; also Vlastos 1991, ch. 7, esp. 180–190.

29. Vlastos 1991, ch. 7, 181–190; Blundell 1989, 50. Although Mytilene escaped this sort of fate, Scione, Torone, and Melos did not. Blundell (1989, 55) notes that enmity and revenge were accepted as natural motives for lawsuits, and that revenge could be endowed with respectability if it was argued that revenge was being sought on behalf of the *polis* (e.g., Lys. 1.47).

30. For references to possible precursors of Socrates' rejection of the *talio*, see Blundell 1989, 56 n. 146.

31. On this inference and its connections with the rest of Socrates' moral theory, see e.g., Vlastos 1991, ch. 7. Vlastos (1991, 195 n. 52, and also, e.g., 1971, 2) understands Xenophon's Socrates to endorse the ancient "Help friends and

harm enemies" ethos (at, e.g., *Mem.* 2.6.35). For a cogent response, see Morrison 1987, 16–18 (and cf. *Mem.* 4.8.11).

32. As Crito wonders (*Cri.* 45c–46a), for example, if we fail to inflict harm on an opponent aren't we doing to ourselves that very thing which the opponent wishes to do to us (viz., "unjustly" deprive ourselves of goods)?.

33. See Guthrie 1950, 27–109; Lloyd—Jones 1971, 176; Nilsson 1940, 38–75; G Murray 1930, ch. 2.

34. Lloyd-Jones 1971, 174–184.

35. Sophocles, for example, mentions *Zeus araios* ["Zeus who listens to curses"] (*Phil* 1183) and makes Heracles threaten Hylus with *theôn ara* ["the curse of the gods"] if he fails to obey his father (see also *Il.* 9.456; *Laws* 931b–c, 854b); see Watson 1991, ch. 1.11–1.13.

36. Lloyd-Jones 1971, 179.

37. Watson 1991, ch 1, esp. 1.12.

38. Note, for example, Euthyphro's use of what must have been a well-recognized moral tension when he affirms that "Human beings themselves believe that Zeus is the best and most just of the gods, while at the same time they agree that he bound his own father" (*Euth.* 5e5–6a2).

39. Hesiod, for example, is willing to describe Zeus as at one point *deceived* by Prometheus (*Op.* 48; cf. *Mem.* 1.1.19) and in the *Euthyphro* the traditional gods are thought to possibly *misjudge* the correctness of some actions.

40. Parker 1996, 256–257; Watson 1991, ch 1. There also existed many affirmations of the justice and morality of the gods, gods with such appellations as "Zeus Meilichios" [kindly Zeus], "Zeus Xenios" [Zeus the guardian of strangers and oaths], and "Delphic Apollo who cannot lie" (and who is foremost among the gods to encourage the notion that the gods underwrite just behavior among humans). See Lefkowitz 1989a, 244; Burkert 1985, 246–250, 273; Mikalson 1983, 3–5, 64; Nilsson 1940, 34; Yunis 1988, 55–56 nn. 40, 43.

41. See, e.g., Hes. *Op.* 256–262, where we learn that Zeus punishes those who offend his daughter, Justice, by telling slanderous lies.

42. While also acknowledging the traditionalist gap insofar as it distinguishes the gods as radically superior to humans in knowledge and power. For further discussion, see McPherran 1996, chs. 2, 3, and 4.

43. Cf. Vlastos 1991, 162–165; Brickhouse and Smith 1994, ch. 6.2.1. The latter perceptively note (n. 6) that Vlastos 1991, 163–164, is incorrect to think that the gods' goodness does not simply follow from their perfect wisdom, since for Socrates no one can know the good and fail to do it (e.g., *Cri.* 49c; *Prt.* 352b–d, 358c–d; *Rep.* 335a–d; Xen. *Mem.* 3.9.5, 4.6.6; Arist. *Nic. Eth.* 1145b25). We never see Socrates offer elenctic arguments for the goodness of the gods; rather, to all appearances he simply *assumes* this, or derives it from their having wisdom in the above fashion. The attribution of wisdom to them, in turn, is either simply assumed or is elicited (perhaps) from "the very meaning of what it means to be a god." See McPherran 1992 and Smith 1992, 401–402.

Note that Euthyphro's conventional assertion that among the gods there exist many disagreements and battles similar to that experienced by Kronos and Zeus (6b5–6; 6c5–7) is met by swift incredulity on Socrates' part (6a–c). Indeed, he indicates that whenever anyone has said such things about the gods he has responded with a disbelief so unmistakable that he speculates that public awareness of this disbelief may be what has prompted his indictment on charges of impiety (6a6–c4).

44. These conditions are taken from Yunis 1988, 42–45, 50–58, who provides extensive textual support for them.
45. JACT 1984, 158; Mikalson 1983, 85, 94; Rhodes 1972, 36; Yunis 1988, 26, 43, 52; Watson 1991, 8.
46. For further argument and discussion, see McPherran 1996, ch 3.
47. Lloyd-Jones 1971, 156–164.
48. By, e.g., visiting educational punishments on wrongdoers.
49. See Tate 1936, 144.
50. Lloyd-Jones 1971, 134; Burnet 1924, 114; Dodds 1951, 141–143; Kerferd 1981, 167; Momigliano 1973, 566; A. E. Taylor 1933, 147; Yunis 1988, 39.
51. Lloyd-Jones 1971, 109.
52. It is also noteworthy that none of these particular thinkers appears to have suffered from religiously based persecution (Lloyd-Jones 1971, 130).
53. Vlastos 1991, 176. Vlastos's argument assumes that since "there is one good product they [the gods of Socrates] *can't* produce without human assistance, namely, good human souls," the *ergon* of the gods is this very production (my emphasis) (Vlastos 1991, 175, and 1989, 233–234; see also C. Taylor 1982, 113). Hence, he concludes, the one way in which we are truly able to serve the gods (and so be pious) is by attempting to improve our souls via Socratic self-examination. For my critical response, see McPherran 1996, 68–69.
54. Vlastos 1991, 176. For a modern application of this sort of argument—namely, that petitionary prayer is pointless if we posit the existence of an omniscient, omnipotent God—see Stump 1979, 81–85.
55. It does seem clear, however, that the Greeks would have found Vlastos's characterization of *do ut des* offerings as constituting a form of *bribery* quite offensive, since they would have regarded such offerings as *honors*, to which we hope or expect the god(s) to respond (see n. 61 below) As we will see, Socrates also has an account available to him that will explain why the gods might require us to so honor them before they respond to our prayers (without, again, our sacrifices and prayers amounting to "bribes").
56. Note, for example, Plato's account of Chryses' imprecation for revenge to Apollo, where Chryses uses his past sacrifices as establishing a basis for a "return" of favors from the god (*Rep.* 394a; cf. *Il.* 1.375–385). See also Yunis 1988, 43, 54 n. 35; cf. Vlastos 1991, 166; Connor 1991, 56.
57. Note also the prayer cited in Parker 1996, 258: "Protect our city. I believe that what I say is in our *common interest*. For a flourishing city honors the gods." (my emphasis)
58. Rhodes 1972, 36–37.
59. See Watson 1991, ch. 1, esp. 1.7.
60. Burkert 1985, 274; Mikalson 1983, 100–102; Parker 1996, 259; Yunis 1988, 51; Hes. *Op.* 336 (quoted in *Mem.* 1.3.3); cf. *Alc.* 2 149b; Arist. *Nic. Eth.* 1164b5 ff. Connor (1991, 53) is thus too extreme when he claims that Socrates' view that the size of a sacrifice is irrelevant to the gods is threateningly *non-traditional*.
61. Mikalson 1983, 89; Parker 1996, 259. Note also *Il.* 6.297–311 where Pallas Athena rejects Theano's prayer, lovely robe, and proffered sacrifice of twelve excellent heifers.
62. See, e.g., Hes *Op.* 336; Yunis 1988, 54–55. Although the primary term for offering a sacrifice is *thuô*, one often also sees *timaô* or *timê*, which carry the sense of paying honor to the gods (see, e.g., *Mem.* 4.3.17).

63. See, e.g., *Charm.* 161a; *Prt.* 313a–b; *Cri.* 47e–48a; *Grg.* 512a; *Euthd.* 278e–281e. See also Brickhouse and Smith 1994, ch. 4, for further discussion.

64. This passage even portrays Socrates as quoting Hesiod's *Op.* 336 ("render to the immortal gods according to your ability") on this point.

65. Of course, causing others the sorts of harm typically requested in curse-imprecations—harm such as loss of material goods, pain, illness, and destruction of human life (that is, harm which is not necessarily harm to the soul)—*might* be acceptable in at least some instances for a true Socratic. After all, such maledictions were commonly thought to work by informing a god of some *injustice,* enrolling the god in one's cause (often employing material sacrifice: e.g., *Il.* 9.456), and such harm *could* be imagined to be productive of moral reformation. But here, then, is one clear incompatibility: Socrates' gods (esp. Zeus) have no need to be made aware of injustices since, unlike the traditional deities, they already know everything (see, e.g., *Mem.* 1.1.19) and, being perfectly just, they have no need to be "enrolled" in any just cause (and so have no use for material sacrifices accompanied by *that* sort of intention). Secondly, the justice most commonly appealed to is that of the negative *talio* (e.g., "May those who killed me meet a like fate, O Zeus, god of guests") and, as we have seen, Socrates rejects the negative aspect of the *talio.* Moreover, it seems clear that the *talio* invoked in many curses is of the particularly objectionable sort which confuses personal revenge with justice conceived of as a rectification of debt where the retribution envisaged includes harm, often gratuitous harm, to innocents (e.g., an enemy's children or an opponent's chariot driver). Socrates, then, seems bound to take at least a skeptical if not an utterly outraged view of many "just" curses. See McPherran 1996, 153–155.

66. In this, Socrates could be seen as following in the footsteps of critics such as Heraclitus, who, for example, finds praying to the statue of a divinity as rather like our addressing another person's house rather than its owner (DK 22 B5).

67. In McPherran 1996, ch. 2.2, I argue that if a person does something just, then whether it is to be counted pious or not is a matter of whether that person really has the inner intention to serve and honor the gods or not. Nonetheless, correct intentions—thought of as being no more than conscious desires to achieve some good end—should not be thought sufficient for doing something virtuously and should not be identified with the possession of a virtue. I have argued elsewhere (McPherran 1987) that Socrates is opposed to behavioral accounts of the virtues, thinking that one cannot specify a complete set of action-types by reference to physical criteria that would identify a virtue such as bravery in all circumstances. Rather, the description of an action as virtuous must specify the "single power" (Socrates says) that makes every brave person brave, where this power produces the aims (conscious or not) productive of their consequent brave behavior. On this account, then, if Socrates gets up in the morning without *per impossibile* the aim of helping the gods, then he is not acting piously, especially because he fails to help the gods by aligning his soul in the ways of virtue by producing or discovering correct aims within himself. For Socrates virtue is knowledge or wisdom, but possession of this for Socrates means more than just possessing a complete definition of a virtue; rather, it also has to do with possessing a state of soul that aims at a good end and possesses the skill to discover useful means for producing or obtaining it. Hence, accidentally dropping some money on the floor and thereby repaying my debt to you is neither just nor pious, but if I repay what I owe with the single aim

(conscious or not) of merely discharging my debt to you—supposing this could happen—then I have done something just, yet not something loved by the gods in the way that a pious action is loved. However, if my aim in doing this is *also* service to the gods—say, improving my soul and yours—then I also do something pious and loved by the gods.

68. For justifications of these claims, see, eg., McPherran 1985, 1996, ch. 2; and C. Taylor 1982.

69. See also *Mem* 1.1.19, 1.4.10–18, 4.3.13–14; Xen. *Symp.* 4.48–49. Note that Aeschines of Sphettus, a close friend of Socrates and an author of Socratic dialogues, ascribes this same view to Socrates (see Field 1913, 149) as well as the view that "the fine and good get a better deal from the gods because of their greater piety" (H. Dittmar, Fr. 8, 61–62); Reeve 1989, 67–68 n. 80.

70. Were it otherwise, piety would be the rejected *emporia* of *Euth.* 14e6–7, and the gods as mere "evil moneylenders" (*Alc.* 2 149e4–5); cf. Reeve 1989, 68.

71. This principle is a fundamental tenet of the Greek ethos. It was thought an evil not to reciprocate a good for a good (Dem. 20.6), and if no material return was possible, one repaid a gifted good with honor, esteem, and loyalty (*Nic. Eth.* 1163b10–14) (see Blundell 1989, 33–34, for further evidence and discussion of this). Like other expressions of traditional morality (e.g., the inviolability of oaths), we never see Socrates reject it; if he had, Plato would hardly have kept that from us while showing Socrates hammering home his objection to the negative side of the *talio*, the return of one harm for another. See also n. 75 below.

72. To honor them would involve acknowledging their great wisdom and power, expressing gratitude for their gifts, and so on. See also the argument in the *Crito* (48d–54d) where Socrates attempts to establish our obligation to our civil "master," the laws of the state. Socrates would likely argue along such lines that since we have received many blessings from the gods since birth, we have thereby entered into an implicit contract with them to obey their command to be honored; see also *Mem.* 4.3.13–17.

73. *Mem.* 4.3.13, 16; cf. *Laws* 716–717 where Plato makes clear that he approves of ritual *veneration* of the gods.

74. *Mem.* 1.1.9, 1.1.19, 1.3.3, 1.4.15–19, 4.3.16–17, 4.8.11; *Symp.* 47–49. Note especially how at *Mem.* 4.3.12 Socrates does not demur when Euthydemus claims that the gods must be very friendly with him—more friendly than with others—because *even when they are not asked* they assist him. Also, at 2.1.28 Socrates asserts that to acquire *the favor* of the gods you must worship them, and that the gods give nothing good to man without toil (although this seems at odds with the view that all good things come to humanity from the gods even when unasked and unworshipped [e.g., *Euth.* 14e–15a]).

75. As Nicholas Smith has pointed out to me, the account of friendship in the *Lysis* seems to show that Socrates had no problem with a moral notion (friendship) being based on a mutual exchange of benefit. Also, Socrates' eudaimonism implies that to do good just is to pursue benefit (of a non-material kind).

76. For a justification of this analogy, see, e.g., McPherran 1985 and 1996, ch. 2.2.

77. Plato, at any rate, is willing to credit to Socrates a prayer that supports the above view:

> Dear Pan, and all you other divinities that dwell in this place, grant that I may become fair within, and that such outward things as I have will not war against the spirit within me. May I count him rich who is wise, and as

for gold, may I possess only so much of it as a temperate man might carry. (*Phdr.* 279b8–c3)

78. Dodds 1951, 141. Wise only in knowing that he lacks complete wisdom (*Ap.* 23a–b), Socrates would not dismiss practices that are compatible with his foundational propositions (e.g., that the gods are entirely wise), and will accept in a weak sense those that seem likely and/or have the backing of custom (readily accepting, of course, those beliefs which the *elenchos* has warranted [e.g., those beliefs that have repeatedly been tested in an elenctic encounter with hostile interlocutors]). As Plato has Socrates say in the *Phaedrus,*

> I should be quite in the fashion if I disbelieved [the story of Boreas and Orithyia], as the men of science do. . . . I don't bother about such things, but accept the current beliefs about them, and direct my inquiries. . . . to myself. (229c6–230a3 cf. Brickhouse and Smith 1989, 188–189)

79. Cf. Stump 1979, 86–91.
80. McPherran 1996, chs. 2.2 and 4.2.
81. And rewarded accordingly since, as Xenophon has it, with Socrates, the gods were even more friendly than with other men. (*Mem.* 4.3.12).
82. On this view, then, Socrates' associate, Aristippus, may have been going the Master just one step better, and neglecting the Socratic considerations seen above, when he said that it was ridiculous to make requests of the gods since they already know what ought to be sent (this is a paraphrase of Aristippus fr. 227 from Guthrie 1971, 177; cf. *Mem.* 1.3.2 where Socrates is said to hold that we ought to pray for no specific thing since the gods already know what is good for us).
83. E.g., the sort of motivation Socrates captures in his ironic characterization of Euthyphro's last account of piety as a kind of cosmic barter (*Euth.* 14e); and, again, see Plato's contempt for this view of piety in the *Laws,* e.g., 885b ff.
84. For further discussion, see, e.g., Brickhouse and Smith 1994, ch. 4, esp. 134–136.
85. Yunis 1988, 49.
86. Brickhouse and Smith 1994, 184–188. See also their replies to Vlastos 1989b in the letters column of the *Times Literary Supplement* (Brickhouse and Smith 1990a, 1990b). Note, however, Kraut's claim in his 1995 that Brickhouse and Smith do not acknowledge in their 1994 the way in which Socratic piety put traditional cult practices into doubt and do not explain adequately how their own understanding of Socratic piety—the knowledge of how to give aid to the gods in promoting wisdom in other human beings (1994, 178)—is compatible with the rituals of Greek religion.
87. We also surely do not wish to make out that Meletus, who may well be the religious zealot Meletus who prosecuted Andocides, has no religious concerns at all regarding Socrates.
88. It is worth noting that Socrates can always be found guilty on *some* interpretations of the formal charges and, as Brickhouse and Smith themselves observe, it is the *prosecutor's* interpretation of the charges that are the legally relevant ones. Socrates, then, *need only reply* to *that* specification of them, not to "any possible interpretation of the charges" (1989, 119). Not coming to grips with all those many other interpretations is not, as some (like Brickhouse and Smith 1994, 184–188) suggest, tantamount to *evasion* of relevant issues. So I think Socrates can both plead innocent to the legal charges—as he, Meletus, and most jurors construe them—while remaining guilty on the charge of non-

recognition of the Athenian gods in the eyes of those (few?) jurors who construe that charge as violated by someone who does not endorse the idea that these gods respond reliably to particular, material petitionary sacrifices, especially those *involving requests that run contrary to justice* (Socratically conceived) and who are perceptive enough to see that Socrates' theological position puts him in this camp.

89. Although Socrates may not have used all the time allotted for his defense speech, that is perhaps best explained by his having supporters (*sunēgoroi*) who spoke on his behalf (*Ap.* 22; D. L. 2.41; Brickhouse and Smith 1989, 75–76). Socrates, knowing this in advance, may have counted on them to address those worries that might be held by a minority of jurors—e.g., the worry that Socrates is in some way or other an opponent of traditional religious practice.

90. Cf. Jackson 1971, 34: "Plato never has a character pray in connection with a sacrifice. I would suggest that this separation of prayer from sacrifice . . . results from Plato's wish to avoid even the suggestion that in prayer one asks for payment for a service rendered." See also Irwin 1977, 46–47; McPherran 1987, 126–129.

   Note also that not long after Socrates' death, it could be averred on the stage that

> Anyone who believes that he secures the god's favor by sacrifice . . . is in error. For a man must be useful by not seducing virgins or committing adultery or stealing and killing for money. (*Menander* fr. 683; see also Isocrates, *To Nicocles*, ii 20, that no offering or worship is superior to the effort to live a virtuous life; cf. Xen. *Ages.* 11.2.)

91. Cf. Parker 1986, 255, who notes that popular Greek religion

> reflected and supported the general ethos of Greek culture. It discouraged individualism, a preoccupation with inner states *and the belief that intentions matter more than actions*; it emphasized the sense of belonging to a community and the need for due observance of social forms. (my emphasis)

92. The sketch of Socrates' religious position in respect of his fellow citizens offered in Parker 1996, ch. 10 (reprinted in this volume), is in many respects supportive of the one I provide here. However, his conclusion that "Socrates' actual religious position would never, surely, have caused him to be singled out as a target for attack" (203) is not based on a full consideration of how Socrates' moral tenets actually undermine traditional motivations for engaging in prayer and sacrifice. Asli Gocer's similar take on this matter (Gocer, 2000) rests on a series of problematic claims. In particular, she argues that if Socrates did (in some sense) renounce public religion but continued to participate in traditional religious forms, then his practice shows that his philosophical views were either immaterial or non-threatening in respect of the general practice of cult; hence, that we have no reason to think that his views were considered revolutionary or changed Athenian religion. But, as I hope to have shown, Socrates' own participation in traditional religious forms would most likely have rested on a reinterpretation of those forms, one that would have been found threatening by those Athenians able to grasp the implications of his moral theory (whether or not he was actually considered revolutionary). I make no claims as to how Socrates' views—independent of their impact on Plato—might have contributed to changes in later popular Athenian religion.

93. Or "from himself" in an earlier, Socratic, period of his career.

94. Morrow 1993, 401.
95. For, says the text following,

> In god there is no sort of wrong whatsoever; he is supremely just, and
> nothing is more like the divine than he who has become as just as it lies in
> human nature to be. . . . The penalty of injustice . . . is not, as they [the
> unjust] imagine, stripes and death, which do not always fall on wrongdo-
> ers, but a penalty that cannot be escaped. . . . In doing injustice, they are
> growing less like one of these patterns and more like the other. The penalty
> they pay is living the life that corresponds to the pattern they are coming
> to resemble. (176c8–177a3)

• • •

From *Plato's Socrates*

THOMAS C. BRICKHOUSE AND NICHOLAS D. SMITH

5.3 SOCRATES AND POLITICAL THEORY

5.3.1 Athenian Politics

In the last years of the fifth century B.C., what had been a long-standing
tension became bitter and violent. On the one side were the oligarchs, rich
landowning aristocrats, who regarded themselves as superior to the δῆμος,
or common people, and hence, constantly sought ways to disenfranchise
the common people. On the other side were the democrats, whose most
revered leaders were also from among the wealthiest economic class in the
state, but whose political ideology was more inclusive: all adult male citizens, according to the democrats, had an equal right to participate in governing the state.[1]

The government of Athens in Socrates' time was a constitutional
democracy whose principal governing body was the popular Assembly,
which paid up to (but not beyond) its quorum of 6,000 citizens to attend.[2]
Payment was on a first-come, first-served basis; the constitution recognized no special privileges for the wealthy, the famous, or the well-born,
though in practice no doubt each faction protected its favorites. All decisions made in the Assembly were made by a simple majority of those present. The Council of Five Hundred, a smaller body, did little more than set
the agenda for the Assembly. Moreover, those who served on the Council
were selected by lot—fifty men from each of the ten official tribes.[3] The
presidency of the Council rotated regularly from tribe to tribe, and one
man could serve on the Council only twice in his lifetime.[4]

Thomas C. Brickhouse and Nicholas D. Smith, from *Plato's Socrates* (New York:) Oxford University Press, 1994), pp. 155–175, 179–189.

One other extremely important element in Athens' government was the jury-court system. Jurors volunteered for duty, and 6,000 of these volunteers were selected by lot for service for one year.[5] Specific juries would be assigned to each case by lot; those that were actually assigned to a case were paid for their service.[6] To prevent tampering, juries were made large (no fewer than 200 jurors were assigned to any trial; sometimes, as many as 1,000 or even more might be assigned),[7] though by the beginning of the fourth century various changes were made precisely because the old system did not always achieve even the minimal requirements of procedural justice.[8] One problem seemed to be that litigants could find out which juries would be working which cases in advance of the actual litigation.[9] Even the most important cases were decided in a single day; as many as four minor cases might be decided in one day.[10] In most cases, the trial was initiated by a private citizen (and not a magistrate),[11] and the litigants spoke for themselves; there were no professional prosecutors or defense lawyers, though speeches might be written by professionals for presentation by the litigants.[12]

The effect of this form of government was that every adult male citizen could expect to have a substantial role in both legislation and litigation. But twice in one decade at the end of the fifth century, this government was overthrown by the oligarchic faction. In 411, a group of 400 oligarchs took power for nearly a year, until the democracy was restored and the oligarchs themselves were exiled. After Athens lost the war with Sparta (in 404), one of the conditions of the peace agreement was that these exiles be permitted to return to Athens. Within a year—and with the help of threats from the Spartan general, Lysander—thirty of these men were installed in power during one of the bloodiest periods in Athens' history. Like the earlier one, this oligarchy did not last long; the democrats regained power only eight months later after a civil war.

5.3.2 Socrates versus Democracy

Socrates lived the last years of his life in this atmosphere of violent partisan politics and disastrous foreign and civil wars. It is natural for us to wonder with which side Socrates sympathized.

Many scholars have concluded that, to one degree or another, Socrates must be counted among those loyal to the oligarchic faction.[13] Two general sorts of reasons are given for this conclusion: (1) careful scrutiny of the various ancient testimony reveals a variety of powerfully anti-democratic points of view within various statements Socrates explicitly makes, or implied by them; and (2) prosopographical study of Socrates' associates shows a clear majority to be from among Athens' oligarchic faction—indeed, some of the most violent and dangerous of these men may be counted among Socrates' closest associates. We wish to dispute scholars' understandings of both sorts of evidence. Let us look first at the philosophical views Socrates expresses, and try to see what political philosophy they represent. Then we will turn to his relationships with others.

Before we are in a position to assess Socrates' own ideological commitments regarding democracy, we must first identify which texts will—and which texts will not—count as appropriate evidence. Because we have elected in this book to focus on Plato's early dialogues and the Socrates whose views are represented therein, however, we have already decided this issue. On the question of Socrates' political sympathies, this selection of texts is critical, for if we are right, there can be no reconciling the Socrates who speaks in Plato's early dialogues with the one we find in Plato's middle period works or the one we find in the works of Xenophon. Plato's middle period Socrates and Xenophon's Socrates are simply hostile to democracy.[14] Because our focus is the Socrates of Plato's early dialogues, however, we shall adhere to the principle we have followed thus far: when other ancient sources conflict with views attributed to Socrates in Plato's early dialogues, we shall accept the version found in the early dialogues. Our question, then, is this: What is Socrates' attitude toward democracy in Plato's early dialogues?

5.3.3 A Look at the Texts

Scholars who have concluded that the Platonic Socrates sympathized with the oligarchs have pointed to a number of passages that seem plainly to express views inconsistent with the political ideology of Athenian democrats.

5.3.3.1 The Importance of Experts

• *Ap.* 24e4–25c1: Meletus claims that all men make the young better (except, of course, Socrates), whereas Socrates argues that it is much more likely that those capable of making the young better are but one or a few, whereas most people would make them worse. Socrates makes this argument by comparing the treatment of the youth to the training of horses.

• *Cri.* 47a2–48c6: Socrates says that in regard to questions of "right and wrong, shameful and noble, good and bad" (47d9–10), one should disregard the words of the many, who have no special training and heed instead only the one who knows (47c1–2).

• *La.* 184c9–e9: Laches and Nicias disagree on whether Lysimachus should train his sons in heavy-armed fighting. Socrates is asked to cast the deciding vote, but demurs, saying that one should pay no heed to the majority but instead ask the one who knows, and ignore the others. If no one can be found who is an expert on the subject, one should go on looking for one who is.

Each of these passages reveals Socrates' commitment to the view that nothing—not even a huge majority—can outweigh or override the single opinion of an authentic expert. Plainly, Socrates assumes that moral expertise will not be found in the greater masses of people, but rather only in one or a few people, if any have it at all. Contrary to popular democratic ideology, Socrates regards the teaching of virtue to be no different from the teaching of any other expertise—such teaching is the sole province of the expert.

5.3.3.2 The Democratic Ideology

• *Prt.* 319a8–328d2: Socrates claims that he regards civic virtue as unteachable. Protagoras responds with a great myth according to which everyone is innately capable of instructing others in civic virtue to some degree, though some are more capable than others. This, he explains, is why everyone's opinion is worth something in questions of what is just and lawful (327b2–4).

• *Meno* 92d7–94e2: Anytus, later one of Meletus' supporters in the accusation of Socrates, argues that people learn virtue from their elders, and that most people teach it to their children. Socrates angers Anytus by responding that none of the great Athenian leaders has managed to teach virtue to his children, and concludes that it must not be teachable.

Socrates' view is clearly in contrast to Protagoras' compelling expression of democratic ideology in his great myth, according to which everyone has some expertise in judging civic issues and so no one's opinion should be overlooked. Socrates makes no secret of the fact that he does not accept Protagoras' theory. The above two passages also show that Socrates did not regard virtue as teachable in the way Athenian democratic ideology insisted it was. Protagoras (in the *Protagoras*) and Anytus (in the *Meno*) voice the popular democratic opinion that every one (or nearly everyone) taught virtue to the young. (Socrates' accuser, Meletus expresses the same view in the passage from the *Apology* cited above in 5.3.3.1. In the *Protagoras* and *Meno,* Socrates insists that virtue cannot be taught at all precisely because there are no experts in virtue.

5.3.3.3 The Many Failings of the Many

• *Ap.* 31el–32a3: In this passage, Socrates says that he thinks that no one "who genuinely opposes you or any other populace and prevents many injust and illegal things from happening in the state" will survive for long.

• *Cri.* 48c2–6: Socrates regards "the many" as valuing any number of things that are morally irrelevant, and characterizes them as those "who carelessly put people to death and bring them back to life again, if they could, without thinking."

• *Cri.* 49c10–d5: Socrates says that one ought never to return wrong for wrong nor do evil to any person, but also says that "there are few who believe these things, or ever will. So those who do and those who do not have no common counsel, but must necessarily despise one another, in view of their respective views" (49d2–5).

• *Grg.* 471e2–472d1: Socrates introduces the two modes of refuta-tion—the rhetorical and the dialectical (discussed in section 5.1.4)—and identifies the rhetorical as capable of producing the greater number of wit-nesses at any given time, but "worth nothing with regard to the truth" (471e7–472a1). Socrates also allows that on the point under dispute, Polus will find "nearly all, Athenians and foreigners, are in agreement with what you say, if you want to bring forward witnesses against me, testifying that I do not speak the truth" (472a2–5).

These passages show that Socrates regards "the many" as committed to a number of immoral and unjust points of view. These passages show that Socrates thought there was bitter opposition between "the many," on the one hand, and, on the other, "the few" who accept the truth and stand for justice and law. We find the antagonism between "the many" and "the few" is likely to lead to the death of "the few" good men. So democracy—the government by "the many"—is certain to be dangerous to "the few" good men whose points of view are in opposition to the immoralities "the many" accept. This is not a temporary problem: Socrates obviously thinks it is unlikely that "the many" will ever be brought to accept the correct moral view.

5.3.3.4 Famous Democrats

• *Gorgias* 472a5–b3: In his dispute with Polus, Socrates names a few famous men on whom Polus could count to give such false witness, including Nicias and his brothers, Aristocrates, and the whole house of Pericles.

• *Meno* 92d7–94e2: In the same passage in which he confronts Anytus, Socrates explicitly mentions Themistocles, Aristeides, Pericles, and Thucy-dides (son of Melesias), as having failed to teach their sons to be virtuous.

• *Grg.* 515c4–517a6: Socrates argues that the most distinguished politicians of Athens' past—Pericles, Cimon, Miltiades, and Themisto-cles—all made the citizens wilder and less controlled.

Socrates regards the most famous and influential men of the demo-cratic faction with disdain. All three passages mention Pericles, perhaps the most beloved leader of the democrats; but others are mentioned as well. We learn how seriously the Athenians regard failing to take proper care of their children from Crito's appeal to Socrates on behalf of Socrates' children: "Either one ought not to have children, or be willing to suffer hardship for them, bring them up, and educate them" (*Crito* 45d4–5). Because Socrates regards the understanding of virtue as a matter of such importance that it is "most honorable to have it and most disgraceful to lack it" (*Grg.* 472c7–8), the great Athenians' inability or neglect as regards their sons' educations would qualify as a terrible embarrassment, or worse. No wonder Anytus, an influential democrat, was offended.

The evidence we have surveyed supports the following conclusion regarding Socrates' politics: Socrates not only rejects any number of fea-tures of Athenian democratic ideology, he regards "the many" as morally corrupt and as dangerously hostile to genuine morality and to "the few" good men who would seek to promote genuine morality. Socrates also repeatedly used Athens' greatest and most beloved democratic leaders as examples of moral, political, and pedagogical inadequacy. Such views might well have tarred Socrates as a subversive in the eyes of the radical democrats.

5.3.4 Socrates versus Oligarchy

With the possible exception of Socrates, whose position we are now trying to understand, those who rejected democracy in ancient Athens typically supported oligarchy; democracy and oligarchy were generally perceived as the only two realistic options for Athens' government. Scholars have no doubt relied on this fact in noting the sort of textual evidence we have discussed above and going directly from that evidence to the conclusion that Socrates was an oligarchic ideologue, involved "in a conspiracy against the democratic constitution of Athens"[15] and seeking "the replacement of the . . . democracy by the rule of an aristocratic-oligarchic elite."[16]

But it is worth noting that Socrates' frequent attacks on specific democrats and on democratic ideology are never balanced in Plato's early dialogues by praise for specific oligarchs or by endorsements of specific aspects of oligarchic ideology. We find no calls, for example, for a return to "the ancestral constitution";[17] there are also no celebrations of the virtue or wisdom of specific members of the oligarchic faction (in contrast to Socrates' many denigrations of democratic leaders), no claims to the effect that oligarchs were able to give their sons the education that Pericles could not give his sons. No specific "few" are ever identified who could rule the state in such a way as to avoid the "many injustices and illegalities" that happen in the democratic state. Instead, we find Socrates expressing any number of opinions a doctrinaire oligarch would never express. Let us now turn to these.

5.3.4.1 Praise and Blame for Other Famous Politicians

• *Grg.* 526a2–b3: Socrates says that there have been a few very powerful leaders who have nevertheless been good men and thus deserve special praise—"for it is hard, O Callicles, and deserving of much great praise when one who has great power to do injustice lives a just life" (526a3–5). Though there have been few such people, Socrates identifies one of them as Aristeides, son of Lysimachus. (See also *Meno* 94a1.)

• *Meno* 92d7–94e2: In this passage, cited above in 5.3.3.4, Socrates singles out a number of famous Athenians who were unable to teach their sons virtue. Aristeides and Themistocles are mentioned; so are Pericles and Thucydides.

• *Grg.* 515c4–517a6: In this passage, also cited above in 5.3.3.4, Socrates notes that a number of famous Athenians made the citizens wilder and less controlled after they came to power. Pericles, Cimon, Miltiades, and Themistocles are named as examples.

In the first passage, Socrates offers what appears to be the highest praise we ever find him offering to any man—to Aristeides, a man who, according to Socrates, remained good even though he held great power in the state. Aristeides was one of the early leaders of the democratic faction, in no way associated with the later oligarchic movement.[18] Socrates offers such praise despite the fact that Aristeides is also included in the group of men who were not able to educate their sons in virtue, and despite the fact that Aristeides was once ostracized.[19] Socrates' admiration for Aristeides, then, must have to do with Aristeides' private moral character—and not his political or pedagogical expertise—but nonetheless, praise of Aristeides is not at all what one would expect from an oligarchic sympathizer.

We might expect, instead, praise of Cimon, whose hostility to the development of the democracy was well known,[20] and of his father, Miltiades. But the passage from *Gorgias* 515c4–517a6 shows that Cimon and Miltiades were no better statesmen, in Socrates' view, than was the man whom the oligarchs would hate above all others, Pericles.[21] And the *Meno* passage shows that even Thucydides, Pericles' bitter political rival within the democratic party in Athens,[22] comes in for precisely the same criticism.

As these passages show, Socrates shows equal disrespect for political rivals from both political factions, and even for rivals who share affinities for the democratic or oligarchic points of view. Aristeides is singled out for praise, as we have seen. But his greatest rival, Themistocles, is identified as "among the best men of earlier times" (*Meno* 93e11) in spite of the fact that he is said to have been unable to train his sons to be virtuous. Elsewhere Socrates indifferently identifies men of such disparate political sympathies as "Pericles and Cimon and Miltiades and Themistocles" (*Grg.* 515d1) as all equally incapable of making the Athenians better. Indeed, Socrates suggests that they have all made the Athenians worse.

The remarkable thing about such passages is that they are so often cited as evidence for Socrates' hostility to democrats and the democracy, while their equal treatment of oligarchs goes unmentioned. In context, moreover, Socrates' point in using such examples is not to single out those whom he regards as the most notorious moral failures, but rather to identify Athens' most notable citizens and leaders on either side of the political spectrum. Socrates' use of such figures seems to be for emphasis: his identification of a number of famous men who surely would have taught it to their sons if such a thing were possible is evidence for his claim in the *Meno* passage that virtue cannot be taught. If anything, Socrates is complimenting such men for being the most likely to have virtue to teach, if only teaching virtue were possible. His remarks do not betray a political agenda or a partisan bias. Similarly, at *Gorgias* 515c4–517a6, his point is to show that none of the most accomplished leaders of Athens had ever really succeeded in practicing what Socrates regards as the "true art of politics." The criticism is made by using a carefully bipartisan selection of what

Socrates regards as failed leaders. If such passages may be counted, as they almost universally are, as evidence for Socrates' disdain for democracy and its most revered leaders, they must count no less for his disdain for oligarchy and its most famous leaders.

But these passages all concern statesmen of former days. What does Socrates think of more recent leaders? At *Gorgias* 503a5–b5, Socrates confesses that he knows of no man who made the Athenians better by his oratory in the state. Callicles concedes the point as regards contemporary orators, but goes on to insist that men from earlier times like Themistocles, Cimon, Miltiades, and Pericles had indeed improved the body of citizens.[23] It follows obviously from this that Socrates has no more regard for any of the political leaders of the end of the fifth century than he has for those of former times.

5.3.4.2 *Breaking Laws*

• *Cri.* 51b3–c3: In this and other passages from the *Crito* (discussed above in section 5.2), Socrates articulates his doctrine of "persuade or obey." According to Socrates, the citizen must treat the state with more reverence and respect than he treats his father or, if he is a slave, his master. Socrates concludes that it is *impious* to use violence against the state—even more than it is to use violence against one's parents.

• *Ap.* 32a9–e1: Socrates describes two of his most dangerous clashes with government. When the democracy was in power, a mob wanted to try the generals of the battle off the Arginousai islands *en bloc*, for failing to remain and gather up those who had been killed.[24] In his role as *prutanis*, Socrates opposed this decision, because, as he says, it was unjust and illegal. Socrates goes on to recall that when the Thirty were in power, they sent for him to go out and bring in Leon of Salamis to be put to death. Socrates did not obey, but simply went home. Socrates characterizes the Thirty's action as an example of their "wanting to infect as many others with their guilt as they could" (βουλόμενοι ὡς πλείστους ἀναπλῆσαιαἰτιῶν—32c7–8). He considers his own response to show that he is the sort of man who would refuse to do anything unjust or impious (32d2–3).

No one has ever doubted that the "Laws" Socrates refers to in the *Crito* are the democratic laws currently in effect in Athens, even if, as some have argued, they are these laws in a somewhat purified or clarified sense.[25] It follows that any Athenian who violated the laws of Athens, according to Socrates in the above *Crito* passage, commits impiety and injustice. Moreover, we see from the *Apology* passage that Socrates was willing to risk everything against those of the democratic faction who acted contrary to these laws, and describing the acts of the Thirty, who overthrew these laws, with obvious and unmixed hostility. This is not at all the tone we would expect from a man who sympathizes with those who seek "the replacement of . . . democracy by the rule of an aristocratic-oligarchic elite," as some have said.[26] Rather, it would appear that Socrates is inclined to obey completely (see section 5.2), and to defend and protect—even to revere—the democratic laws of Athens as if they were his parents and masters.

Further evidence for this conclusion comes from another passage in the *Crito,* where Socrates makes no objection to the Laws' characterization of him as completely satisfied with them and as having shown no interest in other cities or other laws.

- *Cri.* 52b1–c3: Socrates, speaking for the personified Laws of Athens, claims that he has shown himself to be satisfied with the Laws and the city of Athens, by never leaving the city even though he was always free to go (except on military duty), and by having children in Athens, showing that it pleased him. The Laws claim that Socrates "had no desire to know other cities or other laws, but [was] contented with us and our city" (52b7–c1). At 52d6–7, Socrates and Crito are forced to agree that what the Laws have said is true.

No oligarch could honestly speak this way. Moreover, there is no evidence, from Plato or any other source, that Socrates ever took part in any of the activities designed by the oligarchs to help topple the democratic state.

5.3.4.3 *Socrates on Common Crafts and Craftsmen*

- *Grg.* 489e2–491e1: Callicles holds that the truly superior person is none other than the powerful person, and means by this the one most able to take more than his share. Callicles claims that such a person deserves the greatest share he can take. Socrates compares this to the absurdity that the best weaver deserves the largest cloak, or the best shoemaker deserves the biggest shoes. Callicles responds that Socrates can never stop talking about cobblers and fullers, cooks and physicians, and denies that the subject of superiority has anything to do with such people. Instead, Callicles has the man powerful in public affairs in mind.

- *Ap.* 21b1–22e5: In his attempt to discern the meaning of the oracle to Chairephon, Socrates goes to those who have a reputation for wisdom and first discovers that the "public men" knew nothing that was fine and good, but thought they did; indeed, "those with the greatest reputation seemed to me to be nearly the most deficient . . . and others who were held as more base seemed to be superior as regards intelligence" (22a3–6). The poets and prophets, too, knew nothing of value; their poetry and prophecy was the result of divine inspiration, not wisdom. Finally, Socrates went to the craftsmen, who did indeed "know many fine things" (or have much fine knowledge—πολλὰ καὶ καλὰ ἐπισταμένους [22d2]), but who wrongly supposed that because they were able to practice their crafts well, they were also wise about "the most important things" (22d7)—a faulty assumption. Socrates thus concludes that even though he does not have the wisdom the craftsmen have (knowledge of their crafts), because he also lacks their folly (about "the most important things"), he is wiser than they are.

One feature of the oligarchic ideology was the view, expressed very plainly by a number of our best sources on the historical Socrates,[27] that manual labor stunts one's ability to deliberate effectively about moral or political issues. Yet we find no trace of this bias expressed by the Socrates of Plato's early dialogues. On the contrary, Socrates actually appears to look with a certain degree of approval on the craftsmen. Callicles regards them, it is clear in the *Gorgias*, as beneath notice; he is interested only in the great and powerful men. Socrates, on the contrary, regards the very men whom Callicles reveres and admires as "nearly the most deficient" (*Ap.* 22a3–4) in wisdom, whereas the craftsmen do genuinely "know many fine things" (*Ap.* 22d2). The craftsmen, of course, are still less wise than Socrates because they think their craft-knowledge makes them wise in ways they are not. But unlike the great politicians, at least they have some worthy knowledge— knowledge of their crafts. The great politicians have none at all.

In Socrates' notorious use of craftsmen and the crafts they practice as models for the philosophical and political knowledge he seeks, there is no trace of the oligarchic doctrine that manual labor is morally corrosive. Socrates lends no support whatever to those who would insist that for a man to be good, he must be a man of leisure. Moreover, Socrates himself must not be mistaken for a man of leisure, if leisure requires any significant wealth. Although he practices no craft, he toils ceaselessly in his philosophic mission, and is "in great poverty due to [his] service to the god" (*Ap.* 23b9–c1). This is no model of an oligarch's life. Socratic philosophy never equates wealth and leisure with moral nobility.

5.3.5 A State without Politicians?

The evidence we have surveyed in the last two sections shows that Socrates could not be counted as a partisan democrat or as an oligarch; he was, then, not a man of factional affiliations. Because he also respected the ultimate authority of civil law, moreover (see section 5.2), he was anything but an anarchist. It is plain enough that Socrates would regard a government by moral experts to be the ideal. But he was also convinced that no moral expert could be found. How, then *should* decisions be made in the state? Did Socrates think that all or most of the choices "public men" made on behalf of the state were *moral* choices, and hence, choices for which no expert could be found? And did Socrates believe that there were choices that had to be made one way or the other in the state, for which no experts could be found?

In fact, a number of texts very strongly suggest that Socrates believed that most of the choices a city makes ought not be decided by ideology or partisan politics. For many questions, we should neither take a vote or pick lots, as the democrats would do, nor look to the wealthy land owners and patrician families as the oligarchs would do. Instead, wherever experts were available, all of the relevant decisions should be left to them.

> When the city has an assembly to choose physicians, or shipbuilders, or any other group of craftsmen, the orator will not give advice, will he? For it is plain that it is necessary to choose the most skilled person

in each case. And in regard to building walls, or the equipment of harbors or dockyards, we call on none but the architects. And in choosing generals, or in regard to arranging soldiers for battle against the enemy, or on an occupation force to be left behind, the generals give advice, but the orators do not. (*Grg.* 455b2–c2)

This passage leaves little doubt about how Socrates thinks these issues should be decided (see also *Grg.* 503d5–504a6, 512b3–d6, 514a5–e10). It follows that the State has little need for the advice of Gorgias and the other rhetoricians.

But if not, then, by the rhetoricians, who *should* be the ones to make decisions in the state? Remarkably, it seems that Socrates thinks that all decisions about carrying out a goal must be made by those craftsmen who have that goal as the object of their craft; everyone else should keep out of it. Thus if the goal is to erect a public building, the city architect alone should decide how it is to be constructed. The sort of political structure Socrates favors—if it can be called a structure at all—is in a way oligarchic and in a way democratic. It is oligarchic insofar as each distinct decision will not involve "all the people" or even "the many"; instead, each decision will be made by "the few" qualified craftsmen, including the decision as to who the qualified craftsmen are (see *Grg.* 455b7–8). All others should not meddle in such decisions, but should mind their own business. But because each decision would require a different "few," a great many people, from all walks of life, will be called upon to make decisions for the state.

Socrates never tells us anything more about how such a system could be made to work, but it is clear that such a system could be put into place within a variety of constitutional schemes. There would no doubt still have to be managers to oversee the process and, given limited resources, to decide which projects to promote and which to delay. In all such administrative matters, important evaluations would still need to be made, and the fact is that Socrates does not tell us how or by what structure he thinks such decisions would best be made. It is clear, however, that Socrates sees no use for what the Athenians and the rhetoricians mean by "the public man," for Socrates regards this person as having nothing to offer the state at all.

It is tempting to see in Socrates' remarks in the *Gorgias* about the proper role of craftsmen in the state a forecast of Plato's "one person, one job" principle on which the ideal state depicted in the *Republic* is based (see, for example, *Rep.* IV. 433d7–434c7). Indeed, what is often regarded as the greatest novelty introduced in the *Republic* is that Plato seems to have come to believe that master statecraftsmen could come into existence—the philosopher-kings—who could then rule the state in the way Plato's Socrates of the early period all along said they should, if only they existed. So the real difference seems only to be that Plato thinks it is possible to establish what Socrates thought unlikely. No doubt, this difference derives from Plato's "discovery" of a new method of inquiry, which replaces the *elenchos* in the middle period. From this new method Plato thinks genuine wisdom could be produced.[28]

So instead of Plato's philosopher-kings, we find no one at all as the captains of Socrates' ship of state. Most of what would ordinarily be called political decisions, we find, should be made by non-politicians. No one is qualified to make the remainder of the decisions that would presumably need to be made, but Socrates does not doubt that they will be made anyhow—by proud and dangerous incompetents. This is why, no matter where he might find himself, the good man should not try to live as a "public man," for it is among "public men" that he will most surely find the most arrogant and ignorant—and, hence, the most dangerous—of men.

5.4 SOCRATES' PERSONAL ASSOCIATES AND THE TRIAL

5.4.1 Birds of a Feather?

Earlier (5.3.2), we said that two sorts of evidence had been cited for supposing that Socrates was an enemy of democracy—his philosophical opinions about Athens' "public men" and the ideals they stood for, on the one hand, and the political affiliations of his own friends and associates, on the other. We have now looked at the first sort of evidence: the opinions he actually expressed as well as their implications. We found that Socrates was no more an enemy of democracy than he was of oligarchy. Having completed our review of his views of Athens' public men and on political philosophy, we can now turn to the claim that Socrates' political ideals are betrayed by his associations with other people, whose political views and activities are not in doubt.

In fact, we think there is little or nothing to recommend the value of such evidence. "Guilt by association" is obviously not a secure method by which to decide such matters, especially when, as in this case, no corroboration of the guilty verdict can be found in anything said or done by the one being judged. Moreover, we are not only unimpressed by the evidence usually cited regarding Socrates' associates; we also think that in Socrates' case, there are special reasons for resisting such evidence.

We should begin by reminding ourselves that Socrates saw himself as Athens' gadfly, working his philosophical mission in the public places of Athens. As he tells his jurors, he will talk to anyone, "young and old" (*Ap.* 30a2–4, 30a8), "foreigner and citizen" (*Ap.* 30a3–4), "rich and poor" (*Ap.* 33b1–2). He does not carry out his mission by talking only to the members of one political faction; nor is it his mission to discuss factional ideologies or to promote oligarchy. Instead, his mission is to tell the Athenians

> not to care for your bodies or for wealth more than for the perfection
> of your souls, or even so much; and I tell you that virtue does not come

from wealth, but from virtue comes wealth and all other good things
for human beings both in private and in public. (*Ap.* 30a8–b4)

This message is not masking some political agenda: it applies to all Athenians, no matter what their political affiliation.

It may nonetheless turn out that Socrates is somewhat more effective at targeting the wealthier and more powerful Athenians in the actual practice of his mission (about which we shall have more to say in section 5.4.3). But this is not to say that he shunned the democratically inclined craftsmen. Let us recall that when he first heard the oracle given to Chairephon, Socrates spoke to the craftsmen (*Ap.* 22c9–e5), individuals who did not have the leisure to follow him every day and engage in elenctic arguments. It is the fact that the practice of philosophy requires free time, and not shared political sympathies, that explains why Socrates' most visible following included "the young men who have the most leisure, the sons of the richest men" (*Ap.* 23c2–3). The attraction Socrates apparently had for certain "wealthy, young men," then, need have nothing whatever to do with shared political sympathies.

5.4.2 Socrates' Associates

When scholars indict Socrates on the evidence provided by the affiliations and careers of his associates, usually men like Critias, Charmides, and Alcibiades top their lists. Critias, the leader of the notorious Thirty Tyrants, appears in Plato's *Protagoras* (316a5, 336d6, 337a2) and is one of the principal interlocutors in the *Charmides* and the late dialogues, the *Timaeus* and the *Critias*. Though we may legitimately doubt the historical value of these later dialogues, Plato plainly depicts Critias in the *Charmides,* an early dialogue, as having been acquainted with Socrates for quite some time (see 156a7–8). Socrates is shown to be attracted to the young Charmides—later also one of the Thirty—in Plato's *Charmides* (155c7–e2) and *Symposium* (222a8–b4). Closest of all was Socrates' tie to Alcibiades: that the two were lovers in some sense or another[29] is clear from many texts (*Prt.* 309a1–b2; *Grg.* 481d1–4; *Symp.* 213c6–d6, 214c8–d4, 216e7–219e5, 222c1–d3; see also *Prt.* 316a4–5). But these were not the only evil men among Socrates' associates: unsavory characters populate many of Plato's dialogues.[30] From the fact that a man frequently speaks with criminals of various stripes, however, we cannot draw the inference that the man himself is a criminal or a traitor. Obviously, everything depends upon why the person is associating with such bad people.

We have already established, in section 5.3, that as far as we can tell from the evidence of Plato's early dialogues, Socrates was not conspiring with these men to commit similar acts of crime or treason. In fact, as we have argued, Plato's Socrates would eschew both treason and crime as violence to the state he regarded as his parent and master (see *Cri.* 50e1–51c3, and section 5.2, above). Moreover, the evidence we reviewed also showed that Socrates could not even be counted as agreeing with the ideals of such men.

It is also seldom noted in this connection[31] that Chairephon must be counted among the associates of Socrates. It was to Chairephon that the Pythia at Delphi gave the famous oracle about Socrates' wisdom (*Ap.* 20e8–21a8). Indeed, Chairephon is the only historical person directly associated with Socrates in Aristophanes' *Clouds* (104, 144–47, 156, 1499, 1505) and *Birds* (see esp. 1296, 1554–64), a man whom Socrates identifies as having been a friend (or associate—ἑταῖρος) since their youths (*Ap.* 20e8–21a1).[32] But their friendship is significant because Chairephon went into exile during the reign of the Thirty and returned with the democrats, making his political affiliations perfectly clear (see Socrates' attribution at *Ap.* 20e8–21a2).

According to Plato's *Laches*, Socrates was also on friendly terms with the Athenian generals Nicias[33] and Laches, whose military careers both ended in disaster,[34] but neither of whom was involved in either of the oligarchic coups (of 411 and 404). Of course, this fact alone hardly tells us anything about their political leanings, since both were dead by the time of the first of these oligarchic upheavals. J. K. Davies speaks of a "family taint of oligarchic sympathies" regarding Nicias' grandson by the same name,[35] but he also notes that Nicias' brother, Eucrates,[36] and Nicias' son, Niceratos,[37] were both murdered by the Thirty. In fact, Davies says Nicias' own "relationship with the old aristocracy is tenuous."[38] There is, moreover, no oligarchic "taint" on Laches at all.

Socrates also seems to be on good terms with a certain Callias, son of Hipponikos, at whose house most of the dialogue of the *Protagoras* takes place (*Prt.* 311a1–2; see also *Ap.* 20a5).[39] Again, although Callias would not be the sort of man whose friendship one would point to with pride,[40] his political associations, such as they were, seem to have been with the democrats against the oligarchs.[41]

If we look at all of Socrates' associates, then, contrary to what is often assumed, we do not find a tight clique of oligarchic revolutionaries. And though most are wealthy men, many have ties to the democracy. But even if we look just at those among Socrates' associates whom scholars usually cite—Critias, Charmides, and Alcibiades—we will not find clear evidence of an oligarchic faction, for though Critias and Charmides were among the Thirty, Alcibiades, who died before the second coup, fought *against* the four hundred and helped to return Athens to democracy after the first coup.[42]

Moreover, when Charmides is present among Socrates' associates, he is depicted as a youth for whom Socrates feels a strong physical attraction (see esp. *Charm.* 154d1–5, 155c7–e2), but about whose moral character Socrates is agnostic (*Charm.* 154d7–e1, 175e6–176a5). We are told that Charmides was to continue to learn from Socrates (*Charm.* 176a5–d5), but we find no trace of evidence for supposing that their relationship continued to be close once Charmides became an adult. We know of at least two lessons Charmides did not learn from Socrates: Charmides decided to become a "public" man, in conspiring with Critias and the other members of the Thirty. And in conspiring with the Thirty, Charmides did violence to the laws of Athens. In this, as we have seen, he could not have been following Socrates, who condemned such things.[43]

Even if we accept that at one time Socrates and Critias had been close,[44] there is also ample evidence for great strain in Socrates' relationship with Critias by the time the latter had become the leader of the Thirty. In Plato, we learn that the Thirty hoped to implicate Socrates in their evils by ordering him to go out and arrest Leon of Salamis (*Ap.* 32c4–e1). Socrates disobeyed and simply went home, which he says put him in great danger (*Ap.* 32d7–8). In this passage it is clear that Socrates has nothing good to say about the Thirty, which is what we would expect from someone who regarded violence against the established constitution of Athens as an even greater impiety than violence against one's parents (*Cri.* 51c2–3). This and other stories of friction between Socrates and the Thirty may be found in a number of ancient texts by various authors.[45]

Looking closely at the many and various associates of Socrates in Plato's early dialogues, then, we find little support for the view that Socrates was sympathetic to oligarchic rule or committed to the overthrow of the Athenian democracy. Socrates was, at least at some time, on friendly terms with some of those who were oligarchic extremists and revolutionaries. But he was also on good terms with many other men whose political commitments were directly opposed to those of the oligarchs. Unless we ignore many of Socrates' associates, then, including some of his closest friends (such as Chairephon), we will find no political ideology that is common to all of Socrates' associates.

5.4.3 Why Socrates Sought Association with Such Bad Men

We have argued that Socrates' associations cannot support the view that Socrates was a dangerous oligarchic revolutionary. But there is something about Socrates' associates that may well suggest something wrong. Plato does, in fact, make an astonishingly large number of Socrates' interlocutors "traitors and criminals."[46] If we add "notorious failures" (such as Nicias) to this characterization, we will find blameless men represented only very rarely among those with whom Plato's Socrates speaks. Perhaps scholars have sensed this taint, and sought to explain it in political terms. If it is not the sign of some political association, then, why does Plato so persistently put Socrates in the company of such bad men?

Let us return to Socrates' own characterization of the mission he believes the god commanded him to pursue in Athens. Socrates says that when he first heard about the oracle given to Chairephon, he was astonished because he could not believe that what it appeared to be saying could be true—surely there must be someone wiser than he (*Ap.* 21b3–9).

His first response, in attempting to discover the meaning of the oracle, was to seek out those with the greatest reputation for wisdom and to examine them so as to find out how to solve the oracle's riddle. Socrates' first targets were the "public men," those with the greatest authority and influence in the state. He tells of the first such encounter as follows:

> So examining this one—I don't need to call him by name, but he was a politician . . . and in discussing with him, it seemed to me that this man was thought to be wise by many other people, and, most of all, by himself, but was not. And then I tried to show him that he thought he was wise, but was not. From that time, I have been hated by him and many of those present. (*Ap.* 21c3-d1)

Socrates says he then went to another such man—one even more highly regarded for wisdom than the first—and got the same results he had achieved the first time (*Ap.* 21d7-e2). After a number of such trials, Socrates concludes that "those with the greatest reputation seemed to me nearly the most deficient . . . and those others who were held to be baser seemed to be superior men as regards intelligence" (*Ap.* 22a3–6). From these surprising results, Socrates moves on to examine the poets and the craftsmen, with similar consequences.

At the end of his research, Socrates comes to the conclusion that he really is the wisest of men, for according to his understanding of the oracle he alone recognizes how impoverished he is with regard to wisdom. His mission on behalf of the god, then, becomes (among other things) a mission to seek out those who are the most in need of enlightenment, the high and powerful men whose reputations for wisdom—and whose authority in convincing others to do their bidding—were the greatest. As Socrates says, those with lesser reputations were not as much in need of Socratic humiliation (*Ap.* 22a5–6), although none are as wisely humble as Socrates himself.

The result is that Socrates seeks out those who think they are wise about the most important things when they are not. Those most self-satisfied with their own wisdom are those most likely to make mistakes regarding the most important things in their lives. Such men are especially likely to go wrong in particularly catastrophic ways. And because one's reputation among other men tends to support one's own self-image, those most prone to catastrophe, in Socrates' view, would be those who not only are self-satisfied, but whose smug self-image is buttressed by the admiration and supporting esteem of others. Such men are likely to be the very worst men in any society; and Socrates regards associating with and examining such men—attempting to show them that they are not wise—as crucial to his mission. So if we were to "read the indictment" of this criticism of Socrates as if it were a legal indictment (see *Ap.* 19b3–4), we would read that "Socrates does wrong by associating most closely with the most evil of men." To such a charge, we should suppose, Socrates would eagerly admit his guilt: He has aggressively pursued such associations, as we see documented in Plato's depictions of Socratic conversations, precisely because such men more than any others are in need of being stung by Socrates, the gadfly.

Moreover, when we do see Socrates conversing with such men, we do not find him either cozying up to their most egregious moral or political commitments, or offering to them further grist for their most arrant aspirations and values. Perhaps one of these men depicts Socrates' real goals most vividly; Nicias warns Laches about speaking with Socrates:

> You do not seem to me to know that whoever is closest to Socrates and draws near into a discussion with him, if he would but begin to discuss something else, will necessarily not stop being led around by him in the discussion until he falls into giving an account of himself—of the way he is living now and of the way he has lived in the past. (*La.* 187e6–188a2)

Socrates, let us recall, *refutes* the people he speaks with; he shows them that they do not know what they supposed they knew. Because his entire approach in discussion is adversarial and *ad hominem*, therefore, we should understand that Socrates' interlocutors do not stand for points of view Socrates agrees with. If anything, therefore, the positions for which his interlocutors are best known are those most likely to be targeted and refuted by Socrates. In this peculiar way, then, the characters of Socrates' associates tell us more about what Socrates is *not*—what he *does not believe* and *does not stand for*—than they do about anything he is, believes, or stands for. No doubt Socrates would know of such men, and seek them out, precisely on the basis of their most notorious or extreme points of view. And no doubt Plato would select such interlocutors in portraying Socrates at work—in inventing "Socratic conversations" (as he almost certainly did)—precisely because the most notorious men would provide especially good and fitting moral contrasts to Socrates himself.

A final reason for Socrates' seeking out the worst of men might be seen in Socrates' own search for the truth. As we said in section 1.3.3, Socrates is convinced that he can discover important moral truths by challenging a variety of people whose beliefs differ, and by determining which beliefs, upon reflection, they regard as true. Over time, as he practices the *elenchos* on a wide variety of persons, Socrates comes to have increasing confidence that the positions to which people are driven as a result of elenctic examination are genuine moral truths. Accordingly, some of the most valuable interlocutors for Socrates' search are those whom we should rightly regard as the most thoroughly corrupt, those most disdainful of commonly accepted moral points of view. Such people are particularly useful for Socrates' searches because if he can show that even these people turn out to accept some Socratic moral proposition, on examination, the proposition is given especially revealing support; others might simply agree to the principle out of a sense of shame (see, for example, *Grg.* 482d2–e2).

Accordingly, Socrates is delighted when the most shameless of those present (in the *Gorgias*)—Callicles—becomes engaged in the discussion:

Soc.: If I happened to have a soul made of gold, O Callicles, don't you think I should be delighted to find one of those stones with which they test gold, the best one, which—if I were about to bring my soul to it and it agreed with me that my soul had been well taken care of—would give me complete assurance that I am in good condition and in no need of other test?

Call.: Why do you ask this question, O Socrates?

Soc.: I will tell you: I am thinking in coming upon you I have come upon such a godsend.

Call.: How so?

Soc.: I know well that whenever you agree with me about anything that my soul believes, this must indeed be the truth itself. (*Grg.* 486d2–487a1)

It is fair to conclude that Socrates had nothing in common with evil men with whom is he is often associated. In fact, quite the reverse is true. We are on safer ground in concluding that the persons he sought out served as so many philosophers' stones: proud, powerful, and shameless men by whom Socrates could test the metal (and the mettle) of his soul. Such associations help to define Socrates by contrast to them; no doubt this is why Plato chose to portray the conversations he did. Whether or not most of these conversations ever took place, the cast of characters, it seems, was just what Socrates himself would have prescribed.

5.4.4   Socrates' Trial

We cannot leave this subject until we look briefly at the evidence provided by Socrates' trial. Virtually every scholar who has written about the trial of Socrates has agreed that the real motivation behind the prosecution was political,[47] a claim we have disputed in detail elsewhere.[48] The evidence we have discussed in this chapter, however, should be enough to call such a claim into question. (In the next chapter, we shall attempt to show just how religion was the real issue at Socrates' trial.) We have shown that neither Socrates' own views nor his associations support the view that he was a political threat to Athens. This is, however, unfortunately quite compatible with his having been *seen* as such a threat.[49] Certainly, the very same doctrines and associations have led a number of scholars to endorse the same prejudices. Let us look, then, at the trial itself, to see to what degree politics played a part.

Although there is some ancient support for supposing there to have been a political motivation in the prosecution of Socrates, it is striking that we find absolutely none of this evidence in what are almost certainly our most important sources on the trial—Plato's *Apology* and Xenophon's *Apology*. Xenophon does later (in *Mem.* 1.2.9–64) discuss the political motives of "the accuser." Like most other scholars, however, we take "the accuser" to refer not to any of Socrates' actual prosecutors, but, rather, to Polycrates the sophist, who published an accusation of Socrates a number of years after the actual trial.[50] Why, then, would the political motive be nowhere in evidence in Plato's and Xenophon's accounts of the trial itself?

Scholars have imagined a wide variety of reasons why Xenophon and Plato would suppress the political issue, but their accounts, for obvious reasons, are derived with little support from the texts. Moreover, scholars often claim that Socrates' actual prosecutors could not mention the pertinent political issues aloud in court, supposing that such talk would have been outlawed by the Amnesty of 403/2.[51] Accordingly, Socrates himself would be free to pass over them in silence at his trial. But there are a number of flaws in this reasoning. (a) In fact, the Amnesty would not have ruled out open discussion of Socrates' political activities or those of his associates. It ruled out only the possibility of prosecution for crimes committed prior to, or during, the rule of the Thirty, or for the violation of laws that had been nullified by the Amnesty itself.[52] Insofar as the prosecutors might have supposed that Socrates' political activities or associations—before, during, or after the rule of the Thirty—could be used in a prosecution for crimes still being perpetrated after the restoration of the democracy—for example, seditious oligarchic agitation—they were free to speak openly and in detail about them. (b) The Socrates who speaks to us in Plato's *Apology,* at least, not only claims to be eager to discuss any issue that has led to prejudice against him (see *Ap.* 18a7–19a7), but actually does spend a substantial amount of time, in giving his defense, discussing such issues. If there had been such slanders in the air by the time of the trial, he had, as we have seen, ample ammunition with which to rebut any slanders about his political affiliations or associates. Because he was so willing to combat other slanders he regarded as dangerous to him, his utter lack of attention to the political issues scholars have discussed at such length strongly suggests that Socrates did not see these political issues as any threat at his trial. If he had— certainly if the prosecution had made an issue out of these slanders, as well they could have—he would have had to make some clear reply.

Finally, (c) we find it particularly revealing that the actual indictment against Socrates was religious. Those who find a political motive lurking behind the prosecution simply cannot explain why Meletus and his supporters would choose such an unrelated indictment. It is certainly not as if the Amnesty or any other enactment prohibited trials on charges of sedition or other actions against the government. Given the sorts of people and activities scholars have imagined Socrates to have promoted, why would the prosecutors not have indicted him on subversion?[53] In 399 B.C., within months of Socrates' own trial, Andocides quotes from a law that seems made to order:

> If anyone subverts the democracy at Athens, or holds office when the
> democracy has been subverted, he shall be an enemy of the Athenians

and shall be killed with impunity, and his property shall be confiscated and one-tenth of it shall belong to the Goddess; and he who kills or helps to plan the killing of such a man shall be pure and free from guilt. All Athenians shall swear over unblemished sacrifices by tribes and by demes to kill such a man. The oath shall be as follows: "I shall kill, by word and deed, by vote and by my own hand, if I can, anyone who subverts the democracy at Athens, and anyone who, when the democracy has been subverted, holds any office thereafter. . . ." (Andoc. *Myst.* 96–7; trans. MacDowell, 175)

Given the availability of a more suitable charge, if the motivation for the prosecution had been political, it seems that the trial was, after all, a religious one. One advantage of this view is that we do not now need to see Socrates as dithering or slickly avoiding the real issues when he presents his defense in Plato's *Apology*. Instead, his focus is on the genuine concerns his prosecutors represented in their indictment, and about which his "first accusers" have slandered him for so many years: does Socrates or does he not believe in the gods of the state, and if so, how and why he has gotten his reputation as a dangerous atheist? From those, then, who would claim that Socrates' "discussion of his religious views diverts attention from the real issues,"[54] we must beg to differ; it is the scholars themselves who have diverted attention from the real issues.

• • •

6.2 SOCRATIC THEOLOGY

6.2.1 *Omniscience and Omnibenevolence*

The most fundamental tenet of Socratic theology is that the gods are truly wise (*Ap.* 23a5–6; see also Xen. *Mem.* 1.1.19). Because the possession of wisdom guarantees also the possession of virtue, for Socrates,[55] it follows that the gods are completely virtuous. Thus, Socrates thinks we can be assured that the gods are completely good.[56] Socrates proclaims that humans get nothing good that does not come from the gods (*Euthphr.* 15a1–2), including—at least according to a literal reading of the conclusion of the *Meno*[57] emvirtue itself (*Meno* 99b11–100b6).

This line of reasoning also explains why Socrates finds myths portraying the gods as fighting with one another hard to believe (*Euthphr.* 6a6–8), for the only sorts of disagreements that could make gods or men become enemies are disagreements about the just and the unjust, the fine and the foul, good and evil (*Euthphr.* 7b2–d10). If the gods truly are omniscient about good and evil, however, they should not disagree, and, hence, should never fight. Moreover, the gods would never, in Socrates' view, do anything evil or harmful. This, too, follows from their moral omniscience, for, as we discussed in chapter 3, Socrates is convinced that one cannot know the good and fail to do it, or, conversely, know the evil and do it.

Plainly, then, we have no reason, according to Socratic theology, to fear that we shall be visited with any evil from the gods; for everything they do is good. This theology is summed up in Book II of Plato's *Republic*.[58]

> "Is not the god truly good and must one say so?"
> "Of course."
> "Moreover, nothing good is harmful, is it?"
> "It does not seem so to me."
> "Well, then, does that which is not harmful do harm?"
> "Nor that."
> "Does that which does no harm do evil?"
> "Not that, either."
> "And that which does not do evil would also not be the cause of any evil."
> "How could it be?"
> "And what about this? Is the good beneficial?"
> "Yes."
> "And therefore the cause of doing well?"
> "Yes."
> "The good is therefore not the cause of all things, but of those that are well it is the cause; it is blameless for evil things."
> "Completely true," he said.
> "Neither, therefore," I said, "would the god be the cause of all things, as the many say, since he is good; but he is the cause of few things for human beings, for many things he is blameless. For there are many fewer good things for us than evil; and for the good things we must assume that the cause is nothing other than the god, but for the evil things we must search for another cause, but not the god." (*Rep.* II.379b1–c7)

In the *Republic*, Plato's Socrates goes on to say that this is why many of the traditional myths must be rejected within the ideal state, namely, all of those which portray the gods as sources of evil. The early period Socrates does not advocate the abolition of such myths; the most he ever says about them is that he finds them hard to believe (*Euthphr.* 6a6–8).

6.2.2 Socrates and "The Gods the State Recognizes"

Could Socrates' attitude towards such myths have been what landed him in court? The first two specifications of the legal charge against Socrates were that he "did not believe in the gods the state believes in" and that he "invented new divinities."[59] The proper interpretation of these accusations has long been a matter of scholarly debate,[60] but most scholars have claimed that these charges hide the real concern of the prosecutors, which, in their view, was political rather than religious.[61] Because this view falls apart, as we argued in chapter 5, it seems reasonable to look for a genuinely religious motive behind the plainly religious accusations.

Recently, a few scholars[62] have argued for what they regard as the genuinely religious motivation behind Socrates' prosecution, a motivation which they argue was derived from Socrates' moralistic conception of the gods, a conception owing in part to philosophical developments beginning much earlier in Ionia. The "nature-philosophers," as they were called, had already begun to erode traditional Greek religious beliefs by attempting to provide naturalistic explanations for phenomena traditionally explained in terms of divine agency. This tradition, which may have begun with Thales the Milesian,[63] is burlesqued in Aristophanes' *Clouds*, in which Socrates appears as the head-master at a "Think-Shop" at which such inquiries were characteristic. Of course, Socrates did not engage in precisely these sorts of innovations, but might it not be that Socrates' conceptions of the gods as perfectly moral beings was a similarly revisionary move, designed to rationalize Greek religion no less than did the speculations of the nature-philosophers?[64] Because what Socrates did was so plainly revisionary, we are told, to suppose Aristophanes' assimilation of Socrates to these other revisionaries is not surprising. It is also not surprising that Socrates is eventually brought up on religious charges and convicted.

One product of Socrates' revisions, we are told, is that he ends up actually being guilty of the charges—he disbelieves in "the gods of the state," and "invents new gods," gods of a thoroughly moral nature. As Vlastos has put it,

> What would be left of her [Aphrodite] and of the other Olympians if they were required to observe the stringent norms of Socratic virtue which require every moral agent, human or divine, to act only to cause good to others, never evil, regardless of provocation? Required to meet these austere standards, the city's gods would have become unrecognizable. Their ethical transformation would be tentamount to the destruction of the old gods, the creation of new ones—which is precisely what Socrates takes to be the sum and substance of the accusation at his trial.[65]

6.2.3 How Revolutionary Were Socrates' Views?

Because Socrates believes in completely wise gods and because he thinks the highest form of wisdom is practical, he believes the gods are thoroughly moral. Of course, contrasting accounts to this can be—but are certainly not always—found in Greek literature. There is no single, coherent conception of the gods to be found in Greek myths. In poets as diverse as Homer and Hesiod, or Aeschylus and Euripides, the gods are presented as having very different and often conflicting attitudes and motives in acting as they do towards each other and towards mortals, good and evil.

Socrates' understanding of the gods, then, is different from those myth-ical and literary conceptions which portray the gods as beings who often did visit mortals with disaster. But just how different was Socrates' con-ception from those of his contemporaries? The fact is that the ancient sources themselves never suggest that any of Socrates' contemporaries showed any particular concern over his moralizing conception of the gods.

With the exception of Aristophanes, all of the ancient characterizations of Socrates' public or private practice of customary religious rituals make Socrates look unremarkable and ordinary. Xenophon's Socrates, it seems, never misses a chance to perform a sacrifice, and Plato's, too, can occa-sionally be found offering a sacrifice (*Phd.* 118a7–8; *Symp.* 176a1–4), or a hymn to the gods (*Phd.* 61b2–3; *Symp.* 176a1–4), and claiming to have the standard collection of ritual objects (*Euthyd.* 302b4–d5)—not, we may assume, simply for window dressing. Not once is there any suggestion that Socrates thought standard religious practices to be empty gestures or in need of revision.

Of course, Plato and Xenophon were apologists, but even if we turn to Socrates' most vehement critics, we find no trace of evidence that they con-sidered Socrates' moralized conception to be in any way criminal. In the *Clouds,* for example, Socrates is not depicted as having changed the Athen-ian traditional gods in some moralistic way. Instead, Aristophanes assim-ilates Socrates to the Ionian scientific revolution, whose threat to religion is atheism. So, too, in Plato's *Apology,* we find both the "first" and the "later" accusations explicitly tied to Socrates' alleged role in scientific inquiry, and thus atheism ("first accusers": 18a7–19d7; "later accusers": 26d1–e2). Nothing *whatever* can be found that suggests that his accusers took Socrates' belief in the goodness of the gods to be grounds for the legal action they brought against him, and no trace of Socrates' moralizing of the gods can be found in his characterization of the prejudices of his "first accusers." If even Socrates' accusers could not manage explicitly to find fault with his alleged moral innovations to religion, it is hard to believe such innovations actually troubled anyone else. To these accusers, we might add "the accuser" (no doubt, Polycrates)[66] to whom Xenophon responds in *Memorabilia* 1.2. Xenophon's "accuser" finds many faults with Socrates, but religious innovation is not one of them.

Even Euthyphro, a man who is fanatically devoted to a literal under-standing of certain amoral traditional myths, seems unperturbed by Socrates' explicit skepticism about Euthyphro's conception. When Euthy-phro cites myths attributing savage acts to Zeus, Socrates suggests that perhaps the reason he is being prosecuted is that he finds such stories about the gods hard to believe (6a6–8). Euthyphro is eager to tell Socrates a number of other "amazing things" about the gods (6b5–6, 6c5–7), but seems nonplused at Socrates' reluctance to believe in morally repugnant myths. In fact, Euthyphro seems to concede Socrates' point that such myths are hard to believe (though Euthyphro does enthusiastically believe them) by suggesting that he can tell Socrates some myths that are *"even more amazing"* (6b5), as if the myths Socrates finds hard to accept are amazing enough in themselves. When Euthyphro does speculate about the grounds for Socrates' prosecution, he unhesitatingly locates the innovation in question not in Socrates' moralistic conception, but rather in Socrates' claim to have a private divine sign (3b5–7). On this point, the ancient authorities speak in one voice: Plato and Xenophon both clearly identify the charge of innovation as motivated not by Socrates' ethical transformation of the gods, but rather by his claim to have a private "divine sign"—his *daimonion* (Pl. *Ap.* 31c7–d4; Xen. *Ap.* 12). Where the ancients agree, we see no reason not to believe them.

The upshot of our remarks so far, then, is this: there is no ancient evidence for supposing that his contemporaries were troubled by Socrates' alleged ethical transformation of the gods, however revolutionary that transformation may seem to us. We are inclined to take this as evidence against the view that Socrates' moral transformation of the gods was the ground for his prosecution.

6.2.4 What Socrates Himself Says

Those who allege that Socrates' conception of the gods is so revolutionary as to make him stand outside the law must argue that in the *Apology* Socrates carefully avoids the actual formal charge—that he disbelieves in "the gods of the state"—by getting Meletus to construe the charge as one of atheism. This conception of the charge allows Socrates to refute the claim that he is an atheist without actually affirming his belief in the gods *of the state.*[67] The reason for this, we are told, is that Socrates does *not* believe in the gods of the state, for Socrates is aware of having transformed them beyond recognition.[68]

Before we accept such an implication, we would do well to stop and consider the consequences of this view regarding Socrates' behavior at his trial. For example, it follows that Socrates knows full well that he is guilty of (at least one of) the specifications of the formal charge, but because his nominal accuser, Meletus (and perhaps Meletus' supporting speakers, Anytus and Lycon, as well) have stupidly interpreted their own charge in such a way as to leave the *real* problem unstated, Socrates prudently leaves it unstated as well. Socrates does not express innocence of the *real* accusation against him because he does not have to, once it has been more conveniently interpreted for him by Meletus. Of course, the jury must now be distracted from making the connection that Meletus and his fellow accusers have bungled. Is this why we should suppose that Socrates professes his belief in gods so emphatically, then? Does he hope by this sly exchange of the generic term "gods" for "gods of the state" to confuse the jury into supposing that he has refuted the accusations against him when in fact he has not?

This plainly is not the way Socrates behaves at his trial; he openly and repeatedly admits before the jury to holding a number of moralizing beliefs about the gods (21b6–7: it is not the part [οὐ θέμις] of the god to lie; 23a5–6: the god is really wise; 30c8–d1: it is not the way things are [οὐ θεμι-τόν] that a better man be injured by a worse; 30e1–31c3: the god sends Socrates to Athens because the god cares for humans; and so on). So Socrates has hardly hidden his guilt of disbelieving in the gods of the state—if such moralizing beliefs do indeed make him guilty—and it is not as if he would make it difficult for anyone to prove that guilt. Yet at the end of his defense speech, Socrates is amazed to discover how near he came to winning acquittal. The closeness of the vote cannot be because Socrates repeatedly offended the religious sentiments of his jurors.

The view we have been considering, that Socrates' conception of the gods made him guilty of the formal charges, has at least two other very troubling consequences: (a) if Socrates' alleged moralizing innovations had actually been a serious issue in his prosecution, trial, or conviction, Plato's Socrates would be a liar. Moreover, (b) if Socrates' moralized conception of the gods had been the real issue at his trial, the prosecution itself has avoided bringing the *real* issue to light, and has failed to do so for no apparent reason and despite ample opportunities to do so. Let us review each of these points in order.

From 20c4 to 24b2 in Plato's *Apology*, Socrates imagines someone asking him how the prejudices which have led to his appearance in court came into being, if, as he has already claimed, he is not a nature-philosopher and/or a sophist. He responds by telling the notorious story of the oracle to Chairephon, and of his attempt to understand it,[69] through which he comes to conceive of his elenctic activities as a religious mission.[70] He concludes that his activities in examining others for wisdom are what aroused the terrible enmity he now faces. Because the young men like to imitate him, people say that Socrates corrupts the youth (*Ap.* 23c2–d2). But this slander is not the result of Socrates' skcepticism about the capacity of the gods to do evil or injustice; rather, it is the invention of those who wish to hide their shame in having been shown to be ignorant:

> And whenever someone would ask [those who promote the prejudice against Socrates] "by doing or teaching what [does Socrates corrupt the youth]?" they have nothing to say, but do not know, and yet lest they not seem confused, they say those things that are convenient against all philosophers, "the things in the air and under the earth," and "they do not believe in the gods," and "they make the weaker argument the stronger." For I think they would not want to say the truth, that it is being made very clear that while pretending to know, they know nothing. Therefore, inasmuch as they are lovers of honor, and vehement, and many, and speak eagerly and persuasively about me, they have filled your ears for a long time with vehement slanders. (*Ap.* 23d2–e3)

Socrates goes on to say that it is from among these people that Meletus, Anytus, and Lycon have arisen. He concludes his account of the origin of the prejudices against him with the following words:

> That is the truth, O men of Athens, and I speak without hiding anything from you, great or small, or holding anything back. But I know pretty well that I am making myself hated by these things; this is proof that I say the truth and that this is the slander against me, and these are its causes. (*Ap.* 24a6–b1)

If one of the "real" charges against Socrates is that he believes in thoroughly moral gods, as the view we have been considering claims, then in saying these words Socrates is just lying to the jurors; for according to the view we have been considering, the slanders against Socrates must be traced back not simply to his elenctic examinations, but rather—at least in some way "great or small"—to his scepticism about gods who would do evil and injustice. It is one thing for one to say that Socrates has conveniently neglected a dangerous issue; surely it is another to find that he specifically addresses that issue—the *real* source of the prejudice against him—and flagrantly *lies* about it in order to deceive his jurors. Moreover, if Socrates is lying here, he is also lying when he repeatedly vows to his jurors that they will hear nothing but the truth from him (e.g., at *Ap.* 18a5–6, 20d5–6, 22b5–6, 28a6, 28d6, 32a8, 33c1–2). Socrates, it seems, turns out to be precisely the sort of slick and deceptive speaker the prosecution has made him out to be (see *Ap.* 17a4–b8).

Moreover, Meletus, Anytus, and Lycon turn out to be inexplicably incompetent prosecutors. For one thing, it is difficult to believe that Socrates could have told the story of how the prejudices against him had arisen if these men had already made the case that Socrates' rejection of the common belief in immoral gods threatened civic cult. When Socrates interrogates Meletus at the trial, Meletus has a number of opportunities to make this accusation. Yet if we were to accept the view that Socrates' moralized conception of the gods is one of the real issues behind Meletus' prosecution, Meletus consistently and incredibly bungles each opportunity to show the jury that Socrates' conception is criminal. At 26a8–b7, for example, Meletus makes clear that he thinks Socrates corrupted the youth by means of his teachings about the gods. Socrates then seeks clarification from Meletus as to precisely what Meletus thinks these teachings are:

> With regard to these gods themselves, O Meletus, whom the argument is now about, speak more clearly both to me and to these men. For I cannot understand whether you say that I teach and believe that there are some gods, and thus that I believe there are gods and am not a complete atheist and a wrong-doer in that way, and yet that these gods are not the gods of the state, but others, and this is what you accuse me of—believing in others; or do you say that I do not believe there are gods at all and teach this to others? (*Ap.* 26b8–c6)

If the *real* issue were Socrates' moral transformation of the gods, it is hard to imagine why Meletus would unhesitatingly answer as he does: "That is what I say, that you do not believe there are gods at all" (*Ap.* 26c7). Why would Meletus not instead answer that, however Socrates might claim to believe in gods, according to Socrates' teaching the gods would never do evil and, hence, much or all of Athenian cult religion was a sham? Surely, if such moralistic teaching were such an obvious threat to Athens' customary religion, even someone as dim as Meletus could see how to make the threat clear: Socrates' theology is impious precisely because it would destroy Athens' religion.

Moreover, even if we suppose that Meletus was so foolish that he could not make the obvious connection, we know that Anytus was an accomplished and canny politician; surely *he* could see that Meletus was bungling their case, and could now call out his suggestions for the right answers to Socrates' questions. Even if we are to imagine (without benefit of ancient evidence) that Meletus' supporting speakers are under a gag-order during this interrogation, surely the jurors themselves are not.[71] If Socrates' scepticism about the immorality of the gods was so notorious, why do they not call out their suggestions and accusations at this moment? We do not know that they did not, but if they did, it is remarkably foolish of Socrates not to have acknowledged that his attempt to avoid the "real" issue had failed. If the jurors ever did cry out their recognition of Meletus' error surely Socrates would have had to address the issue of how his moral religion fit civic cult, after all. Instead, he continues his interrogation of Meletus on different points, and then turns to other issues in the last part of his speech, which stretches on for another eight Stephanus pages after Socrates is done with Meletus (28a2–35d8).

So we suggest that the best interpretation of the charges, the prejudices that led to them, and to Socrates' being convicted, is precisely what Plato's Socrates says in the *Apology*. Neither Socrates nor his accusers acknowledge the purported significance of the distinction between the expressions "the gods of the state" and "the gods" either because no one present sees the distinction, or because no one present sees it as pertinent to this case. Accordingly, when Socrates does make it clear that he believes in the gods, he is responding to Meletus' charge that Socrates is an atheist, which is the only conception of the charge anyone supposed was relevant to the trial. Only this account makes sense of what we know about the trial.

6.2.5 A Final Issue Considered

What, then, should we think about what Socrates says in the *Euthyphro*, when he wonders aloud if perhaps he has been brought up on this religious charge because he finds myths about the immorality of the gods hard to believe? It appears that Socrates is at least aware that his own views do not entirely cohere with those of (at least some of) his contemporaries. They certainly do not cohere on this point with those of Euthyphro, for example. Let us not forget, however, that his hypothesis about the motives of his prosecutors is offered as a step in Socrates' bid to engage Euthyphro in elenctic argument. Plainly, not all such "bait" must be taken as reflecting a serious Socratic conviction.

But even if Socrates had been convinced, as he stood with Euthyphro before the King-Archon's office, that his skepticism about the traditional myths of divine immorality led to his indictment, if Plato's account in the *Apology* is at all correct, by the time his trial actually began, either Socrates had become convinced that such skepticism was irrelevant to the charges he faced or he had become devious. The fact is that not once at his trial does Socrates mention his difficulty in believing immoral myths. Of course, as he stood before the King-Archon's office with Euthyphro, Socrates did not yet know the exact grounds for the charges against him, so his opinion about the real motive behind the trial at that point was purely speculative. In any case, by the time he spoke before the jury, he knew well what his accusers had to say, and he knew well what prejudices they had sought to employ in their prosecution. Thus, at that time, he knew exactly what the grounds of the actual prosecution were. Given Socrates' own characterization of the "first accusations," it appears (again) that the problem is that he has been assimilated to the nature-philosophers. This has nothing to do with his skepticism about myths regarding the immorality of the gods. And given the testimony of Meletus, it appears that the charge of disbelief in the gods of the state really was intended to make the connection between the science Socrates is depicted as pursuing and atheism. So either Socrates' speculation in the *Euthyphro* turned out to be off the point, or someone—Plato, we must suppose—is willfully misrepresenting how the issue was actually presented to the jury.[72]

6.2.6 Concluding Remarks

The upshot of our argument is that we also find no evidence for believing that Socrates or any of his peers—friend or foe—saw any threat in Socrates' conviction that the gods were thoroughly moral beings. Moreover, we cannot find any evidence that whatever tension may have existed between Socrates' conception of the gods as moral beings and established religion in Athens actually motivated any of the accusations against him. The only religious tension we do find alleged in the accusations is between Socratic philosophy and theism, a tension Socrates eagerly and, all things considered, quite effectively disputes as based upon a slanderous distortion of what he does in his philosophizing.

The idea that Socrates might not be dangerously critical of his culture's religious attitudes—and especially the idea that he might genuinely believe in dreams and oracles and signs and voices, as we shall argue later in this chapter—is very troubling to some scholars precisely because Socrates has for centuries been held up as the hero of reason. Professional philosophers routinely hold him up as a model of the sort of thinker they try to encourage their students to become—free to question anything, constrained by nothing but reason itself. So Socrates has become the perfect philosophical martyr: he gave up everything else to live the life of philosophical reason, despite all its dangers, and the mob killed him for it. The problem with the ordinary representation of this view is that it is based upon a very anachronistic conception of what "the life of philosophical reason" is taken to be.

Unlike contemporary philosophers, Socrates saw no need to investigate religious beliefs per se. As Aristotle tells us, Socrates confined his philosophical attentions to ethics (*Metaph.* A, 987b1–4,) and so it should not be surprising to us that Socrates seems to have attended to theological issues only insofar as they related to ethical concerns. In fact, Plato himself characterizes Socrates as one who cannot possibly live up to our own image of the religiously critical contemporary philosopher. Socrates' lack of interest in questioning religion in general is starkly evident in his response to Phaedrus' expressions of skepticism.[73] Phaedrus asks if Socrates really believes the old myth about Boreus, and Socrates responds by saying that he regards "the wise ones" (*Phdr.* 229c6) who attempt to explain away the old myths by providing rationalistic interpretations of them, as "clever, hard-working and not completely fortunate men" (*Phdr.* 229d4), for they find themselves in the position of having to go on to explain away all kinds of other mythical creatures and stories (*Phdr.* 229d4–e1). Socrates concludes his response in such a way as to betray an astonishing lack of intellectual interest in critical inquiry regarding religion.

> And if someone who doesn't believe in these things would seek to explain each of them in accordance with probability, by using a bumpkinish sort of wisdom, he will need much leisure. But I have no leisure for these things at all. And the reason, O friend, is this: I cannot yet, as the Delphic inscription has it, know myself. So it seems laughable to me, when I do not know these things—to investigate the still unknown—and purposeless. So I do not pursue these things, but in accepting what is believed about them, as I said just now, I investigate not these things but myself. . . . (*Phdr.* 229e2–230a3)

No twentieth-century philosopher could give this response to Phaedrus. So we should not look to Socrates as a model for the sort of religious criticism or rationalization we now take for granted among philosophers. Instead, we should understand that, for the most part, Socrates unreflectively accepted and intellectually ignored the jumble of myths that constituted the intellectual component of Greek religion, and even regarded the attempt to look critically at these myths as a vanity—a "bumpkinish sort of wisdom"—for which he had no leisure. It does not follow that he believed in the literal truth of these myths; indeed, the insistence that Socrates had to have some very specific and clearly defined commitment one way or the other is itself an anachronism. As he puts it in the passage just quoted, he follows the customary beliefs uncritically and without so much as the leisure or interest to pursue how much or whether he should believe in them. This sort of relation to religion is, we believe, quite common among unreflective people even now; religion has to become an intellectual issue before one even becomes aware of the degree or depth of one's religious beliefs.

NOTES

1. Strauss actually counts "a minimum of six leading factions" within the political spectrum in Athens in the postwar years (1987, 104). These factions and their members would not doubt differ in the ways they regarded issues of importance to the oligarchic-democratic split, which makes an easy identification of a policy along this division somewhat more tricky than it would be if there had been only two parties. The characterizations that follow, therefore, are intended only as rough sketches, to help identify the scholarly issue regarding Socrates' own sympathies rather than to offer a precise picture of Athens' politics at the time in question.
2. Sinclair 1988, 67.
3. Roberts 1984, 53.
4. Jones 1969, 105–6.
5. MacDowell 1978, 34.
6. Ibid.
7. Ibid., 35–40.
8. Ibid., 36, 38.
9. Ibid., 38.
10. Ibid., 249.
11. Ibid., 237.
12. Ibid., 250.
13. These include Stone 1988, 117–39; Grote 1888, vol. 7, 144–46; Guthrie 1971, 61–64; Vlastos 1983, 495–516; A. E. Taylor 1933, 103.
14. See, for example, *Mem.* 2.6.26, 3.1.4, 3.7.5–9, and 3.9.10.
15. Winspear and Silverberg 1960, 84.
16. Wood and Wood 1978, 97.
17. For an excellent discussion of the anti-democratic sentiment behind this phrase during the gigarchic upheavals during the latter part of the fifth century, see Andrewes 1974, 212–13.
18. See Bury 1962, 249, who calls Aristeides one of the "three most prominent" of "the progressive democratic statesmen" of the time.
19. Ibid.
20. Ibid., 328.
21. For the political rivalry between Cimon and Pericles, see ibid. 329.
22. Ibid., 349.
23. Callicles' own selection of great leaders is also bi-partisan. But just as we should not be surprised to see Socrates' indifference to party politics, Callicles' own is not puzzling. Callicles does not hold a political ideology; rather, he seeks involvement in public affairs to promote his own private interests. Accordingly, he would approve of anyone who held political power, no matter what faction the powerful person represented.
24. See Brickhouse and Smith 1989, 174–79.

25. See, for example, Woodruff 1982, note on *Hip. Ma.* 284d6–7, 41; and Colson 1989. We are convinced that the Laws for whom Socrates speaks are none other than the unmodified statutes of Athens.

26. Wood and Wood 1978, 97.

27. See, for example, Pl. *Rep.* VI.495d4–e2, *Laws* 919c3–d2; Xen. *Oec.* 4.2–3; Arist. *Pol.* 1328b39–1329a2, 1337b5–15.

28. For a discussion of this transformation in Plato's thought, see Vlastos 1991, ch. 4.

29. We learn from the *Symposium* (217a2–219d2) that Alcibiades was terribly frustrated by the chastity of the relationship, which Socrates seems to have maintained as a primarily (if not completely) intellectual one. See also *Prt.* 309a1–d2, where Socrates' attraction to Alcibiades is completely eclipsed by the opportunity to have a searching conversation with Protagoras.

30. Mogens Herman Hansen counts "about a half" of those who talk with Socrates in Plato's dialogues as "criminals and traitors." These quotations are from a letter from Hansen to N. Smith dated February 2, 1987, in which Hansen refers to his argument for this conclusion in his article (1980, see esp. 73–76 and nn. 81–91). Since neither of the authors of this book reads Danish, we would not have been able to cite Hansen's work here without his generous assistance. As will become obvious, however, we do not agree with the conclusions Hansen draws from this evidence.

31. In making this comment, we do not have in mind Hansen, who does recognize Socrates' friendship with Chairephon (1980, 74). For an example of the sort of oversight we are criticizing here, see Chroust, who writes 34 pages (1957, 164–97) on what he calls "the political aspects of the Socratic problem" without once mentioning Socrates' longtime friendship with Chairephon.

32. Socrates' description of Chairephon as an "ἑταῖρος" may itself have political significance. Athens' ἑταιρεῖαι were recognized as having strong political roles—they were, according to Thucydides, "associations for the management of lawsuits and elections" (8.73.3). Socrates' identification of Chairephon as an "ἑταῖρος," therefore, would perhaps be surprising if Socrates could be counted among the oligarchic faction; instead, it could actually suggest a democratic affiliation. On the political role of the ἑταιρεῖαι, see Strauss 1987, 20.

33. Socrates also identifies Nicias, at *Grg.* 472a5–6, as one who would be willing to give false testimony on Polus' behalf. This would appear to be some evidence against a very close relationship between Socrates and the general; it certainly distances Socrates from what he takes to be Nicias' moral views.

34. For summaries, see Bury 1962, 453–63 (Nicias) and 448 (Laches).

35. J. Davies [1971], 406.

36. Ibid., 404; see Lys. 18.5; Suda *A* 3069.

37. J. Davies [1971], 405; see Lys. 18.6, 19.47; Plut. *Mor.* 998b.

38. J. Davies [1971], 404.

39. Ibid., #7826, 254–70.

40. J. Davies refers to Callias' "urbane extravagance and aristocratic fecklessness" (ibid., 261).

41. See Strauss 1987, 102, who makes this inference from what Callias' oligarchic opponent, Andocides, does and does not say at Andocides' trial (see Andoc. *Myst.* 117 ff.).

42. Thucydides tells us that Alcibiades initially supported the abolition of the democracy in the hopes that he might be restored at Athens if the democracy

under which he had been sentenced to death in absentia were removed. But later, it is plain that Alcibiades worked with the enemies of the four hundred to restore the democratic government, and was restored as his reward. See Thuc. 8.45–97. Given the use to which Socrates' association with Alcibiades has been put, it is remarkable that one of the principal texts cited in support of the claim that this association put a political taint on Socrates—Xenophon's *Memorabilia* (1.2.12)—distinguishes the activities of Critias under the oligarchy from the "hubris and violence" of Alcibiades under the democracy.

43. Xenophon's claim that it was Socrates who persuaded Charmides to go into politics (*Mem.* 3.7.1), which is repeated by Diogenes Laertius (2.29), simply cannot be squared with the Platonic Socrates' proscription of such activities. It is not our purpose here to argue for the greater historical reliability of the Platonic portrait.

44. Vatai suggests that Socrates and Critias had been lovers (1984, 65), but cites no text to support this claim.

45. Regarding the Thirty's order to arrest Leon, see also [*Epist.* 7] 324d8–325a3, 325c1–5; Xen. *Mem.* 4.4.3. Other sorts of conflicts are reported in Xen. *Mem.* 1.2.29–38; Diod 14.5.1–3. Because these other incidents are not discussed in Plato, they do not concern us here. We do discuss them, however, in Brickhouse and Smith 1989, 181–84.

46. The phrase is Hansen's. See n.65, above.

47. See, for examples, Barker 1951, 93–94; Bonfante and Raditsa 1978; Burnet 1924, note on 18b3; Bury 1926; Chroust 1957, 26, 164–97; Hansen 1980; Lofberg 1928, 602; MacDowell 1978, 202; Montuori 1981, 167–68, 177–86; Roberts 1984, 243–46; Seeskin 1987, 75–76; Stone 1988; Vlastos [1983]; and especially Winspear and Silverberg 1960; esp. 64–85. Zeller (1963, 217) and Guthrie (1971, 62–63) take the more cautious view that the trial was only partly the product of a political motive. Perhaps I. F. Stone, in his recent book on the trial, puts this point of view most succinctly. Stone proclaims that "it was the political, not the philosophical or theological, views of Socrates which finally got him into trouble. The discussion of his religious views diverts attention from the real issues." (1988, 138–39). In Brickhouse and Smith 1989, 69–87, we argue against these scholars. A few other scholars have also questioned the relevance of politics at Socrates' trial; see, for example, Cohen 1988, Finley 1968, ch. 5; Hackforth 1933, 73–79; and Irwin 1989, who advances a view in many ways similar to ours on this topic.

48. See n.82.

49. So Vlastos 1983, for example, argues that Socrates did not deserve to be condemned as a "crypto-oligarch," but remains convinced that such a prejudice fueled the prosecution.

50. For a detailed reconstruction of Polycrates' accusations, see Chroust 1957, 69–100. In addition to Xenophon's *Mem.*, the ancient sources include Aisch. Rhet. 1.173; Isoc. *Bus.* 5; D.L. 2.38–9; Libanius, *Ap*. The only scholar we know of who rejects the identification of Xenophon's "accuser" with Polycrates is Hansen (1980, 59–64). At least some support for the established view, which we follow, may be found in the fact that when Xenophon mentions the one or ones who actually did prosecute Socrates, he does not refer to "ὁ κατήγορος" ("the accuser"—1.2.12, 26, 49, 51, 56, 58), whom he identifies in all of the passages in which political issues are raised, but rather to "οἱ γραψάμενοι" (1.1.1) or "ὁ γραψάμενος" (1.2.64)—"the one(s) who wrote the indictment." This would appear to distinguish those who would qualify as "γραψάμενοι" namely, Mele-

tus, Anytus, or Lycon, from Xenophon's "κατήγορος" namely, Polycrats. We argue in Brickhouse and Smith (1989, 84–85) that Polycrates was in all likelihood the primary source of all of the ancient evidence for there having been a political motive behind the prosecution of Socrates. Later writers simply echoed or responded to Polycrates' accusations.

51. See, for example, Allen 1975, 12; Burnet 1924, 101; Bury 1940, 393; Davies 1971, 187; Navia [1985], 14 and 39, n.20; Roberts [1984], 245.

52. See our discussion in Brickhouse and Smith [1989b], 32 n. 113, and 74; see also Loening 1981, esp. vii.

53. See MacDowell 1978, 175–91, for a review of such laws.

54. See Stone 1988, 139.

55. This follows because of the unity of the virtues. Commentators disagree about just what Socrates is committed to with the unity of the virtues thesis. Vlastos (1978 and 1991, ch. 8) denies that Socrates thinks that "courage," "wisdom," "temperance," "justice," and "piety" all name the same thing. The contrary view is defended by Penner 1973 and 1992; Irwin 1977, 86–90; and C.C.W. Taylor 1976, 103–8. Although Kraut thinks that virtue terms name the same thing, he denies that they have the same scope (see Kraut 1983, n.28, 261). We describe and defend our own view of the unity of the virtues in Brickhouse and Smith 2000, 158–173.

56. See Vlastos (1989a, revised as 1991, ch. 6; in the remainder of this discussion, we will refer only to the more recent [revised] version, unless otherwise specifically noted). Vlastos claims that Socrates' ascription of beneficence to the gods does not simply follow from his view that they are perfectly wise. Vlastos argues, "To allow one's gods infinitely potent intellect is not of itself to endow them with flawlessly good will" (1991, 163–64). But one of the most notorious features of Socratic philosophy is the tenet that one cannot know the good and fail to do it (see our discussion of this in 3.5). Given this thesis, it *does* follow, in Socratic philosophy, that omniscience entails omnibenevolence.

57. Some may not accept our employment of this part of the *Meno* to aid our understanding of the philosophy of Plato's early period Socrates, on the ground that traces of a number of middle period doctrines may already be found in that dialogue. We agree that caution is required in general. However, we also regard the specific claim we are considering here consistent with, and one possible extension of, the claim made at *Euthyphro* 15a1–2.

58. Although we do not regard this part of the *Republic* as among the early dialogues with which we are specifically concerned in this book, we find the doctrine Plato's Socrates articulates in this passage entirely consistent with what Plato's Socrates says about the gods in the early period dialogues.

59. See n.1, above.

60. For a summary of the various positions, see Brickhouse and Smith 1989b, 30–36.

61. See Brickhouse and Smith 1994, ch. 5, n.81, for references.

62. See Connor 1991; McPherran 1990 and 1991; Vlastos 1991, chapter 6.

63. Vlastos says that Thales' younger associate, Anaximander of Miletus, was "the true founder of Ionian *physiologia*" (Vlastos 1991, 159, n. 13), but gives no reason for not considering Thales. Thales' pair of primary principles—that "everything is full of gods" (Arist. *De An.* A5, 411a7–9), and that the first principle of all things is water (see Arist. *Met.* A3, 983b20–27)—certainly tempt one to think that a rational and naturalistic restructuring of divinity had already

begun in his philosophy. There is too little evidence to make any conclusive judgment on this matter, however.

64. See Vlastos 1991, 162; McPherran 1991.

65. Vlastos 1991, 166. See also Connor 1991, 56.

66. This identification is defended in Brickhouse and Smith 1989, 71–72, 84.

67. Vlastos makes the following point about Socrates: "that he believes in the gods is clear enough; that he believes in the gods *of the state* he never says" (1991, 166, n.41, his emphasis).

68. See above n. 17. McPherran 1990 also accepts this point.

69. Some have argued that even here Socrates betrays a kind of impious skeptical disrespect for the god. So Burnet claims that Socrates "tries to prove the god a liar" ([1924], note on 21b8), and Nehamas speaks of "Socrates' effort to prove the oracle wrong" ([1986], 306) and says that Socrates "tests the oracle's wisdom as rigorously as he tests the wisdom of those by means of whom he tests the oracle itself" (1986, 305). What such scholars miss is that Socrates begins his inquiry into the meaning of the oracle with the conviction that although the god can speak in riddles (*Ap.* 21b3–7), it is not within the god's nature to lie (*Ap.* 21b6–7).

70. For discussion and explication of the process by which this transformation takes place, see Brickhouse and Smith 1989, sec. 2.5.

71. It was not uncommon for jurors to create a disturbance during trials. In Plato's account of the trial, Socrates repeatedly pleads with the jury not to do so—see *Ap.* 17d1, 20e4, 21a5, 27b1, 27b5, 30c2, 30c3. For a discussion of such disturbances, see Bers 1985.

72. In fact, we do not need to suppose even that Socrates is represented in the *Euthyphro* as actually believing that this is the source of the accusation. He may say what he does only to express his doubts about such stories in such a way as ironically to underscore his own fallibility and vulnerability on such issues, thus emphasizing his "need" for Euthyphro's instruction. Certainly, nothing more is made of this issue regarding the actual legal case, in this or any other ancient source.

73. In general, we believe that middle and late period dialogues cannot be used to interpret earlier works except when they supplement or clarify positions already established as Socratic in the early period works (see nn. 7 and 8, above). We believe that this passage in the *Phaedrus* may be cited as evidence of the views of Plato's Socrates as opposed to the views of Plato because the passage fits the general principle we follow regarding the use of middle period works to help interpret the early period works.

CHAPTER 8

Socrates and Obedience
to the Law

From *Socrates and the State*

RICHARD KRAUT

AN INCONSISTENT SOCRATES?

According to one common interpretation of the *Crito*, the Laws leave no room whatsoever for justified disobedience. Rather, they require "absolute submission," "blind obedience," "strict and complete compliance."[1] The problem for such an interpretation is that it makes Socrates contradict himself. He says that we must never do what is unjust, a point made more forcefully in the *Crito* than anywhere else (49a4–b8). What if a law or an order requires the citizen to perform an act that he correctly believes is unjust? If Socrates is committed to blind obedience, then the act must be done. If he calls upon us never to act unjustly, then the act must not be done. Obviously, a Socrates who will always obey the city, no matter what it commands, is an inconsistent Socrates.

   The contradiction can be avoided by a philosopher who believes that somehow or other law and virtue cannot conflict. Such a doctrine might be attractive to Thrasymachus, since he wants to recognize no standard of justice other than the decrees of a particular city.[2] But Socrates is worlds apart from such a position. He thinks there is an objective standard of justice;[3] this means that it is possible for human beings to make mistakes about what

Richard Kraut, from *Socrates and the State* (Princeton, NJ: Princeton University Press, 1984), pp. 11–24.

is just; and obviously if those who have political power go wrong about justice, they will make defective laws.[4] The possibility that moral blindness might coincide with political power is for Socrates no merely theoretical possibility. As we have seen, he insists that the democratic majority and the politicians of Athens have no moral expertise. If a law or decree has been adopted by a large popular vote, that does not give Socrates the slightest reason for thinking that it is a good or a just decision. Accordingly, he is the last person in the world who would have been surprised at the existence of unjust legislation and unjust commands in Athens. We should expect his objective conception of ethics and his contempt for the many to lead him to the conclusion that sometimes in a democracy a virtuous man will have to disobey his city's commands. And that is precisely what he does say, in the *Apology*. He assures the jury that if they were to order him to give up his philosophical mission, he would disobey them (29b9–d5). Furthermore, democracies are not the only political systems in which a virtuous citizen might have to defy the state. He reminds his audience that when he was commanded by the Thirty Oligarchs to bring in Leon of Salamis to be executed, he merely walked away, because he thought their order impious and unjust (32c4–e1). Evidently, Socrates was clearheaded enough to see that you cannot be unconditionally committed both to justice and to obedience. He insists that when an order calls upon a citizen to act in a way that conflicts with virtue, he must refuse.

None of this shows, of course, that the *Crito*, like the *Apology*, recognizes the need for disobedience. That issue can only be resolved by an examination of the text. Nonetheless, the evidence of the *Apology* forces the responsible reader to adopt a certain interpretive policy toward the *Crito*. Suppose, when we turn to the speech of the Laws, we find certain ambiguities: certain statements might be taken to mean that disobedience is sometimes justified, or they might also be given a more authoritarian interpretation. Should this occur, we will have good reason to adopt the more permissive reading. If possible, the *Crito* ought to be interpreted in a way that makes it consistent with the *Apology* and the other early Platonic dialogues.[5]

PHILOSOPHY BANNED

It could be argued that in the *Apology* Socrates is not nearly so defiant of authority as I have made him out to be. Consider his statement that he would disobey the court were it to order him to abandon philosophy:

> . . . Suppose you should say to me, "Socrates, for now we will not be persuaded by Anytus, but instead we will release you—on this condition, however, that you no longer spend your time on inquiry or philosophy. But if you should be caught doing this, you will die." If, as I say, you were to release me on these terms, I would say to you, "I have

the utmost regard and affection for you, Athenian gentlemen, but I will obey the god rather than you, and so long as I breathe and am able, I shall not cease from philosophizing. . . . (29c5–d5)

Socrates is certainly threatening to disobey[6]—but would he be violating a legal command?[7] If the order to give up philosophy is *illegal*, then perhaps our passage tells us less than we had thought.

Two uncontroversial points about Athenian law are relevant at this point.

(A) There was no fixed penalty attached to certain crimes, including those of which Socrates was accused. In such cases, the appropriate form of punishment had to be chosen by the jury. But the jury had to decide on the question of guilt or innocence before it could consider the question of punishment. If the defendant was judged innocent of the charges against him, the court no longer had authority to issue penalties or stipulate conditions for release. Accordingly, Socrates' jurors could not declare him innocent and then order him to refrain from philosophical inquiry. Such an order would have no legal standing.[8]

(B) If an Athenian jury found a defendant guilty as charged, and if punishment was not fixed by law, then the jury had to decide between two penalties; the first was proposed by the prosecutor and the second by the defendant. A jury had no other choice but to decide between these two—it could not invent a third alternative of its own.[9] Accordingly, Socrates' jurors could not have assured him that they would vote him guilty but then release him on easy terms. Had they ignored the proposed penalties of Meletus and Socrates, and voted instead for a ban on philosophy, that ban would have had no legal force.

Armed with these two points, someone might argue that Socrates is not being as defiant as we might have thought. The court is thinking of acquitting him and then restricting his activity, or it is proposing to find him guilty and punish him by banning further inquiry. In either case, the jury's order would be contrary to law. Therefore, when Socrates says that he will obey god rather than the court, he may only mean that he will refuse to abide by an illegal order. In that case, he might still subscribe to a doctrine of submission to all *lawful* commands.

But I do not think there is much plausibility to this proposal. Our passage tells us that Socrates "shall not cease from philosophizing" so long as he is alive, and throughout the *Apology* Socrates repeats the point that his practice of cross-examining others is required by god.[10] His commitment to philosophy is therefore so strong that it has to take precedence over any civil command, whether legal or illegal. And we should realize that a legally valid ban on the practice of philosophy would not be an impossibility in democratic Athens. The Assembly would merely have to pass a law, by a simple majority, prohibiting all persons from challenging conventional beliefs in public places. This would be an outrageously vague decree, but Athens had no Supreme Court to strike down broad restrictions on speech. Since Socrates is unconditionally committed to obeying god and practicing philosophy, he would have to violate such a ban on inquiry, despite its legality.

If we need any further assurance on this point, we can find it in a famous passage that occurs later in the *Apology*. Socrates has been found guilty, Meletus has proposed that he be put to death, and now a counter-penalty is in order (36b3–4). Should he propose exile? Socrates says (37c4–e2) that this would have some chance of acceptance. But he nonetheless refuses to recommend it, for if he goes to other cities and continues to ask philosophical questions, he will receive the same treatment Athens is giving him. He can hardly expect other communities to be more tolerant of philosophy than his native city. And so, if he continues to practice philosophy, he will be exiled from one city after another—a life in which he sees no value. But what about proposing exile and then giving up philosophy? Once again, Socrates reminds the jury that this is unacceptable.

> Perhaps someone might say, "Can you not leave us and live in peace and quiet?" On this point it is most difficult of all to persuade some of you. If I say that this is disobeying the god and that for this reason it is impossible to keep quiet, you will not be persuaded, but will think I am being ironical. If I go on to say that this happens to be the greatest good for man—to construct arguments every day about virtue and the other things about which you hear me conversing as I examine myself and others—and if I say that an unexamined life is not worth living for man, you will be even less persuaded. (37e3–38a6)

Notice that Socrates would have to give these same arguments were Athens to adopt a legal prohibition on philosophical activity. Obviously, such a decree would be designed to hound Socrates out of the city; and if Athens were to use this legal weapon against him, other cities, which are no more tolerant of criticism, would follow suit. Socrates therefore has no alternative: faced with a law against philosophy, he could not give it up, and he would not leave the city; he is unavoidably committed to disobeying a valid law, if need be.

Still, a sense of puzzlement may remain. Admittedly, Socrates is prepared to disobey even lawful decrees prohibiting philosophy. But why does he express this point by threatening to defy a court order that would in fact be illegal? Doesn't the unlawfulness of that order weaken the force of his statement? I think we can answer this question if we consider a point Socrates makes in the sentence immediately preceding our passage. It reports a statement Anytus had made to the jury: either Socrates should not have been brought to court, or, since he is being tried, there is no alternative to finding him guilty and sentencing him to death (29c1–3). What is important here is the fact that the prosecutors have already announced that they are going to recommend the death penalty, for this must have raised a poignant difficulty for many of the jurors. They are not convinced that Socrates deserves to die; he later says, as we have seen, that exile might be acceptable to them (37c4–5). On the other hand, they really think that Socrates is undesirable, if not downright dangerous, and they wish they could muzzle him in some way. Accordingly, many jurors must have been tempted to vote for acquittal, in the hope that his trial would be enough to scare Socrates into quiescence. But such a strategy would certainly be risky, since nothing could assure the court that the defendant would in fact change his ways. Thus many jurors must have found themselves thinking, "If only we could let Socrates go this time and order him to give up philosophy, on pain of death." Socrates realizes that his audience is ambivalent, but he does not want them to vote for acquittal in the hope that he might stop philosophizing. He wants them to know just what sort of person he is, and so tells them that he is not going to abandon philosophy, no matter what they do. They might as well stop wishing that they had the power to forbid further inquiry, for he would disobey any such order. True, the court's ban on philosophy would be unlawful, but that is not relevant to the point Socrates is making, and he therefore does not even mention the issue of legality.

I suggest that when we read our passage with this background in mind, it makes perfect sense. And I conclude that Socrates was clear-headed enough to see where his uncompromising principles led him. Unwilling to leave Athens, religiously dedicated to a philosophical way of life, he realizes that he would have to disobey any order or decree prohibiting him from examining himself and others.

LEON AND THE THIRTY

It will be helpful to take a more careful look at the other case in which Socrates expresses a willingness to disobey a city's orders. In this instance, his defiance is not hypothetical but real. It occurred after the close of the Peloponnesian War, some five years before his trial, when the Spartan general Lysander pressured Athens into adopting a new oligarchic regime.

> . . . When the oligarchy came into being, the Thirty sent for me and four others to come to the Rotunda, and ordered us to bring from Salamis Leon the Salaminian, so that he would be killed. Such orders they gave to many others, since they wanted to spread the blame as widely as possible. However, I then proved, not by talk but by action, that—to put it in an uncultivated way—death doesn't mean a thing to me; rather, to do nothing unjust or unholy: that is my whole concern. That government, powerful as it was, didn't scare me into doing anything unjust. When we came out of the Rotunda, the other four went to Salamis and brought in Leon, but I walked away and went home. And perhaps I would have been killed because of this, if the government hadn't been overthrown soon afterwards. (32c4–d8)

The implications of this passage are clear: Socrates was given an order by the government in power, and he disobeyed because he refused to commit an unjust act. Generalizing, we may say that he will not do what is contrary to virtue, even when he has been given a command by the Athenian government. Is there any reasonable objection to drawing this conclusion?

(A) Burnet says: "There is no inconsistency . . . between the attitude of Socrates in the *Crito* and his disobedience to the arbitrary orders of the Thirty some years earlier. . . . The Thirty were a temporary body appointed . . . to revise the laws, and they had no legal authority to do anything except what was necessary to carry out this duty."[11] Evidently, Burnet thinks that according to the *Crito* citizens must obey all laws and all *lawful* commands. Since the order to arrest Leon was *un*lawful, Socrates could consistently disobey it and still subscribe to a highly authoritarian political philosophy.

Whether Burnet is right about the *Crito* is an issue we shall soon discuss at length. Let us see whether he is right about the *Apology*. If we have to decide whether the command to arrest Leon was in fact lawful, we enter a thicket of historical and conceptual questions. Was the authority formally given to the Thirty by the Assembly so broad and vague that they did have some legal basis for arresting and condemning such men as Leon?[12] When a new regime arises through force of arms, is the distinction between legal and illegal applicable? If a revolutionary government issues orders that circumvent the legal machinery of the prior constitution, is it in effect creating a new legal system? Fortunately, we need not be led astray by these difficult questions, for what matters to us is the justification Socrates gives in the *Apology* for having disobeyed the Thirty. Did *he* believe that this order was illegal? It would be absurd to answer this question by first deciding whether in fact the order was illegal and then assuming that Socrates would agree with us. We can simply look at the *Apology* and see why he thought disobedience justified in this case. He tells the court that the order of the Thirty was unjust, and says nothing whatever about its legal status.[13] Socrates did not have to worry about the issue of legality, since the injustice of arresting Leon gave him all the reason he needed to disobey. In this passage, the *Apology*, like the *Crito*, upholds the view that one must never commit an unjust act.

If we need any further support for this interpretation, we can find it in the lines that immediately precede our passage. In them (32b1–c4), Socrates reminds his judges that several years before the democracy was overthrown, he had opposed a motion in the Assembly to try ten generals as a group for having failed to pick up the survivors in the battle of Arginusae. Such a collective trial, Socrates says, was unjust and illegal, and that is why he opposed it. The fact that Socrates emphasizes the trial's illegality (he repeats the point twice) makes it all the more significant that he says nothing, in the lines that follow, about the legal status of the Thirty's order to arrest Leon.[14] His silence suggests that he either thinks their order legal, or he does not care to discuss the issue. In either case, the wrongfulness of their command was enough to justify his defiance.[15]

(B) Woozley says: ". . . while Socrates should have had no difficulty in allowing . . . that . . . an executive order might require a man to do what was unjust, it is perhaps less certain that he would have said the same thing of a *nomos* [law]; and *nomos* is the word used uniformly throughout the *Apology* and the *Crito*. . . . It would have been impossible for Socrates to believe that in disobeying their [the Thirty's] order to bring in a man for summary execution he was disobeying the law."[16]

I agree that the Thirty's order was merely that—an order, and not a law. But Woozley proposes that for Socrates this is a distinction that makes all the difference, and that I cannot accept. We have just seen that Socrates does not challenge the legal authority of the Thirty; he objected to their order because it required an unjust act, not because that government had no right to issue orders. He apparently believed that Leon had done no wrong, and he refused to collaborate in the murder of an innocent person. Now, since Socrates says in the *Apology* that he would never commit an injustice, he surely would have refused to arrest Leon even if such acts had been sanctioned by statute. If what an order calls for is a wrongful killing, then it remains wrongful even if it is required by law. Furthermore, we already know that Socrates is committed to disobeying the law, if need be. As I have argued, he would have violated a law prohibiting philosophical inquiry. Since Socrates believes that lawbreaking is sometimes justified, and since he is committed to avoiding all wrongdoing, he could not have submitted to a law that calls for wrongful killing.

I want to correct one other mistake Woozley makes when he says that ". . . *nomos* [law] is the word used uniformly throughout the *Apology* and the *Crito*. . . ." I take him to be suggesting that the *Crito* is about disobedience to the *law,* rather than obedience to orders, decrees, or any other political decisions that have a lower status than the law.[17] His idea is that although the *Crito* might require blind obedience to the law, it would still leave room for disobeying orders, since it simply does not discuss this topic; and thus the submissiveness of the *Crito* can be reconciled with defiance of the Thirty. But Woozley is simply wrong to suggest that the *Crito* does not discuss disobedience to orders. Consider the dialogue's statement that the citizen must "either persuade or do what the fatherland commands . . ." (51b3-4). In what way does Athens (or any other city, for that matter) issue commands? Only through its laws? Not at all, since the supreme political power in the city, the Assembly, delegates the right to command to those who occupy various legal offices and fulfill various legal functions. A court, for example, is given the authority to order individuals to submit to certain penalties if they are found guilty of specified offenses. And similarly a general is given the right to issue orders to his subordinates and soldiers. Therefore, when the *Crito* says that citizens must "either persuade or do what the fatherland commands . . . ," it is as much talking about obeying a court or a military officer as it is about obeying a law. This comprehensiveness is explicitly advertised by the text: ". . . one must neither yield nor run away nor leave one's post, but in battle and in court *and everywhere* one must do what the city and fatherland commands, or persuade it as to the nature of justice . . ." (51b7–c1, my emphasis). In this passage, the *Crito* is striving for generality. It wants to say something about every case in which a citizen might disobey the city, and therefore its political philosophy is extended to every situation in which a citizen is given an order by a legal official or body, whether that be the Assembly, a court, a military officer, or a magistrate.[18] So the *Crito* confirms the point I made earlier: for Socrates, the distinction between a law and an order is of little significance. He is interested in the perfectly general question of when a citizen should do that which his city, through its legal institutions and officers, tells him to do.[19]

(C) When Socrates tells the story of Leon, he calls the Thirty an oligarchy, and he reminds his audience that the regime they replaced was democratic (32c3–4). It might therefore be suggested that he saw nothing wrong with disobeying the Thirty because he thought power should reside in the hands of the many and not the few. But I see no merit in this idea. When Socrates explains why he disobeyed, he only refers to the injustice of the order to arrest Leon. What he objected to in this oligarchy was the way in which it used its power; we have no evidence that he believed thirty to be an unduly small number when it comes to rulers. We saw earlier that according to Socrates the many are unalterably corrupt, and he would therefore have no objection in principle to a sharp reduction in the number of those holding power in Athens. When he disobeys the Thirty, he does so because of the content of their commands, and not because of the oligarchical form of their government.[20]

Later, I will present a more thorough examination of Socrates' attitude toward democracy. For now, I conclude that when he disobeys the Thirty, his reason has nothing to do with the legality of their order; nothing to do with the fact that it was merely an order and not a law; and nothing to do with the fact that they were only thirty in number. Plainly and simply, he disobeyed because their order called upon him to do an unjust act. It is safe to generalize and say that according to the *Apology* Socrates will disobey any law or order of any government, if that law or order calls upon him to perform an act he considers unjust.[21] This general principle also stands behind his refusal ever to abandon his role as a moral critic of Athens. To disobey the god's command would have been an act of impiety, according to Socrates, and since impiety is injustice toward the gods (*Euphr.* 12c10–d4), giving up a philosophical life would have been an act of injustice. Socrates insists upon doing what is just, according to his understanding of justice, and he clearly recognizes that such an attitude can lead to trouble with the law. Our two examples of defiance in the *Apology* show us that Socrates did, in fact, draw the conclusion we would in any case have expected of him: since he will always do what he believes to be just, and since his city's conception of justice will not always match his own, he will sometimes have to disobey.

If Socrates is clearheaded enough in the *Apology* to recognize that political orders can conflict with virtue, we should expect comparable lucidity in the *Crito*. Since he applauds the speech of the Laws, he presumably interprets it in a way that leaves room for his principle that one must never act unjustly. So we too ought to look for parts of that speech that open the door to justified disobedience. And once we find them, we must see how they can be integrated into the rest of the speech to form a consistent theory.

NOTES

1. "Absolute submission" is Grote's phrase (1875, 303), "blind obedience" (une obéissance aveugle"), Romilly's (1971, 130), and "strict and complete compliance," A. E. Taylor's (1936, 168).

2. See *Rep.* 338c1–339b8. Note especially 339b7–8: justice is obedience to the rulers. Socrates immediately forces Thrasymachus to abandon this extreme position. *Tht.* 175c–177d also rejects the doctrine that whatever a city establishes as just really is just for it. For philosophical treatments of Thrasymachus and further references to the philosophical literature, see Irwin 1977, 289 n. 23; Annas 1981, 34–49, 57–58.

3. I take it to be an uncontroversial matter that Socrates has an objective conception of ethics. That is, he assumes that there are independent truths about the good, and that we must come to know them if we are to become virtuous. The craft analogy of Plato's early dialogues and the search for definitions presuppose the objectivity of ethics.

4. The point is well put by Allen 1980 89: "The Biblical injunction that thou shalt not follow a multitude to do evil is one which Socrates would most emphatically have accepted . . . and it is deprived of meaning if what the multitude do, when organized, is by definition good."

5. It might be objected the *Crito*'s apparent authoritarianism is consistent with the authoritarianism of the *Republic,* and that the former work should therefore be considered a middle dialogue, or at least a transitional work. According to this hypothesis, the *Crito* represents Plato's quarrel with Socrates, rather than the latter's quarrel with himself; and therefore there is no reason to try to interpret the speech of the Laws in a way that makes it consistent with the *Apology*'s tolerance for disobedience. In reply: The *Republic* never suggests that citizens owe absolute obedience to their city, whatever the merit of its political leaders. Rather, the *Republic*'s claim is that in a philosophical state, governed by moral experts, the rulers must always be obeyed. So if the *Crito* advocates unconditional obedience to the rulers of one's native city, regardless of the wisdom of those rulers and regardless of the content of their orders, then it is expounding a political philosophy that is far more authoritarian and morally objectionable than anything we find in the *Republic*. I see no good reason to read the *Crito* as Plato's move away from Socrates. The common view among scholars, that this

dialogue belongs squarely in the early period, is surely correct. For a useful survey, see Ross, 1951, 1–2.

6. Contrast Woozley, 1979, 44–46. He suggests that Socrates is merely telling the jury that he will not be persuaded by them. Against this, see Kraut 1981, 658–659.

7. The issue was raised by Brickhouse and Smith in a paper read to the 1981 Western Division meeting of the American Philosophical Association. " . . . We show that the jury directive Socrates vows to disobey would have been illegal, a legal fact which has gone wholly unnoticed in the vast literature on the issue." See Brickhouse and Smith 1981, 513. I am grateful to the authors for allowing me to see a copy of their paper. I treat this issue briefly in Kraut 1981, 657–658.

8. For a summary of the legal procedure, see MacDowell 1978, 247–254.

9. Ibid., 253.

10. See too 28e4–6, 30a5, 30e2–6, 37e5–6.

11. Burnet 1924, 173.

12. The facts are summarized in Bury and Meiggs, 1975, 318–322; and Sealey 379–384. For a list of ancient sources, see Sealey 1976, 385 n.4. For a fuller treatment, see Krentz, 1982.

13. See Santas, 1979, 37.

14. Similarly Woozley 1979, 52; but note the change of direction on 54–55. As Woozley says, p. 52, Xenophon's treatment of this event is significantly different from Plato's: *Mem.* IV iv 3 implies that Socrates disobeyed the Thirty because their order was illegal. Curiously, Burnet cites this passage to support his interpretation of Plato's *Apology*. See his 1924, 174.

15. Allen comes to the same conclusion, 1980, 106.

16. Woozley 1979, 54.

17. For the distinction between a law (*nomos*) and a decree (*psēphisma*), see MacDowell 1978, 44–45.

18. See Santas 1979, 26.

19. A number of Greek texts suggest or assert that nothing should count as a *nomos* (law) if it conflicts with some higher ethical standard. See *H. Ma.* 284d1–7, and *Minos* 314b8–315a3, 317c1–7. But no such suggestion is made in the *Crito*. Evidently, this dialogue wants to discuss the general question of whether the citizen must do whatever the city commands, and the terminological point that unjust commands cannot be laws would not help decide this matter. Two further points should be noticed: (A) At 54b8–c1, the *Crito* says that Socrates has not been treated unjustly by any law. It might be suggested that according to this passage no law could possibly do injustice to a citizen (presumably because laws are just by definition). But that interpretation goes well beyond the text: the fact that no law *has* wronged Socrates is compatible with the fact that laws *can* wrong a citizen. (B) It was not a point of general usage, at the time of Socrates, that no law could be unjust. See Ostwald 1969, 37–40; Dover 1974, 306–309.

20. Contrast Santas 1979, 38. He tentatively suggests that according to Socrates one need obey a ruler only when "ruler" means "properly constituted authority in a democratic regime." As he points out, Socrates says in the *Apology* that he *obeyed* an unpopular law (in the trial of the Arginusae generals) when Athens was *democratically* ruled, but *dis*obeyed the rulers after the democracy

had been overthrown. See *Ap.* 32c3–4. But this need not be taken to mean that according to Socrates the democratic nature of a government gives us reason to obey it. As we will see in VII.1, there are too many antidemocratic statements in the early dialogues to justify Santas' interpretation.

21. It is sometimes said that according to the *Apology* one must always obey the city unless one has been given a contrary command by a god. Thus Murphy 1974, 17. However, Socrates never says that his disobedience to the Thirty was divinely sanctioned. I do not think any statement in the *Apology* commits him to the view that political orders can be violated ony when divine orders supersede them. However, a philosophy of blind obedience to political orders (in the absence of divine commands to the contrary) might be read into the following two passages:

> (A) Wherever someone stations himself, thinking it to be best, or is stationed by a ruler, there he must—as it seems to me—remain and run the danger, taking into account neither death nor anything else, in preference to what is shameful. (28d6–10)
>
> (B) To do an injustice and disobey a superior [*beltion*], whether divine or human: that, I know, is bad and shameful. (29b6–7)

But (A) does not address itself to the crucial issue. What if a ruler orders you to do something that is shameful? Should you obey the authority, even if you believe his orders to be evil? Nothing in (A) or its immediate context answers that question, and we should not press these lines for more than they can deliver. Socrates is merely trying to get across the idea that he will obey the god's command to practice philosophy even if this should result in his death.

What of (B)? These lines seem to assume that a "superior"—whether divine or human—would never require the performance of an unjust act. It is easy to understand why Socrates would say this of a god (see *Ap.* 21b5–7), but how can he say it of a *human* superior? Everything depends on how we take *beltion* ("superior"). If someone is superior merely by being in a position of political power or authority, then Socrates is committing himself to an extremely conservative political doctrine—and he is also contradicting the position he took when he disobeyed the Thirty. After all, they were his "superiors" in the sense that they were his rulers. (See *Ap.* 32d4 and 8: Socrates concedes that the Thirty were the government [*archē*], and so he would have no qualms about calling them his rulers [*archai*].) But a "superior" can mean someone who is more virtuous (*Protag.* 320b3, cf. *ameinon* at *Ap.* 30d1), and surely that is what Socrates means here. He will always obey someone who is at a higher moral stage than the one that he has reached, for he assumes that such a person will never give orders that are contrary to justice. (Woozley 1979 49, also adopts this interpretation.) I think this doctrine does have authoritarian implications, which will be explored later (VII.4, 8). Socrates is committed to obeying moral experts, if there are any, but that does not in any way commit him to obeying each and every political order of a government in power. For a different treatment of (A) and (B), see Santas 1979 33–40. I briefly discuss his interpretation of (B) in Kraut 1981, 654–655.

From *Plato's Socrates*

THOMAS C. BRICKHOUSE AND NICHOLAS D. SMITH

5.2 THE SOCRATIC DOCTRINE OF "PERSUADE OR OBEY"

5.2.1 A Problem of Interpretation

> . . . in war and in court and everywhere one must do what the city and country commands, or you must persuade it as to what is naturally just. (*Cri.* 51b8–c1).

In this passage and others like it in the *Crito*, Plato's Socrates expresses what has come to be known as the "persuade or obey" doctrine. A straightforward reading of the passage suggests that there are only two proper courses of action a citizen may follow in response to a command by the state: either obey the command or persuade the state to rescind its command. But scholars have resisted this reading and proposed a variety of other ways to construe what Socrates says about the citizen's obligation to obey the law.[1]

One reason for scholars' reluctance to accept the *Crito*'s doctrine at face value is that it appears to conflict with various other things Socrates says in the early dialogues, especially Socrates' famous absolute prohibition of injustice (see, e.g., *Cri.* 49d5–9). Surely the state could command an injustice which, it is argued, Socrates' interest in justice would require him to disobey.

Nearly everyone[2] has also agreed that a specific case of the relevant sort of conflict is identified by Socrates himself: Socrates seems all too willing to disobey legal authority when he tells his jurors in the *Apology* that he would disobey them if they required him to give up philosophizing:

> If you should say to me, "Socrates, we will not now be persuaded by Anytus, but will let you go on this condition: you will not any longer spend your time in this investigation or philosophizing, and if you are found doing this again you shall be put to death." If you should let me go on this condition, I should tell you, "Men of Athens, I hold you in high regard and I love you, but I will obey the god more than you, and just as long as I breathe and am able, I will never cease from philosophizing or from exhorting you and from declaring my views to any of you I should ever happen upon." (*Ap.* 29c5–d6)

Thomas C. Brickhouse and Nicholas D. Smith, from *Plato's Socrates* (New York: Oxford University Press, 1994), pp. 141–155.

We could not effectively review and specifically refute each of the many interpretations that have been put forward on this issue—there have been too many of them. Instead, we propose to look closely at the relevant texts and their contexts, allowing them to motivate an interpretation unlike any we have found in the vast literature on this topic. Let us first consider carefully what Socrates says in the *Crito*.

5.2.2 Civil Disobedience in the Crito?

A number of scholars have tried to show that the arguments of the *Crito* can be understood as leaving Socrates room to accept certain forms of disobedience to the law.[3] We think this is a mistake. The problem with this view, we think, can be found in the way Socrates characterizes the authority of the state over its citizens.

Though has urged Socrates to violate the law, Crito is no anarchist. His concern is only that in this case civic authority is in conflict with Socrates' (and others') welfare, through no fault of Socrates. So Socrates does not need to argue *that* the state has authority; he must instead try to convince Crito about the *extent* of its authority.

At 50e3–51c3, Socrates compares the authority of the state over the citizen to two other recognizable forms of authority, that of parent over offspring and master over slave. These two forms are hardly equivalent: parents do not *own* their offspring; parents do not use children for their own purposes; children are reared and nurtured and trained to become citizens in their own right. So the relation of master to slave is not the same as that of parent to child.[4] But Socrates does not insist that these forms of authority are alike in every respect. He requires only that each is a recognizable relationship of an authority to an inferior with respect to that authority.

In comparing the master-slave and parent-child relationships to that of state and citizen, Socrates tells us nothing about the former pairs. They are the models—assumed by the argument to be well understood—by which the problematic pair of state-citizen is to be made clear. This requires Socrates to construe the model relationships (at least for the purposes of this argument) in a conventional way; otherwise neither Crito nor Plato's readers will comprehend the comparison to them.

Now given this understanding of the model relationships, Socrates' point is simple: the authority we should recognize in the state's relationship to the citizen is *even more complete and one-sided* than what we conventionally accept in the models:

> . . . could you say, first, that you are not our offspring and slave, both you yourself and your ancestors? And if this is the case, do you think justice between you and us arises from equality, so that whatever we try to do to you, do you think it is just for you to do the same in return to us? Between you and your father there was no equality arising from justice, or your master if you happen to have one [. . .] or are you so wise that it escapes you that your country is more estimable, more

worthy of respect, more holy, and held in higher regard by the gods
and by men of intelligence than your mother and your father and all
of your ancestors. . . . (*Cri.* 50e3–8, 51a7–b2)

It is plain that conventional wisdom would not permit a minor child to disobey his or her parent, or a slave to disobey his or her master. If there can
be moral grounds within Socratic philosophy for a citizen to disobey the
state, then, they are certainly not evident at *Crito* 50e3–51b2.

5.2.3 Is There an Apology/Crito *Problem?*

At *Apology* 28d10 and following, Socrates compares his mission in Athens
to the military posts to which he was stationed at Potidaia, Amphipolis,
and Delion. "I would have done a terrible thing," he says, "if I remained
where [the commanders whom you chose to command me] stationed me,
like anyone else, and risked death, but when the god stationed me [. . .] I
deserted my post through fear of death or anything else whatever"
(28d10–29a1). Socrates points out to his jurors that the fear of death is
really "the basest sort of ignorance" (29b1–2), for no one really knows if
death is bad or good (29a6–b1). At 29b2–7, Socrates concludes:

> In this also, perhaps I differ from many people, and if I were to say that
> I am wiser, it would be in this: that not knowing sufficiently about
> what's in Hades, I don't think I know. But I do know that it is evil and
> disgraceful to do injustice and to disobey one's superior, whether god
> or man. (*Ap.* 29b2–7)

Though there have been a number of ingenious efforts to interpret
Socrates' words here as identifying only his *moral* superiors,[5] it is clear in
context that included in the class of "human" superiors would be the likes
of his commanders at Potidaia, Amphipolis, and Delion, whose authority
over him was legal and military. Given Socrates' negative appraisal of his
fellow human beings' moral wisdom, it seems most unlikely that he
would count his former military commanders as his *moral* superiors, or
indeed, that the class of Socrates' moral superiors would have any members.[6] The upshot of Socrates' remarks here in the *Apology*, then, reflects the
same view we find in the parent-child, master-slave, and citizen-state comparisons of the *Crito*: Socrates, it seems, believes it is never right to disobey
the legitimate commands of civil authority. Perhaps even more remarkable
than this is the fact that Socrates' notorious profession of ignorance seems
not to apply in this case—for all he does not know, Socrates says he *knows*
this.[7]

But Socrates is also the one who argues repeatedly that one ought
never to do an evil or injustice, even in return for evil or injustice done to
one.[8] Is it not evident that the two principles—never do evil and never disobey civil authority—could be made to compete? Is it not obvious that one
could be commanded by civil authority to do an injustice or other evil?

Most scholars have supposed that precisely such a command is contemplated by Socrates in his famous hypothetical vow to disobey the jury in the *Apology* (29c5–d6). There, Socrates imagines the jury letting him go on the condition that he give up philosophy, to which he says his response would be to disobey. But his vow in the *Apology* can be construed as pertinent to the arguments of the *Crito* only if there is some plausible way to understand his vow as committing him (even hypothetically) under some specifiable circumstance or other to disobeying a valid command of an authentic civil authority.

In fact, we have argued at length elsewhere that Socrates' words at *Apology* 29c5–d6 in no way commit him to civil disobedience.[9] Socrates makes his vow as he stands before an Athenian jury, indicted for impiety and under threat—as a specific part of the indictment itself—of execution. His trial is an ἀγὼν τιμητός,[10] the trial procedure in which the penalty for committing the crime in question is not prescribed in advance by the law. So the jury must first decide whether the defendant is guilty or innocent. Then, if they find him guilty, they will be asked to decide between the prosecution's penalty, which must be specified in advance of the trial in the indictment, and whatever counter-penalty the now-convicted defendant might propose. The prosecutor may not change his proposed penalty after he has submitted the indictment, nor may the jury assign any penalty other than one of those proposed by the litigants themselves.

Socrates makes his vow not to comply before he has been convicted (and hence before he has offered his counter-penalty), but after the penalty proposed by the prosecution has been stated. At *Apology* 29c5–d6, he imagines the men sitting in the jurors' seats (whom he fails throughout his defense speech to address by the title "jurors")[11] offering to let him go free on the condition that he give up his philosophical mission. If he is caught philosophizing again, however, he shall be put to death. Socrates says he will obey the god rather than the "men of Athens" to whom he speaks. But what precisely does Socrates have in mind here? Is he imagining that they agreed to find him innocent on the condition that he promise to abandon his mission? If so, we needn't worry that his disobeying their "order" would cause conflict with what he says in the *Crito*. Juries were neither legally nor even practically empowered to make such conditional acquittals (they did not even have a formal opportunity to discuss the case among themselves, much less to negotiate conditions with the litigants).[12] So if Socrates were freed and then disobeyed the condition his jurors offered him, he would not be guilty of disobeying any valid command of an authentic legal authority. Neither would he be violating a just agreement, for as Socrates clearly says, he would never agree to such a condition, precisely because he thinks it would be wrong to do so.

Perhaps instead we should imagine that Socrates' jury is threatening to find him guilty and then assign quitting philosophy as his penalty. This could be the case, however, only if Socrates himself offers abandoning philosophy as his counter-penalty, which he obviously would never do (see *Ap.* 37e3–38a6). Recall that the penalty proposed by the prosecution is already fixed and cannot be changed. Since the jury can only choose between the penalties proposed by the litigants themselves, the jury could not legally assign the abandonment of philosophy as Socrates' penalty. If somehow they did so, Socrates would be under no legal obligation to obey the jury's command.[13]

The simple fact is that what Socrates says at *Apology* 29c5–d6 does not create conflict with the most straightforward reading of the "persuade or obey" doctrine he articulates in the *Crito.* In saying this, however, we are not claiming that Socrates is making a legal point in response to his jurors in this passage. Socrates is not saying that he would disobey the jurors *because* they would have no legal authority to command him in the relevant way. Rather, we are claiming only that in saying he would disobey them, the legal context is such that his disobedience to the jury involves no direct or implied violation of the law or legal authority. To put it another way, law and legal authority have *nothing whatever* to do with this passage, either in its assumptions or in its implications.

Socrates does not have to assume that the "men of Athens" to whom he speaks at *Apology* 29c5–d6 have the legal authority to make such a command;[14] they do not, and we may suppose that Socrates knows perfectly well that they do not. Nor does Socrates have to assume that these "men of Athens" are so confused about Athens' laws as foolishly to presume they have that authority. Socrates imagines only that these "men of Athens" have the power to kill him if he should disobey their order, not that they have the legal authority to do so. Accordingly, the legal status of the "men of Athens" whom Socrates imagines ordering him to cease philosophizing—and the legal status of this order—are never specified. And Socrates' answer is appropriate: he does not lecture them as to the legal impropriety of their command, for they need not be mistakenly assuming any specifically legal authority when they contemplate such a command. Because what is morally appropriate and not what is lawful is the explicit issue here, Socrates' reply to the jurors' hypothetical command is not an evasion. Instead, Socrates confronts the Athenians directly: he says he would obey the god rather than them, and so would prefer to die than to give up philosophizing, were these his only choices.

5.2.4 Reinventing the "Problem"

At this point, one might concede that our understanding of the legal circumstances is correct but nevertheless dismiss the significance of those circumstances by insisting that whether or not the particular command Socrates hypothesizes the jury issuing could be legally made, surely *some command proscribing philosophizing could be made by an appropriate legal authority.* Perhaps such a command would be legally binding if it were

passed by the Assembly.[15] One might suppose that Socrates would disobey such an order. Hence, we are back to the original question: is there
not an inconsistency in Socrates' principles?

We believe that the supposition behind this concern cannot be supported under Socrates' understanding of Athenian law. For Socrates, in
order for a command of the Assembly to be binding, it is not enough that
the majority of Athenian citizens agree to it; as Socrates clearly says about
the mass trial of the Arginousai generals (*Ap.* 32b1–c3), general agreement
about something—even where enforced by irresistible power—does not
make what is agreed upon legal. Before Socrates would find himself in the
awkward position of having to choose between his duty to philosophize
and his duty to the state, any command to cease philosophizing would
have to be genuinely legal. But since Socrates believes that he has a pious
duty to philosophize, any law proscribing philosophy passed by the city
of Athens would—in Socrates' eyes, at least—be in direct conflict with the
already established law proscribing impiety.[16] So even if the *Athenians* saw
no direct conflict between a "law" prohibiting the practice of philosophy
and the law proscribing impiety, *Socrates* would.

Now what would Socrates make of such a case? It seems he would
have but four choices: (1) he could treat each of the conflicting laws as
equally valid and obey whichever one he felt like obeying at a given time;
(2) he could treat each law as equally invalid and behave however he chose
to, on grounds other than obedience to law; (3) he could regard the new
law as invalidating the prior law; or (4) he could regard the new law as
invalidated by the prior law. That Socrates would make the first choice
(namely, that both laws were equally valid) seems unlikely, since it
involves maintaining an inconsistent position regarding the pair of the
candidates. Even if he did regard both laws as equally valid, it seems reasonable to suppose that the law he would inevitably obey would be the
law he took to require him to philosophize, namely, the law proscribing
impiety. We could expect the same behavior from Socrates if he made
choice (2), according to which neither conflicting law would be regarded
as valid; for Socrates thinks he has good reasons to philosophize independent of what he construes the law to require on this issue.

So let us imagine for the moment that the Athenian Assembly actually
did pass a new decree proscribing philosophy. On either option (1) or (2)
Socrates might simply consider himself free to ignore the new decree, convinced as he would be that it conflicted with the law forbidding impiety.[17]
If so, he might be arrested, tried, convicted, and condemned to death—just
as he was for practicing his mission under the current laws. So long as his
arrest, trial, conviction, and execution are performed according to due
process, Socrates would have no more moral ground for resisting than he
finds he has during his discussion with Crito in the Prison of the Eleven.
He might well argue at his trial that he could not be held responsible for
breaking the law on the ground that the relevant laws conflicted. But convincing the jury might be just as impossible as it was at his historical trial.

What about choices (3) and (4)? We can think of at least one good ground for thinking that of these two options, Socrates would select (4) and not (3); that is, he would regard the prior law as having precedence. The Athenian legal system, through a procedure called a γραφὴ παρανόμων/ *graphē paranomōn*, allowed a citizen to challenge a newly proposed law on the ground that it violated a prior law. If the suit were successful, the new law would be struck from the books and a fine would be assessed against its sponsor in the Assembly.[18] This shows that when conflict arose between laws, the principles of Athenian law gave precedence to the prior law. Now we have no reason to think that Socrates would not have accepted this tenet of Athenian law, and we have good reason for thinking that Socrates generally accepted the tenets of Athenian law. Hence, were a case to arise in which Socrates would feel the need to decide which one of the conflicting laws was legitimate, we would expect him to treat the prior law as the valid law. Accordingly, in the situation we have been considering, Socrates would see the new law as illegal precisely because what it required would be against the prior law proscribing impiety. If he disobeyed the new "law," in this hypothesis, he would disobey no *valid* law.

One might suppose that instead of simply refusing to obey the new law, Socrates would think he needed to swear out a *graphē paranomōn* against the new law. It is easy enough to imagine that the effect of his doing so might be that the Athenians would be unmoved by Socrates' argument, and vote to uphold the new decree. Socrates, however, might well remain convinced that the new "law" is illegal. But having tested the new law by a legally correct procedure, Socrates would no longer have any legal means of resisting the new law. That is, he would now have attempted, but failed, to persuade. According to our reading of the "persuade or obey" doctrine, Socrates would now have to obey the new law or leave Athens, as he says the Laws have always permitted him to do if he were no longer satisfied with them (*Cri.* 52a8–d7).

Precisely because Socrates never imagines a case such as this, one can only speculate as to what his decision would be. On the one hand, he could surely no longer be satisfied with the laws of Athens, as he is said to be in the *Crito*, in which case leaving Athens would certainly hold more appeal than it did without such a new law. On the other hand, unless we know more about exactly what was and was not prohibited by the new law, we cannot be certain that Socrates could not continue to call the new law into question in the hopes that it might soon be rescinded. He may not willingly violate the new law, of course, but it is not clear precisely what the new law is supposed to prohibit. Plainly, any legislative decree prohibiting calling laws into question would itself be of questionable legality, and in any case it is most unlikely that such a law would ever pass the Assembly. So even if the Assembly were to prohibit the practice of philosophy, there would nevertheless be a number of legally permissible tacks Socrates could take to pursue the nullification of the command. Perhaps he would see his mission as requiring that he attempt to get the law nullified.[19] As he deliberated about what he should do in such a circumstance, his *daimonion* might come into play: even if he thought he had good reason to make one decision, it might well be that a daimonic alarm would compel him to reverse himself.[20] But unless he would be prepared to change the position he announces in the *Crito*, one avenue would not be open to him in our view: even though he has (*ex hypothesi*) made a sincere attempt to persuade the state to rescind the new law, he may not now disobey it, any more than a minor child may disobey his parent or a slave may disobey his master.

5.2.5 Socrates and Political Activity Again

In order to get this far in our speculation about Socrates' response to a legal ban on philosophy, however, we have had to make a number of great leaps away from the texts. In fact, we believe that at least one of the suppositions that got us this far is not true to Socrates' character. Socrates, let us recall, is the man whose *daimonion* has prevented him from aggressively pursuing institutional politics, that is, from attempting to play any role in Athens' recognized political arenas other than those for which he is conscripted or selected by lottery (as, for example, when he ends up a Prutanis during the aftermath of the Arginousai affair). He might well see some new decree (for example, one prohibiting philosophy) as conflicting with a prior law; but what action would he feel required to take? In the past, he has taken no legal action when he saw Athens go wrong, which he suggests has happened often when he tells his jurors: "no one will save himself who genuinely opposes you or any other populace and prevents many unjust *and illegal* things from happening in the state" (*Apology* 31e2–4).

With these words, which we discussed at length in section 5.1, Socrates explains his life as "a private, not a public man" (*Ap.* 32a2–3). We may infer that Socrates does not believe he must take formal steps in opposing what he sees as "many unjust and illegal things" that occur in the state. The mere fact, then, that Socrates would see the prohibition of philosophy as illegal, therefore, would not be sufficient inducement for him to play what is to him the unfamiliar role of "public man" by opposing the new decree with a *graphē paranomōn*.

It might be argued, however, that a decree prohibiting philosophy would be different from the "many . . . illegal things" Socrates has ignored in the past. The other illegalities, one might suppose, have never directly obligated *Socrates* to take any particular action. But a law prohibiting philosophy would have direct consequence on the way Socrates lives his life. Now, in fact, the text neither explicitly says nor implies that the injustices and illegalities Socrates ignored in the past were restricted to acts to be undertaken by others. Thus, any attempt to show that Socrates would regard a prohibition of philosophy as importantly different from the many illegalities he has ignored in the past simply has no textual basis.

But the texts also tell us what Socrates would do in a situation where he is directly given a command to act in a way he does not find acceptable:

when the Thirty ordered him to go out and arrest Leon of Salamis, Socrates did not protest their order or create a disturbance—he simply went home (*Ap.* 32c4–d7). His behavior has been taken by some[21] as showing that Socrates would never obey even a legal command to do what Socrates conceived as an injustice. Such a conclusion involves a very dubious argument from silence: by Socrates' not explicitly stipulating to his jurors that the Thirty's order was illegal—as he had in the case of the trial of the Arginousai generals under the democracy—he shows either that he construed the Thirty's order as legal or that its legal status had no effect on his deliberations. We have disputed this at length elsewhere.[22] Without repeating our arguments again here, it is worth noting that nothing requires Socrates to preach to the choir; let us recall to whom he is speaking on this matter. He must insist on the illegality of the trial of the generals precisely because many of those on the jury might have initially supposed the decision to try the generals *en bloc* was a legal one. But no one on the democratic jury would need Socrates to emphasize the supposed illegality of anything having to do with the Thirty. (The obvious partisan identification of the jurors is indicated at *Ap.* 20e8–21a2.) Accordingly, Socrates' silence on this point hardly cries out for attention, and the inference from it is insecure even for an argument from silence. Moreover, we need not think that Socrates' disobedience of the Thirty had anything to do with his conception of legal authority; rather, he was free to do what he personally thought was just precisely because there was no legal impediment to his making up his own mind.

If we are right about this case, therefore, we may suppose that Socrates' reaction to what he considered to be illegal decrees would be the same whether or not they included his own actions within their scope: he would simply ignore them and continue his mission as a private person. In failing to obey the decrees he was convinced were illegal, moreover, he would in no way force upon us a reassessment of his arguments in the *Crito*. Plainly, the same goes for cases where the relevant laws conflict, for, as we said elsewhere, "when two laws contradict one another, even the most steadfast adherent to civil authority cannot find a way to comply with both."[23] Scholars have insisted that the texts provide an answer to the question: What would Socrates do if a legal ban were to be placed on philosophy? But the fact is, the texts do not answer this question. They do not even begin to put Socrates in the position of having to ask it. The entire issue, we believe, is an artifact of scholarly speculation.

5.2.6 Just Obedience versus Obedience to Just Laws

We do not need to try to reconcile the *Crito*'s doctrines with a legal ban on philosophy, then, for Socrates would not believe there could be a legal ban on philosophy without radically changing the laws to which Socrates refers in the *Crito*.[24] But it is not unfair to ask what Socrates would do about a law which does not conflict with any prior law, but which Socrates would conceive as commanding an injustice. It is tempting to imagine that the Laws who speak to Socrates in the *Crito* are not the actual positive laws of Athens—flaws and all—but rather an idealized version, purified of any injustice.[25] The problem with this account is that the Laws who lecture Socrates in the *Crito* are plainly capable of making an error of judgment regarding justice; otherwise the "persuade" disjunct of the "persuade or obey" doctrine would be no more than rhetorical window dressing. Because the citizen might well recognize a moral error in the Laws, the Laws do not simply command obedience—the citizen is invited to persuade them when they err. But the Laws do not guarantee that they will change even if a citizen presents them with a morally compelling reason for doing so. So what would Socrates do if an unjust law were enacted and all legal challenges to it were turned back?

It is, perhaps, revealing that in Xenophon's account, Socrates simply identifies the just and the lawful (*Memorabilia* 4.4.12–25; see also *Cyropaedia* 1.3.17). One might be tempted to infer from such evidence that Socrates supposed simply that there could be no unjust laws, and hence that any "law" that was unjust would in fact be no law at all. But this is artificial. First, as we have just seen, the Laws Socrates personifies in the *Crito* are plainly capable of making mistakes with respect to justice. Second, even Xenophon's Socrates recognizes that the laws might change (*Mem.* 4.4.14), and so insists that the issue is not the justice of the laws themselves (for if a law is revoked, either the law or its revocation must be just—not both), but rather the justice of *obedience* to the laws. According to Xenophon's Socrates, it is always just to obey the law—both the law before it is revised, and the law after it is revised (*Mem.* 4.4.15–16).[26] It is also plain that Plato's Socrates does not approve of *all* the laws he feels constrained to obey (see *Ap.* 37a7–b2).

But does it make sense to distinguish between the justice of *obeying* the laws and the justice of the *laws themselves?* To see that it does, let us return to the models Socrates offers for the relationship of citizen to state in the *Crito.* Suppose a master were to order his slave to commit what even the slave is convinced (let us imagine rightly) is an immoral act. Perhaps the slave would protest the command. But suppose the master is adamant and will not rescind the command. If we are right, Socrates' view—both in Xenophon and in Plato—would be that moral duty requires the slave to obey the master. *Ex hypothesi*, the act in question is unjust; but whose injustice is it?

A case can be made that the slave is actually guilty of wrongdoing only if the slave is regarded as an independent moral agent. But to the Greeks of antiquity, the slave plainly is not independent of his master, morally or legally. What is important is not merely that the slave was coerced (we can well imagine there being some implication of threat to the slave if he should disobey the master's command), but rather that the slave's actions are performed under the master's authority. If there is blame to be assessed, it must apply solely to the master. That this *is* the conventional understanding of such a case is clear from Athenian law, which held the masters responsible for what slaves did under their masters' orders.[27] The case is plainly similar if we imagine a minor child acting under orders from his or her parent.[28] The responsible agent in such cases is not the child or the slave, but rather the parent or the master. Where such authority is involved, the superior alone is culpable.

It is surely sensible, then, to understand Athenian conventions as holding that minor children and slaves were supposed always to obey their parents and masters respectively. Moreover, in obeying their parents or masters, neither children nor slaves ever do wrong—even when what they are commanded to do *is* wrong—for when they are under the commands of their superiors, *they* are not responsible for the wrong they do. The same transference of responsibility would apply, we may obviously assume, in assigning credit for any good done by a child or slave under orders: the child or slave might rightly be praised for obedience; but credit for any good done would go solely to the parent or master who commanded that the good-producing action be done.

Socrates explicitly conceives of the authority of parent over minor child and of master over slave as similar in the relevant way to that between state and citizen. Accordingly, the citizen may have exceptionless duties to obey legal authority and never to do wrong, and these duties may be seen to be perfectly consistent. Unjust laws may be passed; but in obeying them, the citizen does not act unjustly.

Scholars who have attempted to provide exceptions to Socrates' doctrine of legal obedience have done so mainly because they saw an inevitable conflict between such a doctrine and Socrates' famous prohibition against injustice. We are now in a position to see why there need be no such conflict. In our view, Socrates can consistently require that the citizen never act unjustly and that the citizen never disobey the law even when the law itself is unjust and even where the citizen's actions in accordance with the law will produce injustice. The reason for this is that the responsible agent of injustice in such cases is the state, and not the citizen acting as the state's "offspring" or "slave."

5.2.7 The Moral Consequences of Socrates' View

One might detect in the view we have attributed to Socrates a precursor to those who, accused of war crimes, attempt to appeal to the fact that they were "only following orders." This consequence is to some degree mitigated by the way Socrates conditions the doctrine for which he argues in the *Crito*. In fact, anyone reading the *Crito* will notice that Socrates' arguments are explicitly subjected to a number of provisions, and we are in no position to guess what Socrates would say if one or more of these provisions were removed. The "Laws" to which Socrates says he owes obedience are the laws of Athens, the laws by which his parents married and under which Socrates himself was raised and nurtured. They are laws with which he has made a just agreement, and with which he has been manifestly satisfied, which all along had allowed him to leave Athens with his possessions, and to which (by undergoing the process of δοκιμασία)[29] he has sworn allegiance. Socrates' political doctrine, such as it is, is never generalized to other people, living under other legal systems, in other states. Attempts to discern what he would say about such things seem hopelessly speculative.

Nothing significant follows from the fact that Socrates did not leave Athens when the notorious Thirty were installed in power. It surely does not follow that he regarded the reign of the Thirty as legitimate. Even if he had initially been willing to consider the new government's legitimacy, it does not follow that he saw any of their subsequent excesses as permitted by the principles of their original constitution.[30] The Tyrants held power for only eight months; Socrates hardly had time to show that he was satisfied with their government (cp. *Cri.* 51d1–e4, 52b1–c3). In fact, he did not even last that long before coming into dangerous conflict with those in power (see *Ap.* 32c4–d7).

Far more troubling is Socrates' commitment to political passivity; he views engagement in the political affairs of his *polis* to be a sure route to an early demise (*Ap.* 31e2–4). It is for this reason, then, that he does not attempt to persuade his state to refrain from committing genocide on Scione and Melos,[31] or from any of the other "many unjust and illegal things" (*Ap.* 31e4) he sees happening. It would be comforting if we could suppose that the Athens to which Socrates explicitly claims to owe absolute obedience was a just and merciful place. But it was not always so, and Socrates knew all too well that it was not.

5.2.8 Was Socrates an Authoritarian?

If our interpretation of the relevant passages in the *Apology* and the *Crito* is correct, Socrates' remarks about the duty of the citizen to obey the law are consistent with his other doctrines. But some may object that our interpretation comes only at a very high cost, since in our view Socrates thinks the citizen who fails to persuade the State to rescind a legal command must fully abandon his autonomy to the authority of the State. According to our reading of the *Crito*, Socrates makes no allowance for the justified disobedience of a citizen who, unable to persuade the State to withdraw its command, is nevertheless convinced that the command is unjust. Where the citizen fails to persuade, he must obey, regardless of how odious the State's command. Some might suppose this leaves Socrates with an unacceptably authoritarian view.

It is important to keep in mind that there is no reason to think that Socrates was ever asked to carry out a legal order to engage in any of the many evils the city of Athens committed. Nor is there any reason to think that Socrates ever actively supported the commission of any of those evils. By removing himself from the arena of organized politics, he effectively takes himself out of the ranks of those in authority who promoted immoral policies. And if those policies ever required Socrates' own personal involvement in their implementation, the fact that he merely followed orders is pertinent, for surely the defense that "I was only following orders" has some validity, provided that the person carrying out those orders occupies an inferior position in an institutional hierarchy issuing the orders, and did not in any way amplify the evil created by the carrying out of those orders. If we add that the inferior actually in some way opposed the order he carried out, his defense becomes even stronger.

Just how authoritarian, if at all, is Socrates' view? Plainly, he would be an authoritarian if his view would prohibit any dissent or criticism of legal commands by those subject to them. But this is *not* Socrates' position. Socrates, by contrast, says that the Laws actually invite criticism and recognize their fallibility (51e7–52a3). Moreover, the Laws never claim that when a citizen fails to persuade them to rescind a command, that failure is evidence of the rightness of what they have ordered. Even in rejecting attempts to persuade, the Laws make no claim of infallibility.[32]

The Laws, instead, are more like a modest umpire or referee in a sports contest who recognizes his own fallibility as well as that of the players and who also welcomes attempts by players to persuade him whenever they believe that he has erred in a call. But regardless of how open an umpire or referee is to protests and to reconsidering his calls when they are protested, in the end the game cannot proceed if any player is free not to count the umpire's or referee's ultimate decisions as authoritative. When no one is empowered to make authoritative calls in a sports contest, the problem is not that the nature of the game is altered; the problem is that the game simply cannot be played. Similarly, we think that Socrates recognizes that, despite the fallibility of the Laws, the city simply cannot survive if there is no source of authoritative decision making which can conflict with and even override the opinions of individual citizens. It is precisely for this reason that the Laws think they must upbraid Socrates for contemplating escape:

> Do you think it is possible for that city to exist and not to be overthrown in which the sentences arrived at have no force but become invalid and are overturned by private persons? (*Cri.* 50b2–5)

Socrates' point is that the State itself can survive only if its commands are regarded as ultimately authoritative. This does not mean that Socrates thinks that dissent is never appropriate, or that ineffective dissent could never be morally correct. Moreover, Socrates' view leaves open the question of whether a particular State such as Athens ought to survive, just as the reason why the umpire's calls must be obeyed leaves open the question of whether the game of baseball (or any particular game of baseball) should continue to be played. We can imagine umpiring becoming so bad that, while the game can still be played, it is not worth playing any longer.

So, similarly, although Socrates seems satisfied with the Laws he imagines in the *Crito* (50c9–e1), we can imagine a State whose commands are so corrupt that the State is not worth preserving. Perhaps a State in which philosophy was forbidden by law would qualify as not worth surviving in Socrates' eyes. But that, as we noted above, is a very different situation from the one Socrates actually faces in the *Crito*.

Scholars have assumed that either we must understand the "persuade or obey" doctrine as leaving open the possibility of justified disobedience or we must convict Socrates of authoritarianism and self-contradiction. We can see now why these are not the only options. In this section, we have defended the consistency of Socrates' position, and also sought to show that, despite the strength of his parent-child and master-slave models, Socrates does not endorse blind obedience or authoritarianism. Perhaps Socrates erred in recognizing no justified disobedience. But even if so, we hope we have shown that scholars need not be so eager to avoid the most straightforward understanding of Socrates' arguments. The position he articulates in the *Crito* is not only consistent with what he says in the *Apology* and elsewhere; it is also not so implausible that we should feel charitably compelled to revise it through creative interpretation.

NOTES

1. A list of the various major interpretations may be found in the bibliography of Kraut 1983. Kraut also discusses a number of different interpretations in 1983, ch. 3.
2. To our knowledge, we are the only ones who have ever denied the relevance of the following passage to the issue of Socrates' attitude toward legal obligation. See Brickhouse and Smith 1984 and 1989, 137–53.
3. See, for example, Woozley 1979; see also Woozley 1971, 306–8; Vlastos 1974; Kraut 1983; Reeve 1989, 115–121; Santas 1979, ch. 2.
4. For the comparison Socrates makes, however, it must be that there is something common to the two relationships, and it is clear that what is common is that each is a strongly authoritarian relationship. Indeed, it seems that Socrates has chosen these two relationships precisely because they were the most authoritarian relationships he could think of, excluding that of state to citizen, which is the relationship under dispute. So we must not suppose, contrary to what Kraut claims (1983, 94–105), that the "offspring" Socrates has in mind are only adult or even nearly adult "offspring." Rather, the "offspring" are intended to be understood as young children. Otherwise, the implied likeness between a child and a slave would be absurd.
5. See, e.g., Kraut 1983, 23, n.36.
6. Moreover, unless one understands the phrase to refer to one's moral superiors *only when their commands reflect such moral superiority*, it is not at all clear that Socrates would accept the claim. After all, one's moral superiors need not always be right—and inferiors need not always be wrong—when their points of view conflict. But if this were supposed to provide the meaning of Socrates' phrase, it reduces to the triviality that one ought always to do what is right.

7. For discussions of this issue, see Vlastos 1985; Brickhouse and Smith 1989, secs. 2.6 and 3.2, and 1994, ch. 2.

8. See, e.g., *Cri.* 49d5–9.

9. See Brickhouse and Smith 1989, sec. 3.3.

10. See MacDowell 1978, 253; Harrison 1971, vol. 2, 80–82; Lipsius 1905–1915, 248–262.

11. See Brickhouse and Smith 1989, 210–212. We do not think there is any special significance in Socrates' form of address, though the fact that he does not address the jurors by their legal title, δικασταί, certainly leaves open the possibility that what Socrates says to them does not always take their legal role into account. In saying, as he does at *Apology* 29c5–d6, that he would disobey these "men of Athens," then, we are not required to assume that he is addressing them strictly as jurors.

12. See MacDowell 1978, 251–252.

13. Yet another possibility has been proposed by Spiro Panagiotou 1987. According to Panagiotou, the situation Socrates has in mind is that he would be found guilty, condemned to death, but then pardoned on the condition that he give up his mission. We do not find this convincing. First, the jury was not empowered to suspend sentences or to grant pardons; these functions could be performed only by the Assembly, as Panagiotou himself notes (1987, 40; 41–42, n.7). Moreover, the legal procedure by which a pardon might be granted would have to be initiated by the convict himself, and any condition according to which the pardon would be granted would have to be explicitly accepted in advance by the convict. Plainly, Socrates would not propose quitting philosophy as a condition for his pardon. "Refusing" to accept such a condition would hardly constitute legal disobedience.

14. Contrast the view of Reeve, who claims that Socrates' hypothetical vow to disobey the jury can only be understood as conceding "even *per impossible*" the legal authority of the jurors to make the command that Socrates says he would disobey (1989, 116). We find it quite implausible for Reeve to claim that Socrates would require the jurors to assume an impossibility in order to make his point. A detailed criticism of Reeve's view may be found in Smith 1992.

15. This is precisely the line taken by Richard Kraut 1983, 13–17.

16. See Brickhouse and Smith 1989, sec. 3.3.6.

17. We argue for this option in Brickhouse and Smith 1989, sec. 3.3.4.

18. See MacDowell 1978, 50–52. We discuss this in Brickhouse and Smith 1989, 151.

19. See Xenophon's account in *Mem.* 1.2.31–37, in which Socrates confronts a law against teaching "the art of words."

20. See *Ap.* 31c8–d1, 40a4–6, c2–3, 41d6; *Euthphr.* 3b5–7; *Euthyd.* 272e4; *Rep.* VI.496c4; *Phdr.* 242b8–9; and [*Theages* 128d2–131a7 (see also [*Alc.* I] 105d5–106a1). For a discussion of the workings of the *daimonion*, see Brickhouse and Smith 1989, sec. 5.5. Gregory Vlastos argues (in 1989a, revised in 1991, ch. 6) that Socrates would always follow his own reasoning, even where divination was involved. Accordingly, Vlastos seems to think that Socrates always provides a convenient interpretation of the *daimonion*'s alarms. On the contrary, we think that if a daimonic monition opposed Socrates (for example, if he was about to go address the Assembly because he thought it would be best for him to argue against some law they were likely to pass—see *Ap.* 31c8–d1), he would always modify his own reasonings according to his daimonic promptings; by its very nature, the *daimonion* often shows Socrates that

the ways he intends to act, and hence in some way or ways the reasons he may have for acting as he intends, are incorrect. The texts provide no grounds for doubting that Socrates would always follow the *daimonion*'s promptings no matter what course of action or pattern of reasoning it opposed. This does not mean that Socrates became unreasonable; it means rather that he would re-evaluate and adjust his reason to what he considered the indisputable fact, revealed by the *daimonion,* that he had been about to act in some improper or wrongful way. We provide additional arguments against Vlastos's position in sec. 6.3.

21. See Colson 1985;, Kraut 1983, 17–24. See also our reply to Colson's argument in Brickhouse and Smith 1989, 185–193.

22. See Brickhouse and Smith 1989, sec. 4.3.5.

23. See Brickhouse and Smith 1989, 152.

24. See Brickhouse and Smith 1989, 152–53, for a discussion of how much distortion is required to generate the kind of case scholars have imagined.

25. See, for example, Woodruff 1982, note on *Hip. Ma.* 284d6–7, 41; and Colson 1989.

26. The same equation of just with lawful can be found articulated by Aristotle at *EN* 5.1129a32–34. We take such evidence to show that the view we are attributing to Socrates is one that would be familiar to the Greeks. See also Soph. *Philoctetes* 50–53, 1144 (see Blundell 1987, 311–12, for a commentary on this passage); Lys. 12.28; Dover 1974, 147f., 155. Even in the late dialogue, the *Politicus,* Plato advocates complete obedience to existing laws (see 300e11–301a4). The identification of obedience to the law and justice is represented by Thrasymachus (*Rep.* I.338e3–6, 339b7–9, 339c10–12) and Glaucon (*Rep.* II.359a3–4) as the common opinion of justice. The mutability of Athenian law was a frequent source of humor in Aristophanic comedy—see Ar. *Hipp.* 267f.; *Eccl.* 577ff., 586f., 797f.

27. See MacDowell 1978, 81. We are indebted to Charles Young for calling this to our attention.

28. See MacDowell 1978, 84.

29. See Kraut 1983, 154–158.

30. See Brickhouse and Smith 1989, 186–192.

31. See Thuc. 5.32, 5.116.

32. See also *Rep.* I.339c1–6, and perhaps *Ap.* 37a7–b1. Socrates is plainly not committed to the view that the laws are inerrant. Katsutochi Uchiyama first pointed out to us that our view of Socrates did not make him an authoritarian.

CHAPTER 9

Did Plato Tell the Truth about the Death of Socrates?

The Death of Socrates

CHRISTOPHER GILL

THE scene at the end of the *Phaedo,* in which Plato describes how Socrates dies by poisoning from hemlock, is moving and impressive. It gives us the sense of witnessing directly an actual event, accurately and vividly described, the death of the historical Socrates. There are, however, certain curious features in the scene, and in the effects of the hemlock on Socrates, as Plato presents them. In the *Phaedo,* hemlock has only one primary effect: it produces first heaviness and then numbness in the body. The numbness begins in the lowest part of the body, the feet, and then proceeds gradually upwards, to the groin and then the heart, death occurring when the heart is affected. The only other symptom is a single movement (ἐκινήθη, 118 a 12) immediately prior to death. The symptom of numbness in the lower legs is one that we meet in other ancient accounts, for instance in Aristophanes' *Frogs* (when Dionysus and Heracles are discussing possible routes to Hades),[1] and in the *Alexipharmaca* of the second-century writer Nicander.[2] But that is only one of a number of symptoms Nicander lists. He also speaks of disturbed consciousness, rolling eyes, choking in the throat and windpipe, gasping for breath, and contracted arteries. Accounts of hemlock-poisoning in modern medical authorities recount more effects of this kind. They speak of salivation, nausea, vomiting, as well as dryness and choking in the lower throat; the pupils are dilated, the vision and hearing become imperfect, and the speech is thick. Paralysis occurs in the arms as

Christopher Gill, "The Death of Socrates," *Classical Quarterly* NS 23 (1973), 25–28.

well as the legs, and is often accompanied by spasms and convulsions.[3] Thus, Plato's description gives only one or two of the symptoms of hemlock-poisoning. Furthermore, the death scene in the *Phaedo* gives a quite different impression of the effects of the drug from the medical accounts. In Plato's picture, the penetration of hemlock into the body is a process of calm, almost rhythmic regularity. Contrast this with the hectic impact of the drug, as Nicander presents it: ' . . . the eyes roll, and men roam the streets with tottering steps and crawling upon their hands; a terrible choking blocks the lower throat and the narrow passage of the windpipe; the extremities grow cold; and in the limbs the stout arteries are contracted; . . . the victim draws breath like one swooning, and his spirit beholds Hades' (tr. Gow and Scholfield). Modern accounts, with their emphasis on nausea and unsteadiness of movement, give a similarly torrid picture of the physical collapse the drug induces.[4]

How should we explain this discrepancy between Plato's description, which seems to give such an accurate and detailed account of Socrates' death, and medical accounts of hemlock-poisoning?[5] One possible explanation might be that the kind of hemlock used by the Athenians in Socrates' day was different from that known two centuries later by Nicander, and from that used in modern experiments; or, that the dose used in Socrates' case was smaller than that in more recent cases. (The question of the amount of hemlock ground up to make the poisonous drink occurs twice in the dialogue; on the second occasion the poison-mixer explains that he prepares only as much of the drug as is needed for the fatal dose, 63d 5–e5, 117b6–9.) It is inherently unlikely that the type of hemlock used would differ between Socrates' and Nicander's time. And, if Socrates' dose were smaller, the result would surely be all the usual symptoms on a smaller scale, not a reduced number of symptoms. In fact, a poisonous dose of hemlock is likely to be roughly the same, in amount as well as kind, at all periods.

One might try to explain the unusual character of Plato's account by arguing that he describes all the symptoms that would be visible to an eyewitness. Many of the symptoms omitted are internal: the choking in the throat, impairment of senses, pain and contraction of blood-vessels and muscles. The dilation of pupils might not be perceptible in Socrates' naturally protruding eyes; in any case, we are told that Socrates covered his face (presumably with a piece of his clothing) for most of the time the drug was acting on him (118a6). However, Plato goes out of his way to disclose one of the internal symptoms, the numbness spreading from the lower legs. He tells how the poison-mixer pinched Socrates' feet, and then his shins, and so on, asking if he felt anything; in each case Socrates said no, thus showing how sensation was gradually leaving the body (117e6–118a2). If Plato had wished to emphasize internal symptoms other than just this one, revealing the more general collapse of the bodily functions that was actually taking place, he could have done so. Similarly, the holding up of a piece of clothing throughout much of the process would not have concealed wholly the slurring of speech, the gasping, salivation, and perhaps vomiting, that the drug induced. We have to conclude that the picture given in the *Phaedo* is not that of an observant eye-witness preserving every detail of Socrates' death. (Indeed, Plato makes it clear at the start of the dialogue that he was not himself present on this occasion, 59b10.) The special features of the act of dying depicted there reflect the selectiveness of the narrative, and of the author.

On what principle has Plato made his selection of symptoms: why did he describe the effects of hemlock in the way he did? In minimizing the effects of the poison, Plato may have wished to show Socrates' physical toughness and stoicism, the control of his mind over his body which is also stressed in Alcibiades' speech in the *Symposium* (220a ff.). Other men exhibited various features of physical collapse: Socrates merely covered his face except for one final ironic remark. This may very well be one motive behind Plato's description; another may have been the desire to eliminate the more unattractive results of hemlock-poisoning from his picture of Socrates' end. But the physical details Plato does give, and the way the poison-mixer, as well as Socrates, is used in the composition of the scene, can be seen as having a positive purpose, that of illustrating a major theme in the *Phaedo*: the liberation of the soul from the body.[6] Of the various indices of physical collapse produced by hemlock, the one isolated in the *Phaedo* is the paralysis or numbness spreading from the feet upwards into the body (not, as in some accounts, affecting other extremities like the arms).[7] The demonstration in which the poisonmixer pinches one part of the body after the other presents the spreading paralysis as the passing of sensation out of the body, proceeding stage by stage. The word ψυχή, usually translated 'soul', had a number of meanings, as the essential functions of life were variously identified.[8] Sensation, however, was generally seen as a property of *psyche*, particularly by the natural philosophers;[9] for Plato, sensation is an activity in which the *psyche* uses the body as its instrument.[10] Since Homer, loss of sensation, in fainting and death, had been described as *psyche* leaving the body. The gradual loss of sensation, then, would be seen as the departure of the *psyche* from the body (a process emphasized by its measured slowness)[11]—departure, in this case, having a special significance. The word used by the poison-mixer in explaining the point in the poisoning process at which Socrates will die is οἴχεσθαι, a word often used to mean 'die', but whose primary significance is 'go away' or 'leave'. A little earlier in the dialogue, Socrates makes some play with this ambiguity in οἴχεσθαι, stressing to Crito that, at what the others regard as death, he, that is his *psyche*, will not stay but will 'go away'.[12] Throughout the argument of the *Phaedo*, it is repeatedly emphasized that, in what is normally thought of as death, the *psyche* is not destroyed along with the body, but is released or purified from the body, and goes from it into independent, non-corporeal existence.[13] What Plato presents, I think, in the death of Socrates, is the purification of the *psyche* from the body. The *psyche* begins its journey from the physically lowest region, the feet; in

Plato's account, it was when the *psyche* had passed out of a bodily region that was 'low' and 'physical' in another sense, the groin, the area of sexual lust and generation, that Socrates uncovered his face to make his last ironic remark, that he owed a cock to Asclepius, since he had now recovered from the sickness of being alive.[14] The soul 'gathering itself to itself' (to use a phrase from the discussion of the *Phaedo*),[15] comments detachedly on its release from the burdens and pressures of bodily existence.[16] The final movement of Socrates' body is the last index of the *psyche's* presence, perhaps the movement of its actual departure. The quietness, the calmness, the regularity of the effects of the penetration of poison into Socrates' body (so different from the chaos, squalor, and collapse described by Nicander and modern toxicologies) is the quietness of a ritual, the *katharmos* or purification of the soul from the prison of the body. The vivid and detailed picture of this death that Plato gives is not that of a man reproducing an actual event in every particular, but of an author selecting and embellishing those features which will illuminate, in visual form, the intelligible meaning of his argument.[17]

This instance, in which a historical event is transformed into a representation of a philosophical idea, should alert us to the possibility that many of what seem to be authentic glimpses into the life, and death, of the historical Socrates may in fact be illustrative pictures, attached or inset, like the myths of the dialogues, into Plato's arguments.[18]

NOTES

1. εὐθὺς γὰρ ἀποπήγνυσι τἀντικνήμια (126). Professor Fitton-Brown points out to me that artistic selectiveness (which I find in the *Phaedo*'s account) may have determined Aristophanes' choice of symptoms also. The whole section plays on comic oppositions, as Dionysus criticizes various routes to Hades: hanging is stiflingly *hot* (πνιγηράν, 122), it chokes the throat, hemlock is much too *cold* (ψυχράν, 125), it freezes the legs. The choking in the throat that hemlock also induces is omitted, to sharpen the contrast with hanging.

2. Gow and Scholfield 1953, 186–194.

3. Dwight 1904, 259 Kobert 1906, 1079–1080 Witthaus 1911, 924–925 McNally 1937, 517 von Oettingen 1952, 317.

4. e.g. McNally 1937, 517: 'Poisonous doses produce the general symptoms of weakness, languor and drowsiness, but not actual sleep. Movements are weak, slow and unsteady, and the gait is staggering. Generally there are nausea and vomiting, with profuse salivation . . . There are tremors and febrillary contractions of the muscles, with occasional convulsions.'

5. This disparity is noted by Burnet 1911, App. 1, pp. 149–150. He finds it puzzling; and, since he presupposes that the account is historically accurate, he wonders if the drug was indeed hemlock. He is reassured on this point by 'an eminent pharmacologist, my colleague Professor C. R. Marshall', who affirms: '. . . Personally, I am decidedly of opinion that his death was due to conium (i.e. hemlock-juice). It is difficult to be absolutely positive on this point, as

conium is somewhat peculiar in its action, and the symptoms produced vary with the dose and probably with the individual.' This vague reply satisfied Burnet but leaves the puzzle where it was. Poisonous doses of hemlock, to judge from the toxicologies, regularly produce a number of symptoms: some of these Plato omits. That is the problem. To say 'the symptoms . . . vary . . . *probably* with the individual' (my italics) is not enough.

6. 66b ff., 80d ff., 114e.
7. e.g. Witthaus, 1911.
8. Cf. Claus 1969.
9. e.g. Philol. 13, Diog. Apoll. 4, cf. Arist. *de An.* 405^{b}11.
10. *Phd.* 79c, *Tht.* 184c ff.
11. Contrast the rapidity of the exit of the Homeric *psyche*: ψυχὴ δ᾽ ἐκ ῥεθέων πταμένη Ἀϊδόσδε βεβήκει *(Il.* 16. 856, 22. 362), ψυχὴ δὲ κατ᾽ οὐταμένην ὠτειλὴν ἔσσυτ᾽ ἐπειγομένη *(Il.* 14. 518), ψυχὴ . . . πεπότηται *(Od.* 11. 222).
12. εἶπεν ὅτι, ἐπειδὰν πρὸς τῇ καρδίᾳ [ἤψυχρότης] γένηται αὐτῷ, τότε οἰχήσεται, 118a3–4. Cf. ἐπειδὰν πίω τὸ φάρμακον, οὐκέτι ὑμῖν παραμενῶ, ἀλλ᾽ οἰχήσομαι . . . 115d3–4.
13. 115d. Cf. καθαρεύωμεν [τὴν ψυχὴν] ἀπ᾽ αὐτοῦ [sc. τοῦ σώματος] 67 a, κάθαρσις, καθαρμός 69b–c; 84a–b; 106e–107a.
14. The usual interpretation of the remark, 118 a 8–9.
15. [τὴν ψυχὴν] αὐτὴν . . . εἰς αὑτὴν συλλέγεσθαι, καὶ ἀθροίζεσθαι, 83a7–8, cf. τὸ χωρίζειν ὅτι μάλιστα ἀπὸ τοῦ σώματος τὴν ψυχὴν καὶ ἐθίσαι αὐτὴν καθ᾽ αὑτὴν πανταχόθεν ἐκ τοῦ σώματος συναγείρεσθαί τε καὶ ἀθροίζεσθαι . . . τοῦτό γε θάνατος ὀνομάζεται . . ., 67c6–d4.
16. Compare Sophocles' calm pleasure at having escaped, through old age, the λυττῶντά τινα καὶ ἄγριον δεσπότην of lust, *Rep.* 329c4.
17. It also reinforces the argument. This measured and ordered picture encourages us to see the *psyche* as an entity separable from the body, not just the 'harmony' of the physical parts while they are all working together (85e ff.), but the inner centre of sensation and cognition visibly separating itself from its shell.
18. This article was read as a 'communication' at the Classical Association A.G.M. in Bristol, April 1972, and is summarized in the *Proceedings,* 1972. I am grateful to Professor E. A. Havelock for suggesting, in conversation, the basic idea of this article.

• • •

Hemlock Poisoning and the Death of Socrates
Did Plato Tell the Truth?

ENID BLOCH

INTRODUCTION

The closing pages of Plato's *Phaedo* provide a stunning picture of the effects of poison upon the body of Socrates. Plato describes a slowly ascending paralysis, beginning in Socrates' feet and creeping steadily up his legs toward his chest, with Socrates' mind remaining clear until the end. Death arrives calmly and peacefully. It is a remarkable account, rich in emotive power and in clinical detail. But is it true?

Let us recall once again those final hours. After Socrates drank the poison, "he walked about and, when he said his legs were heavy, lay down on his back, for such was the advice of the attendant." The jailor then began to examine Socrates, much in the way a modern physician might do.

> The man . . . laid his hands on him and after a while examined his feet and legs, then pinched his foot hard and asked if he felt it. He said 'No'; then after that, his thighs; and passing upwards in this way he showed us that he was growing cold and rigid. And then again he touched him and said that when it reached his heart, he would be gone. The chill had now reached the region about the groin, and uncovering his face, which had been covered, he said—and these were his last words—'Crito, we owe a cock to Asclepius. Pay it and do not neglect it.' 'That,' said Crito, 'shall be done; but see if you have anything else to say.' To this question he made no reply, but after a little while he moved; the attendant uncovered him; his eyes were fixed. And Crito when he saw it, closed his mouth and eyes.[1]

So vivid is this process of dying, most readers through the ages probably have accepted Plato's account without question, its very attention to clinical detail sufficient evidence of its veracity. Yet it has hardly gone unchallenged. In the 1970s the classicist Christopher Gill and the pathologist William Ober, writing in the *Classical Quarterly*[2] and the *New York State Journal of Medicine*,[3] respectively, suggested that Plato had deliberately distorted the truth for his own dramatic or philosophic purposes. Hemlock poisoning, they claimed, would have produced a far nastier and more violent end. Because Plato wished to portray the philosophic idea of the soul departing peacefully from the body, he needed to envision a quiet, dignified unfolding of symptoms.

"The quietness, the calmness, the regularity of the effects of the penetration of poison into Socrates' body," Gill proposed, "is the quietness of a ritual, the *katharmos* or purification of the soul from the prison of the body."[4] Plato "tampers with the facts," Ober contended, because "he wanted to preserve the noble image of his friend and teacher," with "no undignified details to obscure the heroic manner of his death. He was writing literature, not an historical annal."[5] In 1991 these same arguments would be repeated by Bonita Graves et al.[6] in a paper claiming to shed "twentieth century scientific light" on the death of Socrates.

The issue is important, not only for reasons of historical curiosity, but for the sake of our general trust in Plato's veracity. If Plato had indeed tampered with the medical facts of Socrates' death, then his entire picture of the life and personality of Socrates, as well as many other of his observations, also must come under deep suspicion. Gill had suggested as much.

"This instance, in which a historical event is transformed into a representation of a philosophical idea, should alert us to the possibility that many of what seem to be authentic glimpses into the life, and death, of the historical Socrates may in fact be illustrative pictures, attached or inset, like the myths of the dialogues, into Plato's arguments."[7]

But why would Plato have expected his readers to accept so bold a distortion?[8] Socrates' death had hardly been a secret affair. Not only had his final hours been witnessed by a large group of talkative friends, in politically volatile Athens such executions were a frequent event. Would it not have made much more sense for Plato to write honestly and accurately about a poison with which he and his contemporaries already were far too familiar?

It might seem a simple matter to resolve this issue, perhaps with one phone call to a physician, poison hotline, or botanical garden. But accurate knowledge of hemlock is hard to come by these days, and to discover it one must navigate a veritable thicket of botanical, toxicological, neurological, linguistic, and historical complexities. In this paper, I report the results of such a journey. Plato not only told the truth, I conclude, but much more of it than anyone has recognized. The calm, peaceful death of the *Phaedo* was a historical reality.

Until now, Gill, Ober, and Graves have enjoyed the last word on the subject. Yet these writers reached their conclusions after having made only the most cursory examination of the medical and historical literature. Gill and Ober consulted among the ancients only Nicander and from modern medicine only a few timeworn and inaccurate lists of symptoms. Graves cites an equally problematic list of symptoms, further confusing the issue by offering information about nicotine instead of hemlock.[9]

In contrast, I have found it necessary to explore the writings of Theophrastus, Pliny, Dioscorides, and many other ancient authors, as well as the scientific works of such seventeenth-through nineteenth-century figures as Wepfer, Störck, Linnaeus, Christison, Bennett, and Harley,[10] piecing together their bits of information like a huge jigsaw puzzle. I have also spoken at length with practicing neurologists and pathologists,[11] researched the recent medical and even veterinary literature, and brought plants from Cornell University's Poisonous Plants Garden into my own home,[12] growing familiar enough with their features to make sense of the ancient writings.

Determining the likely ingredients in Socrates' cup proved in itself a difficult task, for Plato never identified hemlock, κώνειον (*kōneion*) in Greek, as the actual poison, speaking only of τὸ φάρμακον (*to pharmakon*), "the drug." How can we be sure it was hemlock? And which hemlock? A number of plants with different properties are called by that same name. Plato's Greek also presents a challenge. What exactly did he mean when he stated that Socrates' legs were "growing cold and stiff," ψύχοιτο τε καὶ πηγνῦτο (*psuchoito te kai pēgnuto*)? Should we understand "cold" as an actual drop in temperature, a subjective feeling of chills, or simply a lack of energy? Does "stiff," or "congealed" in the Greek, imply a rigid paralysis or a flaccid one? In the answers to these questions lies all the difference between central and peripheral nervous system pathology, and therefore between toxins from a plant like water hemlock, which attack the brain and spinal cord, and those from poison hemlock, which target peripheral nerves.

In the end I have been able fully to align Plato's description with modern medical understanding. Socrates suffered a peripheral neuropathy, a toxin-induced condition resembling the Guillain-Barré syndrome, brought about by the alkaloids in *Conium maculatum,* the poison hemlock plant. Plato proves to have been entirely accurate in every clinical detail, while Gill, Ober, and Graves were mistaken in the violent demise they imagined for Socrates.

HOW MANY HEMLOCKS?

Most ancient writers seem to have known very well which herb they were talking about when they spoke of hemlock, and they did not question its ability to provide a peaceful death. According to Theophrastus,[13] the speed and ease of hemlock's effects depended on the thoroughness of its preparation. Many people had once simply "shredded up" their hemlock for use, he observed, but now "they bruise it in the mortar, and, after putting it through a fine sieve, sprinkle it on water and so drink it; and then death is made swift and easy."[14]

Hemlock must often have been combined with other drugs in an attempt to enhance its virtues. Theophrastus tells us of a certain Thrasyas of Mantineia, who discovered "a poison which produces an easy and painless end; he uses the juices of hemlock, poppy and other such herbs, so compounded as to make a dose of conveniently small size."[15] We can well imagine Socrates' jailor doing likewise. It is evident that he crushed the hemlock, for when Socrates asked him to "prepare" the poison, he used a form of the verb τρίβω (*tribō*), which means to crush, as in a mortar.

Yet as time passed, the identity of the Athenian plant grew less certain. The great Greek herbalist Dioscorides,[16] writing in the first century A.D., and his Roman contemporary, Pliny the Elder,[17] still possessed a great deal of information about the plant and its powers. Indeed, their accounts would be regarded as authoritative for many centuries to come. Yet with the translation of Greek κώνειον into Latin *cicuta* and then into English "hemlock,"[18] the name took on a more or less generic meaning.

In English, "hemlock" refers not only to poison hemlock, but to water hemlock, hemlock water dropwort, lesser hemlock (fool's parsley), and other herbs as well, all resembling each other in their lacy, umbrella-like flowers and tiny fruits. They are members of the *Umbelliferae* plant family, a very large and widespread group that includes such edible vegetables as carrots, celery, dill, parsley, and parsnips. It is easy for the various hemlocks to be mistaken for these vegetables, often with dire results. The root of poison hemlock, for example, looks like a white carrot or parsnip, and its leaves, especially in the first year of the plant's two-year cycle, closely resemble parsley.

Through the centuries Latin *cicuta* became virtually an English word, a synonym for all types of hemlock. At the same time it acquired a somewhat more scientific veneer, for botanical works were written in Latin all the way through the eighteenth century. With no agreed-upon system of plant names, each botanist not only used the names however he wished but invented more of his own. By the seventeenth and eighteenth centuries the confusion of the hemlocks was enormous, with literally dozens of different plants assigned various versions of the names *cicuta* and *cicutaria*, in scores of botanical works. No one could keep up with it anymore.

Linnaeus brought some order to the world of plants with his great scheme of plant classification, but paradoxically, when it came to the confusion of the hemlocks, he seems to have made matters even worse. For he separated Greek κώνειον and Latin *cicuta*, assigning the name *Conium* to poison hemlock and *Cicuta* to water hemlock.[19] But the Greek and Latin terms had traveled together through the ages, and they could not so readily be divorced, whether in popular language or in general medical discussions. Information about the plants was thus all the more confounded, with facts about *Cicuta* injected into descriptions of *Conium*. Indeed, the difficulty continues to our own day. Ask a modern emergency room doctor about poison hemlock, and he is likely to answer, "Cicuta, right? It produces seizures."

Even as late as the eighteenth century botanists tended to assume the various hemlocks all shared the same poisonous qualities and effects, if in lesser or greater amounts. Though eventually realizing this was not quite so, they still possessed little accurate knowledge of the true differences. Question arose, especially in England, as to whether poison hemlock was poisonous at all, a doubt apparently shared even by Linnaeus.

In light of this history it is easy to understand why so many people have mistakenly associated seizures with poison hemlock, for it takes an expert to tell the various plants apart, and reports of poisonings have so frequently been attributed to the wrong species. As lists of symptoms were handed on, various pieces of information fell out or were tacked on, until misinformation took on an historical tradition of its own. Modern toxicology texts unfortunately still draw upon these older compilations, and scholars who rely upon them unwittingly reproduce their centuries-old errors.

Poison hemlock is in fact a unique plant, with chemical properties different from any other of the thousands of members of the *Umbelliferae* family. For it is the only one, apparently, among these many thousands, that produces the toxic substances known as alkaloids. The toxins in all other poisonous *Umbelliferae* are acetylenic compounds.[20] This striking botanical fact is little known even today, and it certainly was not recognized in the past. Could this profound chemical difference be the reason poison hemlock, of all the hemlocks, is the only one to attack primarily the peripheral nervous system, rather than the central?

ABOUT NICANDER

Even in the ancient world the identity and properties of κώνειον had not remained entirely clear. Nicander, possibly a Greek-speaking Roman army doctor of the second century B.C., composed a poem on poisons and their antidotes, the *Alexipharmaca*.[21] In it, he presented a gruesome picture of κώνειον poisoning:

> Take note of the noxious draught which is hemlock, for this drink assuredly looses disaster upon the head bringing the darkness of night: the eyes roll, and men roam the streets with tottering steps and crawling upon their hands; a terrible choking blocks the lower throat and the narrow passage of the windpipe; the extremities grow cold; and in the limbs the stout arteries are contracted; for a short while the victim draws breath like one swooning, and his spirit beholds Hades.[22]

A fearsome portrait indeed, and one upon which Gill and Ober heavily depend in their attempt to refute Plato. But why should Nicander's account be credited above that of Plato? Not only was Nicander writing a good two centuries after Socrates' death, he was describing illness, not execution. The victim in Nicander's poem is not a prisoner, forced to ingest a toxin known at the very least to his executioner, but a man free to wander about and "totter" through the streets. We are not told how he came to be poisoned. Would an observer have been able to say which substance, if any, had been responsible for his condition? Nicander was writing at a time of high anxiety about poisons, when any acute episode of appendicitis, or asthma, or choking, in the absence of other explanation, was likely to be deemed a surreptitious murder.

Nor was Nicander regarded as much of an authority even in his own day. There has to be "doubt," report Nicander's modern translators, A.S.F. Gow and A.F. Scholfield, "whether the poet knew what he . . . was talking about," for "his descriptions do not always tally with the known habits of the plants of which he is supposed to be speaking."[23] His information was mostly derivative, they note, rather than the product of personal observation or study. "No doubt the mythological and other ornaments are his own . . . but the bulk of his matter is borrowed."[24] Indeed, the great Greco-Roman physicians of the following centuries were largely to ignore his work.

Most important, we cannot simply assume that Nicander and Plato were talking about the same plant. In an important article in the 1936 *Journal of Hellenic Studies*,[25] R.M. Dawkins warned of the difficulty in establishing ancient plant identifications. The Greeks did not think as we do, and "of Linnaeus and still more of the modern natural system of classification we must completely clear our minds."[26] Plant names in the ancient world emerged not from botanical principles but from the uses of plants, their scent, or sometimes their general appearance. The Greek attitude, Dawkins recognized, was akin to that of English people "who are apt to call any yellow cup-like flower a buttercup," and "indications are that the ancients used plant names in much the same way."[27]

Dawkins cited an interesting example from the ancient Greek-speaking communities of Italy, where the word κάμμαρον (*kammaron*) served as the name for hemlock, while κάμμαρος (*kammaros*) referred to aconite. Dawkins found even a third variant, κάμμαρι (*kammari*), the big tree spurge, still in use in the modern Greek-speaking village of Bova in Calabria. Since all three plants are highly toxic, Dawkins drew the conclusion that in one form or another κάμμαρον had always pointed to some sort of poisonous plant, with no careful distinction as to type.[28]

If κάμμαρον had enjoyed such multiple use, why not κώνειον? Could Nicander have been thinking not of hemlock but of an entirely different plant when he described the effects of κώνειον? Aconite, perhaps? Significantly, nineteenth and twentieth century reports of aconite poisoning correspond almost exactly with the symptoms portrayed by Nicander. Modern aconite victims suffer burning of the mouth, constriction and pain in the throat and chest, greatly labored breathing, vertigo, diminished vision or blindness, slight convulsive twitching, and a sense of impending doom.[29] Surprisingly, Nicander's account appears to have been remarkably accurate, but only if we recognize the κώνειον of the *Alexipharmaca* as aconite rather than hemlock.[30]

SEIZURES AND SWELLINGS

Confusion among the hemlocks has long fueled a scholarly debate over the death of Socrates. Modern writers like Gill, Ober, and Graves seem unaware of their predecessors, but the controversy over the demise of Socrates has in fact been going on for centuries, ever since the appearance in 1679 of Johannes Wepfer's monumental treatise, *Cicutae aquaticae historia et noxae*.[31]

Wepfer, a Swiss physician, had been deeply impressed by the effects of water hemlock on eight local children. After eating various amounts of its root the children had suffered horrendous seizures, and two of them died terrible deaths, with backs arched and jaws clenched, foaming at the mouth. Wepfer interviewed surviving children and their parents, and his treatise provides what still today are the classic descriptions of water hemlock poisoning. His work was a scientific masterpiece, bringing all the known botanical literature together with his own toxicological experiments and observations.

Behind Wepfer's inquiries lay a fundamental question. His treatise is filled with references to the *Phaedo* and the death of Socrates, about which he expressed the gravest doubts. Hemlock could not have been a "cold" poison as reported in all the ancient works, he contended, for the experiences of the eight poisoned children proved how very "hot," that is, conducive to violent seizures, it actually was. It did not occur to Wepfer that his studies of water hemlock might be irrelevant to the hemlock of the Athenians, for he was convinced all varieties of *cicuta* shared similar toxic properties. Wepfer's treatise set the stage for the ensuing debate, and throughout the seventeenth, eighteenth, and nineteenth centuries scores of physician-botanists, some of them the best scientific minds of their age, were to weigh in on the issue.[32]

In the middle of the eighteenth century medical interest shifted away from water hemlock to poison hemlock, thanks to the enthusiasms of the Baron Anton von Störck, a Viennese physician convinced *Conium maculatum* could cure cancer and all other manner of "swellings."[33] No doubt he had arrived at his ideas after reading in Pliny and Dioscorides of hemlock's reputed power to shrink breasts and wither testicles.[34] Störck fed extracts of poison hemlock to his patients and proclaimed his efforts a total success. It was not long before physicians all across Europe were following his lead, and by the beginning of the nineteenth century doctors were routinely prescribing hemlock for a vast range of illnesses, as the pharmacological dispensaries of the period amply reveal.

TREASURE TROVE

No one, not even the ancients, knew more about the effects of poison hemlock than did a group of nineteenth-century physicians and toxicologists, who together amassed a veritable treasure trove of first-hand observations. These men were poisoning humans and animals right and left—and they were keeping records of it. Especially in the first half of the century, doctors not only were feeding extracts of hemlock to their patients, toxicologists were deliberately poisoning themselves and dispatching huge numbers of laboratory animals as they studied the plant's physiological effects, and chemists were breathing its vapors as they sought to isolate its alkaloids.[35] The resulting poisonings were carefully documented, as were deaths through ingestion of the plant growing wild.

This hard-won knowledge, culled from the misfortune of so many victims, soon would be entirely forgotten. Today's physicians and toxicologists remember nothing of their nineteenth-century colleagues, but for our purposes their prolific experiments and precise observations are priceless. We may use the cases they describe, especially those reported by the three great Scottish toxicologists, Robert Christison, John Hughes Bennett, and John Harley, to establish beyond the shadow of a doubt the truth of Plato's account.

In virtually every one of these experimental or accidental cases, whether human or animal, a flaccid paralysis began in the distal parts of the body and moved progressively toward the trunk. Consciousness was preserved throughout, though in animals it was sometimes hard to tell. Death arrived when paralysis reached the muscles of respiration, preceded by a terminal seizure due to lack of oxygen to the brain. The seizure appeared mild, for the already paralyzed muscles of the body could not strongly convulse. But death was not always inevitable. If the amount of poison was insufficient to paralyze breathing the victim survived, slowly recovering over a period of hours. Toward the end of the century, after the discovery of cardiopulmonary resuscitation, victims could be saved by supporting their breathing through the critical period of respiratory failure.

HARLEY'S ACCOUNT

John Harley, an avid proponent of hemlock's medicinal use and a careful student of its physiological effects, did not hesitate to poison himself. He described his adventures in *The Old Vegetable Neurotics*,[36] published in 1869:

> After taking three drachms of the *succus conii* of the 'British Pharma-copoeia,' I set out walking; and three-quarters of an hour after the dose, I felt a heavy clogging sensation in my heels. There was a distinct impairment of motor power. I felt, so to speak, that 'the go' was taken out of me. It was not that I felt fatigued just then, but it seemed as if a drag was suddenly put upon me, and that it would have been impossible to walk fast, if urged to do so. After walking about a mile up-hill, this sensation was very decided; and on putting a foot on the scraper at the door of the hospital, the other leg was shaky, and felt almost too weak to support me. My movements appeared clumsy to myself, and it seemed necessary that I should make an effort to control them. At the same time, there was a sluggishness of the adaptation of the eye. My vision was good for fixed objects; but, when an uneven object was put in motion before the eyes, there was a haze and dimness of vision, producing a feeling of giddiness. The pulse and pupils were unaffected. These were the whole of the effects; and, after continuing for an hour, they rapidly disappeared, and left me in the possession of my usual vigour.[37]

On another occasion, Harley had ingested even more of the drug:

An hour and a quarter after taking the dose, I first felt decided weakness in my legs. The giddiness and diminution of motor power continued to increase for the next fifteen minutes. An hour and a half after taking the dose, these effects attained their maximum. . . . The legs felt as if they would soon be too weak to support me. There was a positive diminution of voluntary power in every part of the muscular system, and this nearly amounted to complete paralysis as far as the hamstring and levator palpebrae muscles were concerned. At one time, the greatest exertion was required to elevate the eyelids. The mind remained perfectly clear and calm, and the brain active throughout; but the body seemed heavy, and well-nigh asleep. After continuing for about half an hour at their maximum, the symptoms began rapidly to decline, and within three hours and a half of taking the dose they had totally disappeared.[38]

Could he have come any closer to Socrates' own experience?[39] Harley was luckier perhaps than he realized in having escaped the same fate. He went on to poison many of his patients, finding hemlock especially helpful in treating unmanageable children, those whom we today would call hyperactive. The drug did indeed slow them down.

THE UNFORTUNATE GOW

In 1845 a poisoning occurred that would capture the attention of leading toxicologists. A poor Scottish tailor named Duncan Gow had enjoyed a sandwich lovingly made for him by his children, from what they thought to be parsley growing wild.

In from fifteen to twenty minutes there was loss of power in the lower extremities; but he apparently suffered no pain. In walking, he staggered as if he were drunk; at length his limbs refused to support him, and he fell. On being raised, his legs dragged after him, and when his arms were lifted they fell like inert masses, and remained immovable. There was complete paralysis of the upper and lower extremities within two hours after he had taken the poison. There was a loss of the power of swallowing, and a partial paralysis of sensation, no convulsions, but only slight occasional motions of the left leg; the pupils were fixed. Three hours after eating the hemlock the respiratory movements had ceased. Death took place in three hours and a quarter; it was evidently caused by gradual asphyxia from paralysis of the muscles of respiration; but the Intellect was perfectly clear until shortly before death.[40]

Gow died in the Edinburgh hospital where John Hughes Bennett practiced medicine. Bennett immediately recognized the significance of the case for the ongoing debate over the death of Socrates, and he carefully interviewed all who had witnessed any aspect of Gow's demise, whether passers-by in the street, police officers, or hospital attendants. Bennett performed an autopsy on the body, carrying the stomach contents to Robert Christison, who confirmed absolutely that Gow had ingested *Conium maculatum*. Reporting the case in great detail, Bennett emphasized its remarkable correspondence with the facts of the *Phaedo*.[41] For a while, at least, the long debate seemed all but settled. Poison hemlock could indeed bring on the symptoms of Socrates' death.

COLD AND STIFF

Christison was at that time the world's authority on hemlock poisoning. Yet until the case of Gow he himself had doubted *Conium maculatum* was the plant responsible for Socrates' death. The difficulty for him lay in Plato's description of Socrates' legs as "growing cold and stiff," ψύχοιτό τε καὶ πηγνῦτο . Though neurology in Christison's day had not yet advanced to the point of clearly distinguishing central and peripheral nervous system pathology, he nevertheless knew enough from his own experience with poisons to recognize that "cold and stiff" did not make much sense together with the ascending paralysis of Socrates and his clear mind.

Christison was correct, for lowered temperature in the extremities indicates a reduced blood circulation, and it usually is accompanied by impaired consciousness, for the circulation to the brain has been compromised as well. And rigidity in the legs is a sign of central nervous system pathology. Instinctively Christison understood that a poison which paralyzed the extremities but left the mind clear had to have produced a flaccid paralysis, not a rigid one.

In 1835 Christison had addressed the issue directly. "I think it will puzzle the most learned toxicologist," he told the Royal Society of Edinburgh, "to point out any poison which has the property of occasioning coldness and stiffness of the limbs, proceeding gradually upwards, and proving fatal without causing either pain or sopor. There seems, then, no alternative but to conclude, either that the description of Plato . . . is not a detail of facts, but an embellished narrative, written for effect; or that, although we are now acquainted probably with fifty times as many poisons as the ancient Athenians, and with many which are fifty times as active as any in their list, we have lost acquaintance with one with which the ancients were quite familiar, and which differs totally from every known poison in its action."[42]

It had never occurred to Christison or his colleagues that the translation of Plato's words might be wrong, or that the implications of "cold and stiff" in English might not be the same as in the original Greek. Even Bennett, despite noting the flaccid paralysis of Gow, still thought Plato had been talking about rigidity, and thus he admitted he could not explain the "cold and stiff" reference in the *Phaedo*, despite having found so many other aspects of Gow's case fully in accord with Plato. Today's scholars persist in this same mistake. Graves et al. point to the supposed coldness and stiffness of Socrates' legs as proof that Plato's account could not have been medically accurate.[43]

But the problem immediately disappears when we remember that Plato lived in his world, not ours, and when we correct our English translations accordingly. ψύχοιτο, from the verb ψύχω, "to make cool or cold," and πήγνυτο, from πήγνυμι, "to congeal," reverberated in Greek ears with a resonance that is not easy to recall, for these words connoted nothing less than the fundamental structure of the universe.

Like others of his time, Plato conceived of the cosmos in terms of the four great elements, fire, air, water, and earth, and of their associated qualities, hot, cold, wet, and dry. In various combinations and proportions these elements and qualities made up almost everything in the cosmos. A number of times in his writings, especially in a cosmological work like the *Timaeus*, Plato used πήγνυτο and other forms of πήγνυμι to indicate the way elements and qualities are transformed from a looser to a firmer consistency and from a greater degree of activity to a lesser.[44]

As part of this deep sense of the structure of the world, πήγνυμι did not necessarily imply rigidity, but pointed more to the action of congealing than to the thing that is congealed. Milk curdles, water freezes, pudding thickens—all are "congealing." We do not get the feeling, either in Plato or elsewhere, that the congealed substance itself is necessarily rigid or hard to the touch, just that it is relatively thick, and most important, that it stays put, not flowing or changing shape like a liquid. Homer, for example, sang of spears flung into the hearts of enemies, which then stick out of their chests, or, having missed their target, stick into the ground. It was not the rigidity of the spears as such, but the characteristic way they retained their position without coming unstuck, that Homer seems to have had in mind.[45]

πήγνυμι in the sense of congealing is even more evident in Hippocratic writings. Phlegm, for example, is described as a congealed "cool" substance, which if not sufficiently dispersed on entering the "warm" bloodstream will thicken the blood as well. When such thickening prevents πνεῦμα (*pneuma*), the very breath of life, from getting through to the body, the result is the convulsions of epilepsy or even death, if the blockage is severe enough. Hippocrates depended upon ψύχω and πήγνυμι, the very same verbs employed by Plato, to describe "cold" and "congealing."[46] He certainly did not mean to imply that phlegm is solid or that blood becomes rigid, just that both may thicken. Had any of these writers wished to describe something that felt hard to the touch, or to specify the rigidity of muscular contractions, they could have called upon other far more suitable words, such as σκλήρος (*skleros*) and σπάσμα (*spasma*).

Both πήγνυτο and ψύχοιτο were associated with a reality that was as much psychic as it was physical. People's characters and emotions, the humors of their bodies—black bile, yellow bile, blood and phlegm—as well as their food and drink, all involved precarious combinations of hot and cold and wet and dry, which constantly were in danger of imbalance. Illness, both physical and emotional, resulted from such imbalance. Thus the practice of medicine consisted largely of restoring proper proportions of hot, cold, wet, and dry, whether through purgings, drugs, or diet.

In this larger sense, "hot" and "cold" did not so much refer to temperature as to a level of physical and emotional energy or activity. "Warmth" implied strength, motion, or strong feeling, whereas "cold" suggested passivity, restraint, and lack of feeling. There is a hint of temperature in all of this, of course, for cold does tend to inhibit activity and heat to speed it, yet something much more fundamental was really being invoked by these terms. Interestingly, we ourselves sometimes still speak in this ancient way, as when we refer to a "hot-tempered" person or to one with a "cold" heart. We do not mean that the bodily temperatures of such people are any different from those of others, just that their irritability, explosiveness, or sensitivity may be more intense or less so.

Thus it was not the rigid flexion of Socrates' muscles or a drop in body temperature that Plato meant to imply by "cold and stiff," but a lack of movement, energy, or feeling. Socrates' legs were "stuck" or "congealed," remaining fixed where they were. They were "cold," that is, inert, lacking in activity or energy, unable to move and unable to feel. In other words, Socrates' legs were paralyzed.

SPEAKING OF PARALYSIS

Why then did Plato not simply say so? Paralysis, after all, is a good Greek word. But when we look carefully we see that it had not been available to him, for it belonged to a somewhat later period in the development of Greek medicine.

The noun παράλυσις (*paralysis*) stems from the verb λύω (*luō*), which means "to loosen or set free." In a metaphoric sense, λύω had long implied the traumatic onset of paralysis, as in Homer's references to mortally wounded soldiers whose limbs were "loosed" in the moments before death.[47] But the meanings of λύω, one of the most common of Greek verbs, were multiple and general, certainly not technical or medical. Even in prefixed form, as παραλύω (*paraluō*), its usage remained broad, referring to any "loosing" of something "from the side," as in unhitching a horse or dismissing a soldier from the ranks.

As a noun rather than a verb, and as the technical name for a specific physical disability, παράλυσις would be a long time in coming. We encounter it for the first time in a fragment from Theophrastus,[48] and not until the first and second centuries A.D., in the texts of Galen, Aretaeus, and others of the great Greco-Roman physicians, do we find its consistent and authoritative use.[49] Interestingly, *paralysis* by that time must have entered folk language as well, for Dioscorides in the first century would list it as one among many regional names for hemlock.[50]

A related noun, ἀποπληξία (*apoplexia*), did exist in Plato's day, for we find it in Hippocratic writings. *Apo-* means "from" or "away from," and *plexia* denotes a sudden striking, as when a lyre is struck with a *plectrum.* Thus *apoplexia* referred either to something like a stroke, in which one side of the body was affected, or to a sudden loss of consciousness. Plato might also have turned to παραπληξία (*paraplexia*), but this too would have implied a sudden event, such as sunstroke. The gradually ascending paralysis that Plato needed to describe, with its symmetrical effect on Socrates' limbs, could not have been suggested effectively by either of these words. And so Plato called upon the most evocative terms he could find, and these were ψύχοιτο τε καὶ πηγνῦτο.

Plato's choice of words was not an unusual one. Indeed, in his comedy *Frogs,* Aristophanes had employed almost identical terms to describe the effects of hemlock poisoning.[51] In the play, the protagonist Dionysos has been looking for a way to kill himself in order to visit the underworld. Heracles suggests suicide by hanging, but Dionysos rejects that method as "too hot." All Heracles then has to do is hint at a "beaten path," by mortar and pestle, for Dionysos immediately to respond, "hemlock, you mean?" But he dismisses that idea as well, declaring it "too cold and wintry, already the stiffness (congealing) is reaching the shin." In Greek, Dionysos' words are: ψυχράν γε καὶ δυσχείμερον. εὐθὺς γὰρ ἀποπήγνυσι τἀντικνήμια. ψυχράν (*psuchran*) and δυσχείμερον (*duscheimeron*) mean "cold and wintry," ἀποπήγνυσι (*apopēgnusi*), from πήγνυμι, connotes something being "made to congeal," and τἀντικνήμια (*tantiknemia*) refers to "the shin."

Socrates' symptoms exactly, are they not? Yet Aristophanes first produced *Frogs* in 405 B.C., six years *before* the death of Socrates. How then does it make any sense to accuse Plato of fabricating these very same effects? Far from trying to deceive their audiences or their readers, Aristophanes and Plato were employing the ordinary language of their day, building their jokes and their dialogue upon the shared experiences of their fellow Athenians. Aristophanes evidently expected his audience not only to recognize the symptoms of hemlock poisoning, but to understand how the toxin was prepared, by crushing the plant in a mortar. Why should Plato have expected any less?[52]

Plato knew also that a number of his readers would be approaching the *Phaedo* with medically sophisticated eyes. Hippocrates, the great master of clinical observation, had lived at the same time as Socrates, and he had taught his skills to others. Plato not only was aware of the Hippocratic school of medicine, he seems to have been following their methods. Though his gorgeous literary style contrasts sharply with the clipped manner of Hippocratic case presentation, Plato and the Hippocratic writers were using much the same approach, identifying a set of symptoms and carefully tracking the onset, course, and outcome of disease in an individual patient.

Interestingly, we cannot turn directly to the Hippocratic corpus to verify the symptoms of hemlock poisoning, for overt discussions of poisoning do not appear in Hippocratic writings. Hippocrates distinguished sharply between the practice of medicine and the use of poisons, and in subscribing to the Hippocratic Oath ancient physicians were promising never to use a drug, or instruct others in its use, for the purpose of bringing about death.

This Hippocratic injunction may well be the reason Plato employed the general term, τὸ φάρμακον, in the *Phaedo,* rather than identifying hemlock by name.[53] It is also possible that Plato simply was unsure of the full ingredients of Socrates' cup. If Thrasyas of Mantineia had added poppy, dill, and other substances to his hemlock, might not Socrates' jailor have cooked up his own favorite recipe? If so, the most likely additional ingredient would have been opium from poppies.[54]

GUILLAIN-BARRÉ SYNDROME

Once Plato's language is properly translated, there is absolutely nothing in what he reports of Socrates' demise that cannot be aligned both with the experimental evidence of the nineteenth-century toxicologists and with the requirements of modern neurological understanding. Were Socrates brought today to a hospital emergency room, the attending physicians would immediately recognize his ascending paralysis as a peripheral neuropathy of the Guillain-Barré type. They would support his breathing when the paralysis reached the muscles of respiration, and he would have survived the experience. Had Socrates' friends only known CPR, they too could have saved him.

But Socrates stopped breathing, and with his brain deprived of oxygen he suffered a terminal seizure. Though the seizure was generalized it would have appeared quite mild, for with his limbs already paralyzed Socrates could not have convulsed in any dramatic fashion. In Plato's simple term, ἐκινήθη (*ekinpēthē*), "he moved."[55] A Guillain-Barré patient whose respiration has ceased would expire in this same way.

And yet, none of the modern doctors would think to associate Socrates' condition with hemlock poisoning. For in neither their modern texts on peripheral neuropathy and the Guillain-Barré syndrome, nor in their training, would they ever have come across references to poison hemlock. It is a strange failure, especially since the syndrome of "acute ascending paralysis" was first identified in the mid-nineteenth century, when reports of hemlock poisoning abounded in the medical literature. The physicians who defined the "new" syndrome, four French neurologists, apparently were unaware of the writings of Christison and his colleagues—or those of Plato, for that matter.

"Acute ascending paralysis" was first described in 1859 in a landmark paper by Octave Landry. Commenting on five cases he had observed for himself and five he had found in the literature, he set forth a set of symptoms which we may once again recognize as identical to those of Socrates:

> The sensory and motor systems may be equally affected. However the main problem is usually a motor disorder characterised by a gradual diminution of muscular strength with flaccid limbs and without contractures, convulsions or reflex movements of any kind. . . . One does not observe any symptoms referable to the central nervous system. . . . The intellectual faculties are preserved until the end. . . . The weakness spreads rapidly from the lower to the upper parts of the body. . . . The first symptoms always affect the extremities of the limbs and the lower limbs particularly. . . . The progression can be more or less rapid. It was eight days in one and fifteen days in another. . . . More often it is scarcely two or three days and sometimes only a few hours. When the paralysis reaches its maximum intensity the danger of asphyxia is always imminent.[56]

In 1916, a second landmark paper appeared, by Georges Guillain, Jean-Alexandre Barré, and André Strohl.[57] Interestingly, these men wondered whether a toxin or infection might be responsible for the syndrome, but they did not think about hemlock. Eventually Strohl's and even Landry's names receded, and "acute ascending paralysis" came to be known as the "Guillain-Barré Syndrome," or GBS.

Technically speaking, Socrates' paralysis is not a case of GBS, for neurologists in recent years have restricted the label to conditions in which a known toxin is not involved. Most cases of GBS are assumed to have been caused by viral infection, or are labeled "etiology unknown." Nevertheless, there is surely much that might be learned by bringing hemlock poisoning into the neurological discussion.[58]

SPOTS, ROOTS, AND ODORS

Christison had expressed two further reservations about *Conium maculatum* as the hemlock of the Greeks. "Both Pliny and Dioscorides have left tolerably minute descriptions of the plant,"[59] he noted, yet their observations did not accord with his own. The poison hemlock with which he himself was so familiar sported a solid root and a purple-spotted stem, but both of the ancient writers had called the root of the hemlock "hollow." And neither had mentioned the spots, "a character so obvious, that one can scarcely imagine an ancient herbalist omitting it."[60] How then could these be the same plants?

The answer may well lie in the changed physical appearance of the plant in its different seasons of growth. As Dioscorides advised long ago:

> It behooves anyone who desires to be a skilful herbalist, to be present when the plants first shoot out of the earth, when they are fully grown, and when they begin to fade. For he who is only present at the budding of the herb, cannot know it when full-grown, nor can he who hath examined a full-grown herb, recognize it when it has only just appeared above the ground. . . . Therefore the man who will observe his herbs oftentimes and in divers places, will acquire the greatest knowledge of them.[61]

Christison certainly was correct that the spotted appearance of poison hemlock is fully "obvious," but only at certain times. During the first year of the plant's growth, when its leaves remain close to the ground like parsley, it is difficult to see small spots on the thin, delicate branches. And even in the second year, when the plant grows to eight or ten feet high, the spots are not always visible. At the height of the summer they are certainly prominent, but by the fall they have entirely faded away. Given such variability, might not an ancient author have decided to omit any mention of spots, assuming he himself had even seen them?

But what about the "hollow" root? As Christison pointed out, the root of the poison hemlock plant is indeed entirely solid. Indeed, in the full-grown plant its texture is so tough, only with great difficulty can it be cut or sawed apart. And yet the solidity of the root is hardly the issue, for once again the problem lies not with a disparity between ancient and modern observations but with our English translations from the Greek.

What the ancient botanists most likely had been talking about were not "hollow" roots but "curved" or "bent" ones. Greek κοίλη (koilē) and Latin concava, the words used by Dioscorides and Pliny, do not imply an enclosed space so much as a concave or yielding shape. While a curved shape might indeed produce a hollow, as in the hold of a ship, it is the curvature itself to which the word is referring. Significantly, to the word κοίλη Dioscorides had added καὶ οὐ βαθῆῖα, "and not long," or, "and not deep."[62] In other words, the roots of the hemlock plant, growing in the rocky soil of Greece, were "bent, unable to grow deep."[63] Water hemlock, on the other hand, does sport a hollow rootstock, a fact that may have led many through the centuries to believe that water hemlock, rather than poison hemlock, was the κωνειον of the Greeks.

One feature of the plant that every commentator has noted, from ancient times to the present, is its noxious odor. Dioscorides and Pliny mentioned a "heavy" or "strong smell," and many others through the centuries have compared its odor to that of "mice, or the urine of cats."[64] To a modern observer it might seem more like a very heavy, peculiar tea, clinging obnoxiously in the mouth and nose, as if it has entered the body and will not let go. Just one strong whiff immediately brings on a sensation something like car-sickness, and a mild but sharp headache.[65] This very same odor, no doubt, had emanated from Socrates' fatal cup, and when he drew the poison into his mouth, it must have filled his senses.

CONCLUSION

The long, persistent controversy over the death of Socrates may finally have reached its end. By moving back and forth between the ancient and modern records, by uncovering the many layers of botanical and linguistic confusion, by learning the lessons of modern neurology, and by entering fully into the centuries-old debate, we have been able to bring every piece of the puzzle together. After so much complexity, the answer is almost simple. Socrates died gently and peacefully, just as Plato said he did. For Plato not only told the truth, he did so with astounding medical accuracy.

Socrates welcomed hemlock as a friend, allowing it to send him drifting gently off toward the Isles of the Blessed. We who seek the historical Socrates should welcome it, too. For in the precision and accuracy with which Plato described hemlock poisoning lies some assurance he told the truth in other respects as well. Did Plato always portray Socrates as faithfully in life as in death? We may never entirely know, but in the matter of hemlock at least, we have found our answer, and it is a powerful piece of evidence.

NOTES

1. Plato, *Phaedo* 117E–118A. The English translation appears on 401–403 of the Loeb Library edition, Harvard University Press (Cambridge, 1990).
2. Gill 1973.
3. Ober 1977.
4. Gill 1973, 28.
5. Ober 1977, 257.
6. Bonita M. Graves et al., 1991.
7. Gill 1973, 28.
8. Nicholas Smith (private communication) comments on the literary insufficiency of "the Gill-Ober interpretation," which "makes little sense of the fact that Plato gives the description of Socrates' symptoms to the *executioner*. If Plato's point were to ascribe to Socrates a miraculous and unusually calm reaction to a poison well-known to cause violent seizures, why make the executioner (who surely would know better) guilty of giving what would (allegedly) be a patently false symptomology? It seems that Plato would do a far better job of emphasizing Socrates' heroic strength of character by having the executioner either not discuss the symptoms at all (as well known to the ancient Greeks, anyway), or perhaps even better, having him warn of the allegedly well-known horrible symptoms, only to be miraculously contradicted by Socrates' heroic restraint, even as he lay dying. If Plato were writing fiction,

accordingly, I find his fictionalization quite foolish and poorly conceived. I'd just as soon not accuse Plato of that!"

9. Graves et al. are seriously in error in regarding the toxins in *Conium maculatum* as all but identical to nicotine in their chemistry and poisonous effects. Of the five alkaloids in poison hemlock, they focus on only one, γ-coniceine, regarding it as most toxic. In actuality, it is coniine that is present in largest amounts, especially in the developing fruits, the most poisonous part of the plant and the part most likely to have been used to make Socrates' poison. With the isolation of coniine by organic chemists early in the nineteenth century coniine became the standard substance employed by toxicologists in their hemlock experiments and by physicians in treating their patients. Though two of the four authors of the Graves paper hold medical degrees, their description of the nervous system seems quite crude. They posit an excess of neurotransmitters as the sole mechanism in both hemlock and nicotine poisoning, and do not consider demyelination, derangement of the axonal transport system, or any other of the pathological processes which peripheral neuropathy may involve. Indeed, they do not think in terms of peripheral neuropathy at all, so convinced are they that hemlock attacks the central nervous system. While γ-coniceine may in fact do so, the same is not true of coniine.

10. For extensive, unflagging help and guidance in tracking down old botanical and medical writings, I am profoundly grateful to Lilli Sentz, former curator of the Robert L. Brown History of Medicine Collection at the University at Buffalo's Health Sciences Library, and to her student assistant Kristin Stoklosa. I also wish to thank the New York Academy of Medicine for opening its remarkable collection of original manuscripts to my perusal.

11. I am deeply indebted to neuropathologist Dr. Barbara Zaias for patiently explaining, through many lengthy phone calls, the basic workings of the nervous system, especially the relationships of rigid and flaccid paralysis to the central and peripheral nervous systems. Without her warm response to the naïve questions of a non-physician, this work could never have been accomplished. I also wish to thank biochemist and friend of many years, Dr. Janice Sufrin of the Roswell Park Cancer Institute, for much advice and encouragement.

12. Krissy Faust, ornamental gardener at Cornell Plantations, introduced me to poison hemlock, water hemlock, and other toxic plants under her care at the Poisonous Plants Garden of the College of Veterinary Medicine, Cornell University. Ms. Faust generously shared her intimate knowledge of these plants and provided specimens for me to take home, making possible my observation of poison hemlock at close range.

13. Theophrastus, friend and successor to Aristotle, is credited with having founded the science of botany almost single-handedly. Some herbals preceded his, notably that of Diocles of Carystus, but the encyclopedic information Theophrastus gathered, and his efforts to describe and classify hundreds of plants, were altogether monumental in scope. Theophrastus lived from 372/1 to 288/7 BC.

14. Theophrastus, *Enquiry into Plants*. 9.16.9.

15. Theophrastus, *Enquiry into Plants*. 9.16.8.

16. Dioscorides' περὶ ὕλης ἰατρικῆς (*Materia medica*), a work of five books composed in the first century AD, describes about 700 plants and more than 1000 drugs and their physiological effects. Dioscorides' medicinal judgments were regarded as authoritative until at least the sixteenth century. His information

on hemlock appears in Book 4.79, or in English translation, Gunther 1968, 477–8. All further references to Dioscorides refer to this edition.

17. Pliny the Elder lived from 23/4 to 79 AD. A prolific author, he brought together in *Natural History* a vast compendium of the knowledge of his day. His information on hemlock appears mostly in Book 25, 94.151–5. The English translation of these sections may be found in Vol. VII of the Loeb Library edition, pp. 245–7.

18. It is possible to discern a connection between Latin *cicuta* and English "hemlock" as early as the seventh century AD. Four very old manuscripts, known as the Epinal, Erfurt, Corpus, and Leiden Glossaries, dating from the seventh, eighth, and ninth centuries, consist of lists of Latin words and their English equivalents, drawn up by scribes examining Latin religious or literary books, probably in the libraries of monasteries. The scribes were recording what they saw of English words written in the margins of the Latin books or inserted as interlinear translations. The scribes may also have been working from Latin-English "class-glossaries," that is, lists of words for classes of plants, animals, or other natural objects, drawn up by the first missionaries to England. In these old glossaries, *cicuta* is translated as "hymblicae," "huymblicae," "humlice," and other Anglo-Saxon spellings of "hemlock."

19. Carolus Linnaeus, *Species plantarum* (1753), 243, 255–6.

20. See Hegnauer 1971, and Fairbairn, 1971.

21. Nicander's *Alexipharmaca* appears both in Greek and in English translation in Gow and Scholfield 1953. 186–194. According to Gow and Scholfield, the difficulty in determining Nicander's dates "hardly admits of final solution." They place him "not in the third, but in the mid-second century or somewhat later." (8.) Nicander wrote a second poem, *Theriaca,* about animal toxins.

22. Nicander in Gow and Scholfield 1953, 106–7.

23. Ibid., 24.

24. Ibid., 18.

25. R. M. Dawkins 1936.

26. Ibid., 6.

27. Ibid., 7. Gow and Scholfield 1993 make the same point in their introduction to Nicander's poem. "It is plain moreover that . . . in ancient times as in modern Greek the same name was often used for different plants, and that the same plant often had more than one name" [p. 24]. How easy it is for plants to be confused is evident from the propensity of people in our own day to misidentify the "hemlock" of the Greeks as a "hemlock tree." The evergreen they have in mind is neither poisonous nor in any other way related to the various hemlock herbs. Experienced translators of the classics have made this same mistake, calling the hemlock of the Greeks a "fir tree."

28. Ibid., 4. Pliny tells us that some people in his day called aconite by the name *cammaron,* because its root resembled the crayfish, *cammarus.* See *HN,* 27.2.9, or Vol. 7, p. 395 of the Loeb Library edition.

29. Superb descriptions of aconite poisoning can be found in Bentley 1872, 997–1004, and Christison 1845, 662–670.

30. Readers may object to my conclusion that Nicander's hemlock actually was aconite on the grounds that Nicander wrote specifically about aconite poisoning elsewhere in his poem. But in ancient times (and still today) the same name, aconite, referred to several plants quite different in appearance. Nican-

der may well have known one of these under the name aconite (ἀκόνιτον) and anther as hemlock (κώνειον).

31. Wepfer 1679.

32. A number of these botanists are listed in Imbert-Gourbeyre 1875. So far as I am aware, this volume is the only book-length discussion of Socrates' physical death ever to have been published. Imbert-Gourbeyre consulted a great many botanico-medical sources, from ancient times through the Renaissance and beyond, but he himself did not delve deeply into either botany or medicine. His analysis included many important points, but it was fundamentally in error in the toxic properties it attributed to the various hemlocks. The only distinction Imbert-Gourbeyre made was that between water hemlock on the one hand and terrestrial hemlocks on the other, for he assumed all terrestrial hemlocks shared the same toxins. This left him in the paradoxical position of claiming correctly that *Conium maculatum* had been the poison of the Athenians, yet wrongly asserting the plant had been capable of producing *both* the slowly ascending paralysis reported in Christison's experiments *and* the delirium with convulsions observed in victims after ingestion of various other terrestrial hemlocks.

33. von Störck 1760.

34. In the wonderful 1655 translation of Dioscorides by John Goodyer in Gunther 1968, we read of hemlock's powers: "It doth extinguish ye Herpetas, & ye Erysipelata being smeared on. And ye herb, & ye hair being beaten small and smeared on about ye stones doth help wanton dreamers, & seed shedders, & doth enfeable ye genitals being smeared on, & drive away milk, & forbids ye breasts to grow great in time of virginity & makes ye stones in children unnourishable" (478). Pliny had offered similar information: "It forms an ingredient of eye salves, and it checks all catarrhs generally. The leaves also relieve every kind of swelling, pain or flux. Anaxilaus is responsible for the statement that if the breasts are rubbed with hemlock from adult maidenhood onwards they will always remain firm. What is certain is that an application of hemlock to the breasts of women in childbed dries up their milk, and to rub it on the testicles at the time of puberty acts as an antaphrodisiac." *NH*, 25.95.154, pp. 245–7, Vol. VII of the Loeb Library edition.

35. There are five alkaloids in poison hemlock, coniine, γ-coniceine, conhydrine, pseudoconhydrine, and N-methlconiine Coniine was the first alkaloid in the world to be isolated, a feat accomplished in the 1820s. It was synthesized in 1886. In the first half of the nineteenth century, when the science of organic chemistry was just getting underway, laboratory accidents seem to have been common. There are vivid reports in the literature of lab assistants or medical students breathing in the vapors of boiling *Conium maculatum* and succumbing to a paralysis that began in their limbs. They were put to bed and survived when the effects of the poison slowly reversed themselves. Medical patients who overdosed on extracts of the plant often were not as fortunate.

36. Harley 1869.

37. Ibid., 3.

38. Ibid., 4–5. See also Harley's delightful descriptions of a poor little mouse, a horse, and other creatures which succumbed but recovered from hemlock poisoning. Harley observed in these animals very much the same physical effects he had noted in himself. Harley's colleagues poisoned many other animals,

almost always with the same results. The animals, unfortunately, could not report their own experiences.

39. There are interesting problems of scientific method in assessing the effects of drugs upon oneself. According to endocrinologist Dr. Gerald Bargman (private communication), modern toxicological research does not credit the self-reporting of drug effects, for the perceptions of a drugged person may have been altered by the drug itself. Yet it is precisely Harley's impressions, distorted or not, that are so valuable in reconstructing Socrates' own subjective experience, which had to have been very similar.

40. S. Smith, 1948, 683.

41. For Bennett's full presentation of the case of Gow see Bennett 1860, 413–418.

42. Christison 1836, 407. Christison's great work is Christison 1845.

43. Graves et al., 1991, 165–6.

44. See, for example, *Timaeus* 46D, where Plato speaks of "cooling and heating, solidifying and dissolving," ψύχοντα καὶ θερμαίνοντα πηγνύντα τε καὶ διαχέοντα, as fundamental processes transforming the four elements into each other. Plato in a sense was deeply criticizing this notion, pointing out that it left no room for "reason" or "mind," but he could not escape thinking that way himself when it came to the physical aspects of the universe. Nicander employed the same terminology, *e.g.* lines 310–11 of the *Alexipharmaca*, where πηγνυμένου refers to milk curdling in a pail (114, *Nicander*).

45. Two examples among many are *Iliad* 4.260, when Antilochus drives a spear into the forehead of the Trojan Echepolus, ἐν δὲ μετώπῳ πῆξε, and *Iliad* 22.283, when Hector admonishes Achilles not to plant a spear in his back, ἐν δόρυ πήξεις. See pp. 186–7 of Vol. I and pp. 474–5 of Vol. II, Loeb Library edition of the *Iliad*. Both πῆξε and πήξεις are forms of πήγνυμι.

46. Hippocrates, "The Sacred Disease," especially 10.30–11.26. "The patient suffers all these things when the phlegm flows cold into the blood which is warm; for the blood is chilled and arrested. If the flow be copious and thick, death is immediate, for it masters the blood *by its coldness and congeals it.*" ψύχει καὶ πήγνυσιν, 10.44–48. "Little children when attacked by this disease generally die, if the flow come on copious and with a south wind; for the minor veins being thin cannot admit the phlegm because of its thickness and abundance, but *the blood is chilled and congeals,* causing death," ἀποψύχεται καὶ πήγνυται τὸ αἷμα., 11.1–6, pp. 154–7, Loeb Library edition of Hippocrates, Vol. II (my italics).

47. For example, *Iliad* 4.469, "he loosed his limbs," λῦσε δὲ γυῖα, and *Iliad* 7.16, "his limbs were loosed," λύντο δὲ γυῖα. pp. 186–7 and 302–3, Loeb Library edition of the *Iliad*, Vol. I. These are but two of many similar uses of λυω in the *Iliad*.

48. Theophrastus, *Fragments* 11. Theophrastus' writings have to be placed some two generations or more after those of Plato. When Theophrastus was born in 370 BC, Plato already had reached some sixty years of age. When Plato died in 347 BC, Theophrastus was only a young man in his early twenties. He would be fated to live a good forty more years beyond Plato.

49. Aretaeus the Cappadocian's medical writings are extraordinary in their precision and sophistication. His discussion of paralysis and other neurological disorders reads almost as if it had been written in our day rather than his. See, for example, his wonderful distinctions between apoplexy, paraplegia, paresis, and paralysis in Book I, chapter 7, "Of Chronic Diseases," in Adams 1972, 305–309.

50. κώνειον, "which some call Aegynos, some Ethusa, some Apolegousa, some Dolia, some Amaurosis, some Paralysis, some Aphron, some Creidion, some Coete, some Catechomenion, some Abioton, some Apseudes, some Ageomoron, some Timoron, some Polyanodynos, some Dardanis, some Catapsyxis, Osthanes Babathy, ye Egyptians Apemphin, ye Romans Cicuta, sends out a knotty stalk, like as Fennil, great, but leaves like to Ferula, but narrower, & of an heavy smell, & on ye tops, excrescencies, and tufts, a whitish flower, ye seed like to Annisseed whiter, ye root hollow, & not deep." Dioscorides 4.79, 477–8 in Gunther 1968.

51. Aristophanes, *Frogs,* 116–126, pp. 304–7 in Vol. II, Loeb Library edition of Aristophanes.

52. Xenophon, too, was aware of hemlock's effects, for in his *Apology* he depicts Socrates commenting on the easy death it would provide. I am grateful to Nicholas Smith for reading a draft of this paper and bringing the following lines from Xenophon to my attention: "Perhaps . . . God in his kindness is taking my part and securing me the opportunity of ending my life not only in season but also in a way that is *easiest* [ἡ ῥᾷστα]. For if I am condemned now, it will clearly be my privilege to suffer a death that is adjudged by those who have superintended this matter to be *not only the easiest* [ῥᾴστη] but also the least irksome to one's friends and one that implants in them the deepest feeling of loss for the dead. For when a person leaves behind in the hearts of his companions no remembrance to cause a blush or a pang . . . how could such a one fail to be sorely missed?" Socrates "escaped the hardest part of life and met the *easiest sort of death* [τῶν δὲ θανάτων τοῦ ῥᾴστου ἔτυχεν]" *Apology* 7 and 33, Loeb Library translation (emphases added by Smith). "I think," Smith writes, "there can be no question of what Xenophon means by emphasizing how 'easy' Socrates' death will be for him, and I also think that a death preceded by hideous convulsions of the imagined sort would most certainly qualify as an episode that 'implants' in his friends a remembrance 'to cause a blush or a pang.' I take this as further confirmation of the unanimity in the most proximate ancient sources, which you cite in the accounts of Plato, Aristophanes, and Theophrastus about this issue" (private communication).

53. Plato did call κώνειον by name in *Lysis,* 219E, commenting on the relief a father would feel if a jug of wine were standing nearby, ready to be administered as an antidote had his son ingested hemlock (accidentally, we may presume). Since this was a matter of counteracting a toxin and of saving life rather than seeking to take it, Plato is unlikely to have felt any Hippocratic qualms about identifying the poison. Like other ancient commentators, Plato believed that hemlock, as a "cold" poison, could be countered by a "hot" substance like wine or pepper. He no doubt was thinking of unmixed wine, which might even have worked, not because it was "hot," but because in large enough quantity it probably would have induced the young man to vomit. Plato specifically mentions three pints of wine.

54. Not only might opium have enhanced hemlock's powers, bringing on death more quickly, as Thrasyas of Mantineia long ago discovered, as a stimulant it might also have helped Socrates awaken after dozing off. I base the probability of such synergistic effects upon experimental results reported in 1950 by J. de Boer of the Pharmacological Institute, University of Utrecht. Boer injected first coniine and then coniine combined with opium into laboratory animals.

He found the addition of opium not only minimized convulsive activity, it also increased the wakefulness of his animals. "The rats could be awaked very easily after coniine plus opium." Though in my judgment Boer's experimental method and some of his results cannot fully be trusted, his findings are certainly interesting. See de Boer 1950.

55. *Phaedo*, 118A.

56. Landry 1859. Quoted in Hughes 1990, 1–2. An English translation of Landry's full paper may be found in Rottenberg and Hochberg 1977, 298–308.

57. Guillain, Barré, and Strohl 1916. A full English translation may be found in Rottenberg and Hochberg 1977, 309–316.

58. There appear to be many neurological mysteries still to be uncovered in the study of GBS. Why does paralysis begin in the most distal parts of the body, advancing slowly toward the trunk? No one really knows for sure, though theories abound. The largest cells in the human body are the peripheral nerves extending from the spine all the way to the toes. Several feet in length, these individual cells may be especially vulnerable to damage in their most distal portions, for the farther a nerve reaches out from the spine the narrower its circumference may become and the more open to attack it may be. Among suggested pathological mechanisms for GBS are damage to the neuromuscular plate, disruption of the axon transport system, and demyelination of the nerve coating due to viral, allergic, or autoimmune processes. Two excellent texts in the large literature on GBS are Hughes 1990 and Ropper, *et al.* 1991. With the virtual elimination of polio, GBS is the most common paralysis in the world, and researchers studying the condition have decried the lack of a good experimental model. Why not poison hemlock? Might not the death of Socrates yet point the way, not so much to ancient means of taking human life, as to modern ones of saving it?

59. Christison 1836, 399.

60. *Ibid.*, 400.

61. Book 1, "Introductory," 3–4 in Gunther 1968.

62. Dioscorides, 4.78, and Pliny, *HN* 25.95.151.

63. When Cornell gardener Krissy Faust pulled poison hemlock plants out of the ground for me to take home, she apologized for the appearance of their roots. In loose or sandy soil, she explained, they would have grown straight down like carrots. But in the hard clay of Ithaca, New York, the roots had taken on a gnarled, crooked appearance, bending back up upon themselves at odd angles. Ms. Faust's remark, and the strange deformity of the Ithaca roots, provided the crucial clues for deciphering the ancient botanical meaning of κοίλη καὶ οὐ βαθῆια, "bent, and not deep."

64. Never having lived either with mice or cats, I cannot testify to the similarity in odor. But Ms. Faust tells me it is true that the mice in her woodpile do smell exactly like hemlock.

65. I have on several occasions brought fresh branches of poison hemlock into my Socrates classes. After warning students of its possibly toxic effects, I have offered them the opportunity to sniff the odor if they wished. All who volunteered (virtually everyone) reported the same immediate feeling of car-sickness and mild but sharp headache. I myself would describe the slightly nauseous feeling more like that of morning-sickness than car-sickness, an observation most of my students were ill-equipped to make.

Works Cited

Adams, Francis, ed. 1972. *The Extant Works of Aretaeus, the Cappadocian.* Unabridged replication of the edition of 1856. Boston.

Allen, R. E. 1970. *Plato's 'Euthyphro' and the Earlier Theory of Forms.* London.

———. 1980. *Socrates and Legal Obligation.* Minneapolis.

———. 1975. "The Trial of Socrates: A Study in the Morality of the Criminal Process." In *Courts and Trials: A Multi-Disciplinary Approach,* ed. M. L. Friedland. Toronto. 3–21.

Andrewes, Antony. 1974. "The Arginousai Trial." *Phoenix* 28: 212–22.

Annas, Julia. 1981. *An Introduction to Plato's Republic.* Oxford.

Babut, D. 1969. *Plutarque et le Stoïcisme.* Paris.

Barker, Ernest. 1951. *Greek Political Theory: Plato and His Predecessors.* 4th ed. New York.

Barnes, J. 1979. *The Presocratic Philosophers.* London.

Bennett, John Hughes. 1860. *Clinical Lectures on the Principles and Practice of Medicine.* New York.

Bentley, Robert, ed. 1872. *Dr. Pereira's Elements of Materia Medica and Therapeutics.* London.

Bers, Victor. 1985. "Dikastic *Thorubos.*" In *Crux: Essays Presented to G. E. M. de Ste. Croix on His 75th Birthday,* Special Festschrift Edition of *History of Political Thought* 6: 1–15.

Blumenthal, H. J. 1973. "Meletus the Accuser of Andocides and Meletus the Accuser of Socrates: One Man or Two?" *Philologus* 117: 169–178.

Blundell, M. W. 1989. *Helping Friends and Harming Enemies.* Cambridge.

Boegehold, A., and Scafuro, A., eds. 1994. *Athenian Identity and Civic Ideology.* Baltimore.

de Boer, J. 1950. "The Death of Socrates: A Historical and Experimental Study on the Actions of Coniine and Conium Maculatum," *Archives internationales de pharmacodynamics* 83: 473–490.

Bonfante, L., and L. Raditsa. 1978. "Socrates' Defense and His Audience." *Bulletin of the American Society of Papyrologists* 15: 17–23.

Bowie, A. M. 1993. *Aristophanes.* Cambridge.

Breidert, W., ed. 1994. *Die Erschütterung der vollkommenen Welt.* Darmstadt.

Bremmer, J. 1995. "Religious Secrets and Secrecy in Classical Greece." In *Secrecy and Concealment,* ed. H. G. Kippenberg and G. Stroumsa. Leiden. 59–78.

Brickhouse, Thomas C. and Nicholas D. Smith. 1981. Abstract for "Socrates and Disobedience to the Law." *Proceedings and Addresses of the American Philosophical Association* 54: 513.

———. 1984. "Socrates and Obedience to the Law." *Apeiron* 18: 10–18.

———. 1989. *Socrates on Trial*. Oxford and Princeton.

———. 1990a. Letter to the Editor. *Times Literary Supplement*. Jan. 5–11:11.

———. 1990b. Letter to the Editor. *Times Literary Supplement*. Jan. 26–Feb. 1:89.

———. 1994. *Plato's Socrates*. Oxford.

———. 2000. *The Philosophy of Socrates*. Boulder, Colorado.

Buck, R. J. 1994. *Boiotia and the Boiotian League*. Alberta.

Burkert, Walter. 1985. *Greek Religion*. Cambridge, Massachusetts.

———. 1986. "Der Autor von Derveni: Stesimbrotos περὶ τελετῶν?" *Zeitschrift für Papyrologie und Epigraphik* 62: 1–5.

Burnet, John. 1911. *Plato's Phaedo*. Oxford.

———. 1924. *Plato's Euthyphro, Apology of Socrates, and Crito*. Oxford.

Burnyeat, M. F. 1988. Review of Stone 1988. *The New York Review of Books* March 31: 12–18.

Bury, J. B. 1926. "The Trial of Socrates." *Rationalist Press Association Annual*. London.

———. 1940. "The Life and Death of Socrates." In *Cambridge Ancient History*. 3rd ed. Vol. 5, ch. 13.4. 386–397.

———. 1962. *A History of Greece*. New York.

Bury, J. B., and Russell Meiggs. 1975. *A History of Greece to the Death of Alexander the Great*. 4th ed. New York.

Christison, Robert. 1836. "On the Poisonous Properties of Hemlock, and Its Alkaloid Conia." *Transactions of the Royal Society of Edinburgh* 13: 407.

———. 1845. *Treatise on Poisons*. Philadelphia.

Chroust, Anton-Hermann. 1957. *Socrates, Man and Myth*. Notre Dame, Indiana.

Claus, D. 1969. "Psyche: A Study in the Language of Self before Plato." Dissertation, Yale University.

Cohen, David. 1988. "The Prosecution of Impiety in Athenian Law." *Zeitschrift der Savigny-Stiftung für Rechtsgeschichte (Romanistiche Abteilung)* 118: 695–701.

———. 1991. *Law, Sexuality, and Society: The Enforcement of Morals in Classical Athens*. Cambridge.

Colson, Darrel D. 1985. "On Appealing to Athenian Law to Justify Socrates' Disobedience." *Apeiron* 19: 133–151.

———. 1989. "*Crito* 51A-C: To What Does Socrates Owe Obedience?" *Phronesis* 34: 27–55.

Connor, W. R. 1991. "The Other 399: Religion and the Trial of Socrates." In *Georgica, Greek Studies in Honor of George Cawkwell*. Bulletin Supp. 58 of the Institute of Classical Studies, 49–56.

Craik, E. M., ed. 1990. *Owls to Athens: Essays on Classical Subjects Presented to Sir Kenneth Dover*. Oxford.

Davies, J. K. 1971. *Athenian Propertied Families: 600–300 B.C.* Oxford.

Davies, M. 1989. "Sisyphus and the Invention of Religion ('Critias' TrGF 1 (43) F19 = B25 DK)." *Bulletin of the Institute of Classical Studies* 36: 16–32.

———. 1990. "'Popular Justice' and the End of Aristophanes' *Clouds*." *Hermes* 118: 237–242.

Dawkins, R. M. 1936. "The Semantics of Greek Names for Plants." *Journal of Hellenic Studies* 56.

Decharme, P. 1904. *La critique des traditions religieuses chez les grecs.* Paris.

Derenne, E. 1930. *Les procès d'impiété intentés aux philosophes à Athènes au Vme et au IVme siècles avant J.-C.* Liège-Paris.

Dodds, E. R. 1951. *The Greeks and the Irrational.* Berkeley.

———. 1973. "The Religion of the Ordinary Man in Greece." In *The Ancient Concept of Progress* E. R. Dodds ed. Oxford. 140–155.

Dover, K. J. 1968. *Aristophanes Clouds.* Oxford.

———. 1974. *Greek Popular Morality in the Time of Plato and Aristotle.* Berkeley and Los Angeles.

———. 1975. "The Freedom of the Intellectual in Greek Society." *Talanta: Proceedings of the Dutch Archaeological and Historical Society* 7: 24–54.

———. 1988. *The Greeks and their Legacy.* Oxford.

Drachmann, A. B. 1922. *Atheism in Pagan Antiquity.* London.

Dwight, E. 1904. *Toxicology.* Philadelphia.

Dykman, Aminadav and Wlad Godzich, eds. 1996. *Platon et les poètes:hommage à George Steiner.* Geneva.

Elton, G. R. 1974. *England under the Tudors.* 2nd ed. London.

Engelmann, H. 1975. *The Delian Aretalogy of Sarapis.* Leiden.

Fahr, W. 1969. ΘΕΟΥΣΝΟΜΙΖΕΙΝ. *Spudasmata* 26. Hildesheim.

Fairbairn, J. W. 1971. "The Alkaloids of Hemlock (*Conium Maculatum* L.) (or *Conium Maculatum* L: The Odd Man Out)." In Heywood 1971, 361–368.

Festugière, A. J. 1972. *Études de religion grecque et hellénistique.* Paris.

Finley, M. I. 1968. *Aspects of Antiquity.* London.

Garland, R. 1992. *Introducing New Gods.* Ithaca, New York.

Gerson, Lloyd P. 1990. *God and Greek Philosophy.* London.

Gocer, Asli. 2000. "A New Assessment of Socratic Philosophy of Religion." In *Reason and Religion in Socratic Philosophy,* ed. Nicholas D. Smith and Paul B. Woodruff. Oxford. 115–129.

Gow, A. S. F., and A. F. Scholfield. 1953. *Nicander: Poems and Poetical Fragments.* Cambridge.

Graves, Bonita M., G. M. Graves, A. K. Tsakopoulos, and J. P. Anton. 1991. "Hemlock Poisoning: Twentieth Century Scientific Light Shed on the Death of Socrates." In *The Philosophy of Socrates,* ed. K. J. Boudouris. Athens. 156–168.

Grimm, J. 1965. *Die literarische Darstellung der Pest in der Antike und in der Romania.* Munich.

Gronewald, M., Maresch, K., and W. Shäfer. 1985. *Kölner Papyri 5.* Opladen. 33–53.

Grote, George. 1875. *Plato, and the Other Companions of Socrates.* 3rd ed. Vols. I and II. London.

———. 1888. *A History of Greece,* 10 vols. London.

Guillain, G., J. A. Barré, and A. Strohl. 1916. "Sur un syndrome de radiculo-revrité avec hyperalbuminose di liquide céphalorachidien sans réaction cellulaire." *Bulletin Société Médicale des Hopitaux* 13: 1462–1470.

Gunther, R. T. 1968. *The Greek Herbal of Dioscorides: Illustrated by a Byzantine A.D. 512, Englished by John Goodyer A.D. 1655, edited and first printed A.D. 1933.* London.

Guthrie, W. K. C. 1950. *The Greeks and Their Gods.* Boston.

———. 1969. *A History of Greek Philosophy.* Vol. III. Cambridge.

———. 1971. *Socrates.* Cambridge.

———. 1975. *A History of Greek Philosophy.* Vol. IV. Cambridge.

Habicht, C. 1994. *Athen in hellenistischer Zeit.* Munich.

Hackforth, R. 1933. *The Composition of Plato's Apology*. Cambridge.

Hansen, Mogens Herman. 1980. "Hvorfor Henrettede Athenerne Sokrates." *Museum Tusculanum* 40: 55–82.

Harley, John. 1869. *The Old Vegetable Neurotics: Hemlock, Opium, Belladonna and Henbane*. London.

Harrison, W. W. R. 1971. *The Law in Athens*. 2 vols. Oxford.

Hausrath, A., ed. 1970. *Corpus Fabularum Aesopicarum*. 2nd ed. Vol. I, book i. Leipzig.

Havelock, E. 1952. "Why Was Socrates Tried?" In *Studies in Honor of Gilbert Norwood*, ed. M. White, (*Phoenix* suppl. 1). Toronto. 95–109.

Heath, M. 1987. *The Poetics of Greek Tragedy*. London.

Hegnauer, R. 1971. "Chemical Patterns and Relationships of Umbelliferae." In Heywood 1971, 267–277.

Henrichs, A. 1975. "Two Doxographical Notes: Democritus and Prodicus on Religion." *Harvard Studies in Classical Philology* 79: 93–123.

Heywood, V. H., ed. 1971. *The Biology and Chemistry of the Umbelliferae*. Supplement 1, *Botanical Journal of the Linnean Society* 64.

Hornblower, S. 1985. *The Greek World 479–523*. London.

Hughes, Richard A. 1990. *Guillain-Barré Syndrome*. London.

Imbert-Gourbeyre 1875. *De la mort de Socrate par la ciquë*. Paris.

Irwin, T. H. 1977. *Plato's Moral Theory*. Oxford.

———. 1989. "Socrates and Athenian Democracy." *Philosophy and Public Affairs* 18: 184–205.

Jackson, B. D. 1971. "The Prayers of Socrates." *Phronesis* 16: 14–37.

Jacoby, F. 1959. *Diagoras Ο΄Αθεος. Abhandlungen der preuβ. Akademie d. Wissenschaften zu Berlin* no. 3: 20.

JACT (Joint Association of Classical Teachers). 1984. *The World of Athens*. Cambridge.

Jaeger, W. 1947. *The Theology of the Early Greek Philosophers*. Oxford.

Jones, A. H. M. 1969. *Athenian Democracy*. London.

Kahn, Charles. 1960. *Anaximander and the Origins of Greek Cosmology*. New York.

Kendrick, T. D. 1956. *The Lisbon Earthquake*. London.

Kerferd, G. B. 1981. *The Sophistic Movement*. Cambridge.

Kobert, R. 1906. *Lehrbuch der Intoxication*. Vol. 2. Stuttgart.

Kopff, E. Christian. 1990. "The Date of Aristophanes, *Nubes* II." *American Journal of Philology* 111, 318–329.

Kraut, Richard. 1981. "Plato's *Apology* and *Crito*: Two Recent Studies." *Ethics* 91: 651–664.

———. 1983. *Socrates and the State*. Princeton.

———. 1995. Review of Brickhouse and Smith 1989. *Ancient Philosophy* 15: 619–625.

Krentz, Peter. 1982. *The Thirty at Athens*. Ithaca, New York.

Lacey, W. K. 1968. *The Family in Classical Greece*. Ithaca, New York.

Landry, Octave. 1859. "Note sur la paralysie ascendante aiguë." *Gazette hebdomadaire* July 29: 482–488.

Lefkowitz, M. R. 1989a. "Commentary on Vlastos' 'Socratic Piety'" In *Proceedings of the Boston Area Colloquium in Ancient Philosophy* 5, ed. J. Cleary. 239–246.

———. 1989b. "Impiety and Atheism." *Classical Quarterly* NS 39: 70–82.

Lieberg, G. 1982. "Die Theologia tripartita als Formprinzip antiken Denkens." *Rheinisches Museum für Philologie* 125: 25–53.

Lipsius, J. H. 1905–1915. Das attische Recht und Rechtverfahren. Leipzig.

Lloyd-Jones, H. 1971. *The Justice of Zeus*. Berkeley.

Lofberg, J. O. "The Trial of Socrates." *Classical Journal* 23: 601–609.

Luck, G. 1985. *Arcana Mundi*. Baltimore and London.

MacDowell, Douglas M. 1978. *The Law in Classical Athens*. Ithaca, New York.

Macleod, C. W. 1983. *Collected Essays*. Oxford.

de Mahieu, W. 1964. "La doctrine des athées au Xe livre des *Lois* de Platon." *Revue belge de philologie et d'histoire* 41: 16–47.

Mansfeld, J. 1980. "The Chronology of Anaxagoras' Athenian Period and the Date of his Trial, II: The Plot against Pericles and his Associates." *Mnemosyne* 4th ser., 33: 17–95.

Marshall, M. 1990. "Pericles and the Plague." In Craik 1990, 163–170.

McNally, W. 1937. *Toxicology*. Chicago.

McPherran, Mark L. 1985. "Socratic Piety in the *Euthyphro*." *Journal of the History of Philosophy* 23: 283–309.

———. 1987. "Commentary on Woodruff." In *Proceedings of the Boston Area Colloquium in Ancient Philosophy* 3, ed. J. Cleary. 116–130.

———. 1990. Letter to the Editor. *Times Literary Supplement* Feb. 16–22:171.

———. 1991. Review of Brickhouse and Smith 1989. *Ancient Philosophy* 11: 161–169.

———. 1992. Review of Reeve 1989. *The Philosophical Review* 101: 827–830.

———. 1996. *The Religion of Socrates*. University Park, Pennsylvania.

Mikalson, J. D. 1983. *Athenian Popular Religion*. Chapel Hill.

———. 1984. "Studies Presented to Sterling Dow." *Greece, Rome and Byzantine Studies* 10: 423–431.

Momigliano, A. 1973. "Impiety in the Classical World." In *Dictionary of the History of Ideas*, Vol.2, ed. P. Wiener. New York. 565–566.

Montuori, Mario. 1981. *Socrates: Physiology of a Myth*. Trans. J. M. P. Langdale and M. Langdale. Amsterdam.

Morrison, D. 1987. "On Professor Vlastos' Xenophon." *Ancient Philosophy* 7:9–22.

Morrow, G. 1993. *Plato's Cretan City*. Princeton.

Müller, C. W. 1967. "Protagoras über die Götter." *Hermes* 95: 140–158.

Murphy, Jeffrie G. 1974. "Violence and the Socratic Theory of Legal Fidelity." In *Violence and Aggression in the History of Ideas*, ed. P. P. Weiner and J. Fisher. New Brunswick, New Jersey.

Murray, G. 1930. *Five Stages of Greek Religion*. Oxford.

Murray, O. 1990. *Sympotica*. Oxford.

Navia, Luis E. 1985. *Socrates: The Man and His Philosophy*. Lanham, Maryland.

Nehamas, Alexander. 1986. "Socratic Intellectualism." In *Proceedings of the Boston Area Coilloquium in Ancient Philosophy* 2, ed. J. Cleary. Lanham, Maryland. 275–316.

Nilsson, M. P. 1940. *Greek Popular Religions*. New York.

Nussbaum, Martha. 1980. "Aristophanes and Socrates on Learning Practical Wisdom." In *Aristophanes: Essays in Interpretation* (*Yale Classical Studies* 26), ed. J. Henderson. 43–97.

Ober, William. 1977. "Did Socrates Die of Hemlock Poisoning?" *New York State Journal of Medicine* 77: 254–258.

von Oettingen, W. F. 1952. *Poisoning*. New York.

Ostwald, M. 1969. *Nomos and the Beginnings of the Athenian Democracy*. Oxford.

———. 1986. *From Popular Sovereignty to the Sovereignty of Law: Law, Society and Politics in Fifth Century Athens*. Berkeley.

———. 1992. "Athens as a Cultural Centre." In *Cambridge Ancient History*. 2nd ed. Vol. 5. Cambridge.

Padel, Ruth. 1992. *In and Out of the Mind: Greek Images of the Tragic Self.* Princeton.
———. 1995. *Whom the Gods Destroy: Elements of Greek and Tragic Madness.* Princeton.
Panagiotou, Spiro. 1987. "Socrates' 'Defiance' in the *Apology.*" *Apeiron* 21: 39–61.
Parke, H. W. 1961. "Chaerephon's Inquiry about Socrates." *Classical Philology* 56: 249–250.
———. 1977. *Festivals of the Athenians.* London.
Parker, Robert. 1983. *Miasma.* Oxford.
———. 1986. "Greek Religion." In *Greece and the Hellenistic World,* ed. J. Boardman, J. Griffin, and O. Murray. Oxford. 254–274.
———. 1992. "The Origins of *Pronoia*: A Mystery." In *Apodosis: Essays Presented to Dr W. W. Cruickshank to Mark his Eightieth Birthday.* London. 84–94.
———. 1996. *Athenian Religion.* Oxford.
Penner, Terry. 1973. "The Unity of Virtue." *Philosophical Review* 82: 35–68.
———. 1992. "What *Laches* and *Nicias* Miss—And Whether Socrates Thinks Courage is Merely a Part of Virtue." *Ancient Philosophy* 12: 1–27.
Pouilloux, J. 1954. *La forteresse de Rhamnonte.* (Bibliothèque des Écoles françaises d'Athènes et de Rome 179). Paris.
Pritchett, W. K. 1979. *The Greek State at War.* Vol. 3. Berkeley.
Radermacher, L. 1898. "Euripides und die Mantik." *Rheinisches Museum für Philologie* 53: 497–510.
Reeve, C. D. C. *Socrates in the Apology: An Essay on Plato's Apology of Socrates.* Indianapolis.
Rhodes, P. J. 1972. *The Athenian Boule.* Oxford.
Richardson, N. J. 1975. "Homeric Professors in the Age of the Sophists." *Proceedings of the Cambridge Philological Society* 21: 65–81.
Roberts, J. W. 1984. *City of Socrates.* London.
de Romilly, Jacqueline. 1971. *La loi dans la pensée grecque, des origines à Aristote.* Paris.
Ropper, Allan, et al. 1991. *Guillain-Barré Syndrome.* Philadelphia.
Ross, W. D. 1951. *Plato's Theory of Ideas.* Oxford.
Rottenberg, David, and Fred Hochberg, eds. 1977. *Neurological Classics in Modern Translation.* New York.
Rudhardt, J. 1960. "La définition du délit d'impiété d'après la législation attique." *Museum Helveticum* 17: 87–105.
Santas, Gerasimos X. 1979. *Socrates: Philosophy in Plato's Early Dialogues.* London.
Schachermeyer, F. 1968. "Religionspolitik und Religiosität bei Pericles. Vorunter- suchungen zu einer Monographie über Perikles und seine Zeit." *Sitzungs- berichte, Österreichische Akademie der Wissenschaften* (Vienna), Philosophisch- historische Klasse 258.
Sealey, Raphael. 1976. *A History of the Greek City–States ca. 700–338 B.C.* Berkeley.
Seeskin, Kenneth. 1987. *Dialogue and Discovery: A Study in Socratic Method.* Albany.
Sheils, W. J., ed. 1984. "Persecution and Toleration." *Studies in Church History* 21: 1–28.
Sinclair, R. K. 1988. *Democracy and Participation in Athens.* Cambridge.
Slack, P. 1985. *The Impact of Plague in Tudor and Stuart England.* London.
Smarczyk, B. 1990. *Untersuchungen zur Religionspolitik und politischen Propoganda Athens im Delisch-Attischen Seebund.* Munich.
Smith, Nicholas D. 1992. Review of Reeve 1989. *Ancient Philosophy* 11: 399–407.
Smith, Sydney, ed. 1948. *Taylor's Principles and Practice of Medical Jurisprudence.* 10th ed. Vol. 2. London.

Sourvinou-Inwood, Christiane. 1988. "Further Aspects of Polis Religion." *Annali del Seminario di studi del mundo classico, Sezione di archeologia e storia antica* (Naples) 10: 259–274.

Stone, I. F. 1988. *The Trial of Socrates*. New York.

von Störck, Anton. 1760. *Libellus, quo demonstratur cicutam no solum usu interno*. Vienna.

Strauss, Barry S. 1987. *Athens after the Peloponnesian War: Class, Faction, and Policy, 403–386 B.C.* Ithaca, New York.

Stump, Eleonore. 1979. "Petitionary Prayer." *American Philosophical Quarterly* 16: 81–91.

Tate, J. 1936. "Plato, Socrates and the Myths." *Classical Quarterly* 30: 142–145.

Taylor, A. E. 1911. *Varia Socratica*. Oxford.

———. 1933. "Socrates and the Myths." *Classical Quarterly* 27: 158–159.

———. 1936. *Plato: The Man and His Work*. New York.

Taylor, C. C. W. 1976. *Plato's Protagoras*. Oxford.

———. 1982. "The End of the *Euthyphro*." *Phronesis* 27: 109–118.

Todd, S. C. 1993. *The Shape of Athenian Law*. Oxford.

Usener, H., and L. Radermacher, eds. 1904–1929. *Dionysii Halicarnasei opuscula*. Leipzig.

Vatai, Frank Leslie. 1984. *Intellectuals in Politics in the Greek World*. London.

Versnel, H. S. 1981. "Religious Mentality in Ancient Prayer." In *Faith, Hope and Worship: Aspects of Religious Mentality in the Ancient World*, ed. H. S. Versnel. Leiden. 1–64.

———. 1990. *Ter Unus*. Leiden.

Vial, C. 1984. *Délos indépendante*. Paris.

Vlastos, Gregory, ed. 1971. *The Philosophy of Socrates*. Garden City.

———. 1974. "Socrates on Political Obedience and Disobedience." *Yale Review* 63: 517–534.

———. 1978. Review of Irwin 1977. *Times Literary Supplement* Feb. 24: 230–231.

———. 1983. "The Historical Socrates and Athenian Democracy." *Political Theory* 2: 495–516.

———. 1985. "Socrates' Disavowal of Knowledge." *Philosophical Quarterly* 35: 1–31.

———. 1989a. "Socratic Piety." In *Proceedings of the Boston Area Colloquium in Ancient Philosophy* 5, ed. J. Cleary, 213–238.

———. 1989b. Review of Brickhouse and Smith 1989. *Times Literary Supplement*, Dec. 15–21: 1393.

———. 1991. *Socrates: Ironist and Moral Philosopher*. Cambridge and Ithaca, New York.

Wallace, Robert W. 1994. "Private Lives and Public Enemies: Freedom of Thought in Classical Athens." In Boegehold and Scafuro 1994, 127–155.

Watson, L. 1991. *Arae*. Leeds.

Wepfer, Johannes. 1679. *Cicutae aquaticae historia et noxae*. Basel.

Wehrli, F. 1961. Review of Jacoby 1959. *Gnomon* 33: 123–126.

von Wilamowitz, U. 1881. *Antigonos von Karystos*. Berlin.

Winiarczyk, M. 1979 and 1980. "Diagoras von Melas. Wahrheit und Legende." *Eos* 67: 191–213, and *Eos* 68: 51–75.

———. 1981. *Diagorae Melii et Theodori Cyrenaei Reliquiae*. Leipzig.

———. 1984. "Wer galt im Altertum als Atheist?" *Philologus* 128: 157–183.

———. 1987. "Nochmals das Satyrspiel Sisyphos." *Wiener Studien* 100: 35–45.

Winspear, A. D., and T. Silverberg. 1960. *Who Was Socrates?* New York.

Witthaus, R. 1911. *Manual of Toxicology.* New York.

Wood, Ellen Meiksins, and Neal Wood. 1978. *Class Ideology and Ancient Political Theory: Socrates, Plato, and Aristotle in Social Context.* New York.

Woodbury, Leonard. 1981. "Anaxagoras and Athens." *Phoenix* 35: 295–315.

Woodruff, Paul B. 1982. *Plato, The Hippias Major.* Indianapolis.

Woozley, A. D. 1971. "Socrates on Disobeying the Law." In Vlastos 1971, 299–318.

———. 1979. *Law and Obedience: The Arguments of Plato's Crito.* London.

Yunis, H. 1988. *A New Creed: Fundamental Religious Belief in the Athenian Polis and Euripidean Drama. Hypomnemata* 91. Göttingen.

Zaidman, L. B. and Pantel, P. S. 1992. *Religion in the Ancient Greek City.* Trans. P. Cartledge. Cambridge.

Zeigler, P. 1969. *The Black Death.* London.

Zeller, Eduard. 1963. *Die Philosophie der Griechen in ihrer geschichtlichen Entwicklung.* Vol. 1. Repr. of 1922 ed. Leipzig.